D1706849

Histories of Postmodernism

Routledge Studies in Cultural History

Histories of Postmodernism

Edited by
Mark Bevir, Jill Hargis,
and Sara Rushing

Routledge
Taylor & Francis Group
New York   London

Routledge
Taylor & Francis Group
270 Madison Avenue
New York, NY 10016

Routledge
Taylor & Francis Group
2 Park Square
Milton Park, Abingdon
Oxon OX14 4RN

© 2007 by Taylor & Francis Group, LLC
Routledge is an imprint of Taylor & Francis Group, an Informa business

Printed in the United States of America on acid-free paper
10 9 8 7 6 5 4 3 2 1

International Standard Book Number-10: 0-415-95613-7 (Hardcover)
International Standard Book Number-13: 978-0-415-95613-0 (Hardcover)

Library of Congress Cataloging-in-Publication Data

Histories of postmodernism / edited by Mark Bevir, Jill Hargis, and Sara Rushing.
p. cm. -- (Routledge studies in cultural history ; 5)
Includes bibliographical references and index.
ISBN 978-0-415-95613-0 (hardback : alk. paper)
1. Postmodernism. I. Bevir, Mark. II. Hargis, Jill. III. Rushing, Sara, 1972-

B831.2.H57 2007
149'.97--dc22   2007003865

Visit the Taylor & Francis Web site at
http://www.taylorandfrancis.com

and the Routledge Web site at
http://www.routledge.com

Contents

Acknowledgments

Histories of Postmodernism derives from a conference that we organized at the University of California, Berkeley, in October 2004. For their generous support of that conference, we thank the Department of Political Science and the Townsend Center for the Humanities. We are also grateful to those who contributed so much to our discussions at the conference, especially David Bates, Fred Dolan, Suzanne Guerlac, and Paul Rabinow.

1 Introduction
Histories of Postmodernism

Mark Bevir, Jill Hargis, and Sara Rushing

The effort to historicize postmodernism will likely raise eyebrows. Historicism and postmodernism might seem to be an odd couple. Postmodernists sometimes associate historicism with the kind of grand narratives to which they are so vehemently opposed. They think of historicism as saturated with Enlightenment beliefs and values, including universality, truth, modern subjectivity, and progress. Hence they might worry that any attempt to historicize their ideas will reduce these ideas to manifestations of some putative law of development allegedly governing social processes. Perhaps they will object that any attempt to historicize postmodernism inevitably entails an imposition upon it of a repressive narrative, logic, or discourse. Equally, historicists might associate postmodernism with a vaguely delimited but obviously scorned set of beliefs and values, including relativism, nihilism, and textual free-play. Hence they might worry that to take postmodernism as seriously as we do is to flirt with (or even to embrace) ideas that preclude the very possibility of serious historical inquiry.

Part of the excitement of *Histories of Postmodernism* derives from the tension between its two principle concepts. Nonetheless, the primary aim of this volume is neither to delimit postmodernism so as to eradicate it, nor to delimit it so as to endorse it, but rather to narrate aspects of its history. No doubt our aim of narrating histories of postmodernism is contrary to the strand of postmodernism that argues each instance is its own interpretation, and so goes on to insist on the unrestrained play of texts. However, we would suggest that some aspects of historicism actually overlap with other strands of postmodernism. Indeed, our introduction begins by arguing that historicists often reject a view of history as linear, progressive, and determined. Historicism, as we conceive it, thus overlaps with the postmodern emphasis on particularity and contingency. After we introduce historicism, we will return to the question of how it might contribute to our understanding of postmodernism.

VARIETIES OF HISTORICISM

All the human sciences were dominated for much of the nineteenth century by a developmental historicism.[1] Although human scientists as diverse as James Bryce, John Burgess, and Leopold von Ranke insisted that scientific knowledge depended on inductive rigor (which they associated with the systematic, impartial, and painstaking collection and sifting of facts), they typically made sense of the facts at which they thus arrived by locating them in developmental narratives. These developmental narratives varied in the extent to which they drew, often eclectically, on sources such as Whig historiography, organic and evolutionary theories, appeals to divine providence, and philosophical idealism. But typically these developmental narratives presented the history of Europe, the west, or civilization as the unfolding of principles such as reason and liberty. They stressed continuity in the gradual triumph of these principles. They suggested that all societies evolved in accord with these principles. And they often interpreted colonialism—thereby moving toward a justification of it—by reference to the cultivation of these principles.

The developmental historicists of the nineteenth century structured their histories by reference to principles that they believed operated through time either as foundational facts or as unfolding ideals. They believed that historical eras are linked by common experiences that appear in the present conceived as a culmination of a developmental process. Hence they understood the past by locating it in relation to a larger whole, the content of which they characteristically derived from their own concepts of nation and liberty. In doing so, they often used these concepts to define a trans-historical reason by which all societies might be understood. Even when developmental historicists pointed to threats to reason or liberty, they still conceived of the triumph of these principles as somehow ensured by an immanent and evolutionary process. They built progress into the order of things—all societies were progressing toward a more complete realization of the very trans-historical reason in terms of which they were to be understood and evaluated.

Developmental historicism had been decisively undermined long before the hey-day of postmodernism. Friedrich Nietzsche and the first modernists had long expressed skepticism toward those principles of reason and progress that played such a prominent role in developmental narratives.[2] World War One eroded the wider cultural support for these principles. Although developmental historicism continued to appear throughout the first half of the twentieth century, its exponents had lost confidence in the principles that informed their narratives. Their narratives sounded like nostalgic laments. Novelists and poets such as E. M. Forster, T. S. Eliot, and Evelyn Waugh, as much as human scientists, wrote in ways that suggested the world to which they referred was somehow a thing of the past—the expansive confidence of the nineteenth century in reason and progress was no more.[3] This nostalgia took various forms. It could be tempered by ironic detachment, perhaps reflecting recognition that old beliefs and ideals were markedly out of synch with modern politics: one might think here of Forster and the political theorist Ernest Barker. Alternatively, it could be an attempt to reassert old beliefs and ideals by a shrill—and often somewhat insincere—attempt to tie them to a natural or divine law independent of the process of development that suddenly appeared to be moving away from them: one might think here of Eliot and the political theorist Leo Strauss.

The conservative turn to natural or divine law exemplifies one way in which twentieth century thinkers moved away from all forms of historicism. Yet, the twentieth century rejection of historicism was perhaps most apparent in the social sciences. The rise of academic disciplines such as political science and sociology was accompanied by a widespread turn away from historical narrative as an appropriate form of explanation for human affairs. Social scientists turned instead to more atomistic and analytic modes of inquiry.[4] They broke down social life into discrete parts, and they sought to explain these parts by comparison, classification, and correlation. Over time the social sciences has proved fertile ground for innumerable formal and ahistorical theories—functionalism, behavioralism, structuralism, and, most recently, rational choice. A similar rejection of historicism appeared in various strands of twentieth century philosophy. The founders of both analytic philosophy and phenomenology openly rejected the historicism associated with nineteenth century idealism. They concentrated on formal, atomistic and logical analyses of language and mind conceived apart from their histories.

Interestingly, the postmodernists often drew on those twentieth century traditions that opposed historicism. Most of the leading French postmodernists owed a debt to both structuralism and phenomenology, as highlighted in this volume by Robert Resch and Peter Gordon. The clear impact of these traditions on Jacques Derrida, Michel Foucault, and other postmodernists does much to explain the tensions between postmodernism and historicism.

However, while many twentieth century theorists rejected historicism, others redefined it in ways that made it less dependent on developmental concepts of reason and progress. This new, more thoroughgoing historicism really arose only after World War One, although it drew on the heightened concern with context and change that had long characterized historicism.[5] After World War One, historicists such as Ernst Troeltsch and Benedetto Croce rejected the developmental perspective while remaining suspicious of appeals to classifications and structures because of the way they neglected context and change.[6] These new historicists implied that beliefs, actions, and events are radically contingent in that the moment of choice is open and indeterminate. In their view, the ubiquity of change meant that the present might have little if anything in common with the past. Their emphasis on the otherness of the past led to skeptical concerns about the very possibility of objective historical knowledge. On the one hand, skeptical concerns inspired critiques of the ways in which historians obscured the retroactive construction of stability in their narratives. On the other hand, skeptical concerns prompted attempts to avoid a disabling skepticism by appealing to some notion of history itself.

Troeltsch and Croce brought to historicism a greater emphasis on contingency, critique, and uncertainty. They inspired other exponents of a new, more thoroughgoing historicism throughout the twentieth century, including R. G. Collingwood, Hans-Georg Gadamer, and also Antonio Gramsci and the New Left. Where developmental historicists had attempted to bring particular contexts and changes together within grand historical narratives, later historicists worried that these grand narratives tamed the contingency of history. Historicists have become increasingly wary of framing historical developments in relation to any overarching category, let alone of framing them in terms of an apparently natural or progressive movement.

Skepticism toward grand narratives and framing principles raises the question: what concepts referring to what contexts might historians use today? As we have seen, historicists are quick to worry that forcing an aspect of the past into a grand narrative gives it retrospective stability only at the expense of distorting it. Hence they are concerned, on one level, to describe events, beliefs, and the like as best they can—or at least in the best way available to us. They often go painstakingly over a theorist's work in an attempt to piece together its inner structure and its development over time; they offer synchronic and diachronic accounts of webs of belief; they explore the changing content of the ideas of a particular person. Equally, of course, historicists use aggregate concepts to cluster thinkers and, more importantly for our purpose, to provide historical insights into why people held the beliefs they did and, indeed, to ascribe beliefs to people. We suggest that historicists use aggregate concepts such as tradition and problem.[7] Historicists conceive of beliefs, meanings, and actions as contingent in that people reach them and perform them against the background of a particular social inheritance, not on the basis of pure reason or pure experience. Hence they require a concept such as tradition or discourse to denote the inheritances against the background of which people arrive at certain beliefs, meanings, and actions. And they require a concept such as problem to pick out the local contexts within which people modified beliefs, meanings, and actions so as to generate changes within traditions. Now, while we suggest that historicists deploy concepts such as "tradition" or "local context," we should add that such concepts act here not as natural kinds but as pragmatic constructs. Traditions, problems, and local contexts do not exist as self-contained entities with natural boundaries, and historicists should be careful not to reify them as if they did. Rather, historians slice out of an undifferentiated past those traditions, problems, or local contexts that they believe best explain that which interests them.

Collectively, the essays in this volume offer ample illustration of how such aggregate concepts illuminate historical phenomena. Because the essays operate with pragmatic concepts couched at various levels of aggregation, the traditions to which they appeal exhibit different levels of interaction and agreement among adherents to them. The scope of the traditions varies from broad characterizations of patterns of thought, such as the American poetic tradition that Simon Stow identifies as an influence on Richard Rorty, to narrower appeals to networks of scholars, such as the structuralists among whom Resch locates Louis Althusser. The dilemmas and local contexts to which these essays appeal vary similarly from discussions about the importance of social events, such as the protests of May 1968, which Richard Wolin suggests lead various French thinkers to return to human rights, to the importance of philosophical debates among networks of scholars, such as the French debate on the interpretation of Martin Heidegger, which Gordon shows to have played such a role in Derrida's deconstruction, and even to more individual efforts to overcome a contradiction or respond to critics, as Paul Patton argues Derrida did when he expanded on his ethical and political writings.

Whatever the scope of the traditions and dilemmas historians invoke, we might be wary of attempts to equate them with a fixed core and a penumbra that varies over time. Instead we might adopt a nominalist analysis of aggregate concepts. We might replace the idea of a series of discrete and identifiable traditions with that of an undifferentiated social context of crisscrossing interactions, where historians slice a particular context or tradition out of this undifferentiated background in order to explain the set of meanings, beliefs, or actions that interests them. In this view, historians individuate their aggregate concepts in accord with their particular purposes. Once we adopt this view, we will not mistake aggregate concepts for given chunks of the past, as if those concepts alone could appear in the one proper history. Hence we might allow that the criteria for appealing to a tradition, and also for specifying the content of particular traditions, can vary with the purposes of the narrative being told. For example, Stow constructs an "American Poetic tradition" not as a general account of all American poetry but as an aggregate concept, covering Walt Whitman and others, which captures the inheritance that helps to explain Rorty's opportunism and utopianism and so the differences between Rorty and many continental postmodernists.

HISTORICIZING POSTMODERNISM

The ensuing essays historicize postmodernism. They attempt to make sense of various thinkers by situating them against the background of diverse traditions and local contexts. What, readers might ask, do these essays tell us about postmodernism? Part of the answer to that question derives from historicism, with its nominalist approach to the analysis of abstract concepts such as postmodernism. Nominalists deny that abstract concepts (most notably universals) have any existence independent of us. They regard universals, and arguably abstract concepts more generally, as being composed solely of the individuals we locate under them. They deny that such concepts have any essence, although they might allow that the relevant individuals share family resemblances. Hence a nominalist analysis of postmodernism implies—as we said above about traditions and local contexts—that it does not have any fixed, self-contained content by which we might define it and demarcate its boundaries.

Nominalism has two specific consequences for our account of postmodernism. First, we do not draw strict lines of demarcation around those whom one might label postmodern. Instead we appeal to conceptual and historical links between thinkers. That is to say, we conceive of the beliefs and relationships of these thinkers as the things to which we refer when we use the word "postmodernism." We define postmodernism by reference to a loose cluster of themes which have altered over time and none of which is necessarily common to all those thinkers whom we might call postmodern. We trace the changing nature of this loose cluster of themes from several French theorists who are most often associated with postmodernism back to philosophers and movements that influenced them and forward to American academics who have been inspired by them and the debates around them. Second, our nominalist suspicion of fixed definitions inspires an attempt to decenter postmodernism even as we so conceive of it. Hence we challenge a simple narrative in which fixed ideas passed from the precursors through French theory and on to their American disciples. We highlight differences and discontinuities between the various theorists and movements by locating them in their local contexts.

Let us begin our exploration of postmodernism by describing the loose cluster of themes that recur in many of the ensuing essays' discussion of postmodernists. In tracing histories of postmodernism from precursors such as Nietzsche, through French thinkers such as Derrida, Foucault and Jean-François Lyotard, and on to contemporary Americans such as Drucilla Cornell and Rorty, we find that certain themes emerge. No doubt an account of postmodernism in terms of such themes could serve reductive ends. Let us reiterate, therefore, that reductionism is not our aim. To the contrary, themes link ideas through their resemblance to one another or their reasonable association with one another, not by pointing to identical beliefs or the logical consequences of subscribing to them. Hence we elaborate these themes as a prelude to decentering them. In the next section of our introduction, we will examine how local contexts—specific traditions and dilemmas—give different meanings and implications to the themes. The process by which theorists from varied traditions generated a loose cluster of overlapping themes was a contingent historical one, not a necessary one progressing inexorably toward a fixed conclusion in postmodern philosophy. When the essays in this volume explore how the themes emerged and were deployed in diverse traditions to address diverse problems, they do not distract from the task of discussing postmodernism. Rather, they constitute a discussion of postmodernism that recognizes its polyvalence.

The themes that arise out of the following essays and help to provide an account of "postmodernism," are, in many cases, couched as oppositions to other positions, which include: anti-humanism, anti-foundationalism, anti-essentialism, anti-representationalism, anti-historicism, an ethic of self-fashioning, a predilection for irony, and an anti-positivist utopianism. To associate these themes with postmodernism is, of course, neither to say that they are postmodernism, nor to suggest that postmodernism corners the market on them.

The theme of epistemological anti-foundationalism refers to a belief that knowledge cannot be grounded in any indubitable, timeless, transcontextual principles. This belief leads postmodernists to challenge concepts such as neutrality, objectivity, reason, and method in so far as these concepts suggest that there are means by which we might uncover certainties. Postmodernists are skeptical of what is often thought to be a modern or enlightenment faith in mental processes as a way of gaining and organizing knowledge of the world. Postmodernists challenge the authority of science, law, religion, philosophy, and all other master discourses that have been accorded some special access to truth. Epistemological anti-foundationalism also prompts postmodernists to reject the idea (or ideal) that knowledge progresses toward ever greater rational self-consciousness and perhaps even freedom. Postmodernists typically reject the concept of the mind as a "mirror of nature" that could accurately reflect the world—a concept of mind they often associate with a tradition of metaphysical epistemology in which ultimate truths hinge on the quest for knowledge that is self-evident to a rational mind. However, postmodernists rarely make claims to the effect that we can never know anything. They just emphasize that knowledge is produced, not discovered. Here their accounts of the production of knowledge vary from appeals to a pragmatic discursive consensus to accounts of the operations of power.

Anti-humanism refers to the broad claim that the subject or individual person is not an unconditioned or autonomous agent. Many postmodernists associate humanism with the idea that man directs himself and history through his rational will and agency. Their anti-humanism suggests a rejection of a belief that man works at perfecting himself, and a belief that history is progressive. As anti-humanists, postmodernists thus challenge various beliefs that they associate with the modern subject: the beliefs include the sovereign subject, the rational intending self, and the unified conscious individual that pre-exists its own entry into the social and cultural order. Anti-humanism was perhaps of particular importance for many of the leading French postmodernists, such as Derrida and Foucault, for whom the debate on humanism between Sartre and Heidegger represented a galvanizing exchange, as is shown in this volume by Jill Hargis, Gordon, and Wolin.

The theme of anti-historicism refers, as Resch makes clear in his paper, to a "devaluation of historical determination and processes of development." Postmodernists challenge attempts to project a meaning onto historical events in order to establish some kind of progressive teleology. As we suggested earlier, this postmodern anti-historicism rejects developmental concepts of a linear or dialectical progression to history. Indeed, postmodernists tend to see grand narratives of historical development as power-saturated products of the unique moments at which they were articulated. Equally, we might point out that when postmodernists explore just such unique moments they sometimes adopt a practice akin to historicism as we conceive of it; they sometimes seek to delimit the local character of specific cultural arrangements and events.

Ontological anti-essentialism is the belief that being has no ultimate, true nature. Postmodernists generally hold that reality itself is produced through various contexts and contingencies; reality is not discovered as necessity, nature, or God by means of logic or experience. Some postmodernists even suggest that the categorization, classification, or analysis of reality into underlying parts is pointless or even misguided. Their ontological anti-essentialism thus overlaps considerably with an anti-realism that, as Mark Bevir describes in his chapter, entails a denial of any authentic reality lying behind or beyond representation, modern consumer society, or power.

Anti-essentialism and anti-realism open the way to an ethic (or aesthetic) of self-fashioning. Some postmodernists describe aestheticization as a practice of resistance to bourgeois society, as Bevir discusses in his chapter. Others describe it as a practice of resistance to codified sexual and gender norms, as Sara Rushing discusses in hers. For Foucault, the notion of stylized self-fashioning, typically undertaken at the site of the body, was an attempt to break out of particular regimes of subjectivity and to refuse to be normalized into a well-regulated individual. Some postmodernists, following Foucault, appear to suggest that aesthetic self-fashioning involves a kind of turn away from ethics and politics (at least as these are widely conceived) and toward desire, pleasure, and play. Others appear, in contrast, to require any adequate self-fashioning to be a protest against prevailing social norms.

Linguistic anti-representationalism is the belief that language, far from being a neutral medium through which consciousness is manifested, is that through which the world, our understanding of the world, and even we ourselves are continually produced and reproduced. For most postmodernists, language is not a tool that we use to refer to objects that pre-exist it. Rather, objects (and we as subjects talking about them) cohere only in language or social discourses. Postmodernists typically reject the idea that language is instrumental and transparent. They deny that it has a referential relation to an objective world. In their view, language is slippery and opaque; it is constitutive of the world rather than descriptive of it.

The presence of a theme of irony among postmodernists is in large part a response to a bind that arises from linguistic anti-representationalism. On one hand, linguistic anti-representationalism entails a challenge to the use of concepts or words to refer to the world. On the other, we have to use language to convey thoughts, ideas, arguments, and the like. Hence postmodernists face a bind: they deploy concepts that they do not accept (at least not at face value), and they cannot avoid doing so if they are to use language at all. Hubert Dreyfus and Paul Rabinow capture this bind when they say, in a discussion of Foucault, "one has to take the world of serious discourse seriously because it is the one we are in, and yet one can't take it seriously, first because we have arduously divorced ourselves from it, and second because it is not grounded."[8] Derrida responds—both philosophically and stylistically—to the same bind when he places words under erasure; he crosses words out so as to alert his reader that although these words are being used they should not be taken literally. Likewise Rorty describes an "ironist" as "the sort of person who faces up to the contingency of his or her own most central beliefs and desires—someone sufficiently historicist and nominalist to have abandoned the idea that those central beliefs and desires refer back to something beyond the reach of time and chance."[9] Rorty goes on to suggest that ironists thus take philosophical explanations merely to be better or worse descriptions.[10] In general, postmodernists tend to adopt ironic self-consciousness toward the fact that they use words to make arguments while believing that words are not things that authors or agents can use or control in any straightforwardly intentional way. Critics of postmodernism can mistake such irony for frivolity, obfuscation, or irresponsibility. We are suggesting, in contrast, that this irony is a response to specific philosophical binds generated by some of the other themes that characterize postmodernism. Gordon and Patton tackle the critics who suggest Derrida espouses aestheticism or quietisim.[11] Rushing tackles the critics who charge postmodern legal feminists with undermining feminism's commitment to real women's suffering by hiding behind ironic wordplay.[12]

Finally, the theme of anti-positivist utopianism is evident in the desire of many postmodernists to look ahead toward a better set of cultural arrangements. Sometimes this theme sits awkwardly alongside the argument that all knowledge, representation, and ethics are partial, exclusionary, and even laden with power. The more postmodernists stress the latter argument, the more difficult it becomes for them to ascribe content to a utopian vision—a failing Patton points to in Derrida. Foucault expressed this difficulty when he suggested that, "to imagine another system is to extend our participation in the present system."[13] Some postmodernists seem to imply that it is impossible to conceive of an alternative order for which one might offer a justification. Hence some of their critics are able to claim that postmodernism entails an apolitical or cynical orientation.[14] Nonetheless, a number of postmodernists—including Cornell, Derrida, Rorty, and

Edward Said—convey a sincere, if conflicted, hopefulness, which they typically express in intentionally unspecific, futural terms.

DECENTERING POSTMODERNISM

Let us turn now to examine how radical historicism might prompt us to decenter postmodernism. The foregoing narrative of postmodernism overlaps with a conventional one. The conventional narrative tells of a movement of themes such as anti-essentialism from precursors such as Nieztsche and Heidegger, through major French theorists such as Derrida and Foucault, and on to their American legacy in the work of Rorty, Cornell, and others. The conventional narrative is centered on the French thinkers of the 1960s who rejected the formalism and universals of structuralism. It extrapolates from this center back to the precursors and forward to the American inheritance. It can contend that the French postmodernists responded to structuralism in ways that, as one of its narrators writes, "incorporate, develop and respond to Nietzschean and Heideggerian concepts."[15] And it can aspire to establish how American disciples are still carrying on the work of the French postmodernists.[16] Some commentators even describe all these thinkers as sharing a single project that thus appears to be the constitutive feature of postmodernism—to unsettle the enlightenment and grand narratives.

Although the conventional narrative is not without merits, it often implies a greater commonality and coherence than is warranted. It obscures a great deal of the complexity and contradiction—the diversity and discontinuities—among the various thinkers that appear within it. We would suggest, in particular, that one effect of the conventional narrative is a certain border-thinking: who is a postmodernist and who is not? And we would propose that the history of postmodernism might be better conceived as residing in the overlapping and competing ideas that have emerged out of specific local appropriations and applications of earlier theorists and their ideas.

Historicism emphasizes particularity and contingency in a way that draws our attention to the local contexts in which people have inherited and transformed themes associated with postmodernism. People do not simply adopt themes from one another. The themes are always transformed in relation to each thinker's local context. While theorists acquire beliefs against the background of traditions, they then give these beliefs new tones as they use them to respond to particular dilemmas. Historicism thus leads us to explore the ways in which local contexts influenced what themes were appropriated and how they were modified and transformed. When we explore these modifications and transformations, we typically disperse aggregate concepts such as postmodernism; we emphasize the differences and discontinuities between those whom we associate with such concepts.

This spirit of dispersal appears in the way that the essays in this volume decenter postmodernism.

This volume seeks, in contrast to the conventional narrative, to show that the development of postmodernism cannot be explained through a single story of coherent progression. These essays do not attempt to impose some necessary, ascendant logic on the diverse, often conflicted, set of themes and thinkers associated with postmodernism. We do not mean thereby to imply that the oft-asserted connections between thinkers like Nietzsche and Foucault, or Foucault and Said, are not in fact present and worthy of exploration. We mean rather to suggest that it is important to open up the conventional narrative so as to examine other influences, and so as to recognize the discontinuities that are elided in its seamless story. The spaces between (and indeed within) postmodernism's "precursors," "heyday," and "legacies" are characterized by departure and innovation at least as much as by continuity and interpretive fidelity. This volume highlights the ways in which developments in multiple traditions influenced and overlapped with each other to produce the set of themes that characterize much postmodernism.

Histories of Postmodernism is organized in three chronological sections. The first considers precursors of postmodernism—Nietzsche, Heidegger, and the structuralists. The essays in this section situate these thinkers and movements in their local contexts, thereby distancing them somewhat from later appropriations. At times, they explore, more explicitly, contrasts between the work of these theorists, their reception among their contemporaries, and their later reception by postmodern thinkers.

Melissa Lane's chapter— "Honesty as the Best Policy: Nietzsche on *Redlichkeit* and the contrast between Stoic and Epicurean strategies of the self"—examines Nietzsche's subtle treatment over time of self-mastery and honesty. Lane draws our attention away from sterile debates that locate Nietzsche in a transhistorical conflict between a postmodern concern with self-fashioning and a modern one with truth. Instead she seeks to illuminate changes in his thought as he grappled with more specific concerns and more specific intellectual inheritances. Attempts to assimilate Nietzsche to a monolithic postmodernism might capture the anti-historicist and epistemological anti-foundationalist elements of his critiques of specific superordinate foundations such as Christianity. As Lane shows, however, such treatments neglect his persistent concern to find viable standards for virtuous action. Nietzsche drew here on Epicurean and Stoic concepts of truthfulness and honesty to create an understanding of virtue that was based in honest evaluations of reality. Lane argues that ultimately Nietzsche turned to a cognitive, Stoic standard for virtue rather than an emotional, Epicurean one. She thereby disrupts the postmodern interpretation of Nietzsche's self-mastery as based solely on the will to power or overcoming of self. She argues that in his early work, including *Human, All too Human,* he saw value in the Epicurean practice of limiting one's understanding of reality in order to create emotional peace, but that later he rejected this Epicureanism as a "simulation of honesty" and embraced a Stoic concept of *Redlichkeit*. Nietzsche came to advocate a stubborn confrontation with harsh reality. As Lane suggests, Nietzsche's analysis of honesty, virtue, and truth in both Epicurean and Stoic thought is not a theme that finds many echoes in later postmodernists. What is more, Nietzsche's concern with *Redlichkeit* suggests that the notions of self-fashioning and aestheticization that he entertained were not based in any straightforward epistemelogical anti-foundationalism. Rather, his "strategies of the self" were linked to his critical assessments of harsh realities. As Lane concludes, "any would-be postmodern ethic which claims indebtedness to Nietzsche must respect the cognitive constraint of honesty as *Redlichkeit*."

While Nietzsche is often invoked as a proto-postmodernist, postmodernism is typically described as arising out of debates within phenomenology and structuralism. In "Escape from the Subject: Heidegger's *Das Man* and Being-in-the-world," Jill Hargis argues that Heidegger's full legacy for postmodernism has not been acknowledged. She draws attention here to the conservative theory of the public that informed his critique of subjectivity. Heidegger's idea of a modern conforming public reflects his debt to a specific intellectual context of German conservative revolutionaries and Kierkegaard. Hargis explores how this context framed his understanding of subjectivity, and especially his attempt to decenter the subject. She thereby suggests that the anti-humanist critique of subjectivity found in much postmodernism was initially influenced by a fear of the loss of traditional culture to the masses in modern democracy. Heidegger himself drew on a German tradition of conservatism when he renounced humanism and its concept of the subject on the grounds that liberal autonomy resulted in inauthentic conforming masses. Moreover, although when Heidegger influenced later postmodernists they refused his conservative politics, Hargis suggests that postmodernism still carries traces of Heidegger's fear of the public. When postmodernists adopt an anti-positivist utopianism, for example, they often refuse to specify concrete standards for the future in a way that is perhaps a lingering effect of Heidegger's conflation of the problems of *das Man* with a critique of subjectivity.

In "A Rock and a Hard Place: Althusser, Structuralism, Communism, and the Death of the Anticapitalist Left" Robert Resch situates Althusser's thought in its navigation between Marxism, structuralism, and a later poststructuralism. Althusser embraced structuralism, including its critique of the primacy of the autonomous individual, in order to address local dilemmas affecting French Marxism. He bracketed off the "young Marx," with his historicist and humanist ideas, and then brought a "mature Marx" into a "kind of structuralism" by emphasizing their common scientificity. Resch here suggests that Althusser regarded humanism as a form of teleological historicism. Althusser found structuralism helpful in undermining what he conceived as the humanist belief in man as the center of his own world and as the driving force of a salvationist history. Whereas orthodox Marxists espoused historical determinism, Althusser deployed structuralism to suggest that each moment is its own instance and that no particular logic holds all the various moments together. Resch's reading of Althusser complicates the narrative of postmodernism as arising from a break with structuralism. It suggests, to the contrary, that structuralists such as Althusser were already grappling with postmodern themes. Resch concludes by showing how a blurring of the boundaries between structuralism and postmodernism helps us to make sense of Althusser's reception of Derrida. Althusser modified his identification of Marxism as a science so as to suggest that it was instead the site of a continuous struggle between science and ideology.

The second section of this volume explores the "heyday" of postmodernism in France during the 1960s and early 1970s. The essays in this section examine how local contingencies influenced the ways in which thinkers like Baudrillard, Derrida, Foucault, and Lyotard read their predecessors. The essays locate these thinkers in concrete, local movements and debates in philosophy and politics, including French phenomenology, situationism, and human rights. Collectively they go some way toward illustrating the diversity of postmodernism; they illustrate the varied ways in which these French postmodernists drew on their predecessors to address new dilemmas.

Peter Gordon's chapter, "Hammer without a Master: French Phenomenology and the Origins of Deconstruction (Or, How Derrida Read Heidegger)," locates Derrida in the local context of French debates of the 1940s and 1950s over phenomenology and existentialism. Gordon thereby highlights a radical discontinuity between Derrida's own ideas and the ways in which these ideas have been received and appropriated in America and elsewhere. Derrida's deconstruction must be understood as prior to, and distinct from, poststructuralism—a separate movement that did not emerge until the 1960s. Gordon argues that a failure properly to locate Derrida in his local context has led to widespread misunderstandings about deconstruction. In particular, Gordon locates Derrida's rendition of the theme of anti-humanism against the background of the prominent debate between Sartre and Heidegger over the meaning and implications of existentialism and phenomenology. Heidegger's lively challenge to the purported metaphysics of Sartre's voluntarism and subjectivism was a crucial event in the French reception of phenomenology. Gordon shows how the resulting debate over the concepts of "mastery" and "throwness" constituted the setting within which Derrida adopted anti-humanism. In this setting, moreover, Derrida's anti-humanism appears principally as a commitment to anti-authoritarianism. Hence Gordon distinguishes sharply between Derrida's anti-humanism and that of those later postmodernists who turned to the theme of aesthetic self-fashioning. Derrida's deconstruction was a "critical assault" on the themes of subjective mastery and authoritarianism in phenomenology.

In "'A Kind of Radicality': The Avant-garde Legacy in Postmodern Ethics," Mark Bevir similarly locates the theme of aesthetic self-fashioning in a specific debt that some later postmodernists owed to the avant-garde tradition. Bevir describes how some French theorists, notably Barthes and Foucault, responded to Derrida's challenge to structuralism in part by turning to the body in an attempt to develop an ethics without subjectivity. The theme of self-fashioning arose as Barthes and Foucault postulated the body as a site for carrying out strategies of transgressive self-creation, in the style of the avant-garde writers and artists. Bevir traces various sites and strategies of resistance to bourgeois society from Dada, surrealism, and situationism to the work of Baudrillard, Foucault, and Lyotard. These postmodernists participated in avant-garde movements, and they continued to follow the avant-garde tradition in appealing to play and excess, the body and desire, and aesthetic self-creation and stylized transgressions. However, Bevir continues, whereas the avant-garde adopted these sites and strategies as ways of accessing a more real alternative than that offered by bourgeois society, postmodernists renounced the very idea of the real. Hence postmodernists confront the awkward issue of what justification they now might offer for such sites and strategies of resistance.

In "Derrida's Engagement with Political Philosophy," Paul Patton unpacks Derrida's specific rendition of the postmodern theme of anti-positivist utopianism. He effectively counters interpretations of Derrida as apolitical, arguing, to the contrary, that Derrida might provide us with new and interesting ways to think about politics, albeit that these ways of thinking currently remain opaque. Patton traces the commitment to "radical and interminable critique" that Derrida suggests relates deconstruction to Marxist traditions. He then shows how this commitment to critique helped to inspire and direct the explicitly political and ethical themes that appeared in Derrida's work of the 1980s. This type of critique takes the form of aporetic analysis of existing political concepts. Derrida deploys such analyses to expose the productive gap between a contingent or conditioned form of a concept within history—for example, "democracy" as a description of institutions and practices— and an absolute or unconditioned form of a concept—for example, Derrida's favored concept of "democracy to come." Derrida does not highlight these productive gaps solely for the sake of critique; he does so, as Patton argues, as a type of "affirmative deconstruction" that finds in the irreducibility of the unconditional a space for the ever-present possibility of reinventing, reconfiguring or transforming our existing, historically contingent categories, institutions and practices. Patton suggests, moreover, that a close analysis of Derrida's treatment of democracy shows his political philosophy to overlap with both contemporary cosmopolitan theory and the pragmatic liberalism of Rorty. We are left with a Derrida who is a pragmatic "friend of democracy."

Richard Wolin, too, examines the shifting political commitments of postmodernists. In his "From the 'Death of Man' to Human Rights: The

Paradigm Change in French Intellectual Life," he begins by showing how structuralism and Heideggerianism combined to create a distinctly anti-humanist climate in pre-1968 France. He then argues that the student revolts of May 1968 effectively marked a dramatic reversal of that climate. The revolts inaugurated a new local context within which opportunities for human action proliferated and an ethos of human rights came to dominate. Wolin suggests that some postmodernists, most notably Foucault, responded to this new context by turning away from the theme of anti-humanism in practice, even if they did not always make this explicit in their writings. Ironically, as Wolin argues, it was at the very time that humanism was resurgent in France that the idea of the "death of man" began to catch on in the United States. The result of this irony has been the dominance in America of an image of French theory that bears little resemblance to the contemporary French scene. Recognition of the discontinuity between France and America allows for important reflections on specific postmodern themes. Wolin highlights, for instance, the way in which Sartre's theories of agency, will, and progressive historical change have resonated with the student revolutionaries of May 1968 and later French intellectuals far more strongly than have the anti-humanism and futural utopianism that have fascinated American postmodernists.

The final section of this volume addresses the legacy of postmodernism in the United States. The essays included examine the transformation of postmodern themes, and the appropriation of postmodern thinkers, in relation to indigenous traditions and concerns. They explore attempts to read postmodern themes back into a pragmatist tradition, to deploy Foucault in support of a secular and historicist style of literary criticism, and to sustain and develop a somewhat novel emphasis on issues of identity and gender. They show how the U.S. setting has led to a different consciousness and new concerns from those of earlier thinkers associated with postmodern thought.

In "The Democratic Literature of the Future: Richard Rorty, Postmodernism and the American Poetic Tradition," Simon Stow locates Rorty within that tradition in order to explain the particular content Rorty gave to various postmodern themes. Stow examines how Rorty reworked postmodernism so as to align it with an American pragmatic philosophy and an American liberal politics. By locating Rorty in an American Poetic Tradition, Stow also helps to explain why Rorty garnered the wrath of both postmodernists and their opponents: the former disliked his American optimism; the latter rejected his postmodern frivolity. In opposition to those who seek to demonstrate that Rorty either is or is not a postmodernist, or that he either is or is not a pragmatist, Stow traces in detail the ways in which Rorty's continuing debt to an American poetic tradition has led him to change his alignment with postmodernism across specific debates. Rorty flirts with postmodernism. Initially he claimed the label for himself in order to push anti-foundationalism and anti-representationalism in discussions with analytic philosophers. But later, once postmodernism had become associated with aesthetic self-fashioning, he located its ironic stories within the private sphere, and began to pursue a public project of utopian social hope. Here Stow analyzes the specific content that Rorty gives to the postmodern theme of self-fashioning. Although Rorty draws on an interpretation of Nietzschean self-creation as emotional, his rendition of the theme of self-fashioning derives principally from American poets such as Emerson and Whitman, invoking the figure of the spirited poet who inspires democratic vistas with his edifying, potentially transformative—but not necessarily transgressive—words.

David Hawkes' chapter—"The Secular and the Post-Secular in the Thought of Edward Said"—locates Said's concept of the secular against the background of his debt to the kind of historicism found in Vico and also Foucault. Hawkes thereby illuminates the differences between historicist forms of anti-foundationalism, as exemplified by Foucualt and Said, and the quasi-transcendental ones, as exemplified by Derrida. Said's concept of the secular expresses many of the ideas associated with broader postmodern themes, notably anti-foundationalist epistemology and ontological anti-essentialism. The secular is opposed to a variety of essentialist categories such as relations of filiation, nationalism, and conventional uses of religion. It evokes the contingency of human knowledge and human practices. However, Hawkes also argues that Said's concept of the secular owes much to Vico, with his concern to tell the history of the gentile nations in terms of specifically human activity rather than providence. Said here devised a form of historicism—closely akin to that animating this volume—according to which knowledge and action could be understood only within their specific historical contexts. As Hawkes argues, this historicism led Said to oppose Derridean deconstruction and align himself rather more closely with Foucault's genealogical approach.

In "Longing For 'A Certain Kind of Future': Drucilla Cornell, Sexual Difference and the Imaginary Domain," Sara Rushing considers the legacy of postmodernism for North Atlantic feminist thought by examining the concept of "sexual difference" as feminist legal theorist Drucilla Cornell has appropriated it from psychoanalysis, deconstruction and French feminism, and as she has refined and defended it in a series of debates with Judith Butler. Rushing looks at how Cornell performs certain necessary translations and critical juxtapositions of Lacan, Derrida and Irigaray so as to be able to extend from her philosophical engagement with "sexual difference" to a legal theory of equality and right that rivals the limiting and moralizing thrust of MacKinnon's feminist jurisprudence and its reliance on a certain conception of gender. Rushing aims to show how Cornell's theory functions to challenge the monopolization of utopianism that more programmatic feminist theorists like MacKinnon and Nussbaum profess, and how a concept of sexual difference lends itself to emancipatory thinking that is beyond "the here and now" continually reinforced by these programmatic scholars. Postmodern feminism retains a vigorous utopian impulse, Rushing argues, precisely because of its appropriation of insights from Lacan, Derrida, Foucault and others. However the utopian moment in postmodern feminism is a decidedly different species, accompanied as it is by a palpable anxiety, resistant as it is to any sort of substantive description of the future it hopes for, and elaborated as it is within the rights and advocacy-dominated local context of U.S. legal feminism.

AFTER POSTMODERNISM?

To conclude, we want to return to the relation of historicism to postmodernism. Historicism has led us to describe postmodernism in terms of themes that admittedly vary across local contexts. Hence our histories disperse postmodernism. They undermine the lazy notion that postmodernism consists of a monolithic set of ideas. In doing so, they also render somewhat facile the equally lazy question of whether historicists—or anyone else, for that matter—are for or against postmodernism. We might suggest that any such question should specify which postmodern themes are being evaluated and in which local context. It is surely possible, after all, to accept some of the themes that are widespread among postmodernists and to reject others: one might be an anti-foundationalist and yet a humanist. It is also possible to sympathize with one version of a theme and yet to oppose others: one might defend a Nietzschean concept of truthfulness as intellectual honesty against both foundationalist epistemologies and Derrida's concept of indeterminacy.

The historicization of postmodernism leads us, then, to rethink the terms of the question: are we for or against postmodernism? Far too many of the participants in the infamous "theory wars" that took hold of the American academy in the 1980s and early 1990s treated postmodernism as a shared, coherent, trans-Atlantic project aimed at unsettling the enlightenment and grand narratives, or extolling the "death of man," "death of history," and the "death of metaphysics." Advocates of postmodernism promoted it as subversive, and as leading to cultural and political transformations. Critics lambasted it as impotent or nihilistic. In sharp contrast, a historicist approach undermines the idea that postmodernism has any such shared, coherent content. The ensuing studies suggest, as we have argued, that postmodernism consists at most of a set of overlapping themes that have been transformed by a range of different theorists as they have applied them in new contexts, and, moreover, that these theorists have modified their particular beliefs over time—as Wolin shows Foucault did, Patton shows Derrida did, Stow shows Rorty did, and Rushing shows Cornell did. It is possible, of course, that these changes are a sign that postmodernism is dead or at least passé. But it is perhaps more plausible to see them as a sign that, once we recognize that postmodernism is not a substantive "project" but a set of overlapping themes, the debates about "postmodernism" can drift away, enabling the themes themselves to take center stage—and that is just fine.

When we disaggregate the legacy of postmodernism into that of several themes, we might contrast two broad patterns. On the one hand, critics of postmodernism have accommodated themes—such as, we believe, anti-foundationalism and anti-essentialism—so that these themes no longer cause so much controversy. On the other hand, many postmodernists appear to have become dissatisfied with the more provocative versions of the other themes; they have responded to dilemmas that confronted their early statements of these themes by crafting more nuanced and more fruitful versions of them. These two patterns mean that where once—during the "theory wars"—there was a kind of digging in of heels on either side of the divide between postmodernists and their critics, there is now a sense in which that very divide seems to have obscured as much as it illuminated. Today we can ask: after the dissolution of postmodernism as a monolithic project, what remains of its several themes?

The easiest themes to consider are those that have been accommodated by many of postmodernism's critics. Anti-foundationalism—at least when it is conceived as the claim that no transcendent, transcultural, or timelessly true knowledge is possible—has ceased to be a particularly provocative position. The "loss" that people once associated with anti-foundationalism appears to haunt no one anymore. To the contrary, we have learned to see all kinds of theorists as anti-foundationalists *avant la lettre*. Similarly, a kind of anti-essentialism has become commonplace. Even if theorists continue to debate the viability of a naturalist basis to some social concepts, the claim that the social categories of race and gender—or concepts such as democracy and freedom—lack any "core" content is no longer a particularly surprising one.

The other themes—apart from anti-foundationalism and anti-essentialism—are ones that postmodernists themselves have modified, at times without anyone seeming to notice they had done so. Postmodernists offered, or were taken to offer, highly provocative versions of the themes. Later, when they addressed various dilemmas—events, internal issues within their thought, or the caricatures and questions offered by their critics—they often found that the provocative versions of these themes led to dead ends. When they grappled with these dilemmas, they crafted alternative, more fruitful versions of the original themes. In this way, postmodern themes often followed a trajectory from provocation to caricature and on to fruitful modification.

The theme of anti-humanism initially appeared as an apparent rejection of the very possibility of agency. Post-structuralists such as Foucault, Butler, and arguably Derrida, all appeared to want to replicate the structuralist opposition to any appeal to the creative or innovative capacities of individual subjects. "Man" was to disappear apart from as an object of critique. With hindsight, this provocative anti-humanism looks like little more than an over-statement of an underlying suspicion of the alleged neutrality and universality of western, liberal notions of the autonomous self. Indeed, to many critics, it seemed not only implausible but actively to undermine other postmodern concerns. These critics suggested that if anti-humanism entailed a rejection of agency, it undercut attempts to promote an ethic or politics based on either freedom or self-fashioning. As Nancy Fraser asked of Butler: "Why, above all, use an antihumanist rhetoric when one's aim is to explain how *agency* is possible given the constitution of subjects by power regimes? For this purpose, might not such rhetoric be counterproductive."[17] The answer, it seems, was yes, for, as several of the chapters that follow show, many postmodernists have explicitly or implicitly drifted away from their anti-humanism. As Wolin argues, Foucault had modified his anti-humanism to make way for agency and self-fashioning even by the time Butler took it up. Butler's recent work similarly locates "the human" front and center, at least as a normative aspiration. Indeed, the notion of human freedom (of agency under conditions of "unfreedom") that Wolin and others have found in the late work of Foucault appears to be pivotal for Butler's later turn to the topic of responsibility. Yet, the drift away from anti-humanism has not led postmodernists to embrace a view of the subject as autonomous, neutral, or universal. To the contrary, they are better seen as addressing the question of what kind of humanism is still possible after a rejection of the fantasy of autonomy. Said responded to just this question not by rejecting humanism, or scorning it like so many "sophisticated postmodern critics," but by vacating humanistic critique of its individualist and teleological underpinnings.[18] Said suggested that a fruitful or viable humanism had to be articulated in a language of community, interdependence, and the shared human construction of history and understanding. He offered a historical account of humanism that cast it as the "final resistance we have against the inhuman practices and injustices that disfigure human history."[19]

Some postmodernists certainly adopted a version of anti-historicism that treated each moment as its own instance, decontextualized and devoid of any shared meaning. Yet, just as anti-humanism has all but disappeared, so this anti-historicism now appears to have been replaced by overt recognition that there is something between a determined historical development and utter discontinuity and uniqueness.[20] The initial reception of Derrida in the United States certainly owed much to the impression, especially prevalent among scholars of literature, that he offered a way of approaching texts that liberated them from any determinative, historical context: there was just play and inter-textuality. Somewhat differently, Foucault's early work clearly drew on structuralism to assert that a kind of radical discontinuity between epistemes—a bit like Derrida's texts—could be analyzed in terms of an underlying quasi-structure embedded in an idea of representation—or in the very nature of representation. As Foucault moved further and further away from such structuralism, however, he developed historical methods for identifying how bodies of knowledge and belief systems are tied to changing relations of power. Nonetheless, we should not assume that the drift away from an earlier provocative form of anti-historicism ended with postmodernists embracing grand narratives couched as determined historical developments. Rather, several postmodernists came to ask about the nature of historical understanding in the absence of just such necessity. Once again Said provides a pertinent example of the fruitful rethinking of a postmodern theme. As Hawkes argues, Said was emphatically opposed to all grand narratives based on birth and nationalism—he believed that they hindered critical thought and voluntary associations. But he nonetheless cast his historicist concept of the secular against postmodern appeals to quasi-structures or quasi-metaphysics. Said opposed a Foucauldian tendency to separate systems of thought from the beliefs of historical individuals, and a Derridean tendency to divorce texts from their material and historical circumstances. That is, he spoke out against an anti-historicism that "isolated textuality from the circumstances, the events, the physical senses that made it possible."[21]

The theme of aesthetic self-fashioning appeared most prominently in the work of Foucault. Later Butler imported it into the United States when she reworked Foucault's idea of bodily inscription to develop her theory of gender as performative. According to Butler, there is no real inner self that expresses its identity by way of the body, and even bodies have no ontological status or reality aside from the acts, gestures, and enactments that produce them. Rather, we fashion ourselves through interpretive performances of normative categories, with the "stylized repetition of acts" giving a false impression of authenticity, and with political subversion consisting of a parodic recontextualization of such apparently authentic acts.[22] To many critics, such aesthetic self-fashioning lacked content and so normative force. In the absence of any sense of how we were to make ourselves, and in the absence of any justification for subversion itself, postmodernism appeared to have run into a dead end. As Martha Nussbaum wrote, in what became a notorious caricature of Butler, postmodernism implied that all we are capable of are "sexy acts of parodic subversion."[23] Yet the postmodernists, perhaps in response to such critics, have rethought the theme of self-fashioning. Bevir briefly suggests, for instance, that Foucault's commitment to disruptive, stylized transgressions gave way to an account of self-fashioning as an ethical practice—a practice in which we risk our secure place in an established order by challenging the normative horizons of that order so as to engage with excluded others. Similarly, Butler has developed a concern with the problems of living in unchosen communities. She has moved away from a politically neutral notion of parody toward a concept of "critical living." It seems that we are capable not only of sexy acts of subversion, but also, and perhaps more importantly, of living so as to exhibit generosity, humility, and patience toward the Other.

Linguistic anti-representationalism was expressed most provocatively by Derrida in some of his earliest works—*Of Grammatology, Writing and Difference,* and *Speech and Phenomena*—in which he claimed that language always appears as repetition, not representation, and communication is always accidental and unbounded. To his critics and defenders alike, he seemed to be rejecting the very possibility of meaning. Equally Derrida almost immediately distanced himself from the provocative version of linguistic anti-representationalism thus ascribed to him. For example, he wrote in *Deconstruction and Pragmatism,* "all that a deconstructive view tries to show, is that since convention, institutions and consensus are stabilizations (sometimes stabilizations of great duration, sometimes micro-stabilizations), this means that they are stabilizations of something essentially unstable and chaotic."[24] Although Derrida insists that this more "pragmatic" view was part of deconstruction from the beginning,[25] it is hard not to conclude that his casual clarification—"all I was saying was..."—redefines deconstruction in a way that makes it sound a little bit too uncontroversial. There is, after all, nothing earth-shattering, or even particularly novel, in the suggestion that the world is precarious, and that we project a contingent linguistic order onto it so as to be able to function as a community.

Irony was arguably the most caricatured of postmodernism's themes. The novelist David Foster Wallace once described irony as "hip cynicism, a hatred that winks and nudges you and pretends it's just kidding."[26] More generally, critics of postmodernism often moved far too quickly from identifying an ironic tone based on the groundlessness of knowledge, language and reality, to asserting that such irony entailed irresponsibility, a lack of seriousness, and even a quality of deception. To many observers—especially of the American academy—the terrorist attack on the World Trade Tower decisively ended the age of irony. An editorial in *Time* magazine soon after September 11th began: "one good thing could come from this horror: it could spell the end of the age of irony."[27] It is true, moreover, that the post-9/11 commentary of Derrida and Butler—post-9/11 in that it comes after the attacks and responds to the fallout from the attacks—offers a change in tone and emphasis. As Patton suggests, 9/11 provided the context in which Derrida gave the most overtly political account of the role of philosophy: Derrida spoke—with a new seriousness (it seemed to some)—about the relationship of deconstruction to democracy, and he was strikingly less equivocal about his broad support for liberal democratic ideals. Similarly, Butler turned in both *Precarious Life* and *Giving an Account of Oneself* to an ethical vocabulary that remains provisional but is no longer so ironic. Now, when Butler discusses patience, generosity and humility as the basis for a politics of non-violence, there are no quotation marks around her concepts. If the concepts remain open to novel uses for divergent ends, Butler herself seems less concerned continually to say so than she is to expound the normative hopes that she believes they might foster. However, even if the age of irony has drawn to a close, a kind of pragmatic irony remains a present and fruitful theme within postmodern writing. We are talking here of irony as humility and contingency of belief coupled with hope—a form of irony most forcefully expressed by Rorty. The idea that concepts and beliefs are held only contingently, and lack any deep or original meaning, no longer entails nihilism, nor does it require an insouciant "wink and nod." Rather, it provides a starting point for political, and especially democratic, hopes in an all too bleak world.

Hope is, of course, integral to our final theme: post-positivist utopianism. The utopian impulse within postmodernism has often been obscured by critics prone to recognize only cynical nihilism. Even sophisticated interlocutors have concluded, as Seyla Benhabib does, that postmodernism brought a "retreat from utopia."[28] No doubt Benhabib is right if we understand utopia to mean a rationalistic and concrete model of an alternative society. It is far less clear that she is right, however, if we define utopia, as she does, to mean a longing for what is not yet. The problem is that the postmodernists' refusal to offer a concrete model of an alternative society means that their utopianism, at least in its most provocative form, feels like a tease. When Derrida wrote about justice or democracy, it was, as Patton shows, often as something elusive and always "to come." Cornell too argued for a "beyond" the content of which cannot be described because any realization of it would render it present rather than beyond. Butler's early work is replete with phrases such as "normative aspirations" and "futural form of politics," none of which are given any content. Some critics complained that postmodernism thus failed to offer any normative guidelines on what to *do*. Here too, however, postmodernists developed their ideas in fruitful ways. Without giving us programmatic blueprints or principles of justice, they have begun to appeal to concerns, ideas, and values that help to flesh out visions of what is not yet. Radical democracy is a common vision, appearing in the work of Butler and Ernesto Laclau and Chantal Mouffe. Progressive social democracy has taken hold of Rorty. And, Wolin argues, something akin to human rights came to appeal to Foucault. It remains to be seen whether these various hopes are compatible. It also remains to be seen, as Patton reminds us, whether they are really that different from the hopes of liberal democrats.

Many of the themes of postmodernism have been reworked in less provocative forms. Typically, it also remains to be seen whether they are really that different from ideas that can be readily found elsewhere. Although we do not quite want to imply that postmodernism has been "domesticated"—the fear of every good postmodernist a decade ago—we would suggest that historicizing postmodernism serves to deflate it. Deflation may be the end of postmodernism. Alternatively, it may be the start of a more fruitful and widespread debate about what versions of the themes of postmodernism are appropriate for our purposes. As these chapters demonstrate, that debate requires us to consider local contexts: amenable how, to whom, and for what?

NOTES

1. See R. Adcock, M. Bevir, and S. Stimson, eds., *Modern Political Science: Anglo-American Exchanges since 1880* (Princeton, NJ: Princeton University Press, 2007).
2. Compare W. Everdell, *The First Moderns* (Chicago: University of Chicago Press, 1997).
3. For studies of this nostalgia see S. Pederson and P. Mandler, eds., *After the Victorians: Private Conscience and Public Duty in Modern Britain* (London: Routledge, 1994); and J. Stapleton, *Englishness and the Study of Politics: The Social and Political Thought of Ernest Barker* (Cambridge: Cambridge University Press, 1994).
4. Compare Adcock, Bevir, and Stimson, eds., *Modern Political Science.*
5. A broader account of historicism, conceived as anti-metaphysics in the writing of history, appears in D. Roberts, *Nothing But History: Reconstruction and Extremity after Metaphysics* (Berkeley: University of California Press, 1995).
6. Examples of texts that grapple with the problem of universality in the context of a historicist emphasis on particularity include B. Croce, *History: Its Theory and Practice*, trans. D. Ainslie (New York: Russell and Russell, 1960); and E. Troeltsch, *The Absoluteness of Christianity and the History of Religions* (London: SCM Press, 1972).
7. Compare M. Bevir, *The Logic of the History of Ideas* (Cambridge: Cambridge University Press, 1999).
8. H. Dreyfus and P. Rabinow, *Michel Foucault: Beyond Structuralism and Hermeneutics*, 2nd ed. (Chicago: University of Chicago Press, 1983), 105.
9. Richard Rorty, *Contingency, Irony, and Solidarity* (Cambridge: Cambridge University Press, 1989), xv.
10. Ibid., 9.
11. M. Lilla, *The Reckless Mind: Intellectuals and Politics* (New York: New York Review Books, 2001), chap. 6.
12. See, for example, M. Nussbaum, "The Professor of Parody," *The New Republic*, February 1999, 37–45.
13. M. Foucault, Language, *Counter-memory,Practice: Selected Interviews*, ed. and intro. D. Bouchard, trans. D. Bouchard and S. Sherry (Ithaca, NY: Cornell University Press, 1977), 230.
14. See, for example, F. Jameson, *Postmodernism or, the Cultural Logic of Late Capitalism* (Durham, NC: Duke University Press, 1991); F. Jameson, *The Cultural Turn* (New York: Verso, 1998); T. Eagleton, Literary Theory: An Introduction (Minneapolis: University of Minnesota Press, 1996); and T. Eagleton, "Ideology, Discourse and the Problems of 'Post-Marxism,'" in S. Malpas, ed., *Postmodern Debates* (New York: Palgrave, 2001), 79–92.
15. P. Dews, "Postmodernism: Pathologies of Modernity from Nietzsche to the Post-structuralists," in T. Ball and R. Bellamy, eds., *The Cambridge History of Twentieth-Century Political Thought* (Cambridge: Cambridge University Press, 2003), 345.
16. Ibid, 357--360.
17. N. Fraser, *Justice Interruptus* (New York: Routledge, 1997), 215.

18. K. Chance, *Interview with Edward Said*, Bard College, 13 February 2001 at http://www.bard.edu/hrp/resource_pdfs/chance.said.pdf
19. E. Said, "A Window on the World," *The Guardian*, August 2, 2003.
20. Examples include P. Herman, ed., Historicizing Theory (Albany: State University of New York Press, 2004); and D. Myers, *Resisting History: Historicism and Its Discontents in German-Jewish Thought* (Princeton, NJ: Princeton University Press, 2003).
21. E. Said, *The World, the Text and the Critic* (Cambridge, MA: Harvard University Press, 1983), 4.
22. J. Butler, *Gender Trouble: Feminism and the Subversion of Identity* (New York: Routledge, 1990), 179.
23. Nussbaum, "Professor of Parody."
24. J. Derrida, "Remarks on Deconstruction and Pragmatism," in C. Mouffe, ed., *Deconstruction and Pragmatism* (New York: Routledge, 1996), 83.
25. "I recall that from the beginning the question concerning the trace was connected with a certain notion of labour, of doing, and that what I called then programmatology tried to link grammatology and pragmatism." Derrida, *Deconstruction and Pragmatism*, 78.
26. David Foster *Wallace, Interview with Larry McCaffery*, Review of Contemporary Fiction 13 (1993).
27. R. Rosenblatt, "The Age of Irony Comes to an End," *Time*, September 24, 2001.
28. S. Benhabib, "Feminism and Postmodernism," in *Feminist Contentions: A Philosophical Exchange* (New York: Routledge, 1995), 29.

2   Honesty as the Best Policy

Nietzsche on *Redlichkeit* and the Contrast between Stoic and Epicurean Strategies of the Self

Melissa Lane

In *The End of Modernity,*[1] Gianni Vattimo asserted that postmodernism began in Nietzsche's work. Indeed, invocations of Nietzsche in relation to postmodernism are manifold. Thoughts attributed to Nietzsche (including the "new Nietzsche" of the French poststructuralists[2] as well as the "new Nietzsche" of American academe in the 1980s[3]) have been identified[4] as lying behind each of the postmodern ideas identified in the introduction to this volume. In particular, anti-foundationalism,[5] anti-essentialism, anti-representationalism and anti-dualism have in common a concern with the nature and content of truth claims.[6] And it is truth that has become central to recent discussions of Nietzsche and to critics of his relations with postmodernism. Bernard Williams has argued that Nietzsche is not, as postmodernists would have it, a "denier" of truth or indifferent to truthfulness.[7] In contrast, as Paul Patton observes in this volume, Richard Rorty has sought to remove Nietzsche from the arena of truth altogether, relegating his influence to the "private" realm of idiosyncratic self-fashioning.[8] Yet while self-fashioning has become a leading theme of the "postmodern" reading of Nietzsche, and his demand for truthfulness a leading theme of some of its major critics, there has been little discussion of two aspects of these claims: first, the relationship between "truthfulness" and "honesty," and the extent to which Nietzsche marks out a virtue of honesty named *Redlichkeit* from *Daybreak*[9] (1881) onward; and second, the relationship between the intellectual demands of honesty and the attempt to fashion a suitable emotional stance for the self.[10] In both of these concerns, as we shall see, Nietzsche was engaged in an evolving and contrasting evaluation of the role of honesty in the cognitive and the emotional aspects of self-fashioning in the strategies[11] of the ancient Stoics and Epicureans. Thus one cannot assess Nietzsche in relation to postmodern concerns without understanding his own developing position in relation to these Hellenistic traditions of thought, traditions which had become intensely influential again in the early modern period and which had shaped the thinking of the French classical moralists with whom Nietzsche was also deeply engaged.

Previous assessments of Nietzsche on the Stoics and Epicureans have focused almost exclusively on his view of their attitudes toward the emotions.

But comparing their cognitive stances—epitomized in an overt relationship between Stoicism and *Redlichkeit* in the sequence of Nietzsche's books from *Daybreak* to *Beyond Good and Evil*[12] (1886)—reveals the extent to which honesty and intellectual adequacy came to weigh for him on the side of Stoicism. In the contrasts Nietzsche draws between Epicureans and Stoics, and the linking of the latter to the ethic of *Redlichkeit*, we find that honesty as an intellectual policy comes to constrain the range and nature of admirable[13] self-fashioning, just as it did for Montaigne and his fellow French classical writers whom Nietzsche so admired.

The theses of this chapter intersect with recent themes in research on Nietzsche from several angles. First, while I broadly concur with the content that Bernard Williams ascribes to what he calls Nietzsche's cognitive stance of truthfulness, he and other recent writers[14] on cognition and morality in Nietzsche speak interchangeably of "truthfulness" and "honesty" without noting the significance of the distinct trajectories of *Wahrhaftigkeit* (truthfulness), *Redlichkeit*, and another word for honesty, *Ehrlichkeit*, in Nietzsche's texts. These trajectories reveal the ways, and moments, in which Nietzsche felt it necessary to articulate a new virtue of *Redlichkeit* in contrast first with the traditional and unthinking dimensions of *Ehrlichkeit*, and then with the Platonic-Christian entanglements of *Wahrhaftigkeit*. In the process we gain a keener understanding of the cognitive stance that he sought to develop.

Second, and relatedly, my contention that *Daybreak* marks the emergence of two preoccupations—with *Redlichkeit* and with an emerging preference for the cognitive stance of Stoicism in place of an earlier celebration of Epicureanism—which then feature markedly in *The Gay Science*[15] (1882), *Thus Spoke Zarathustra*[16] (1883–85), and *Beyond Good and Evil*, provides a new lens on the question of the unity or sequential division of Nietzsche's published writings. Rather than relegating *Daybreak* to a "middle period" which is superseded by a "late period" somewhere in or after *The Gay Science*,[17] the continuity in their discussions of *Redlichkeit* and the Stoic cognitive stance reveals the extent to which the four texts from *Daybreak* to *Beyond Good and Evil* constitute a consistent sequence and share common preoccupations. Of the major texts, it is only *On the Genealogy of Morality*[18] (1887)—from which these themes are largely absent—that stands apart from this sequence. Whereas from *Daybreak* to *Beyond Good and Evil*[19] Nietzsche is not only criticizing past formations of thought and self-fashioning (such as the Christian) but also developing his own stance of *Redlichkeit* in relation to the productive if problematic stances of the Stoics and Epicureans, *Genealogy of Morality* has a much narrower focus on the main line of decadence from Platonism to Christianity with scarcely any concern either for the development of an alternative Nietzschean virtue or of the Hellenistic roots which might nourish it.[20]

Finally, my evaluation of Stoics and Epicureans in Nietzsche owes much to recent research on the variety and subtlety of Nietzsche's engagement with the ancient schools. Leaving aside his complex and well-documented[21] engagements with Plato, Platonism and Socrates, it is clear that even with respect to the Hellenistic schools neither he nor his hero Montaigne[22] drew exclusively on any one over the others. Rather, important elements of his thought derive from his reflections on Cynicism[23] and Skepticism[24] as well as Stoicism[25] and Epicureanism.[26] Indeed, Nietzsche's understanding of *Redlichkeit*—with its semantic overtones of frank, forthright and uninhibited speech—is flavored both by his understanding of the flourishing of *parrhêsia* in the ancient world (especially but not only in Cynicism, as in *Beyond Good and Evil* 26 and 230)[27] and of its incarnation in the French classical moralists, above all in Montaigne.[28] But the mutual evolution of this understanding of *Redlichkeit* and of Nietzsche's attitude to Epicurus's strategy of cognitive self-constriction for the sake of tranquility, and the contrasting relationship between Stoicism as a non-consolatory, non-delusional cognitive attitude to reality and the Nietzschean virtue of honesty, has not been previously observed.[29]

These, then, are the gaps that the present chapter seeks to fill. It is inspired by a remark in Jean-Luc Nancy's pioneering discussion of the significance of *Redlichkeit* in Nietzsche, in the context of which he says that it involves an "acknowledgement of reality" which is "of the Stoical type, perhaps."[30] And there is indeed a crucial textual link between *Redlichkeit* and Stoicism in *Beyond Good and Evil* 227, although Nancy does not refer to it. Here, *Redlichkeit* is postulated [*gesetzt*] to be "our virtue," the virtue of "we free spirits" which "we cannot get rid of"; and it is said that even if this honesty one day should soften, "we will stay *harsh*, we who are the last of the Stoics! [*bleiben wir hart, wir letzten Stoiker!*]." To appreciate the significance of this connection (while acknowledging that Nietzsche enjoyed playing with such plural self-apostrophe—*Beyond Good and Evil* ends with a question posed about "we mandarins with Chinese brushes"),[31] we must look in turn at Nietzsche's treatment of *Redlichkeit*, the Stoics and the Epicureans, along the way considering the relationship of *Redlichkeit* to *Ehrlichkeit* and then to *Wahrhaftigkeit*.

REDLICHKEIT AND *EHRLICHKEIT*

While Nietzsche uses both *Redlichkeit* and *Ehrlichkeit* at times to mean "honesty," and while he is too fluent a writer to corral himself into any rigid scheme of word choice, nevertheless, we can discern a striking overall pattern in his choices between each of these substantive nouns (and, to a lesser but still significant extent, in his use of the various adjectival forms deriving from them). Underlying this pattern are their quite different semantic overtones in German: *Ehrlichkeit* as the virtue of an upright and honorable man, *Redlichkeit* invoking honesty as frank speech. *Ehrlichkeit* is a preoccupation especially before *Daybreak* in *Human, All Too*

Human[32] (1878–80), where the noun or its adjectival form is the subject of several headings of individual passages. There it bears mixed values, being used both for stances which are presented as admirable and also for figures presented as conventionally honest and honorable but self-deceiving as to the significance of this virtue. (Even Nietzsche's early outburst of admiration for Montaigne's honesty in "Schopenhauer as Educator" is couched in terms of *Ehrlichkeit*).[33] These relatively early writings thus consider the advantages and disadvantages of honesty primarily by using terms deriving from *Ehrlichkeit* promiscuously for both. Meanwhile *Redlichkeit* scarcely appears in any form before *Daybreak*.[34]

It is *Daybreak*—called by Nietzsche in *Ecce Homo* (1888; section on "Daybreak")[35] the launch of his "campaign against *morality*"—that marks a dramatic break with this pattern. There and from then on, in *Gay Science*, *Zarathustra*, and *Beyond Good and Evil* especially, the *Ehrlichkeit* family is used predominantly in the negative sense of the conventionally but deludedly honest and honorable, while *Redlichkeit* is used predominantly to signify a new kind of virtue with which Nietzsche's free spirits and philosophers identify. And this new pattern of partition between the two families of terms is textually marked: while *Human, All Too Human* is pervaded by passage headings invoking *Ehrlichkeit*, *Daybreak* in contrast is pervaded by *Redlichkeit*, the noun alone appearing twelve times whereas in writings before *Daybreak* it had appeared only once.

Daybreak 456 celebrates *Redlichkeit* as "A virtue in process of becoming [*Eine werdende Tugenden*]" and describes it as "among neither the Socratic nor the Christian virtues; it is the youngest virtue, still very immature, still often misjudged and taken for something else, still hardly aware of itself...." In contrast, *Daybreak* 248 diagnoses *Ehrlichkeit* as a virtue that emerged from the simulation of honesty among the "hereditary aristocracies." The contrast is plain. *Ehrlichkeit* is an old and now conventional virtue, which has therefore become liable to self-misunderstanding on the part of those who possess it, in contrast with *Redlichkeit* which is the youngest virtue, still emerging as a virtue, not least in Nietzsche's own texts.

Although, as noted above, the much later *Genealogy of Morality* scarcely attends to the value of *Redlichkeit* per se, when Nietzsche does there consider the cognitive nature and value of asceticism and its intellectual daughter atheism, his choice of terms reveals the same contrasting valorizations of *Ehrlichkeit* and *Redlichkeit*.[36] In *Genealogy of Morality* III.26, Nietzsche is attacking the "objective" historians and idealists who flirt with ascetic ideals, and exclaims, "I have every respect for the ascetic ideal *in so far as it is honest* [*ehrlich*]! So long as it believes in itself and does not tell us bad jokes!" Here, he is speaking of asceticism which remains asceticism, not yet turning its intellectual scrutiny upon itself, but at least behaving honorably in its own terms, and so *ehrlich* is used to mark the conventionality and honorableness of such a stance. In contrast, the very next section, *Genealogy of Morality* III.27, applauds the "[u]nconditional, honest [*redliche*] atheism which is the air "we more spiritual men of the age breathe" and which has precisely taken the next step of turning its discipline in truth-telling fostered by religion against the "*lie entailed in the belief in God*" itself. (Indeed, *Genealogy of Morality* 357 had praised Schopenhauer for having been the first to achieve this "unconditional honest atheism," using the same German phrase.)

This contrast further helps us to understand the famous remarks on Plato's "noble lie" ("'*ehrliche' Lüge*") in *Genealogy of Morality* III.19. Here Nietzsche uses *ehrliche* to capture the virtue- and honor-connotations of Plato's Greek, in which, as G.R.F. Ferrari has remarked, *gennaios* has overtones of "grand or noble" but also colloquially of "massive, no-doubt-about it," while playing in German as Plato does with the Greek with a context of lying in which the sense of "honorableness" and its usual association with "honesty" come apart. [37] And while Nietzsche is observing that such noble lies require the ability to distinguish between truth and falsehood in relation to oneself, the fact that the lie is a lie disbars it from being described in the frank-speaking terms of *Redlichkeit*. When one lies, even if one is right to lie, one cannot be said to display *Redlichkeit*; whereas, as Nietzsche shows here in his choice of translation from the Greek, *Ehrlichkeit* can at a pinch be pushed in the direction of the honorable at the price of the honest. Indeed this may be the seed of his contempt for the conventional *ehrliche*, recalling the way that Montaigne and his contemporaries contrasted the man bound by religious convention with the *honnête homme* who would in German be said to be *redliche* rather than *ehrliche*.

Again, it must be acknowledged that this new distinction between *Ehrlichkeit* and *Redlichkeit* is not universally observed in the texts from *Daybreak* onward. Whereas there appears to be no particular salience to the occasional positive valorizations of *Ehrlichkeit* from *Daybreak* onward, negative uses of *Redlichkeit* in contrast do constitute a significant group: they appear almost exclusively in contexts which treat *Redlichkeit* as an existing social attitude and as an attitude towards other people,[38] in contrast with the positive pattern in which it is considered as an attitude towards oneself or to the world, reality, or knowledge. *Gay Science* 329, for example, clearly distinguishes between *redlich*-demanding attitudes among the present busy bourgeoisie and the genuine *Redlichkeit* which would emerge from solitude. The only other reservation about *Redlichkeit* which emerges after *Daybreak*, particularly in *Beyond Good and Evil*, is that the trumpeting of any virtue, even this new and youngest one, is potentially misleading. Positive invocations of *Redlichkeit* in *Beyond Good and Evil* 227, 230 and 295 are thus followed by warnings that one must not moralize or become complacent as a result of one's commitment to *Redlichkeit*. Nevertheless, with these caveats acknowledged, we will now show that *Redlichkeit* from *Daybreak* to *Beyond Good and Evil* is considered as a new virtue, one linked specifically to a proper cognitive stance exemplified in the consideration of philosophers, knowledge, and *Wissenschaft* or science.

REDLICHKEIT AS A VIRTUE

We have seen already that *Daybreak* 456 proclaims *Redlichkeit* as "the youngest virtue," a claim repeated by Zarathustra, who attacks those who hate "the man of knowledge and that youngest of virtues, which is called honesty [*den Erkennenden und jene jüngste der Tugenden, welche heisst: Redlichkeit*]."[39] We will return to the connection between *Redlichkeit* and knowledge below. First, we must note that *Daybreak* not only proclaims *Redlichkeit* a new virtue, but also gives content to it by offering a significant reinterpretation of the view of the cardinal virtues proposed in *Human, All Too Human* (*The Wanderer and His Shadow* 1880) 64. There, Nietzsche had described four eras of "higher humanity" as each honoring one of the Greek cardinal virtues above the others: in the first era, bravery (*Tapferkeit*); in the second, justice; in the third, moderation; in the fourth, wisdom, concluding the passage by challenging the reader to say in which era "we" and "you" (i.e., the reader) live. He was content to give the classical names and (by implication) definitions of the virtues, the burden of the passage lying not in redefining but simply in prioritizing among them. But in *Daybreak* 556 he advances a new list of "the good four [virtues]" which renames and so (by implication) redefines some of them, drawing strikingly but idiosyncratically on Roman and French sources to do so.[40] The passage reads thus: "*The good four.* — Honest [*redlich*] towards ourselves and whoever else is a friend to us; *brave* [*tapfer*] towards the enemy; *magnanimous* towards the defeated; *polite* — always: this is what the four cardinal virtues [*Kardinaltugenden*] want us to be."[41]

Here, we find a new account of the cardinal virtues—presented adjectivally as attributes of persons rather than as substantive nouns—which revises the previously postulated definitions of three of the four. While bravery or courage is not significantly changed, justice has been dropped in favor of Ciceronian magnanimity or great-souledness (though Cicero himself, *De Off.* I.61, treated magnanimity as an enhancement, not a replacement, for the traditional four cardinal virtues).[42] Moderation is replaced by "politeness": the lineage of politeness here recalls Ciceronian decorum, but is heavily inflected by the French ideal of *honnêteté*, an ideal which incorporated polite sociability into a standard of "honesty" conceived as a kind of global virtue at once moral, social, and still connected to its roots in frank speaking.[43] (*Redlichkeit* in German can also connote a global sort of virtue, one with roots in honesty but extending to a general uprightness.) Most importantly for us, wisdom (*Weisheit* in *The Wanderer and His Shadow* 64), with its overtones of widely recognized and objective knowledge, is replaced by the cognitive virtue of being honest [*redlich*]; compare the way that the eighteenth-century writer Nicolas de Chamfort, whom Nietzsche read avidly especially in 1881–82, had defined the *honnête homme* as "*détrompé de toutes illusions.*"[44] Note that the scope of this virtue is restricted to "ourselves and whoever else is a friend to us." Limiting the scope of honesty to oneself and one's friends makes it not incompatible with lying to outsiders, though lying itself could never (as we observed in relation to *Genealogy of Morality* III.19) be aptly described as *redlich*.

Nietzsche identifies a close connection, verging on a redescriptive identity, between *Redlichkeit* and cruelty: "'wild honesty [*ausschweifende Redlichkeit*]'" is said to be a more "polite" name than "cruelty" in *Beyond Good and Evil* 230. Yet he takes care to warn against the dangers of such cruelty going too far, becoming what *Gay Science* 159 will condemn as the vice of "unyieldingness [*Unbeugsamkeit*]." Zarathustra encounters a man who is making himself bleed by applying leeches to his own skin, who announces that he has learned from Zarathustra to be the "conscientious man" and declares, "Where my honesty [*Redlichkeit*] ceases I am blind and want to be blind. But where I want to know [*wissen*] I also want to be honest [*redlich*], that is, severe, stern, strict, cruel, inexorable."[45] Zarathustra's response to the "conscientious man" is difficult to characterize precisely, but it is clearly critical and negative.[46] That *Redlichkeit*, like any virtue when pushed too far, can turn into a vice is a point which Nietzsche makes in an Aristotelian vein: its corresponding vice is stupidity or boringness.[47] Excessive cruelty in the service of an unyielding honesty is both emotionally and cognitively problematic, for it fails to recognize its own roots and motivations. *Daybreak* 536 warns against the cruelty with which people deploy their particular virtues and enjoins, "let us act humanely with our 'sense of honesty' ['*sinn für Redlichkeit*']"; this is (like) a thumbscrew whose ability to torment all proselytizers "we" have tested on ourselves.

An important generalization of the "conscientious man" story, which argues that dangers lie not only in an excess of honesty (as per *Daybreak* 536) but in the nature of honesty itself, is made in *Gay Science* 107. There, Nietzsche contends that pure and isolated *Redlichkeit* "would lead to nausea and suicide." *Redlichkeit* is portrayed as the attitude displayed in and generating "the insight into general untruth and mendacity [*Unwahrheit und Verlogenheit*]...the insight into delusion and error as a condition of cognitive [*erkennenden*] and sensate existence" which is the result of science [*Wissenschaft*]. But fortunately, Nietzsche avers, *Redlichkeit* now encounters a "counterforce [*Gegenmacht*]" which enables us to avoid these dire consequences of its otherwise unchecked operation. This counterforce is art [*Kunst*], described as "the cult of the untrue" and "the *good* will to appearance." Nietzsche insists that it is only as an aesthetic phenomenon that existence is still "*bearable*" for "us," and that anyone who is "*ashamed*" of himself for this does not yet "belong amongst us."[48]

This important passage helps to clarify the cognitive dimensions of *Redlichkeit* as a Nietzschean virtue. The person with this virtue speaks frankly (that is, without lying) about the whole content of what they perceive, even where that content consists of untruths and lies.[49] In other words, *Redlichkeit* combines the virtues which Bernard Williams[50] distinguishes as Sincerity and Accuracy: combining frank speaking with an unblinking acknowledgement of all the reality which one perceives in relation to a particular subject. (However, it is not uncompromisingly endorsed; it can be dangerous to health and life if pushed too far.) These cognitive aspects of *Redlichkeit* are underscored in Nietzsche's further remarks about its relationship to philosophers and to science (*Wissenschaft*), to which we now turn.

REDLICHKEIT, WISSENSCHAFT, AND PHILOSOPHERS

As we have seen, *Gay Science* 107 strongly, though not uncritically, aligns *Redlichkeit* with *Wissenschaft*, the German word for science or structured body of knowledge, which in its adjectival form has been glossed as "careful, methodical attention to the real facts of the situation being investigated."[51] "Knowledge" (*Erkenntnis*) too is aligned with *Redlichkeit* in a positive vein, especially in *Daybreak*, where in *Daybreak* 84 Christian philologists are criticized for lacking *Redlichkeit*, and in *Daybreak* 482 the men "whom we should call philosophers" are posited in a rhetorical question to be "too serious in their passion for knowledge and for honesty" to seek fame. *Gay Science* 319 indicts insufficient *Redlichkeit* for leading to an inadequate *Erkenntnis* in the founders of religion and similar folk, contrasting these overly credulous men with "we reason-thirsty ones" who "want to face our experiences as sternly as we would a scientific experiment"—*Redlichkeit* and *wissenschaftlichen Versuche* here linked as the path to adequate *Erkenntnis*. And the ideal of science finds its apotheosis in the startling and deliberately amusing passage of *Gay Science* 335, titled "Long live physics!" Here, we must become physicists who know what can and (like the moral worth of an action) cannot be known: "so, long live physics! And even more long live what *compels* us to it — our honesty [*Redlichkeit*]!"

Yet, like the difficult passage of *Gay Science* 344 in relation to truth, *Beyond Good and Evil* 230 will acknowledge that what lies behind the will to knowledge and to *Wissenschaft* is not easy to explain or justify: "Why do we choose it, this insane task? Or to ask it differently: 'Why knowledge (*Erkenntniss* at all?'—Everyone will be asking us this. And we who have been prodded so much, we who have asked ourselves the same question a hundred times already, we have not found and are not finding any better answers...." Moreover, *Daybreak* 550 had already noted the danger that such honesty posed to the great knowledge-loving philosophers of the past (Plato, Aristotle, Descartes, Spinoza): the danger was that their *Redlichkeit* would become a "panegyrist" of all things. That is, insofar as honesty generates (the intense enjoyment of) knowledge, it risks projecting that positive value onto things themselves, forgetting that what is valuable rather is the exercise of honesty generating knowledge itself. And *Gay Science* 110 had made knowledge, *Redlichkeit* and skepticism (again a combination recalling Montaigne) complicit in the evolving fight about the "truths," in which "knowledge and the striving for the true finally took their place as a need among the other needs."

As *Gay Science* 110 shows, it is impossible wholly to segregate *Redlichkeit* from the complex and difficult question of the status of truth, and truths, in Nietzsche. But without being able to enter into that question fully here, we can at least show that *Redlichkeit* as a Nietzschean virtue is related to the cognitive standpoint beyond good and evil. This is manifest in *Zarathustra* "Retired from Service," where the "old" and "last" pope tells Zarathustra that it is his (Zarathustra's) very piety which has engendered his unbelief: "Is it not your piety itself that no longer allows you to believe in a god? And your exceeding honesty [*übergrosse Redlichkeit*] will yet carry you off beyond good and evil, too!" Here it is *Redlichkeit* itself that is credited (albeit by the old pope, whom Zarathustra then invites into his own cave) with enabling one to travel beyond good and evil. This remark encapsulates the importance of *Redlichkeit* in the textual economies of *Daybreak*, *Gay Science*, *Zarathustra* and *Beyond Good and Evil* in particular. Further illumination of the relationship between honesty and truth for Nietzsche can be found by comparing the terms *Redlichkeit* and *Wahrhaftigkeit*, while remaining alert to the complexities of the relationship between the latter (truthfulness) and truth in the texts (e.g., *Daybreak* 73; and on philosophers as friends of "truth," but not dogmatists, *Beyond Good and Evil* 43).

REDLICHKEIT AND WAHRHAFTIGKEIT

In works before *Daybreak*, where as we have seen *Redlichkeit* scarcely appears, *Wahrhaftigkeit* is quite often used in a positive sense. It plays an important role in the conclusion of the second and third essays of the *Untimely Meditations* (1873–76), on history and Schopenhauer respectively, as well as in evaluation of the positive contributions of the Renaissance in *Human, All Too Human* 237. In the Preface to *Human, All Too Human*, added in 1886 (and in the note from 1886-87 first published in *The Will to Power* 945), Nietzsche claims the virtue of *Wahrhaftigkeit* as his personal "luxury." But there are also negative uses of *Wahrhaftigkeit* to be found in *Human, All Too Human*, for example in its book *Assorted Opinions and Maxims* (1879) 32, where in a strikingly Platonic remark it is said that poets who pretend to know and so deceive others about "'real reality [*wirkliche Wirklichkeit*]'" end by becoming "honest [*ehrlich*]" and believing in their own "truthfulness [*Wahrhaftigkeit*]." Here, truthfulness and being *ehrlich* are presented as mutually supportive deceptions, which evolve from deceiving others to deceiving themselves—in stark contrast to the antithesis between *Redlichkeit* and self-deception, and the inaffinity between *Redlichkeit* and deception of any kind, which we have observed.

From *Daybreak* onward, the generally positive valorization of *Redlich-keit* is occasionally shared with[52] or paralleled by[53] a similar valorization of *Wahrhaftigkeit*.[54] And there is the occasional remark that treats *Wahrhaftigkeit* and *Redlichkeit* equally negatively, as in *Daybreak* 418. But the burden of *Beyond Good and Evil*, particularly in its opening sections, is to question both the value placed on *Wahrhaftigkeit* and its very ability to question its own value. In this context of the opening of *Beyond Good and Evil*, important contrasts are drawn between *Redlichkeit* and *Wahrhaftigkeit*. It is as if *Daybreak*'s framing of *Redlichkeit* as a young and new virtue here enables it to play a critical role *vis-à-vis* the old, Platonic and Christian dynamics implicating the virtue of *Wahrhaftigkeit*. So while it is certainly not the case that Nietzsche never invokes *Wahrhaftigkeit* in a valorizing vein, recent treatments of this theme (celebrating his ironic paradox in *Beyond Good and Evil* 177[55] of "*Wahrhaftigkeit*" being something which perhaps no one has yet been *wahrhaftig* enough about) have ignored his several assertions that at least in some contexts it is *Redlichkeit* in contrast to *Wahrhaftigkeit* which he values.

Consider *Beyond Good and Evil* 1 and 5. *Beyond Good and Evil* 1 introduces as the topic the "will to truth," described as "this famous truthfulness [*Wahrhaftigkeit*] that all philosophers so far have talked about with veneration" (compare *Zarathustra* "Of the Famous Philosophers"). And *Beyond Good and Evil* 5 diagnoses "our" mistrust of these philosophers as resulting from the fact "that there is not enough genuine honesty about them [*dass es bei ihnen nicht redlich genug zugeht*]: even though they all make a huge, virtuous racket as soon as the problem of truthfulness [*das Problem der Wahrhaftigkeit*] is even remotely touched upon." Indeed, lacking sufficient honesty and advocating instead prejudices which they call "truths," these famous philosophers lack two specific forms of bravery or courage [*Tapferkeit*: picking up the *Human, All Too Human, The Wanderer and His Shadow* 64 and *Daybreak* 556 terms for the classical cardinal virtue]: courage of conscience to be honest with themselves, and the good taste of courage which would lead them to be honest with others either in warning or in self-satire. A wedge is inserted here between concern with the problem of truthfulness as a philosophical problem, and the virtue of honesty: the former does not entail the latter, and it is the latter that Nietzsche values.

Beyond Good and Evil 5's contrast between (the problem of) *Wahrhaftigkeit* and *Redlichkeit* parallels an important remark in *Daybreak* 456, the passage which we saw identifies *Redlichkeit* as "a virtue in the process of becoming." For *Daybreak* 456 precisely introduces *Redlichkeit* as contrasting with the "level of *Wahrhaftigkeit*" that many "worthy people" have attained, a level of thinking themselves and feeling sincere in asserting the classical or Christian nostrums of virtue and salvation. The point in both passages, *Beyond Good and Evil* 5 and *Daybreak* 456, is that *Wahrhaftigkeit* is a familiar classical, Christian and philosophical virtue, and as such has become a trap: people believing themselves to be truthful and seeking to be truthful are able dishonestly to ignore the roots or consequences of their actions. (Compare *Beyond Good and Evil* 264, in which a contemporary educator who "preach[es] truthfulness [*Wahrhaftigkeit*] above all else these days" to his students is described in manifestly contemptuous terms.) *Redlichkeit* as a new virtue, again, is able to escape these entanglements of the ancient, rooted and complex will to truthfulness.

REDLICHKEIT AND STOICISM

We may now reconsider the link between *Redlichkeit* and Stoicism asserted in *Beyond Good and Evil* 227. In this passage, as mentioned earlier, *Redlichkeit* is postulated as "our virtue," the virtue of "we free spirits" which "we cannot get rid of." Nietzsche avers that even if our (presumably, disposition of) *Redlichkeit* should one day for some reason become "weary" and lead to our craving a "better, easier, tenderer [*besser, leichter, zärtlicher*]" life, nevertheless "we will stay *harsh*, we who are the last of the Stoics! [*bleiben wir hart, wir letzten Stoiker!*]." After some further comments on how others will perceive this *Redlichkeit* and what it might, or should, be called, the passage concludes with the warning that we must not let our *Redlichkeit* degenerate into our stupidity [*Dummheit*], lest we become "saints or tedious bores," which we noticed above in relation to the risk of virtues degenerating into vices.

What does it mean that "we," whose virtue is *Redlichkeit*, are the last of the Stoics? The thought is not that even should our *Redlichkeit* evaporate, we would still remain Stoics. It is rather that should our impulse toward *Redlichkeit* for some reason weaken, our Stoic character of hardness or harshness will restore or preserve it. For far from *Redlichkeit* disappearing from the passage after the thought that it might soften, the rest of the passage is preoccupied by it. One might think that the role of Stoicism here is not cognitive, but solely emotional, as furnishing a harshness of emotional stance that can discipline the will; and indeed, most literature on Stoics and Stoicism in Nietzsche focuses exclusively on this point. But the suggestion that the vice which *Redlichkeit* risks degenerating into is stupidity (*Dummheit*) implies that its fundamental character is cognitive. Moreover, the dangerously craven desire for an easier (*leichter*) life picks up in *Daybreak* 456, where the worthy people at a certain "level of truthfulness" precisely think themselves entitled, when they feel that they are acting selflessly, to take a *leichter* attitude towards the truth [*Wahrheit*]; similarly in *Gay Science* 347, where the masses are said so fervently to crave scientific-positivist "certainty" that the task of proving such certainty is treated "more lightly and negligently [*leichter und lässlicher*]." In these passages, as in *Beyond Good and Evil* 227, we find that the desire for a *leichter*, easier existence risks fostering a flawed cognitive stance. *Redlichkeit* in contrast, insofar as it remains strong, is hostile to such self-indulgent and so self-deceiving emotional, hence cognitive, flaccidity. Instead, its Stoic overtones associate it with a severe and unblinking acknowledgement of nature and reality, of the way things are, which does not attempt to moralize away suffering or harm.

This view of the Stoics is in play in *Daybreak* 546 in a passage entitled "slave and idealist," in which the Stoic sage Epictetus (who had been a slave) is contrasted positively with "our idealists" of today. Epictetus was "brave" (possessing *Tapferkeit*) and "self-sufficient"; unlike later Christians, he lived without either hope or gratitude to the gods. Crucially, Nietzsche links these ethical attributes to his cognitive attitudes and commitments. "The fairest thing about [the Stoic ideal as embodied in Epictetus]...is that it lacks all fear of God, that it believes strictly in reason, that it is no penitential preacher." It is *because* the Stoic believed in reason that he lived in self-sufficiency, without either hope or fear of God, needing neither preaching nor consolation. The achievement of knowledge on the basis of reason enables the achievement of bravery—for reason teaches both that there is nothing supernatural that we need fear and that our natural needs are in fact few.

Consider two further passages where, although the Stoics are not named, they are arguably in view. In *The Wanderer and His Shadow* 37, Nietzsche adjures a group he calls "you dismal philosophical blindworms" not to treat their own oversights of self-fashioning as if they were fated facts about the terribleness of human passions. Instead, he advises that one attend to *kleinen* matters (as it were, the *petits faits*) in order "to *take from* the passions their terrible [*furchtbaren*] character." And he concludes: "let us...work honestly [*redlich*] together on the task of transforming the passions [*Leidenschaften*] of mankind one and all into joys [*Freudenschaften*]." As Nietzsche, who elsewhere calls himself an old philologist, would have known very well, it was a Stoic program to abolish the passions [individually, *pathē*] —which were rooted in and indeed constituted by cognitive errors – but instead to promote a different set of cognitive-emotional stances named in Greek *eupathē*, which are meant to be devoid of the suffering and lack which the "passions" proper involve. For example, the "passion" of pleasure (*hēdonē*) was to be replaced by the *eupathē* of joy (*chara*).[56] So the appeal to "joy" in *The Wanderer and His Shadow* 37[57] is a clue that, while both Epicureanism and Stoicism could be indicated by the claim that the passions are "terrible" and the title of the passage (*Eine Art Kultus der Leidenschaften*), it is Stoicism in particular which is primarily in view. And while *redlich* is playing an adjectival rather than substantive role here, the exhortation to pursue this strategy "honestly" suggests that it could otherwise be undermined by the wrong kind of cognitive stance.

The final Stoic connection to *Redlichkeit* is more speculative. We have already noted the assertion of a "'wild honesty [*ausschweifende Redlichkeit*]'" in *Beyond Good and Evil* 230, followed immediately by a renouncing of the elegant names of virtues such as *Redlichkeit* and "love of truth"

(*Liebe zur Wahrheit*) so as to avoid the danger of feeding "unconscious human vanity" in claiming these virtues as one's own. Nietzsche continues the passage by announcing an appropriate goal for "we hermits and marmots" who have freed ourselves from even the moral bauble of the name of *Redlichkeit*:

> [t]he terrible basic text [*schreckliche Grundtext*] of *homo natura* [italics added] must be recognized even underneath these fawning colors and painted surfaces. To retranslate[58] [*zurückübersetzen*] humanity [*den Menschen*] back into nature; to gain control of the many vain and fanciful interpretations and incidental meanings that have been scribbled and drawn over that eternal basic text of *homo natura* [italics added] so far; to make sure that, from now on, the human being will stand before the human being, just as he already stands before the rest of nature today, hardened by the discipline of science [*hart geworden in der Zucht der Wissenschaft*]....[59]

The passage then concludes with the unresolved self-challenging musing on the question of why one should pursue knowledge at all, which we noticed above.

Note that the reference to becoming hard (*hart*) through the discipline of Wissenschaft picks up the *hart* that "we who are the last of the Stoics" will remain in *Beyond Good and Evil* 227. Nietzsche is musing here on man as part of nature, an important Stoic theme, and in homage to them he seems to have picked up, inverted or perhaps even coined a Latin phrase in order to do so. For *homo natura* is not the common Latin tag that readers might imagine; in fact I have not been able to find a source for this phrase in Latin prose. Its grammatical structure is odd, making sense as an ablative (man in, by or qua nature, normally needing a complement, but compare *servus natura*,[60] "slave by nature," which was the usual Latin translation for Aristotle's discussion of natural slaves) or as a simple equation (man equals nature, man [is] nature; compare *homo mensura*, also a phrase which could be completed by an implicit "*est*").[61] It was indeed a Stoic injunction to view man as part of nature and to understand man in relation to the understanding of nature; and it was equally characteristic of Nietzsche's thinking from *Human, All Too Human* onward, and still influential here in *Beyond Good and Evil*, to insist on treating man as part of nature.

Wissenschaft had already made great strides in Nietzsche's day in the understanding of nature; now he urges that is time for the understanding of human nature to catch up, an injunction with which, if phrased this generally, the Stoics could in principle have agreed. Whether this is the right source, or Nietzsche had simply invented the phrase or found it elsewhere, *Beyond Good and Evil* 230 on my reading is enjoining a Stoic-inspired view of human nature as part of nature, yet its own view of what that nature would be is not necessarily the same as that of the Stoics. Similarly, it is invoking the *hart* cognitive stance that characterizes the Stoics, yet also attacking a particular Stoic philosopher's self-contradiction in attempting to live out the anti-emotional Stoic ideal. These complexities in Nietzsche's attitude to the Stoics are among the tensions and so the caveats that need now to be entered to my general account of Nietzsche's admiration for the Stoic cognitive stance.

THE COMPLEXITIES OF STOICISM
IN AND FOR NIETZSCHE

While we cannot examine all of the texts in which Nietzsche treats the Stoa, we can identify three themes that complicate his account of them. First is the idea of the Stoics as hypocrites or actors. In *Gay Science* 99 Nietzsche quotes approvingly from his own *Untimely Meditations* two lines in which Stoicism and honesty appear to come apart: "That passion [*Leidenschaft*] is better than Stoicism [*Stoizismus*] and hypocrisy [*Heuchelei*]; that being honest [*Ehrlich-sein*] even in evil is better than losing oneself to the morality of tradition...."[62] It may be significant that an *Ehrlichkeit* word is used here instead of *Redlichkeit*: Nietzsche does not choose to drive an explicit wedge between Stoicism and *Redlichkeit*. Nevertheless, it is plain that Stoicism is here aligned with hypocrisy against honesty. Nor is this the only instance of such alignment. As we will see, in *Beyond Good and Evil* 9 the Stoics are called "strange actors and self-deceivers," and in *Gay Science* 359 the "stoicism of gesture" of "bored, weary self-despisers" like St. Augustine is criticized, though this is presented as a veneer of Stoicism rather than a full commitment to it. While the Stoics may strut about vaunting their self-discipline, they risk hypocrisy in their purported denial of the passions while either experiencing them or advocating the only-different-in-name *eupatheiai*. But these points do not undermine their cognitive stance toward reality, only their strategy for handling the emotions. And it is significant to note that Epictetus, Nietzsche's favorite example of a Stoic, is never subjected to any such criticism *in propria persona*. Considering them as an ancient school among other such schools, Nietzsche can acutely perceive the temptations of hypocrisy that would afflict the Stoics; but when admiring Epictetus, he does not try to make any such hypothetical charge stick.

The second theme is that while Nietzsche, as I have argued, admired the unblinking Stoic commitment to the acceptance of nature as a whole, he did not accept the specific dogmatic beliefs to which they believed their knowledge of nature had led them. In *Beyond Good and Evil* 9, he attacks those he calls "you noble [*edlen*] Stoics" (note the second-person here, in contrast to the first person plural in 227) for their ideal of living "according to nature." Nietzsche claims that this is contradictory, since nature is "without purpose," while living is "assessing and preferring"; he diagnoses the Stoics as having projected their morals and ideals "onto nature" to make it over in their own image. The passage concludes by generalizing the point to all philosophies: a philosophy "always creates the world in its own image, it cannot do otherwise; philosophy is this tyrannical drive itself, the most spiritual will to power...." One familiar problem here is that it is not immediately obvious what Nietzsche should find objectionable in the Stoics' stance, given that they are successfully imposing their will to power and creating values.[63] But the criticism seems to be that they deceive themselves about the nature of those values, reifying values as if they derived from nature rather than understanding that they have only created a "nature" in the image of their own values. (Compare *Human, All Too Human, Assorted Opinions and Maxims,* which is headed "'Law of nature' a superstition" and concludes: "Necessity in nature becomes more human and a last refuge of mythological dreaming through the expression 'conformity to law.'"[64]) *Redlichkeit* does not appear here, but its significance elsewhere in *Beyond Good and Evil,* as shown above, helps us to understand the present attack on the Stoics as "strange actors and self-deceivers." It is precisely their self-deception, what *Beyond Good and Evil* 5 called the fundamental lack of honesty in the philosophers of the past, which incurs Nietzsche's attack. Yet the Stoic cognitive stance is not in principle wedded to such self-deception. The latter is the fault of the ancient Stoa's metaphysical commitments, not of their commitment to honesty, which so far as it goes keeps self-deception at bay.

The third theme is that of the Stoic attitude to the emotions and their strategy for self-government in relation to their cognitive commitments. To survey this theme (without repeating the excellent work which has been done on the topic of the emotions in the Stoa) we must assess the changing and complex relationship between Nietzsche's views of Stoics and Epicureans.

STOICS AND EPICUREANS

Nietzsche, at times, emphasized what Epicureans and Stoics had in common over what divided them. For example, *Assorted Opinions and Maxims* 224, "Balm and Poison," describes the pair of Epicurus and Epictetus as representing "the voice of reason and philosophy," and constituting "wisdom in bodily form." Christianity was at best a substitute for the degenerated ancient cultures to live decently when no longer capable of appreciating those sages. *Human, All Too Human* 282 praises Epictetus alongside Pascal, Seneca and Plutarch, while *Assorted Opinions and Maxims* 408 pairs Epicurus with Montaigne alongside Goethe and Spinoza, Plato and Rousseau, Pascal and Schopenhauer. But elsewhere in *Human, All Too Human* Nietzsche is preoccupied by Epicurus to a far greater extent than by any Stoic, and his preoccupation is overwhelmingly positive. Epicurus is praised for discovering that emotional peace need not depend on solving theoretical problems;[65] he is apostrophized as eternal and as a heroic-idyllic kind of philosopher,[66] an image of Arcadian happiness echoed in *Gay Science* 45. In *Daybreak* 72, he is positioned as an anti-Christian insofar as he denied hell and immortality. But while *Gay Science* may, as Martha Nussbaum remarks,[67] be extreme in its critical attitude towards Stoic hardness, we shall now show that it is also newly critical of Epicurean self-deception.

Gay Science 326's conclusion against the "fossilized Stoic way of life"— "Things are *not bad enough* for us that they have to be bad for us in the Stoic style"—is best understood in terms of the comparative judgment of *Gay Science* 306 titled "Stoics and Epicureans." Here Nietzsche contrasts the Epicurean's fastidiousness in avoiding whatever would harm his delicate intellectual constitution, with the Stoic who trains himself to consume the most dangerous and unpleasant things without nausea. Picking up the references to the Stoic as actor discussed above, Nietzsche remarks that the Stoic "likes to act out his insensitivity before an invited audience," while the Epicurean retreats to his garden (Epicurus' Garden being the historical site of the school in Athens). Nietzsche concludes that Stoicism may be necessary where one is dependent on changeable and violent situations or people, but those who can expect longevity do better to take an Epicurean orientation, as "people engaged in work of the spirit have always done": "for it would be the loss of all losses, for them, to forfeit their subtle sensitivity in exchange for a hard [*harte*] Stoic skin with porcupine spines."

While the Stoics do therefore risk becoming too hard and insensitive, this emotional failing would at worst limit their spiritual or intellectual [*geistigen*] sensitivities. In contrast, *Gay Science* 370 charges the Epicureans with not only limiting but distorting their cognitive understanding of the world for the sake of emotional consolation. They are described as implicated in the failings of "romanticism" (now represented by Schopenhauer and Wagner) in which emotional weakness leads to cognitive failure. Because they have a craving for "the conceptual comprehensibility of existence," they allow themselves to experience "a certain warm, fear-repelling narrowness and confinement to optimistic horizons." Nietzsche says here that he has gradually come to understand Epicurus as the antithesis of an (admirable, for Nietzsche) Dionysian pessimist—the latter being able "to allow himself not only the sight of what is terrible and questionable but also the terrible deed"—and the Christian in turn as a kind of Epicurean. Although the Epicurean (who after all denied that the gods were concerned with humans) did not make the mistake of the Christian, who craves and so posits a "savior" god, he did crave "mildness, peacefulness, goodness in thought and in deed" and this craving excluded him from the Dionysian's "sight of what is terrible (*fürchterlichen*) and questionable" in reality.

From *Gay Science* on, Nietzsche's preoccupation with Epicurus and the Epicureans evaporates, and when he does occasionally consider them he does so in almost[68] relentlessly negative terms. (It has been remarked that Montaigne, who tended towards the Epicureans, may have escaped this sort of condemnation because he tended to struggle to be true to himself and to speak as frankly as possible about himself and the world he perceived.)[69] They appear only once in *Beyond Good and Evil*, a text as comparatively preoccupied by the Stoics as *Human, All Too Human* had been by the Epicureans. He repeats the judgment that Epicurus is a pessimist in *Genealogy of Morality* III.17, and that he is a reality-hating decadent in *The Anti-Christ* 30 and 58.[70] And while Nietzsche's unpublished notes (his *Nachlass)* unsurprisingly contain a great deal of mixed evaluations of both Stoics and Epicureans, there is one particular note which is significant for understanding what Nietzsche ultimately could not accept in the Epicureans. This is in the note on "Moral values even in theory of knowledge" from Spring-Fall 1887, which appears as *The Will to Power*[71] 578, where Epicurus is singled out as having "*denied* the possibility of knowledge [*Epikur leugnet die Möglichkeit der Erkenntnis*]," a disastrous move which Augustine and Pascal—for all Nietzsche's respect for the latter[72]—later followed.

CONCLUSION

These late judgments reveal Nietzsche's ultimate conclusion that Epicureanism, for all the greater attractiveness of its emotional strategies, was fatally flawed as a cognitive stance. Epicureans sought to restrict their beliefs in order to achieve happiness and inner peace; Stoics steeled themselves cognitively as well as emotionally to confront reality, to expand their knowledge to include the whole of nature. This then is why Nietzsche associated the Stoics rather than the Epicureans with the *Redlichkeit* that constituted the characterization of his own intellectual stance from *Daybreak* through *Beyond Good and Evil*, even though his own view of the content of "nature" was quite different from the official Stoic view.

Honest acknowledgement of the inconvenient and unpleasant aspects of reality or nature was essential to the Nietzschean stance of *Redlichkeit*, connected to his view of *Wissenschaft*, which was not confined to a purportedly superseded "middle period" but which rather characterizes and unites his mature works from *Daybreak* to *Beyond Good and Evil*. It is a theme that the postmodern readings of Nietzsche as a denier of truth or a celebrator of private self-fashioning, and the attempted defenses of Nietzsche as committed to truthfulness and truth, have equally neglected. The honest acknowledgement of the real by the philosopher of the future (as contrasted with the derided "real reality" of the poets) was a virtue of what Mark Bevir in this volume would call modernism, although Nietzsche more often depicted himself as opposing modernity than as defining an alternative version of it. In *Ecce Homo* he remarked on his project in *Beyond Good and Evil* thus: "This book is in all essentials a critique of modernity, not excluding the modern sciences, modern arts and even modern politics, along with pointers to a contrary type that is as little modern as possible

— a noble, Yes-saying type. In the latter sense, the book is a school for the gentilhomme, taking this concept in a more spiritual and radical sense than has ever been done...."[73]

The virtue of *Redlichkeit* belongs to Nietzsche's school for the gentilhomme. It is young as a virtue compared to its Platonic and Christian forebears, but its German formulation draws on a French tradition of thought in which *honnêteté* was a sum of all the virtues, exuding nobility, and imbuing politeness and good manners with an insistence on frank speaking. In working his way to an admiration of the Stoic model of unblinking acceptance of reality free of the Epicurean search for consolation, Nietzsche also had in mind his mentor Montaigne and his compatriot classical moralists. Theirs was not a virtue that could contemplate a line drawn between private and public pursuits of the kind that Richard Rorty envisages; it was precisely a virtue requiring acceptance of the whole of what is known or experienced. Honesty as the avoidance of self-deception about the real is at once a cognitive and an ethical constraint on the possibilities of self-fashioning, and also on the Rortyan idea that such self-fashioning could be entirely insulated from the public world. As such, although there is more which needs to be said about the relationship between honesty and truth than can be attempted here, we can conclude that the recovery of the centrality of honesty in Nietzsche's thought—achieved here by locating him in relation to the traditions of Hellenistic thought with which he grappled, as well as the models of French classicism which he admired—poses a severe challenge to attempts to appropriate Nietzsche for a postmodernist attack on truth.[74]

NOTES

1. Gianni Vattimo, *The End of Modernity,* trans. J.R. Snyder (Baltimore: Johns Hopkins University Press, 1989), 164–165.

2. French poststructuralists such as Deleuze, Derrida, Foucault, and others, who are central to most accounts of "postmodernism," were profoundly and prolifically affected by Nietzsche in the 1960s and 1970s, responding in part to the challenge posed by Martin Heidegger's work on Nietzsche published in 1961. Heidegger gave lecture courses on Nietzsche from 1936 to 1940, and again in the early 1950s; he also wrote a number of individual lectures and essays on him from 1936 to 1946. In 1961 these were published in two large volumes as *Nietzsche* (Pfullingen: Neske Verlag, 1961), which were quickly translated into French and then later into English, the latter by David Farrell Krell between 1979 and 1987 by Harper & Row. For all Heidegger's influence on the French Nietzsche, however, as Ernst Behler argues, "much of the French work on Nietzsche can be seen as a refutation of Heidegger's interpretation by insisting on the metaphorical character of Nietzsche's writings, his style, his irony, and his masks." See "Nietzsche in the Twentieth Century," in Bernd Magnus and Kathleen M. Higgins eds., *The Cambridge Companion to Nietzsche* (Cambridge: Cambridge University Press, 1996), 281–322, at 316.

3. *The New Nietzsche: Contemporary Styles of Interpretation* is the title of a collection of essays edited by David B. Allison (Cambridge, MA: MIT Press, 1985; first published New York: Dell, 1977), which stressed Heidegger's reading of Nietzsche, though in other hands it refers rather to the French Nietzsche. But as Richard Hinton-Thomas observed in *Nietzsche in German Politics and Society 1890–1918* (Manchester: Manchester University Press, 1983), there have been many waves of "new Nietzsches" from the 1890s onwards.

4. To sketch this sort of list is not to say that these attributions or readings of Nietzsche are justified. It is rather to point out that interpretations of Nietzsche are central, if sometimes hidden, elements feeding most central postmodern claims. For a short but trenchant critique arguing that Nietzsche defined his vision of what would come after modernity substantively, in contrast to the endless play of the postmodernists Lyotard and Derrida which they impute to him, see Wilfried van der Will, "Nietzsche and Postmodernism," in Keith Ansell-Pearson and Howard Caygill eds., *The Fate of the New Nietzsche* (Aldershot: Avebury, 1993), 43–54.

5. In "Nietzsche, modernity, aestheticism," in Magnus and Higgins eds., *The Cambridge Companion to Nietzsche*, 223–252, Alexander Nehamas calls Nietzsche "a postmodern thinker avant la lettre" because he has "abandoned the desire for complete liberation and innovation," but argues that this does not mean he has given up the demand for non-absolute truth or originality. Nehamas has also given an influential reading of Nietzsche's perspectivism in his *Nietzsche: Life as Literature* (Cambridge, MA: Harvard University Press, 1985).

6. Among the other ideas identified are stylistic irony and self-referentiality. A key postmodernist appropriation of Nietzsche, Paul de Man's argument in *Allegories of Reading: Figural Language in Rousseau, Nietzsche, Rilke, and Proust* (New Haven, CT: Yale University Press, 1979) that Nietzsche showed all language to be figural and so incapable of expressing literal truth, is decisively criticized both as a reading of Nietzsche and as a claim in its own terms by Maudemarie Clark, "Language and Deconstruction: Nietzsche, Paul de Man, and Postmodernism," in Clayton Koelb, ed., *Nietzsche as Postmodernist: Essays Pro and Contra* (Albany: State University of New York Press, 1990), 75–90. Likewise, against the postmodernist contention of antihumanism, Kathleen Higgins, "Nietzsche and Postmodern Subjectivity," in Koelb ed., *Nietzsche as Postmodernist*, 189–215, argues that Nietzsche was concerned with subjectivity and so an "implicit critic of postmodernism."

7. Bernard Williams, *Truth and Truthfulness: An Essay in Genealogy* (Princeton, NJ: Princeton University Press, 2002), 18; see generally 5 and 12–19.

8. Richard Rorty, *Contingency, Irony, and Solidarity* (Cambridge: Cambridge University Press, 1989), 83.

9. Friedrich Nietzsche, *Daybreak (Morgenröte)*, Cambridge Texts in the History of Philosophy, trans. R.J. Hollingdale, eds. M. Clark and B. Leiter (Cambridge: Cambridge University Press, 1997). Hereafter cited as D. The German text of works by Nietzsche is taken from the Colli-Montinari KSA or *Kritischen Studienausgabe in 15 Bänden* (Berlin: de Gruyter, 1980). For works not included in the KSA, I refer to the Colli-Montinari KGA or *Kritischen Gesamtausgabe* (Berlin: de Gruyter, 1967ff.), except for notes collected in *The Will to Power*, for which I refer to the Gast edition as reedited by W. Gebhard (Stuttgart: Alfred Kröner Verlag, 1996).

10. Nehamas, *Nietzsche*, 218, emphasizes the emotional connection of honesty to cruelty in *Beyond Good and Evil* 230, on which see also the present text below, but does not consider its cognitive significance. Alan White, "The Youngest Virtue," in Richard Schacht ed., *Nietzsche's Postmoralism: Essays on Nietzsche's Prelude to Philosophy's Future* (Cambridge: Cambridge University Press, 2001), 63–78, focuses directly on *Redlichkeit*, stressing its connection to speech and tracing an interesting genealogy for it in the treatment of identity from the Eleatics to Schopenhauer. He questions, but ultimately accepts, the translation of it as "honesty," and while noting its differentiation from *Ehrlichkeit* and other similar terms in Nietzsche's writings, does not analyze their relationship in any detail.

11. On the practical and strategic aspects of the ancient philosophical schools, see Pierre Hadot, *What is Ancient Philosophy?*, trans. Michael Chase (Cambridge, MA: Belknap Press of Harvard University Press, 2002), Part II: "Philosophy as a Way of Life."

12. Friedrich *Nietzsche, Beyond Good and Evil* (Jenseits von Gut und Böse), Cambridge Texts in the History of Philosophy, trans. J. Norman, eds. R. P. Horstmann and J. Norman (Cambridge: Cambridge University Press, 2002). Hereafter cited as BGE.

13. The role of admiration (*Bewunderung*) and its opposites, disgust (*Ekel*) and contempt (*Verachtung*) in Nietzsche is illuminatingly identified by Raymond Geuss, "Nietzsche and Morality," *European Journal of Philosophy* 5:1 (1997) 1–20, 13–16 with n.14.

14. Williams, *Truth and Truthfulness*, 13, discusses in tandem Nietzsche's "ideal of truthfulness" and his appeal to "honesty and intellectual conscience." His discussion speaks indifferently of "honesty and intellectual conscience" (citing *The Gay Science* 319, which invokes *Redlichkeit*, and 344, which does not), "honesty" (translating *rechtschaffen* in *The Anti-Christ* 50), and "the value of truthfulness (citing BGE 177's play on *wahrhaftig* and *Wahrhaftigkeit*), in his Introduction to his edition of *Gay Science*, xvii. A similar blanket invocation of "truthfulness or honesty, in the sense of the intellectual conscience" is made by Maudemarie Clark, *Nietzsche on Truth and Philosophy* (Cambridge: Cambridge University Press, 1990), 196. Raymond Geuss' discussion of "honesty" in Nietzsche in "Nietzsche and Morality," 8–9, cites only the "'ehrliche' Lüge" passage of *On the Genealogy of Morality* III.19, the unusual features of which are discussed here below. Robert B. Pippin, "Nietzsche's alleged farewell: the premodern, modern, and postmodern Nietzsche," in Magnus and Higgins eds., *The Cambridge Companion to Nietzsche*, 252–278, treats "honesty" as a Christian virtue without attending to its specifically Nietzschean development (259). Peter Berkowitz, *Nietzsche: The Ethics of An Immoralist* (Cambridge, MA: Harvard University Press, 1995), stresses Nietzsche's concern for "intellectual conscience" (*passim*) and his "love of truth" (21) but again without any discussion of "honesty" in particular.

15. Friedrich Nietzsche, *The Gay Science (Die fröhliche Wissenschaft)*, Cambridge Texts in the History of Philosophy, trans. J. Nauckhoff and (poems) A. del Caro, ed. B. Williams (Cambridge: Cambridge University Press), 2001. Hereafter cited as GS.

16. Friedrich Nietzsche, *Thus Spoke Zarathustra (Also Sprach Zarathustra)*, trans. and intro. R. J. Hollingdale (Harmondsworth, England: Penguin Classics, 1982). Hereafter cited as Z.

17. The identification of a distinct "middle period" is often misattributed to Walter Kaufmann, *Nietzsche: Philosopher, Psychologist, Antichrist* (Princeton, NJ: Princeton University Press, 1950), who discussed but on the whole rejected it, while remarking nevertheless on D's "experimental" status. The paradox is that Robert C. Solomon, who so misattributes it, rightly rejects the idea of a middle period, in the course of rejecting postmodern readings of Nietzsche which he thinks appeal to a purported middle period perspectivism (whereas others have called the middle period from *Human, All Too Human* (hereafter cited as HATH) through the first four books of GS "positivistic," so attributed in Arthur Danto, Nietzsche as Philosopher (New York: Macmillan, 1965), 69, and inadequately criticised in favour of a consistently "skeptical" Nietzsche by Beverly E. Gallo, "On the Question of Nietzsche's 'scientism,'" *International Studies in Philosophy* 22:2 (1990), 111–119. In contrast, Ruth Abbey, who correctly identifies both Kaufmann's own view and the origination of the tripartite periodization in Lou Salomé, in my view wrongly defends a distinctive "middle period" stretching from HATH through the first four books of GS. Abbey discusses the "heroism" of science and Enlightenment and also the ethic of care of the self as distinctively middle period concerns, but contrasts them with the "later works" from Z onward, without noticing the centrality of *Redlichkeit* (absent from her index) which as I show unites D, GS, Z and BGE. This sequence should be taken to include and conclude with Book V of GS, which appeared in 1887, the same year as *On the Genealogy of Morality* (the distinction I draw between these works and GM being based not on chronology but content and purpose). See Robert C. Solomon, "Nietzsche, Postmodernism, and Resentment: A Genealogical Hypothesis," in Koelb ed., *Nietzsche as Postmodernist*, 267–293, at 270 with n.5, and Ruth Abbey, *Nietzsche's Middle Period* (Oxford: Oxford University Press, 2000), xi–xii with notes 1–5 and 87–106.
18. Friedrich Nietzsche, *On the Genealogy of Morality (Zur Geneaologie der Moral)*, Cambridge Texts in the History of Political Thought, trans. C. Diethe, ed. K. Ansell-Pearson (Cambridge: Cambridge University Press, 2005). Hereafter cited as GM.
19. In this chapter I primarily consider only the writings published in his lifetime on Nietzsche's own authority. The *Nachlass*, which encompass notes from throughout Nietzsche's working life and which were not edited by him for publication, naturally present a more mixed and complex picture, though I believe that when considered chronologically they broadly bear out the arguments made here.
20. GM, however, at one juncture condemns both Epicureanism and Stoicism. Picking up from the end of GM III.17, where Epicurus is compared to Buddhism as a religion of pessimism, GM III.18 explains how such "hypnotic total dampening of sensibility" depends on the unusual powers of "courage, contempt for opinion, 'intellectual stoicism'" (*Muth, Verachtung der Meinung, 'intellektuellen Stoicismus'*). This joint condemnation of these two Hellenistic schools as pessimistic is at odds with the distinction between their intellectual strategies made in several other texts, as will be shown below, and may best be taken to underscore how comparatively unidimensional the line of argument of GM is.
21. Among many such discussions, see pre-eminently Alexander Nehamas, *The Art of Living: Socratic Reflections from Plato to Foucault* [Sather Classical Lectures, vol.61] (Berkeley: University of California Press, 1998). There are recent articles on the topic in Section III in Paul Bishop, ed., *Nietzsche and Antiquity: His Reaction and Response to the Classical Tradition* (Rochester,

NY: Camden House, 2004). I have discussed it myself briefly in *Plato's Progeny: How Socrates and Plato Still Captivate the Modern Mind* (London: Duckworth, 2001).

22. Although Pierre Villey's classic thesis as to Montaigne's sequential Stoic, Skeptic and Epicurean phases has been problematized, a complex concern with these three Hellenistic schools as well as with Cynicism remains central to the understanding of Montaigne. See Pierre Villey, *Les sources et l'évolution des Essais de Montaigne*, 2nd edition, 2 vols. (Paris: Hachette, 1933), and for example R.A. Sayce, *The Essays of Montaigne: A Critical Exploration*, 149, 166 and passim, references I owe to Neil Kenny. Montaigne himself observed the complicating fact that sometimes Stoics and Epicureans agree in ways that one would not expect, for example that Seneca's advice to Lucilius to give up either the life of luxury or life itself was surprisingly of Epicurean rather than Stoic inspiration (*Essays* I.32). The difficulty of distinguishing sometimes between Stoic and Epicurean themes is addressed in the present chapter, below.

23. A classic study of Cynicism, including important discussion of Nietzsche at 250–277, is Heinrich Niehues-Pröbsting, *Der Kynismus des Diogenes und der Begriff des Zynismus* (München: Wilhelm Fink Verlag, 1979), which is the foundation for the discussions of R. Bracht Branham, "Nietzsche's Cynicism: Uppercase or lowercase?" and Anthony K. Jensen, "Nietzsche's Unpublished Fragments on Ancient Cynicism: The First Night of Diogenes," in Bishop, *Nietzsche and Antiquity*, 170–181 and 182–191, respectively. See also Niehues-Pröbsting, "The Modern Reception of Cynicism: Diogenes in the Enlightenment," in Branham and Marie-Odile Goulet-Cazé eds., *The Cynics: The Cynic Movement in Antiquity and Its Legacy* (Berkeley: University of California Press, 1996), 329–365. As with the convergences between Stoicism and Epicureanism noted above, so there are important Stoic uses of Cynicism, on which see the texts recommended by the editors in Branham and Goulet-Cazé, *The Cynics*, "Selected Bibliography," 422.

24. On Nietzsche and Scepticism (in its Pyrrhonist form), see the discussion in Jessica N. Berry, "Nietzsche and Democritus: The Origins of Ethical Eudaemonism," in Bishop, *Nietzsche and Antiquity*, 98–113, including her references to further bibliography in notes 1–3, and her own forthcoming work.

25. The most influential study of Stoicism in Nietzsche, which however has also served to circumscribe the whole debate on the topics of pity and emotion, is Martha C. Nussbaum, "Pity and Mercy: Nietzsche's Stoicism," in Richard Schacht ed., *Nietzsche, Genealogy, Morality* (Berkeley: University of California Press, 1994), 139–167, which is criticized by Oliver Conolly, "Pity, Tragedy and the Pathos of Distance," *European Journal of Philosophy* 6, no. 3 (1998): 277–296. A more recent general evaluation of Stoicism in Nietzsche is R.O. Elveton, "Nietzsche's Stoicism: The Depths Are Inside," in Bishop, *Nietzsche and Antiquity*, 192–203, which notes briefly the connection between Stoicism and honesty in BGE 227 (194), and brings two important notes from the *Nachlass* to the discussion of Stoicism and emotion (200). See also, as Nussbaum advises, Jonathan Barnes, "Nietzsche and Diogenes Laertius," Nietzsche-Studien 15 (1986) 16–40, who discusses the three long studies which Nietzsche published in 1869 and 1870 on the sources of Stoicism in *Diogenes Laertius: de Laertii Diogenis fontibus, analecta Laertiana, and Beiträge zur quellenkunde und Kritik des Laertius Diogenes*, all now collected in KGA II/1.

26. Epicureanism in Nietzsche's thought is partitioned by Berry, "Nietzsche and Democritus," into a more positive view of Democritus, whose version of *ataraxia* involved "cheerfulness," and a more negative view of Epicurus and the "apathetic" *ataraxia* which was tantamount to nihilism. Berry's recognition of the Democritean strand is valuable, but her treatment of Epicurus himself in Nietzsche's thought is quite brief and general, not noting the dependence of his anti-Democritean passive understanding of apathia on his culpably limited consolatory cognitive stance, nor the evolution of Nietzsche's attitude toward him, and instead bracketing together the Stoics and the Epicureans simply as ascetic (106). No other article in Bishop's valuable collection takes Epicurus as its central theme, but see the remarks below on the section "Plato and Epicurus" in Laurence Lampert, "Nietzsche and Plato," in Bishop, *Nietzsche and Antiquity*, 205–219, at 210–211.

27. Branham, "Nietzsche's Cynicism," 179. Indeed BGE 26 does explicitly connect Redlichkeit to Cynicism—the philosopher is said to be lucky if he meets cynics, because "Cynicism is the only form in which common souls come close to honesty (*Redlichkeit*)." However here we find *Redlichkeit* as the virtue of the common soul, whereas in BGE 227 and elsewhere we will find it connected to Stoic philosophers.

28. Although Montaigne wrote rather than engaging in the public speaking of the Cynics, his practice of not hiding anything gave his writing the flavour of *parrhêsia* even while its written quality must not be neglected. Montaigne would fit into Foucault's definition of "the one who uses *parrhêsia*" as "someone who says everything he has in mind: he does not hide anything, but opens his heart and mind completely to other people through his discourse," as given in "Discourse and Truth: The Problematization of *Parrhêsia*," Lecture 1, from the transcription of six lectures given at the University of California, Berkeley, between October and November 1983, as online at http://foucault.info/documents/parrhesia, last checked July 23, 2006, a reference I owe to Andrea Sangiovanni.

29. Berry concludes "Nietzsche and Democritus" with a description of the role of Democritus in Nietzsche as follows: "the notion of 'cheerfulness' grows up alongside the notion of *ephexis* in interpretation – both integral components of an 'honest' and robust intellectual (or 'spiritual') life" (113), but without giving any textual content to the meaning of honesty in Nietzsche. And Fiona Jenkins, in her exploration of Nietzschean rhetoric in GM ("Rhetoric, Judgment, and the Art of Surprise in Nietzsche's *Genealogy*," in Bishop, *Nietzsche and Antiquity*, 295–309), evocatively describes his stance as "we are 'realists'" (300), commenting that this stance contrasts for Nietzsche with "cowardly misjudgement, erroneous estimation of oneself, of others, of existence as such, misjudgement that honesty and maturity would enable one to avoid" (300), but gives no textual specification for her conception of "honesty."

30. Jean-Luc Nancy, "'Our Probity!' On Truth in the Moral Sense in Nietzsche," in Laurence A. Rickels ed., *Looking after Nietzsche* (Albany: State University of New York, 1990), 49–66, at 70 and 79, respectively.

31. Nietzsche, BGE, 296.

32. Friedrich Nietzsche, *Human, All Too Human (Menschliches, Allzumenschliches)*, Cambridge Texts in the History of Philosophy, trans. R.J. Hollingdale, intro. R. Schacht (Cambridge: Cambridge University Press, 1996). The two parts of the second volume are hereafter identified additionally as AOM, *Assorted Opinions and Maxims (Vermischte Meinungen und Sprüche)*, and WS, *The Wanderer and His Shadow (Der Wanderer und Sein Schatten)*.

33. Friedrich Nietzsche, *Untimely Meditations (Unzeitgemässe Betrachtungen)*, Cambridge Texts in German Philosophy, trans. R.J. Hollingdale, intro. J.P. Stern (Cambridge: Cambridge University Press, 1988), III, 2. Hereafter cited as UM.

34. In fact, a substantive term deriving from *Redlichkeit* appears prior to D only in the form of *Unredlichkeit* in HATH 447 ("Making use of petty dishonesty (*Unredlichkeit*)"), a discussion of the power of the press. The adjective *redlich* appears in HATH 225 and, a positive but basically insignificant incidence, WS 95. More significant is its appearance in WS 37, in relation to a clearly Stoic strategy for transforming "passions" into "joys," which is discussed below.

35. Friedrich Nietzsche, *Ecce Homo*, trans. R.J. Hollingdale, intro. M. Tanner (Harmondsworth: Penguin Classics, 1992).

36. Neither Williams, *Truth and Truthfulness*, 14–15, who discusses GM III.26, nor Clark, *Nietzsche on Truth and Philosophy*, 191, who discusses GM III.27, notes the significance of the contrast or the nuances which it builds into what they each simply refer to as "honesty."

37. Plato, *Republic* 414b8-c1, in the *Oxford Classical Texts* edition, ed. S.R. Slings (Oxford: Clarendon Press, 2003); see note *ad. loc.* in Plato, *The Republic*, ed. G.R.F. Ferrari, trans. Tom Griffith (Cambridge: Cambridge University Press, 2004), 107 n.63.

38. See, for example, BGE 34, 44, 244; See also Friedrich Nietzsche, *Twilight of the Idols (Götzen-Dämmerung)*, trans. R.J. Hollingdale, intro. M. Tanner (Harmondsworth: Penguin Classics, 1990), 12.

39. Nietzsche, Z, "Of the Afterworldsmen."

40. In BGE 284, "you" are enjoined to "keep control over your four virtues: courage, insight, sympathy, solitude [*des Muthes, der Einsicht, des Mitge-fühls, der Einsamkeit*]" because "solitude is a virtue for us." (Note that the voice in this passage changes from addressing the second person singular to invoking the first person plural: see the remarks on Nietzsche's stylistic shifts of voice and the significance of the first-person plural, in GM in particular, in Pippin, "Nietzsche's alleged farewell," 256–258 and 265–267.) If we try to map these onto the cardinal virtues, courage clearly remains identical with bravery in both the WS and D versions; insight corresponds to wisdom (WS) and honesty (D); sympathy now seems to replace justice (WS) and magnanimity (D); and solitude now replaces moderation (WS) and its more social reinterpretation as politeness (D).

41. Nietzsche, D, 556.

42. D 370 makes a requirement of *Redlichkeit* itself that a thinker should "[love] his enemy" in order to praise and confront what can be said against his own thoughts, and does so in relation to the concern for "truth."

43. Nietzsche initially became acquainted with the French moralists inter alia through Friedrich Albert Lange's 1866 book, *History of Materialism*; he was given a copy of Montaigne for Christmas 1870, and throughout his time in Basel was reading the French classical moralists assiduously; his close friend Paul Reé's 1876 book *Psychologische Beobachtung* consisting of "maximes" in the style of La Rochefoucauld was also central to this engagement. On the French moralists, in addition to the works cited below, see generally Emmanuel Bury, *Littérature et politesse: l'invention de l'honnête homme, 1580–1750* (Paris: Presses universitaires de France, 1996); and for a critical view of the historiography on the French influence on Nietzsche, Beatrix Bludau, *Frankreich im Werk Nietzsches: Geschichte und Kritik der Einflussthese* (Bonn: Bouvier Verlag Herbert Grundmann, 1979). On the topic relevant to this paper, Vivetta Vivarelli, "Montaigne und der 'Freie Geist': Nietzsche im

Übergang," *Nietzsche-Studien* 23 (1994) 78–101, overlooks the relationship to *Redlichkeit* in Nietzsche altogether, while David Molner, "The Influence of Montaigne on Nietzsche: A Raison d'Etre in the Sun," *Nietzsche-Studien* 22 (1993) 80–93, confines the relevance of Montaigne's honesty and of his own remark that for Montaigne and Nietzsche "not truth but honesty really matters" (86) solely to the context of literary style. Andrea Sangiovanni called my attention to the significance of the French moralists for this argument, while Neil Kenny helped to educate me about them.

44. Chamfort, *Maximes et Pensées* II, 67ff., as quoted in Williams, *Nietzsche and the French* (Oxford: Blackwell, 1952), 87. As Williams notes, Chamfort's particular form of aphoristic style may also have influenced Nietzsche.

45. Nietzsche, Z, "The Leech."

46. But Zarathustra strikes a more positive note about *Redlichkeit* in Z, "Of the Higher Man," 8. There, he cautions his listeners against exceeding their powers of carrying out what they will, which risks turning them into actors and pretenders and so damaging their honesty, "[f]or I count nothing more valuable and rare today than honesty [*Redlichkeit*]."

47. Nietzsche, BGE, 227. Equally, *Redlichkeit* like any virtue is no proof against corruption by other emotions and motives, for example "one grain of gratitude and piety too much" (D 293).

48. Branham, "Nietzsche's Cynicism," 174, cites this passage as an example of the hostility to shame which Nietzsche learned from the Cynics, though Cynicism does not inform the argument about art and science which is its principal burden.

49. In a similar vein, John Richardson, *Nietzsche's System* (Oxford: Oxford University Press, 1996), 290, remarks that when Nietzsche denies that his truths are "for everyone" he means "not that others will have equal truths of their own but that others can't or won't bear so much truth, and such truth."

50. Williams, *Truth and Truthfulness*, especially Chapters 5 and 6. In his "Introduction" to Nietzsche, *The Gay Science*, ed. Bernard Williams, trans. Josefine Nauckhoff (Cambridge: Cambridge University Press, 2001), xix, Williams astutely comments on WP 822—"We possess art lest we perish of the truth"— that "[Nietzsche] does not mean that we possess art in place of the truth; he means that we possess art so that we can possess the truth and not perish of it."

51. Raymond Geuss, "Thucydides, Nietzsche, and Williams," in his *Outside Ethics* (Princeton: Princeton University Press, 2005), 219–233, at 226.

52. Nietzsche, BGE, 295.

53. Nietzsche, D, 479.

54. BGE 230 aligns *Redlichkeit* with *Liebe zur Wahrheit* and *Liebe zur Weisheit*, among other terms, though in a somewhat critical context in which pluming oneself on these virtues is said to risk feeding pride and "unconscious human vanity."

55. As for example Williams, *Truth and Truthfulness*, 14.

56. See the discussion in Gisela Striker, "Following nature: A study in Stoic ethics," in her *Essays on Hellenistic Epistemology and Ethics* (Cambridge: Cambridge University Press, 1996), 275ff.

57. The association of Stoicism with joy is however challenged in GS 12, where Nietzsche acknowledges that pleasure and pain are intertwined. He says that the Stoics were consistent in seeking as little pleasure for the sake of as little pain as possible. Modern science may either, with the socialist politicians, follow this Stoic path, which makes man "colder, more statue-like, more stoic" and deprives him of his joys [*Freuden*]; or it may choose to inflict great

pain in order to "let new galaxies of joy [*Freude*] flare up." Here, Nietzsche seems to be using joy in a more colloquial sense, rather than in the technical Stoic sense which it is more consistent to impute to WS 37.

58. Owing to Chris Clark's eagle eye I am here correcting the Cambridge translation, which renders *zurückübersetzen* simply as "to translate." Jessica Berry makes the same mistranslation in her otherwise valuable and relevant discussion of the importance in this passage and in HATH generally of Nietzsche's concern that "human beings should be understood as continuous with the rest of nature"; see Jessica N. Berry, "The Pyrrhonian Revival in Montaigne and Nietzsche," *Journal of the History of Ideas* 65, no. 3 (2004): 497–514, at 500.

59. Nietzsche, BGE, 230.

60. This phrase is quoted as a tag for example in *Table Talk of John Selden*, ed. Frederick Pollock (London: Quaritch, 1927), 102, under the heading "Power: State"; it is actually quoted both in the singular and plural, but with accents indicating the ablative (*servus Naturâ, servi Naturâ*). The possible relevance of *servus natura* was suggested by Quentin Skinner; that of *homo mensura* by Malcolm Schofield; Bill Burgwinkle and Neil Kenny also advised me on this point.

61. I have only been able to find two other instances of the phrase homo natura, in both of which however there is a qualification or complement. One is Seneca's "Natura homo mundum et elegans animal est" (Man is by nature a clean and delicate animal), which adds a verb and complement; it does not seem particularly apposite, but the formulation may have caught Nietzsche's eye in that it was quoted by Montaigne in his *Essays* III.13. The other possible source is Cicero's *Academica* (specifically the *Academicorum Priorum*, as the first edition of the *Academica* is sometimes known). Lucullus is describing how Antiochus of Ascalon was infuriated when he received two books by the Academic skeptic Philo: Et quidem isti libri duo Philonis, de quibus heri dictum a Catulo est, tum erant adlati Alexandriam tumque primum in Antiochi manus uenerant: et homo natura lenissimus - nihil enim poterat fieri illo mitius - stomachari tamen coepit. (*Academicorum Priorum* II.11) In Reid's translation of that part of the sentence following the colon: "whereupon though a man naturally good tempered in the extreme — indeed it was not possible for gentleness to exceed his — yet [he] began to get into a passion." Here, as Michael Reeve has pointed out to me, *natura lenissimus* is qualifying *homo*, so the grammatical structure is not the same as that apparently structuring Nietzsche's phrase. But if one conjectures that Nietzsche might simply have been struck by the conjunction of the two words, this also gives an interesting Stoic provenance to Nietzsche's passage, since Antiochus of Ascalon, though the self-proclaimed spokesman of the Platonic "Old Academy," held that Plato, the Peripatetics and the Stoics had essentially agreed. If, as a Stoic sympathizer, he was committed to the extirpation of passion, it is an irony which Nietzsche would have enjoyed pointing out that his dogmatic philosophy was here only a cover for his angry passion (compare BGE 7 on the anger motivating Epicurus against Plato). Although the Stoic individual here does not come out too well, Nietzsche may again have enjoyed the thought of contrasting their individual actions with their call to understand nature as a whole, and also turning a comment about an individual into a tag apparently referring to "man by nature" in general—since unconsciously motivated generalizations of this kind were one of his favorite targets of attack. On this view, *homo natura* would, for Nietzsche, be not the man whom the Stoics had imagined or embodied, but the understanding of

man as part of nature for which they had called even if they had failed to fulfil their own program consistently, man by nature able to acknowledge all that is in his nature rather than clinging to self-deluded dogma. I am grateful to Christopher Clark, Michael Reeve, Malcolm Schofield and Quentin Skinner for discussion of these possible sources and questions of translation, though I have not followed all of their views.

62. Nietzsche, UM, "Richard Wagner," 11.
63. This kind of problem is discussed by Geuss, "Nietzsche and Morality," 7–9.
64. Nietzsche, AOM, 9.
65. Nietzsche, WS, 7.
66. Ibid., 227, 295.
67. Nussbaum, "Pity and Mercy," 164 n.36.
68. Admittedly, in GS 375 Nietzsche explains his heading "Why we seem to be Epicureans," but he speaks ambiguously of "we modern men" who are "cautious...about ultimate convictions" and mistrustful of "every unconditional Yes and No," though he also relates the "almost Epicurean bent of knowledge (*Erkenntniss-Hang*)" to the pride in the "self-control of the rider on his wildest rides" as "our urge for certainty races ahead." And in BGE 7, Nietzsche revels in a malicious Epicurean joke about Plato and the Platonists, coining the term *Dionysiokolakes* or sycophants of Dionysius as a pun on *Dionysokolax* or actor; see the discussion of this passage in Laurence Lampert, "Nietzsche and Plato," 210–211, who further takes it to be an illustration of the philosophical will to power on 215.
69. Williams, *Nietzsche and the French*, 173, on struggle for honesty; Brendan Donnellan, *Nietzsche and the French Moralists* (Bonn: Bouvier Verlag Herbert Grundmann, 1982), 19; he adds that the Epicureans were paradoxically ascetic in paring down their pleasures in order to be sure they only experience pleasure, whereas Montaigne had a more robust enjoyment of many pleasures.
70. Friedrich Nietzsche, *The Anti-Christ (Der Antichrist)*, trans. R.J. Hollingdale, intro. M. Tanner (Harmondsworth: Penguin Classics, 1990).
71. Friedrich Nietzsche, *The Will to Power (Der Wille zur Macht)*, trans. W. Kaufmann and R.J. Hollingdale, ed. W. Kaufmann (New York: Vintage Books, 1968).
72. For Nietzsche's respect and admiration for Pascal as a moralist despite his Christian commitments, see Donnellan, *Nietzsche and the French Moralists*, 38–48.
73. Nietzsche, *Ecce Homo*, 2, commenting on his BGE.
74. I am most grateful to the editors of the volume for inviting me to contribute despite having become unable to attend the initial conference, and to King's College Cambridge for supporting the costs of my foregone travel. I also thank Martin Ruehl for crucial and generous practical aid in relation to the Nietzschean corpus, and him together with those acknowledged in the notes above, as well as Justin Reynolds, Duncan Large, and the attendees of the Monday Seminar in Political Thought and Intellectual History at Cambridge University (Lent 2006, chaired by Quentin Skinner, and invitation extended by him and Annabel Brett) for valuable comments and advice; Trinity College Library; the Centre for History and Economics, King's College, Cambridge, for hosting a research leave during the course of which the paper was conceived; the Rockefeller Foundation and MacArthur Foundation for funding that leave; and my colleagues in the History Faculty of Cambridge University and King's College, Cambridge, for allowing it to me.

3   Escape from the Subject
Heidegger's *Das Man* and Being-in-the-World

Jill Hargis

Heidegger's influence on a multitude of thinkers associated with the traditions of deconstruction, post-structuralism, and postmodernism is established and well documented.[1] It is generally agreed that Heidegger's powerful critiques of modernity, including his claim that Western civilization and philosophy were in crisis due to the denigration of the world and human character in metaphysical thought, "fundamentally shaped" the tradition of French post-structuralism of the late twentieth century.[2] In identifying Western metaphysics as the source of the crisis, Heidegger worked to develop a philosophy that opposed its central tenets, including theories of transcendent reality, timeless truths, and teleological history.[3] These critical positions have contributed to the central themes of the postmodern tradition, including anti-essentialism and anti-humanism. I argue here that because of Heidegger's profound influence on postmodernism, a careful examination of the local context of Heidegger's thought is needed in order to clarify how his negative understanding of the people and their norms as *"das Man"* (the They, or the One—the masses) affects his anti-humanism.[4]

The question of Heidegger's legacy has been pursued mercilessly since the end of World War II and with renewed intensity in the late 1980s when the extent of his commitment to Nazi ideology was made apparent.[5] One way Heidegger's influence has been measured is by tracing his anti-humanism. In this volume Richard Wolin, Mark Bevir, and Peter Gordon analyze various elements of the debate about what it means to be anti-humanist. Each traces the reception of Heidegger's anti-humanism in post-war France. Because anti-humanism was an explicit topic of debate between the traditions of existentialism, phenomenology, Marxism, and later structuralism, this concept, as well as its attendant challenge to subjectivity, has been the focus of considerable interpretation. I suggest that placing Heidegger's theory of *das Man*, in its local context may give us another perspective for seeing what was at stake for Heidegger in his focus on anti-humanism.

For Heidegger, *das Man* referred to the experience of human life lived in conformity with the norms of others, and in particular to what he called the "publicness" of the modern masses. Heidegger's treatment of *das Man* has been used to show his affiliation with the "conservative revolutionaries" of his day, and I do not dispute this tie.[6] In fact, Heidegger's sense of the people of modernity as blindly conforming affected areas of his thought in ways that have not yet been fully examined. I argue here that the standards by which Heidegger judged whether people were conforming to the dictates of *das Man*, and thus their resulting inauthenticity, are grounded in both the strong influence of the tradition of conservative beliefs of Heidegger's Germany, as well as the influence of Kierkegaard. Although Heidegger's *das Man* was intended as an essential ontological category, it is so imbued with the conservative objections to the modern, industrial, urban masses that it operates more as a criticism of modern norms than as an ontological or timeless characteristic. Heidegger's world and Being are fully inter-subjectively constructed as "being-in-the-world" suggests. *Das Man*, however, turns Heidegger's thought away from this basic condition. Instead, he privileged two types of ideal people: the *volk*, the people following traditional cultures and practices who are free from the pressures of modern mass society; and those, like himself, who have a critical perspective beyond the being-in-the-world of modern mass society. Heidegger's anti-humanism recognizes the limitations of the individual subject as contingent upon the context of a limited world, but the negative side of his theory is that the individual's identity and knowledge are controlled by the mass norms of society, which, according to Heidegger, oppressively make up these worlds in modernity. Because of this, subjectivity as a target of criticism is imbued with the Kierkegaardian and conservative fears of modern society. *Das Man* and modern subjectivity come to express a single failure to gain authentic experience and identity.

For this reason, although the standards delineating *das Man*, including its supposed conformity to mass norms, are ideologically driven, they are amongst the foundational ideas for the critique of subjectivity. Conservative ideology, in which there is a great fear of the individual's loss of identity to mass norms, directly informs the way Heidegger's critique of the subject was deployed. Several things result from this slippage between the criticism of modern mass norms and the critique of subjectivity. First, it embeds in the philosophical examination of subjectivity a simplistic and arbitrary condemnation of modern norms merely on the basis of their association with mass society. This in turn tends to create anti-collectivist, solipsistic, and elitist inclinations, in which knowledge and experience are of greater value when created in isolation. These tendencies are evident in much of Heidegger's work, but are not readily identifiable without understanding his work within its local context.

I suggest that the relation between *das Man* and the critique of subjectivity has had important influence on contemporary critiques of subjectivity and foundational thought.[7] For example, I would suggest further exploration into the ways that some in the tradition of postmodernism maintained certain idealistic goals in the areas of aesthetics and literature as well as the idea of individual perfectionism.[8] Despite the general agreement that the world and its norms are inter-subjectively created conventions, ideas are often privileged if they derive from some form or practice resembling the ideal free individual who is apart from convention. It also seems likely that something like the fear of *das Man* has played a role in the hesitancy of those associated with the postmodern tradition to recommend policies —its anti-positivist utopianism. Alternatively, by revealing the bias against mass norms and meanings, I suggest that a thorough-going postmodern critique that does not reject certain norms for fear of their source in mass conformity might avoid these tensions and contradictions.[9]

Others have addressed some of the tensions surrounding *das Man*. Richard Wolin argues that Heidegger's political interests inform his theory as a whole, including his anti-foundationalism and anti-humanism, and therefore his ontology must be rejected.[10] Another kind of argument distinguishes *das Man* as politically motivated and therefore separable from the rest of Heidegger's analysis. One important example of this interpretation is Hubert Dreyfus' argument that for Heidegger, *Dasein's* "world" is made up of all of the norms of any particular person's historical and spatial context.[11] Dreyfus suggests that Heidegger's "world" is constructed by historically contingent everyday norms, which in turn are constitutive of *Dasein* and the individual's consciousness. This implies, against other interpretations of Heidegger's ontology, that the norms themselves are the important target of examination, not the way in which (authentically or inauthentically) the norms are experienced.[12] Dreyfus' analysis makes clear Heidegger's relation to the anti-foundational concepts of postmodernism, but Dreyfus also reduces the role of *das Man* in order to present the clearest non-normative understanding of Heidegger's "being-in-the-world," as contingency and situatedness. This seems to me to be a very important project, the ends of which my argument supports, but at the same time it obscures the role of *das Man* in Heidegger's work and the possibility of its effect on later postmodern thinkers.

The chapter proceeds by first briefly explaining Heidegger's concepts of *das Man* and *Dasein*. In doing so we can see how *Dasein,* as Heidegger's response to "metaphysics," contributed several important means of critique central to the postmodern tradition. And at the same time this analysis shows how *das Man*, although in conflict with elements of Heidegger's *Dasein,* is embedded in the critique that becomes a part of the postmodern tradition. Next, I show how the anti-modernist, conservative influence is reflected in Heidegger's work, specifically in the concept of *das Man*, and how this affects and creates certain tensions within his ontology of "being-in-the-world." I give two examples of how *das Man* as the bias against mass norms comes to dominate Heidegger's authentic individual experience and identity. When *das Man,* dominates, modern subjectivity is in control. The ideas of contingency and conventionality become infused with fears of *das Man,* making the understanding of contingent subjectivity fraught with anxiety and confusion. It is difficult to theorize about shared historical knowledge and meaning (one of Heidegger's goals) within the context of criticism of metaphysics and subjectivity. The first example explains how Heidegger privileged certain norms and practices, such as the use of a hammer, over others, like reading the newspaper, according to whether he believed them to be a part of traditional society or whether they were associated with modernity. Depending on the activity, one will have authentic experience or one will be caught in the subjectivity of *das Man*. For the second, I show how *das Man* is also present in Heidegger's views of language. Language is the place where Being dwells and is to be fully encountered, but language is also the tool of *das Man*, which uses it to enforce conformity to modern, unthinking norms. In the final section of the chapter I argue that Heidegger's treatment of *das Man* creates confusion between criticisms of modern norms as such and an understanding of fundamental and timeless epistemological limitations of the subject. Because *das Man* represents the limitations of subjectivity, this confusion is embedded in Heidegger's critique of the subject.

DASEIN AND DAS MAN

In his first major work, *Being and Time,* Heidegger argued that the whole history of Western metaphysical philosophy had led to the domination of the subjective consciousness, creating a distant, objectifying, and extremely narrow perspective on the world and its meaning. According to Heidegger, reliance on metaphysical thought obstructed experience and knowledge of the world. "Metaphysics" was a term that Heidegger used to identify the problems of both Husserl's transcendental subject and the formalistic methods of the Neo-Kantians.[13] Metaphysics for Heidegger characterized any philosophical position that had strayed from "the question of Being." The book's main contribution is a phenomenological account of how the essence of the human world, Being, is present only in the individual's experience of the world. Heidegger included in the tradition of metaphysics Husserl's transcendental subject-centered phenomenology, which Heidegger countered with a phenomenology that grounded human existence fully within its temporal and physical world and rejected the goal of experiencing a thing-in-itself. His phenomenology also opposed the Neo-Kantians' claims that the natural and human world can only be known through universal laws and values. Against arguments that the essence of beings is eternal and fixed, Heidegger said that beings, or the entities of the physical world, only have meaning as they are created in the context of use and understanding with people. People, in turn, only have meaning in the historical, spatial, and temporal context of the world of entities and other people. The situatedness of human existence Heidegger called *Dasein*. *Dasein* means "there-being," and reflects the quality of being "thrown" into a world of preexisting meanings. How people understand the objects in their particular worlds provide the openings for understanding Being.

Much of *Being and Time* is devoted to showing that every aspect of human existence is derived from the preexisting world created by people together in their "being-in-the-world" and "being-with" others. Heidegger argued that there are no distinct individual subjectivities separate from the phenomenal world, either in an ideal transcendental form or with an objective perspective distinct from the world. Unlike Descartes, for whom individual subjects bring their separate spheres of knowing together to form the inter-subjectivity of the world, Heidegger claimed that an individual's experience of the world, even at its most "primordial," presupposes the presence and understanding of that person within their shared world.[14] This is the first explanatory step in getting beyond the subject/object dichotomy that governs what Heidegger called metaphysical thought. The essence of human being for Heidegger is explained primarily by its "thrownness" into a world of historical meaning, which also positions the individual toward a future of possibility.

For Heidegger, *Dasein* opened up the possibility of seeing the human individual as something other than the subject with a transcendent universal perspective or with an objectifying positivistic perspective on a world distinct from consciousness. Heidegger opposed metaphysical thought because it directed the ontological search for meaning away from the temporal inter-subjective world. For Heidegger, no knowledge, language, or other meaning-giving event exists separately from the world in which a person is living. Heidegger's fundamental ontology is the search for an understanding of the world as the home of being. Being reveals itself only in the world of relations between people and between people and entities in their worlds. *Dasein* can be understood to refer to every individual's context of entities and people and the historical norms that compose the relations and meanings between them. Because these concepts bring the contingency and local nature of knowledge and meaning to bear on questions of epistemology and metaphysics, Heidegger is a clear predecessor to many of the central concepts associated with postmodernism. *Dasein*, as the rejection of metaphysical thought and the positioning of human knowledge fully within the contingencies of history and space, influenced central concepts in postmodern critical thought, including anti-historicism, anti-foundationalism, and anti-humanism.[15]

In Heidegger's ontology, however, *Dasein* is always confronted with *das Man*. *Das Man* is both an inadequate way of encountering the world that is governed by the public, by the masses, and the masses themselves, of which all individuals are unconsciously a part. According to Heidegger, although it appears that an individual or an "I" shows us "who" *Dasein* is in a "phenomenally adequate manner," in fact, ontologically *Dasein* is indistinguishable from the other people of the everyday, or *das Man*. Heidegger said that "the ontical obviousness of the fact that *Dasein* is in each case mine…hides the possibility that the ontological problematic which belongs to it has been led astray."[16] In other words, individual physicality hides the fact that individuals understand Being only as *das Man* does. The ontological problematic here is that each person is originally lost in *das Man* and must recognize this situation in order to struggle against it. Heidegger explained that each individual is largely unaware of the fact that she is governed by *das Man*, so that *das Man* is actually something that one is a part of and contributes to. *Das Man* also constitutes a way of thinking that should be overcome. One is a part of *das Man* when one thinks like *das Man* and therefore cannot see that one is a part of *das Man*. Therefore, this is an ontological problem such that the identity, or "who," of *Dasein* is controlled by others who are most often indistinguishable and unidentifiable within *das Man*. In this way *Dasein* experiences its world according to the dictates of *das Man* rather than experiencing its world authentically.

In *Being and Time*, *das Man* is a way of being open to Being that is inauthentic and one in which all people take part. *Das Man's* way of experiencing its world includes averageness, leveling, idle talk, and superficial curiosity. Everydayness is the primary way *Dasein* encounters its world, and it is Heidegger's way of describing *Dasein's* most common world of involved entities. The everyday is at once the context in which *Dasein* experiences Being, but it is also the place of the public—where "being-with-one-another" and discourse are the means by which understandings are shared, made common, and leveled. According to Heidegger, in the public sharing of ideas *Dasein* is distant from direct and "primordial" experiences.

Das Man is present because of the way *Dasein* encounters its world. In describing the everyday behavior of *Dasein*, Heidegger wrote that in *Dasein's* relations with "Others" "there is constant care as to the way one differs from them, whether that difference is merely one that is to be evened out, whether one's own Dasein has lagged behind the Others and wants to catch up in relationship to them, or whether one's Dasein already has some priority over them and sets out to keep them suppressed."[17] This is "distantiality," according to Heidegger, and it is the basic relationship between people in the everyday that forms the foundation of inauthentic relations to each other and to the world in the public. Instead of experiencing one's world and the Being in it, *Dasein* is distracted by the competitive and petty concerns of modernity, leaving *Dasein* distant from that which should be most important to it. Heidegger's objection to distantiality reflects the conservative idealist commitment that true knowledge is "a complete personal involvement of the knower with the known."[18] Distantiality and the process of leveling is all the more threatening because it is at work without anyone's knowledge of it. Having succumbed to the desire to level the differences between each other, *Dasein* loses itself and its own authentic understanding of itself in its world. "Dasein's everyday possibilities of Being are for the Others to dispose of as they please."[19] And without knowing it one "belongs to the Others oneself and enhances their power."[20] The crisis mentality of the conservative revolutionaries is palpable here. The modern public is dominating the means of thinking and knowing the world.

These are just a few examples of Heidegger's many ways that *das Man* dominates how people understand their worlds. The point is that Heidegger condemned the most common forms of being with others. Being with others in the average day-to-day life hides genuine understanding of oneself and the world, Heidegger implies that authentic encounters occur only in isolation. "When, in our everyday Being-with-one-another, we encounter the sort of thing which is accessible to everyone, and about which anyone can say anything, it soon becomes impossible to decide what is disclosed in a genuine understanding, and what is not. This ambiguity extends not only to the world, but just as much to Being-with-one-another as such, and even to Dasein's Being towards itself."[21]

For authenticity, *Dasein* requires a genuine understanding of its individual potential in the context of its world and the ability to project itself into its future possibilities, but common discourse hides what is unique and meaningful for the individual. "Already everyone has surmised and scented out in advance what Others have also surmised and scented out."[22] The individual is no longer able to distinguish their own possibilities from anyone else's. This is a subjectivity dictated by *das Man*—distant from its world.

DAS MAN, KIERKEGAARD, AND THE CONSERVATIVE ANTI-MODERN TRADITION

The descriptions of conservative German intellectuals by Fritz Ringer and Pierre Bourdieu reveal Heidegger's basic conformity with their thought on modernity and democracy. Ringer explains that a majority of German intellectuals between the late nineteenth and early twentieth-century were in agreement about the threat to their traditionally stratified society by the "masses." Ringer argues that this is unsurprising because these intellectuals were within the primary intellectual tradition of German Idealism that was decidedly anti-democratic in its belief that society should be led by the educated, intellectual elite.[23] By 1890 this elite was imagined to be those capable of succeeding at an education directed at personal "cultivation," a spiritual and philosophical education that was to provide the foundation for the national culture. For example, Karl Jaspers claimed that those aptitudes necessary for cultivation, such as "intellectual and spiritual sensitivity," are not measurable. Therefore, he argued, because the masses are known to have low intelligence, those chosen for university education should come from the tradition of a "cultured family."[24] At the end of the nineteenth century, both the German Romantic focus on cultivating self-perfection and the Idealist belief in absolutes had contributed to the convictions held by many German academics that the state was best perfected according to theoretical norms rather than practical politics, and that the ultimate purposes of government were best devised by the elite who had undergone their own personal cultivation.[25]

The educated elite had been a liberalizing force in the early nineteenth century because of their attacks on the uneducated nobility and efforts to create a legal state governed by a bureaucracy rather than an arbitrary ruler. Wilhelm von Humboldt advocated the idea of self-enhancement as a challenge to social distinction based on birth, and therefore, at least in theory, the broad-based availability of education.[26] By the end of the nineteenth-century, however, the elite academics had become a part of the state as professors and bureaucrats. Having achieved power and status, they became largely defensive of their positions against the "great pushing and shoving from below" by the newly urbanized, industrial working masses.[27] Much of Ringer's book explains how the academic community responded to the industrialization of Germany and why they were a conservative force against the trends toward liberalizing access to education and the increasing influence of industrialists and workers on the government. But the central point here is that their rhetoric reflected their fear of the loss of German national culture of which they saw themselves as both the creators and guardians. Theirs was a sense of "crisis" brought on by the traumas to the nation, as well as the tremendous pressures facing the educational system of Germany.[28]

The descriptions of the people and workers as automatons who cause the "disintegration" of society were plentiful amongst the conservative essayists and academics.[29] For example, Paul Natorp, a neo-Kantian philosopher described by Ringer as moderate, said in 1920 that the factories should be torn down because of the "so-called 'culture' of our urban and industrial age."[30] And from more extreme conservatives there are descriptions such as the following. "As the masses plod along the daily treadmill of their lives like slaves or automatons, soullessly, thoughtlessly, and mechanically...all events in nature and in society appear shallowly mechanized to their technicized and routinized manner of thinking: Everything they believe...is as mediocre and average as the mass products of the factory...."[31]

Because of these widely shared sentiments among academics, non-academic writers had a certain influence in terms of directing their fear and blame.[32] During the early twentieth-century the more extreme conservative cultural critics like Oswald Spengler and Ernst Jünger diagnosed their era as one of malaise and catastrophe. These writers argued that democracy meant chaos and weakness, and they believed that Germany should be led by individuals who would impose order and unity. Heidegger read both Spengler and Jünger, and acknowledged the importance of Jünger's *The Worker* for his own work.[33] It is undeniable that Heidegger's work takes part in the general and popular condemnation of modernity and its destruction of traditional German society and what was understood as "culture," or the true spirit of a people and nation.[34] Both Heidegger's conception of the people as a *Volk*, the romantic vision of the German people who have a common tradition and destiny, and his understanding of the modern public as *das Man*, reveal his deep sympathy with the general academic sentiments and reflect his distaste for the modern formations and movements of the people into urban, political, industrial environments. Heidegger agreed with the idea that most people were blind to the decline in their culture and that a total revolution was necessary.

Heidegger's early education was largely consistent with the general ideology of the conservatives. In accord with his early anti-modernist Catholic education, Heidegger saw people in modern times as divorced from tradition, left isolated and egotistical, and forming alienated aggregate masses.[35] One of his first teachers of note was Carl Braig. Braig, the author of *On Being: Outline of Ontology* (1896) was a theologian at the Freiburg Theological Seminary when Heidegger entered there in 1906.[36] Braig's arguments against modernism and for Christian faith were important to Heidegger's first formulation of a modern atomized people. For example, Braig argued against modern scientific thought and modern civilization, saying that modernism is "blinded to anything that is not its Self or serves its Self."[37] Braig was against the general scientific and epistemological shifts in the philosophy of his time, seeing them as an alternative yet false faith. As evidence that subjective reason cannot replace faith in God he argued "Historical truth, like all truth—and the most brilliantly victorious is mathematical truth, the strictest form of eternal truth—comes before the subjective ego and exists without it...."[38] Braig suggested many of Heidegger's later ideas about how the modern scientific attitude, which was built on the Cartesian idea of autonomous individual consciousness, would in fact blind people to a more authentic experience.

Heidegger found in the Christian philosopher Kierkegaard further support for his concern with the modern situation of people divorced from their traditional understandings of their place in the world. Kierkegaard was a critic of modernism, and in his many philosophical and literary works he explained how the individual strives for an ethical life through faith. The ethical life, which has been compared to Heidegger's authenticity, is the choice of the individual to become herself distinct from the social and moral norms of society.[39] Kierkeggard's formulation of achieving truth individually is very similar to Heidegger's individualizing search for Being. Kierkegaard argued "For a 'crowd' is the untruth. In a godly sense it is true...that 'only one attains the goal'.... It means that every man can be that one, God helping him therein—but only one attains the goal. And again this means that every man should be chary about having to do with 'the others,' and essentially should talk only with God and with himself...."[40] Kierkegaard's distaste for the modern public and crowd is also expressed in his focus on the individual's relation to God as her own experience separate from the beliefs imposed by others. And so for Kierkegaard, one cannot receive truth from others. He said truth is "not nimble on its feet," and it "cannot work by means of the fantastical means of the press...."[41] Truth is only expressed and received by the individual in her arduous relation and experience of God.

Heidegger may also have taken note of Kierkegaard's treatment of subjectivity and objectivity. Kierkegaard claimed he was only interested in the subjective relation of the individual to God and not the objective question of the truth of Christianity.[42] Like Heidegger's rejection of scientific rationality, Kierkegaard saw that objective questioning in search of common truths obscured the more important existential truth found in the individual's experience—for Kierkegaard this was the individual's relation to God. For Kierkegaard the individual had the choice of who to be, which should be made in opposition to the pressures of "the crowd." The concern for objective relations to the external world as dictated by universal methods is one basis upon which Heidegger would criticize the subject of Western philosophy after Descartes.

Kierkegaard wrote that the sharing of values could result in their "banalization."[43] This resembles Heidegger's description of what happens to the individual's experiences once they are shared in communication with others. For Heidegger, the "discovering" of an experience may be valid in its origination as primordial truth, but once it is shared, "passed along," or become common, it loses validity. Heidegger would also take up Kierkegaard's description of the "nothing" and the dread it produces. These are individualizing experiences that awaken a person to authentic relations with God and, for Heidegger, the world.

Heidegger's description of *das Man* shares certain characteristics with Kierkegaard's crowd. For example, Kierkegaard said "A crowd—not this crowd or that, the crowd now living or the crowd long deceased, a crowd of humble people or of superior people, of rich or of poor, etc.—a crowd in its very concept is the untruth, by reason of the fact that it renders the individual completely impenitent and irresponsible, or at least weakens his sense of responsibility by reducing it to a fraction."[44] Heidegger's *das Man* would be "not this one, not that one, not oneself, not some people, and not the sum of them all."[45] The indefinability of *das Man* is a central reason that people are unable to experience their worlds directly and authentically.

From this look at Heidegger's local context, we can see that *das Man* carried several layers of meaning that are not easily separated from Heidegger's contributions to the ideas associated with postmodern tradition. The straightforward condemnations of the modern industrialized urban masses are, in Heidegger's work, folded into a more sophisticated problem of epistemological limits within an ontology of temporal/historical contexts. According to Heidegger, both modernity and the history of Western philosophy have served to detach individuals from their worlds, which results in an increase and rigidity of the subject/object dichotomy. In terms of Heidegger's "cultural" concerns this meant that the people were dislocated from traditional roles in which they had experienced their worlds authentically. Because these philosophical and political questions are intertwined in Heidegger's work, there are several areas where the bias against modern masses is an underlying presence in his anti-humanism and anti-essentialism. The next sections of the chapter look at three places where the tensions and confusions are evident.

ROMANTICIZING THE HAMMER

Although all of Heidegger's descriptions of authentic experiences of Being occur when the individual is in isolation, they are all grounded in the understanding of one's world as inter-subjectively constituted over time. Take for example his description of the authentic encounter with a hammer. Heidegger claimed that *Dasein* understands the objects of its world as "equipment." Understanding entities in the world as equipment entails encountering them in their usefulness or "involvement" in their specific role in the world. *Dasein* encounters this equipment without an explicit consciousness of their presence as an object, instead it is encountered "primordially," meaning that *Dasein* encounters the equipment, like a hammer or a path, without thinking of the object as an object alone in the world. The primordial/authentic encounter is characterized by an "inconspicuous familiarity," and in a basic sense Heidegger believed that "the less we just stare at the hammer-Thing, and the more we seize hold of it and use it, the more primordial does our relationship to it become, and the more unveiledly is it encountered as that which it is—as equipment."[46]

This is a primordial experience because in the use of the hammer there is a history of a network of relations and purposes that make up the meaning of the hammer. Before the current user of the hammer ever held a hammer, people had invented the hammer, designated those who would use the hammer in their day-to-day work, and for what purpose the hammer would be used. And, in using the hammer for carpentry, there is present in the hammer a history of relations that also create opportunities for the future use of the hammer in a complex web of social meanings. The relation of the user to the hammer is not one of subject and object where the subject controls the meaning and representation of the hammer. The inauthentic encounter would entail thinking about the hammer as a hammer—thinking about the hammer as an object rather than the hammer being encountered in a web of relations and purposes, where no entity has its own distinct meaning. In authentically encountering the hammer, one experiences the roles and purposes of the other people who have partaken in making the hammer significant in the way that it is. This is important because Heidegger rejected a subjectivity that denies its own social and historical construction.

And yet because of Heidegger's desire to condemn modernity and its masses, some encounters are determined to be inauthentic simply because of their association with forms of modern association and communication. These associations are described as conforming and routinized rather than primordial. Heidegger argued that the details of the modern everyday world are governed through the regular processes of the public, making the power of *das Man* all the more insidious. "In utilizing public means of transport and in making use of information services such as the newspaper, every Other is like the next. This Being-with-one-another dissolves one's own *Dasein* completely into the kind of Being of 'the Others', in such a way, indeed, that the Others, as distinguishable and explicit, vanish more and more. In this inconspicuousness and unascertainability, the real dictatorship of the 'they' [*das Man*] is unfolded."[47] One loses a sense of other people in these "public" encounters. Although it is probable that all *Dasein* are like the others in the use of the hammer, Heidegger associated modern forms of interaction—mass interactions—with the inauthenticity of *das Man* and the distant subject. These interactions are not the basis for a genuine self-understanding, instead they are the norm-creating limits of the subjectivity of metaphysics.

One way of understanding Heidegger's choices suggests that Heidegger romanticized certain inter-subjective relations, including those activities he considered more traditional such as carpentry, the use of the hammer, and walks along paths in the forest. Despite the fact that everyone uses a hammer in the same way in its everyday purpose, those entities in the modern public that bring people together have a different quality of being-with-one-another, which prevents *Dasein* from encountering the world in terms of its "ownmost possibilities." It is unclear, however, why the more modern inter-subjective relations are necessarily realms of conformity. Why in the use of public means of transportation and the newspaper would *Dasein* be more likely to lose itself and its freedom to encounter Being than it would in the use of a hammer? The historicity of the public transportation system should be just as accessible, and therefore just as open to authentic encounters, as that of the hammer. But the inter-subjective relations between the modern masses are seen as more chaotic and traditionless and therefore without comprehensible meaning. In this fear of losing understanding and predictability rests a facet of the postmodern hesitation to engage in politics beyond criticism.

LANGUAGE: THE HOME OF *DAS MAN*?

A second major tension is the way Heidegger understands language as both a basic constituent element of the world to be interpreted and a means by which *das Man* dominates and levels the world. Language is one of the structures of the shared world and being-with others in the world, and yet language in its everyday form is also the means by which *das Man's* publicness obscures authentic experience of Being. Language is one of the ways by which *Dasein* is led away from primordial authentic experience and toward inauthenticity.[48] Through his recognition of the complex workings of language, Heidegger influenced postmodern linguistic anti-representationalism. But at the same time he loaded it with the negative sense that language is a means by which "others" dominate.

Language provides the basis upon which interpretation is carried out. For Heidegger the hermeneutic circle meant that all interpretation takes place in that which is already understood, so that all interpretation is carried out from within the world in which *Dasein* has its primordial understanding of its norms and relations. Heidegger said that the problem with the circle of interpretation is that people tend to see it as a "vicious" and limiting circle. "But if we see this circle as a vicious one and look out for ways of avoiding it, even if we just 'sense' it as an inevitable imperfection, then the act of understanding has been misunderstood from the ground up."[49]

Heidegger furthered argued that "What is decisive is not to get out of the circle but to come into it in the right way."[50] Regardless of how the world is constituted, whether in traditional or modern ways, it provides the meanings in which individuals live and therefore the material for interpretation. Comparing the hermeneutic circle of interpretation to Heidegger's sense of the world of *das Man* suggests that Heidegger himself did not enter the world of the modern public "in the right way." On the one hand, *Dasein's* world is made up of interpretation and understanding that are only possible because of language. On the other, Heidegger argued that through the domination of *das Man*, language transforms direct experiences into distant and average experiences. Language is both a way of creating meaning and the way by which the meaning of being is made distant from *Dasein*.

In accord with the second, *das Man* dominates *Dasein's* efforts to pass along its interpretations of experience of the world. *Das Man* makes these shared meanings distant and average. Communication (a "derivative" form of language) involves "letting someone see with us what we have pointed out by way of giving it a definite character. Letting someone see with us shares with the Other that entity which has been pointed out in its definite character."[51] Heidegger's example here is the assertion that "the hammer is heavy." Communication can be used to share an understanding of a definite sense of *Dasein's* world, but even in its most immediate form, the communication "narrows" the hammer from its total involvement in the world and reduces it to the character of heaviness. In describing the hammer *as* something, the hammer is objectified and made distant from its original encounter with the person who felt its weight in their direct experience of the hammer.

Everyday language serves to hide the primordial and make it more difficult for those involved in the communications to understand the world more than superficially. In the passing along of ideas, discourse becomes less connected to the direct experience of the world. "In the language which is spoken when one expresses oneself, there lies an average intelligibility.... We do not so much understand the entities which are talked about; we already are listening only to what is said-in-the-talk as such. What is said-in-the-talk gets understood; but what the talk is about is understood only approximately and superficially."[52] And so the average understanding of the everyday is the same as everyone else's. This characterizes the groundless-ness of "idle talk," which is the "possibility of understanding everything without previously making the thing one's own."[53] Heidegger therefore privileged the individual encounter with the world rather than the encounter of the world through the communication with others. Communication reduces the experience of the world to the control of *das Man*. Heidegger portrayed the meanings created by *das Man* and its language as inevitably imperfect and therefore to be avoided. This tendency to individualize and aestheticize experience is a facet of the legacy of this confusion created by the negative portrayal of the masses. Instead of accepting the public-ness of *das Man* as constitutive of the "world" and the hermeneutic circle to be interpreted and understood, Heidegger argued that communication and meaning in the public of *das Man* leveled and made understanding inauthentic.

The tension surrounding language remained in his later work. In the "Letter on Humanism" Heidegger placed great value on the role of lan-guage in the revealing of Being.[54] Because language is the "home of Being," Heidegger reinforced the positive sense of the limited nature of one's world. Heidegger asked that people embrace and open themselves to the limits of their worlds. Language is a fundamental constituent element of ones' horizon. By acknowledging the "restriction to the horizon of unconceal-ment" of what is, Heidegger argued that the ancient Greeks were able to remain open to the revealing of Being.[55] Heidegger compared modernity to the ancient Greek experience of being without the interference and domi-nance of subjectivity. For them dwelling "included and maintained within its openness and in that way to be borne along by it, to be driven about by its oppositions and marked by its discord...."[56] A person who dwells within the limits of her horizon and is open to being in an authentic manner does not require the certainty of the self-asserting and self-determining Carte-sian subject. This individual is open to the manifold meanings of being and is changed by them.

This acceptance humbles the role and place of man. Heidegger examined what he saw as a difference between the metaphysical Cartesian subject that believes that the whole world can be represented and an ancient Greek way of thinking in which the person is only a part of the limited world that they can understand. Within one's horizon and house of language "man dwells."[57] Dwelling is the temporal existence in which a person is open to Being. To this point in Heidegger's argument, the criticism of subjectiv-ity here encourages a way of approaching interpretation, which is neither solitary nor collective. On the contrary, it assumes that the world is created collectively and that the individual has a certain freedom within the limits of that world.

In "The Letter on Humanism," however, the fear of *das Man* appears in Heidegger's response to Sartre's essay "Existentialism Is a Humanism." Heidegger argues that existentialism and humanism, as used by Sartre, are trapped within the metaphysical framework of Western thought. As a part of the subject-centered modern philosophical tradition, both fail to ask the question of Being. Because thought and philosophy are dominated by subjectivity and the public realm, they cannot reach or express Being authentically. Instead thought that is dictated by language of the subject only deals with entities, and therefore it does not have the multidimensionality or freedom to encounter Being. Heidegger argued that "language comes under the dictatorship of the public realm, which decides in advance what is intelligible and what must be rejected as unintelligible."[58] Because the public shares and controls understanding through language that has been divided up into digestible categories or "isms," thought that must be shared in language is reduced to sameness. "The dominance of such terms [-isms] is not accidental. It rests above all in the modern age upon the peculiar dictatorship of the public realm."[59] "[B]ecause it stems from the dominance of subjectivity[,] the public realm itself is the metaphysically conditioned establishment and authorization of the openness of individual beings in their unconditional objectification."[60]

Language, as "the house of the truth of Being," is being subject to a "rapidly spreading devastation" that threatens the essence of humanity. This devastation is due to the fact that language is under the dominance of modern metaphysics of subjectivity, leading language out of its "element" of favoring Being. "...if man is to find his way once again into the nearness of Being he must first learn to exist in the nameless. In the same way he must recognize the seductions of the public realm as well as the impotence of the private. Before he speaks, man must first let himself be claimed again by Being, taking the risk that under this claim he will seldom have much to say."[61] In order for humanity to create a "home for dwelling in the truth of Being," the judging speaking subject and the shared knowledge of the public must be rejected. Prior to modernity the shared understandings of the relations of entities of the world were that which made up the world of *Dasein* and made possible *Dasein's* authentic experience of being in the world. In modernity, however, these shared understandings make up something other than a world where being can be encountered authentically. Not only does Heidegger reinforce the dichotomous goals of experiencing a world constituted by being-with others and escaping the world of the public through isolation, but he also fully links the subject with the public. The limits of the subject are objectionable because they are formed by the modern public.

The question of language gets to the heart of the tension surrounding the public. The qualities of being shared and historically constructed, but interpreted by others, are all the limitations of language and therefore of subjectivity. Language, then, is both what constitutes the positive "house of being" and at the same time the negative limits of subjectivity as constituted in the world and in the public. And so Heidegger searched for a language that is separate from the subject because the subject is constituted by the public through language. Heidegger suggested that we "follow its [language's] trail into what is purely its own."[62] He implied that there is a language purely of the world with no human limitations attached. "Language is the clearing-concealing advent of being itself."[63] But this search for a pure language of the world contradicts everything Heidegger argued about being and the world, namely that being does not exist without human involvement in the world. The figure of the public creates this fundamental contradiction within Heidegger's understanding of language.

DAS MAN AS ONTOLOGICAL CHARACTERISTIC AND CRITICISM OF MODERNITY

The ambiguity of *das Man* arises because it is associated with two distinct goals in Heidegger's writing. The status of inter-subjective relations, language, and historical meaning are unclear because *das Man* represents both the everyday language into which *Dasein* is thrown and which provides a world for understanding, as well as that which dominates, determines, and levels individual awareness in line with modern trends.

In *Being and Time*, Heidegger tried to explain why the question of the meaning of being had been forgotten. The answer reflects Heidegger's two goals. First, *das Man* is always present as a way that people tend to think and communicate. Fallenness, *das Man*, and the public are intertwined as essential and ever-present obstacles to achieving an authentic understanding of one's own self and world. The everyday modes of *das Man* in fallenness allow Cartesian rationality (modern subjectivity) to take hold and dominate over time. In turn, the power of *das Man* grew in part because Cartesian rationality and consciousness exacerbate the tendency to be distant from entities and relations in their full, inter-subjective, and historical meanings. Cartesian thought more fully closed off the possibility of true thinking. Thinking cannot reach Being because Descartes "has narrowed down the question of the world to that of Things of Nature as those entities within-the-world which are proximally accessible. He has confirmed the opinion that to know an entity in what is supposedly the most rigorous ontical manner is our only possible access to the primary Being of the entity which such knowledge reveals."[64] Cartesian rationality claimed that the essence of entities is understood through their most evident properties, which are apparent and constant in mathematics. This objectified perspective regarding the entities of the world is the opposite of Heidegger's theory that the essence of entities is temporal and is best grasped through direct experiences of entities as historical phenomena. According to Heidegger, as

Descartes' philosophical perspective came to inform all ways of thinking, its effects and limitations became harder and harder to see.

The Cartesian objectified and distant understanding of the world is a "passing over the world."[65] This experience of the world is not simply an accident or an oversight, which, as Heidegger said, would be simple to correct. Instead Heidegger argued that this type of thinking has been found in ontologies since Parmenides. Passing over the world is "grounded in a kind of Being which belongs essentially to *Dasein* itself."[66] This kind of Being is the essential characteristic constituting *Dasein* as *das Man* in the everyday public realm. In these descriptions *das Man* is an essential aspect of "the horizon" in which being is revealed.[67]

The two, modern Cartesian thought and the ways of *das Man*, are not, however, always carefully distinguished in *Being and Time*. Heidegger argued that *das Man* is an essential ontological element and therefore prior to the rising influence of metaphysical thought. "Dasein has, in the first instance, fallen away from itself as an authentic potentiality for Being its Self, and has fallen into the 'world.'"[68] This is the basic state of *Dasein* in its everyday existence. The ontological status of *das Man* as distracted and susceptible to conformity allowed metaphysical thought as the way of thinking to be taken up as a historical force that reveals itself overtime. At other times, Heidegger seems to say that even the ontological and essential *das Man* and the public fail to provide a way of thinking that is capable of experiencing the entities of the world in a way that allows Being to reveal itself. "The dominance of the public way in which things have been interpreted has already been decisive even for...the basic way in which Dasein lets the world 'matter' to it. The 'they' [*das Man*] prescribes one's state-of-mind, and determines what and how one 'sees.'"[69] Heidegger's criticism of the way people think in modernity has the same characteristics of the timeless problem of fallenness and *das Man*. Is this coincidence or is this confusion between the epistemological limitations of human knowledge and the fear that in modernity mass forms of communication dictate individual knowledge? By leaving these questions unanswered, Heidegger turned his contemporaries' condemnation of the modern masses into both an ontological status of all humans, as well as a problem of modernity resulting from philosophical trends.

We are left with both questions: whether people in all ages are limited by their horizons of language, history, and culture or whether modernity is to blame because with it mass society has created an overwhelming mass inculcation of norms. In other words, is subjectivity, as a distancing between people and their worlds, a result of conformity to modern norms, including metaphysical thought, or are subjectivity and *das Man* timeless ontological characteristics, meaning that humans are necessarily, but not perhaps unfortunately, required to make due with their historical and limited worlds.

CONCLUSION

These tensions have important implications for interpretations of Heidegger' philosophy, whose efforts were focused on emphasizing that the essence of people is not a self-same identity nor an easily characterized substance. Instead Heidegger described the essence of people as experience, which implies a fluidity that is dependent on being-with-others and being-in-the-world. This conception of the individual is one basis for the critique of subjectivity. By arguing that the public, shared, or common way of understanding the world can be described as a singular particular way of encountering the world that is distant, leveled, and inauthentic, however, Heidegger's work complicated the straightforward critique of subjectivity as contingency. First, there is a general anxiety surrounding the inability to know whether one's individual identity is one's own creation or under the dominion of others. Second, Heidegger's formulation turns thinkers away from a primary (if not the only) source of diverse perspectives and knowledge—communication with others including within the public/mass realm. Instead, Heidegger suggested that all authentic encounters of the world occur from individual experience of the phenomenal, historically constructed world. The idea that engagement with the others of *das Man* "uproots" individuals from their world seems counterintuitive if Being with others constitutes one's world.

Kierkegaard's formulation of the individual's relation to God separate from the public is instructive here. Although Heidegger had rejected the vertical relation to a transcendent God, he maintained the centrality of the individual to the individual world sphere. But Heidegger's individual world sphere is fully inter-subjective. One's world does not exist beyond being-with. It seems consistent with the centrality of the inter-subjective world to claim that there are ways of encountering the world that are lazy everyday ways, which are inauthentic for Heidegger. But it is inconsistent for Heidegger to claim that engagement with others creates the public inauthentic way, because the world is made up of engagements with others, including the everyday engagements. From this conundrum of engagement postmodernism may have earned its reputation for being apolitical.

One suggestion of this chapter has been to show that Heidegger makes thinking more difficult than it needs to be. Heidegger elided elements of the "world" with a faceless all-present public and with the dominating subjective perspective so that the realm in which one should dwell is contaminated by that which keeps one from knowing oneself and one's world. The strange presence of the public seems to be the greatest obstacle in thinking and also seems to be the least necessary for understanding the limits of subjectivity. The limits of human knowledge and language mean that individuals conform or are limited by historical meanings. The idea of conformity with the public therefore is used as the negative way of expressing these limits. Heidegger associated it with democracy, workers movements, industrialization, and loss of elite status, but others have associated it with a variety of historical events, including the rise and power of the mass media, and the success of capitalism. Once we realize that the association of the public and the masses with inauthenticity is arbitrary, political theorists can begin to evaluate specific norms based on standards beyond their status as mass norms.

NOTES

1. See Peter Dews, "Postmodernism: Pathologies of Modernity from Nietzsche to the Post-structuralists," in *The Cambridge History of Twentieth-Century Political Thought*, Terence Ball and Richard Bellamy, eds. (Cambridge: Cambridge University Press, 2003); Richard Wolin, *The Politics of Being: The Political Thought of Martin Heidegger* (New York: Columbia University Press, 1990).
2. Dews, 345. See also Clayton Koelb, *Nietzsche as Postmodernist* (Albany: State University of New York Press, 1990); James Ward, *Heidegger's Political Thinking* (Amherst: University of Massachusetts Press, 1995), xvii.
3. Charles Bambach, Heidegger, Dilthey, and the Crisis of Historicism (Ithaca, NY: Cornell University Press, 1995).
4. "Man" in German is the pronoun one. *Das Man* is often translated "the they," and the translators of *Being and Time* translate it in this way. Martin Heidegger, *Being and Time*, John Macquarrie and Edward Robinson, trans. (New York: Harper and Row Publishers, 1962). Although I will use das Man, I tend to agree with Hubert Dreyfus that "the one" is more appropriate than "the they" because it includes everyone, including the one speaking.
5. See Victor Farias, *Heidegger and Nazism*, Paul Burrell and Gabriel R. Ricci, trans. (Philadelphia: Temple University Press, 1989); and Hugo Ott, *Martin Heidegger: A Political Life*, Allan Blunden, trans. (London: 1994). Many have engaged in the debate about Heidegger's political thought and his reasons for supporting National Socialism. See Otto Pöggeler, *Martin Heidegger's Path of Thinking*, Daniel Magurshak and Sigmund Barber, trans. (Atlantic Highlands, NJ: Humanities Press, 1987); Karsten Harries, "Heidegger as a Political Thinker," in *Heidegger and Modern Philosophy*, Michael Murray, ed. (New Haven, CT: Yale University Press, 1978); Richard Wolin, *The Politics of Being: The Political Thought of Martin Heidegger*; Julian Young, *Heidegger, Philosophy, Nazism* (Cambridge: Cambridge University Press, 1997), Fred Dallmayr, *The Other Heidegger* (Ithaca, NY: Cornell University Press, 1993); James Ward, *Heidegger's Political Thinking* (Amherst: University of Massachusetts Press, 1995).
6. Charles Bambach, *Heidegger's Roots: Nietzsche, National Socialism, and the Greeks* (Ithaca: Cornell University Press, 2003); and Pierre Bourdieu, *The Political Ontology of Martin Heidegger*, Peter Collier, trans. (Stanford, CA: Stanford University Press, 1991), 78–80. "Conservative Revolutionaries" was a term first used in 1927 by Hugo von Hofmannsthal for those who called themselves "neo-conservatives" "young conservatives," "German socialists," "conservative socialists," "national revolutionaries." According to Bourdieu "one naturally includes in this category Spengler, Junger, Otto Strasser, Niekisch, Edgar J. Jung, etc." Bourdieu, 115, fn. 47.

7. In keeping with the historicism of this volume, I do not assert that a historical exploration showing how and why Heidegger developed these concepts proves anything about how subsequent thinkers use these ideas. This historical project only makes claims about Heidegger's local context and understandings. Once this has been shown, however, contemporary political theorists and intellectual historians have a greater chance of understanding the extent to which Heidegger's concept of *das Man* influenced subsequent thinkers—even those who clearly do not sympathize with Heidegger's political and ideological commitments.

8. For example, Michel Foucault's essay "Maurice Blanchot: Thought from the Outside," *Foucault/Blanchot*, Jeffrey Mehlman and Brian Massumi, trans. (New York: Zone Books, 1990), which exemplifies a search for a language and meaning that is outside convention.

9. Michel Foucault approached this position in his later works by acknowledging that power is both a positive and negative force; simply because power creates knowledge does not mean that it must be rejected.

10. Richard Wolin, *The Politics of Being: The Political Thought of Martin Heidegger.*

11. Hubert Dreyfus, *Being-in-the-World: A Commentary on Heidegger's Being and Time, Division I* (Cambridge, MA: MIT Press, 1991).

12. Heidegger's concept of "world" can also be interpreted as the historical context of traditions and values that have been undermined by modernity. In this interpretation *Dasein* stands in for the German *Volk*. Our "world" can be interpreted as any individual's context of entities and people whose relations and meanings have been created over time. Hubert Dreyfus argues that Heidegger's "world" is made up of the norms of any particular person's historical and spatial context. Both interpretations are supported by Heidegger's work, and both are important for understanding the tensions surrounding the concept of the public. The second seems to contribute most directly to the anti-foundational tradition I explore here, but the presence of the first contributes to the ambiguous conception of the people in Heidegger's work. In the discussion that follows, I focus less on the conception of the people as an organic Volk than on Heidegger's negative perception of the atomistic modern people who experience their norms by conforming to them.

13. See Bourdieu's *Political Ontology of Martin Heidegger* for a discussion of the philosophical "field" in which Heidegger positioned himself.

14. For a detailed discussion of Heidegger's being-in-the-world and his anti-Cartesian purpose see Dreyfus, *Being-in-the-World: A Commentary on Heidegger's Being and Time.*

15. For more on this theme, see Peter Gordon, "Hammer Without a Master," Chapter 5 of this volume.

16. Martin Heidegger, *Being and Time*, 152.

17. Ibid., 16. Fritz K. Ringer argues that the idea of "leveling" is ubiquitous in the conservative writings between 1890 and 1933. *The Decline of the German Mandarins: The German Academic Community, 1890–1933* (Hanover, NH: Wesleyan University Press, 1969).

18. Ringer, *The Decline of the German Mandarin*, 104.

19. Ibid., 164.

20. Ibid., 164·

21. Ibid., 217.

22. Ibid., 217.

23. Ibid., 92–102, 129–130.

24. Ibid., 109.

25. Ibid., 120–121. Ringer gives an example of Heinrich Rickert using Ficthe's "Closed Commercial State" as a "model of 'idealistic' politics," 120.
26. Fritz Ringer, *Max Weber: An Intellectual Biography* (Chicago: The University of Chicago Press, 2004), 11.
27. Ringer, The Decline of the German Mandarins, 131, quoting, Freidrich Meinecke, *Politische Schriften und Reden*, Georg Kotowski, ed. (Darmstadt, 1958), 49–50. See generally on this point Ringer, *The Decline of the German Mandarins*, 123–127.
28. Rüdiger Safranski, *Martin Heidegger: Between Good and Evil*, Ewald Osers, trans. (Cambridge, MA: Harvard University Press, 1998), 174, 193. See also Charles Bambach, *Heidegger, Dilthey, and the Crisis of Historicism.* At the national level, the end of the First World War, the Treaty of Versailles, and the occupation of the Ruhr by the French created a strong sense of nationalism based in blood and language (Bourdieu, 7–8). Also between 1918 and 1933, the country faced movements of the people due to industrialization, tremendous inflation, and the great depression of 1929. At the same time, the universities had increasing numbers of students from many sectors of society and a growing number of underpaid instructors. See also Ringer, *The Decline of the German Mandarins*.
29. See Ringer, 214, 222, 249–250 and Bourdieu, 14–15.
30. Ringer, 249.
31. Ibid., 249, quoting Hermann Güntert, *Deutscher Geist: Drie Vorträge* (Buhl-Baden, 1932), 14.
32. Ibid., 223.
33. Bourdieu,18–20. Safranski, 259–260.
34. Safranski, 173–734, 193, 226; *The Weimar Republic Sourcebook*, Anton Kaes, Martin Jay, Edward Dimendberg, eds. (Berkeley: University of California Press, 1994); Richard Wolin, 23–28. Bambach argues that the influence of National Socialist thinkers such as Alfred Bauemler, Ernst Krieck, Franz Bohm, and others reveals itself most distinctly in Heidegger's work between 1933 to 1945. Bambach says that while Heidegger disagreed with their biological racism, he did agree with them on many points during this period. These points of agreement include: modernity and the liberal philosophy of the French Revolution threaten to destroy the great culture of the German Volk; an appeal to the pre-Socratics, Fichte, Hölderlin, and Nietzsche for ways of supporting German nationalism; and a commitment to the idea that German culture and people are properly rooted collectively in the earth and land rather than in modern, atomizing, urban, cosmopolitan settings. Charles Bambach, *Heidegger's Roots: Nietzsche, National Socialism, and the Greeks*, 69–70.
35. Safranski, 16–18.
36. Ott, 55; Safranski, 16
37. Safranski, 17, quoting C. Braig, "Was soll der Gebildete von dem Modernismus wissen?" in *Die Zeit des Selbst und die Zeit danach: Zur Kritik der Textgeschichte Martin Heideggers*, D. Thomä, ed. (Frankfurt, 1990), 37.
38. Safranski, 17.
39. Patricia J. Huntington, "Heidegger's Reading of Kierkegaard Revisited: From Ontological Abstraction to Ethical Concretion" in *Kierkegaard in Post/Modernity*, Martin J. Matustík and Merold Westphal, eds. (Bloomington: Indiana University Press, 1995), 58; and see generally Dreyfus, *Being-in-the-World*.
40. Kierkegaard, "That Individual: Two 'Notes' Concerning My Work as an Author," in *Existentialism from Dostoevsky to Sartre*, Walter Kaufmann, ed. (Ontario, Canada: New American Books, 1975), 94.

41. Ibid., 98.

42. Kierkegaard, "Truth is Subjectivity" in *Kierkegaard in Post/Modernity*, 112.

43. Dreyfus, 276. Dreyfus says, "In Kierkegaard's time everyone was a Christian. It was this banalization of the original insights of Christianity to which Kierkegaard reacted."

44. Kierkegaard, "That Individual," 95.

45. Heidegger, *Being and Time*, 164.

46. Ibid., 98.

47. Ibid., 164.

48. In German the noun "public" is *Öffentlichkeit* and the adjective is *öffentlich*, which literally means openly. In Being and Time Heidegger describes the publicness of *das Man*, and in later works he refers more often to the public and the public realm rather than *das Man*.

49. Heidegger, *Being and Time*, 194.

50. Ibid., 194.

51. Ibid., 197.

52. Ibid., 212.

53. Ibid., 213.

54. Martin Heidegger, "Letter on Humanism," in *Basic Writings*, David Farrell Krell, ed., Frank A. Capuzzi, trans. (San Francisco: Harper Collins, 1993).

55. Martin Heidegger, "The Age of the World Picture" in *The Question Concerning Technology*, William Lovitt, trans. and ed. (New York: Garland Publishing, 1977), 146.

56. Heidegger, "The Age of the World Picture," 131.

57. Heidegger, "Letter on Humanism," 217.

58. Ibid., 221.

59. Ibid., 221.

60. Ibid., 221.

61. Ibid., 223.

62. Heidegger, "The Way to Language," in *Basic Writings*, 398. See also Michel Foucault, "Maurice Blanchot: The Thought from Outside."

63. Heidegger, "Letter on Humanism," 230.

64. Ibid., 133.

65. Ibid., 133.

66. Ibid., 133.

67. Ibid., 133.

68. Ibid., 220.

69. Ibid., 213.

4   A Rock and a Hard Place
Althusser, Structuralism, Communism and the Death of the Anticapitalist Left

Robert Resch

Marxist thought . . . will survive for another powerful reason: the feebleness of current theoretical thinking.—Louis Althusser

History is more imaginative than we are.—Marx

Louis Althusser looms large in the historical traditions of both Structuralism and Marxism. His "Structural Marxism" made him a major figure of the golden age of Structuralism, joining Lévi-Strauss, Lacan, Barthes, and Foucault in the very front rank, yet like his friend Derrida, Althusser broke with Structuralism in 1967 and went on to develop a distinctive "poststructuralist" theoretical position. Unlike the other major figures, however, Althusser was a committed, if critical, member of the French Communist Party (PCF) during the momentous years of its belated confrontation with Stalinism, the challenge posed by the revolutionary events of May, 1968, and its electoral-reformist alliance with the Socialist Party (PS) in the "Union of the Left" during the seventies. It was the theory and politics of the PCF that defined the local context—the specific issues and debates—driving Althusser's synthesis of Structuralist and Marxist traditions. For Althusser, Structuralism was an independent and scientific method for rethinking the "sacred texts" of Marx, as well as a critical theory for undermining the Party's competing theoretical frameworks—"economism" (technological determinism) and "humanism" (ethical idealism). In his poststructuralist writings, Althusser focused more explicitly on class struggle, ideology, and political analyses of the "concrete situation" within the PCF. Critical of the party leadership's position on virtually every major question, Althusser continued to believe in the necessity of the PCF as the organization of the working class and in the importance of being in contact with the worker's political struggles.

Althusser attempted to negotiate a politically revolutionary position between the rock of a Stalinist PCF whose authoritarian, bureaucratic leadership he detested, and the hard place of a Structuralist theoretical tradition whose pessimistic determinism and philosophical relativism undermined his hope for equalitarian, anticapitalist revolution. While Althusser was able to maintain a critical, yet productive distance from the theoretical hard place of Structuralism (and the culmination of its intellectual and political aporias in Poststructuralism), his professional, political, and personal lives[1] were smashed against the political rock of Communism: the failure of the PCF to become the popular and revolutionary party Althusser unwaveringly advocated and the crushing defeats it experienced as a result during the sixties and seventies. Althusser's fate transcends his personal circumstances to exemplify the larger collapse of anticapitalist theory and politics he himself referred to as the crisis of Marxism. Structuralism and Poststructuralism mystified social determination and unleashed the specter of ideological relativism that ultimately eviscerated Marxist social theory, while the PCF pursued a politics of accommodation with capitalism—initially under the direction of Khrushchev's "peaceful coexistence" and "socialist humanism" and then independently under the rubric of Eurocommunism. Both the rock and the hard place have now disappeared, but perhaps it may be of some future value to footnote their role as vanishing mediators in the transition to global capitalist hegemony.

THE DISCREET CHARM OF STRUCTURALISM

Structuralism, Althusser's self-criticism to the contrary, was no mere flirtation; it was deeply influential for his rethinking of Marxist theory. It gave to him, as it did to the social sciences generally, a promise of scientific rigor able to grasp the complex and profound changes being experienced in France, as elsewhere, by rapid capitalist "modernization."[2] For Althusser, Structuralism also meant an assertion of free and independent thinking within the PCF, heretofore a bastion of authoritarian orthodoxy, as well as an opportunity to attack the Party's traditional, simplistic explanation of history in terms of a crude technological determinism or "economism." At the same time, Structuralism's devaluation of subjectivism and voluntarism—the primacy of the autonomous individual who makes history—provided an alternative to the party's new political and theoretical orientation toward "socialist humanism," which Althusser dismissed as ethical idealism, an accommodation to an essentially capitalist ideology.

For Althusser, both economism and humanism were forms of "historicism"—teleological, salvationist projections of ideological meaning onto historical developments.[3] The Structuralist tradition's rejection of just such subjective illusions was important for Althusser. There were problems in a Marxist appropriation of Structuralism, of course; one of the most important being the absence of any connection between objective knowledge (theory) and subjective consciousness (practice)—to paraphrase Marx, explaining the world, is not the same thing as convincing anyone to change it. For the period of his most Structuralist theoretical work, Althusser was content to ignore this problem, offloading political and ideological responsibilities onto the party leadership, while not very surreptitiously supporting Maoist anti-bureaucratic, populist, and revolutionary reforms within the party itself.

In contrast to Althusser, most critics within the Marxist tradition were hostile to Structuralism dismissing it as a technocratic, elitist ideology commensurate with Gaullist authoritarian capitalist modernization. Most famously, Sartre charged Structuralism with being the last stand of the bourgeoisie against Marxism.[4] However, Structuralism was critical of both capitalism and imperialism and could therefore legitimately claim to be on the political Left. Claude Lévi-Strauss rejected not only the superiority of Western cultural values, but also the credibility of all axiological cultural comparisons. Michel Foucault focused on the history of groups whose marginalization or exclusion was integral to Western "progress." Jacques Lacan ridiculed the conformist nature of American "ego psychology," while asserting the "imaginary" structure of conscious rationality and the "symbolic castration" of human beings by the "symbolic order" of language and culture. Roland Barthes mercilessly exposed the myths embodied in Western popular culture and the manipulative processes by which fashion is constituted, while maintaining that Structuralism was the most revolutionary method of all since it operated on language, the basic instrument of revolution. Althusser, of course, aimed to develop a "science of social formations" in order to advance the cause of revolutionary Communism.

Nonetheless, Perry Anderson's view of Structuralism as "politically heteronymous" remains apt: Structuralism had no inherent political values and proved itself quite capable of adapting to different ideological forces.[5] It was not a unified theory to be rejected or accepted in its entirety; but more like a common outlook with similar goals and methods shared across a variety of disciplines. Its local context revealed contradictory possibilities: while it often functioned as a critical theory useful for dissecting capitalist culture, Structuralism also served as a kind of "detox" program for numerous ex-Communists such as Foucault, looking for an alternative explanatory framework promising scientific rigor and exuding an aura of modernity.[6] François Dosse has shown how Structuralism also served as an ideological weapon in the academic trench warfare between the emerging social sciences and the hitherto dominant humanities ensconced in the Sorbonne.[7]

STRUCTURALISM AS A THEORETICAL POSITION

Before addressing the question of Althusser's relation to Structuralism, we should first define the common themes of Structuralist tradition generally. An obvious place to start is the notion of structure as a formal system of rules or laws. Structuralism, according to Barthes, "aims to reconstitute its object in such a way as to reveal the rules by which the object functions."[8] This system of rules constitutes the conditions of existence that make meaning or meaningful action possible. By distinguishing the system of formal rules, the generative matrix of any action, from the content or context of any particular action the Structuralist advances beyond the meaning or truth of the text—literary, mythic, scientific, even sartorial—to the operations that constitute the ability of the text to generate valid meanings in the first place.

A second theme is the predominance of structure over subject. Structuralism's interest in formal, systemic conditions of existence for meaning and activity means a corresponding lack of interest in the subject as agent or the intentionality of consciousness. Structuralists espouse "theoretical antihumanism": individual subjects are not masters of their own actions, rather it is structures that act through subjects who are unaware of the fact. There is little explanatory significance given to the concept of "Man" as an autonomous subject; Foucault points out, "man is merely a recent invention . . . a "wrinkle" in our knowledge," whose illusionary power is rapidly dissipating.[9] Yet theoretical antihumanism has certain weaknesses of its own. How are we to formulate an explanatory link between universal structures and the actual practices of specific individuals? Why this particular practice and not some other? Why this particular person and not another sharing the same structural conditions of existence? While Structuralism is adept at describing and classifying the rules and limits of all practices, it seems incapable of explaining the occurrence of any practice at all. Individual practices by individual subjects are dismissed as superficial, contingent or random eruptions from within an unchanging, universal matrix or "combinatory" of possibilities. If such is the case, then is it legitimate to ask for whom and for what purpose does Structuralism exist? What is the relevance of the knowledge Structuralism produces to the practices of those subjects it treats with such condescension?

The separation of systems of signification from any external referent or reality is a third general theme of the Structuralist tradition. Saussure's truly original insight was neither the priority of the system of language over the individual speech act nor the concept of a sign composed of signifiers (graphic or acoustic images) and signifieds (meanings or ideas). Truly original was his assertion of a differential or relational theory of meaning—that the value or meaning of a linguistic sign resides in its difference from all other signs within the language, not in its correspondence to some real world referent. Despite Saussure's admonition that such a theory of value is inapplicable to non-linguistic structures such as kinship since, unlike language, they were motivated by natural relations and real things, Structuralists often interpreted non-linguistic phenomena as free-floating systems of differential or relational terms. Describing kinship as a communication system (between groups by means of women) enables Lévi-Strauss to isolate the structural determination of the incest taboo from any real-world referent or constraint. Similarly, Lacan asserts that the signified is the result of a contingent, subjective act whereby the ceaseless flux of signifiers is fixed into a given meaning by another, "master" signifier. Obviously, such assumptions push "scientific" Structuralism down a slippery slope toward relativism.

A fourth general theme is "antihistoricism," the devaluation of historical determination and processes of development. Structuralism not only fails to explain historical events and structural transformations, it is uninterested in doing so. In addition to the reasons already noted, Structuralist antihistoricism is motivated by an aversion to "total" or "world" histories: "historicisms" that project a subjective meaning into historical events in order to impose a progressive teleology onto historical development. Historicism posits a predetermined goal (the best of all possible worlds) along with structural processes (biological evolution, technological mastery, the "essence" human nature) and agents (great men, great nations, great ideas) designed to get us there. Historicism is not simply ideological, it is pernicious, tainted by European ethnocentrism, racism, nationalism, and imperialism.

For some Structuralists, e.g., Lévi-Strauss, there is a resigned "posthistorical" sensibility at work within their antihistoricism. "History" is a perpetual hope for a better future that never arrives and whose purpose is precisely never to arrive. History shields us from the meaningless flux of random, superficial events that change nothing in the structural matrix that generates them. Existence is as meaningless for many Structuralists as it is for most existentialists, the difference between them being that the Structuralists lack any concept of heroic self-overcoming through will or engagement. Dosse sees Structuralist pessimism as an important precursor of Postmodernism: the rejection of teleology, the incapacity of human beings to master themselves or their social relations discredits the ideals of Western rationality and evolutionary progress from which it is but a small step to an "ideology of suspicion" of any master narrative and a view of history as eternal recurrence.[10]

Rejecting the concept of progress, Structuralists like Foucault theorized history as a series of accidents, "the iron hand of necessity shaking the dicebox of chance."[11] Foucault not only rejects "total history" as unknowable, he rejects the very idea of such a history as a nascent totalitarian regime of "truth" seeking forcibly to impose itself on believers and unbelievers alike. The best we can hope for, morally as well as epistemologically, are historical fragments—"archaeologies" or "genealogies" that describe historical épistèmes or ideological apparatuses "as if" they were independent monads. Where Lévi-Strauss grounds all myths in a timeless contradiction between nature and culture, Foucault describes random manifestations of an omnipresent will to power: an explanation of power that posits power as an explanation.

ALTHUSSER'S "PECULIAR KIND OF STRUCTURALISM"

Althusser had recourse to other traditions and influences beside Structuralism: Spinoza, who provided a most uncompromising philosophical materialism and concepts of adequate and inadequate ideas consistent with it; French philosophers of science Gaston Bachelard, Jean Cavaillès, and Georges Canguilhem whose conventionalist, historical epistemology Althusser took over; finally, of course, the social theory of Marx himself. However, it is pointless to minimize or deny the profound influence of Structuralism on Althusser's work. One reason for such efforts has been the hostility of Marxists to Structuralism. Conversely, among non-Marxists the dissociation of Structuralism and Marxism erases the uncomfortable fact that a Communist philosopher was able to produce a credible, theoretical synthesis of both traditions. However, rejecting such spurious interpretations is not to say Althusser deployed Structuralist ideas uncritically. In fact, like the other "master thinkers" of the age of Structuralism, he plowed an independent path through a common field of ideas, while cultivating new concepts of his own.

Althusser's "Structural Marxism" contrasts the works of the "young" and the "mature" Marx. In Althusser's view the young Marx was still under the influence of Hegelian dialectics (history as teleological progress, the actualization of reason, freedom, and self-determination, a process motored by contradictions that are "simple" insofar as their resolution is predestined), and Feuerbach's notion of "alienation" (human subjects reconciling themselves to discipline and deprivation by producing religious ideologies that project their desire for happiness onto another, transcendent world). By means of an "epistemological break" with such notions, the mature Marx inaugurated "historical materialism," a new "science of social formations" articulated on the basis of "modes of production." Rejecting evolutionary or moralistic discourses, whether humanist or economist, the mature Marx not only theorized the economic "base" of capitalism and its relation to non-economic, "superstructural" levels and functions, he also developed concepts of non-capitalist modes of production and of the transition from one mode of production to another. Despite the immensity of this achievement, Althusser maintains that Marx never systematically elaborated the scientific revolution contained in his mature work.

The theoretical dimension of the local context shaping Althusser's project involved, first, the systematic specification and extension of Marx's conceptual framework and, second, a defense of its claims to scientificity. A brief summary of key thematic terms will convey both the extent of Althusser's debt to Structuralism and the originality of his revisions of both classical Structuralism and Marxism.[12]

- *Social practice.* Althusser's is a dynamic, diachronic, "genetic" Structuralism within which the idea of transformation through practice is central. Like most other Structuralists, Althusser focuses on the structural determination of individual events, but unlike classical Structuralism, he refuses to conceptualize such events as contingent or insignificant: they are both determined and capable of altering their structural conditions of existence. In a heuristic manner, Althusser specifies three central forms or "instances" of social practices: economic, political, and ideological (with a fourth instance, theoretical practice, emerging as an internal splitting within ideology).

- *Structural Causality.* Althusser thinks of causality in relational terms—both the "structured whole" (that exists only as its elements and their interrelations) and the instances of specific practices (elements whose place and function are assigned by the structured whole). He explicitly rejects both "expressive" causality (all elements of the totality being essentially the same, microcosms of a macrocosm) and "transitive" causality (elements being autonomous and events being the product of random interactions as with the collision of billiard balls). From the synchronic perspective of classical Structuralism, Althusser's "structural causality" may seem self-contradictory. However, the contradiction disappears when we understand Althusser's concept in diachronic not synchronic terms. The determination exerted by the structured whole pertains to the unchangeable past, the simultaneous, combined effectivity of all elements constituting the conditions of existence of the changing present of each individual practice. Since it is in the past, from the present perspective of each instance the structured whole is an "absent" cause—much as our experience of freedom precludes direct awareness of our determination.[13]
- *Overdetermination.* Structural causality operates as a parallelogram of simultaneous but unequal forces. Althusser refers to this complex unity of causes as "overdetermination" (not to be confused with the absence or equality of determinations or with their inherent unknowability). Everything causes everything else, Althusser admits, but like a vector pulled in the direction of a more powerful force despite the weaker pull of another, a social event is a product of the relative strength of its various causes.
- *Relative autonomy.* Althusser also rejects the notion that all practices are perfectly coordinated like mechanism of an orrery. Again distancing himself from classical Structuralism, Althusser posits the "relative autonomy" of each individual instance. Social practices do not emerge at the same time nor for the same purpose and therefore their internal logics are to a greater or lesser degree contradictory, that is "out of synch" with each other. However, this autonomy is not absolute; it is relative to the totality of practices that constitute the structured whole.
- *Economic determination "in the last instance."* Marx's great idea was economic determination, the fact that a social formation

is "articulated" on the basis of a mode of production. However, Althusser rejects the notion of economic determination as "reflection-ist" (all non-economic practices being derived directly from economic structures). Instead the economic instance sets limits on the autonomy of other practices, an ultimately irresistible pressure for them to reach a minimal degree of compatibility or "correspondence" sufficient for the mode of production successfully to reproduce itself. The economy, in other words, exerts the greatest force within the parallelogram of social forces. The qualifying phrase "in the last instance" refers to the fact that when we speak of economic determination we are speaking of a heuristic concept: the economy never exists in isolation from its conditions of existence (the social formation as a structured whole), nor is its causal effectivity on non-economic practices necessarily direct, transparent, or unmediated. In the last instance, however, we all have to eat.

- *Class struggle is the motor of history.* A mode of production is made up of two structural relations: (a) "forces of production" (a labor pro-cess and the technology deployed within it) and (b) "relations of pro-duction" (ownership, that is to say, effective control of the means and results of production). These two relations define the interests and powers of social classes. In class societies the determinant contradic-tion is between a class of owners and a class of laborers who work for them. The central fact of such social formations is the method by which the economic surplus is pumped out of the hands of producers and into the hands of owners. Although classes may be divided into fractions and despite the existence of intermediate classes and status groups, the antagonistic relations between the classes of owners and workers are decisive: class struggle is the motor of history.

- *Dominant instance.* Determination is not exactly the same thing as dominance, although there is often confusion between the two terms. In capitalist democracies, for example, the state may appear to be dominant, but for Althusser it is not since actual dominance always resides with the relations of production. In capitalist social formations, where the political and the economic instances are formally separate (thus "private" property), the relations of production are external to the state. Dominance resides with the capitalist class; the capitalist state, however riven with antagonisms, exists to legitimize capitalism and to facilitate its expanded reproduction. Although a contradic-tion between the "power bloc" and "the people" exists in capitalist democracies, the state is, at most, a lightening rod for dissipating and controlling popular discontents. Even fascist movements—products of capitalist crises and promising an organic, national community where class cooperation under the direction of an authoritarian state will replace class struggle and economic exploitation—must make their peace with capitalism. No fascist regime came to or remained in power by threatening the capitalist class; every fascist regime came to or remained in power by resolving a profound capitalist crisis and thus saving capitalism from itself. Wherever a capitalist mode of production exists, the dominance of the political over the economic instance can only be an ideological illusion.

In a feudal (or "tributary") mode of production, however, the dominance of the political actually exists. In feudalism, the economic instance is composed of forces of production (cooperative labor organized by the peasant village utilizing animal power and manual labor) and relations of production (serfdom, a peasant's right to be on the land in return for obligations of rent and labor to the lord of the manor). Unlike capitalist societies where property ownership is formally separated from state power, feudal "ownership" of the manor is political since tribute-taking aristocracies are organized by relations of lordship and vassalage). In feudal modes of production actual dominance resides in the political instance, but only because it is the site of the relations of production (manorial overlordship and peasant serfdom). The economy is determinant, however, since tribute taking by lords via serfdom is the essence of feudal exploitation. It is this mode of production that explains why feudal societies involve not simply class tensions between lords and peasants, but also "political" tensions between lords (rent takers) and princes (tax takers) over their relative shares of the peasant's surplus. It is also explains the tendency of tributary modes of production to oscillate between political centralization (appropriation by an "absolute" prince governing through a bureaucratic nobility) and decentralization (appropriation by a landed nobility only nominally governed by a weak prince living, for the most part, off the revenues of his own estates).

- *Primacy of contradiction over structure.* As we have already noted, what most distinguishes Althusser's from other Structuralisms is his emphasis on change (diachrony) instead of stasis (synchrony). Because social practices are not perfectly coordinated, and because every social practice is productive, relations of correspondence necessary for structural reproduction are always more or less fragile. Contradictions or non-correspondences are always forcing changes of various forms and magnitudes. Contradictions may be so minor, weak or isolated as to require only minor adjustments, but they may also be so important, so strong and interconnected that they "condense" into a "revolutionary rupture" and perhaps an entirely new social formation.

DERRIDA AND THE CRISIS OF STRUCTURALISM

Although Structuralism was widely criticized for its antihumanism and antihistoricism, the work of Jacques Derrida attacked its claim to scientificity, thus precipitating a genuine intellectual crisis within the movement.

Structuralists deceive themselves, Derrida maintains, by ignoring the fact their own frameworks are no less conventional than those they discover in the representational practices of others. The scientific rigor of Structuralism is an illusion because no independent or objective demonstration of the correspondence between its propositions and reality is possible. Derrida concludes that Structuralism's quest for "truth" is yet another manifestation of Western civilization's compulsive "logocentrism," a metaphysics of "presence" that ignores the conventionality of all linguistic practice.

For Derrida, every attempt to claim a direct, unmediated grasp of a fact or to communicate a fully aware, self-present consciousness of such facts is subverted by the necessity of thinking and expressing facts in language (always already existing concepts and theories). A sampling of Derrida's more well-known "concepts" sufficiently conveys their radically relativistic implications: *"différance"*—written with an "a" not an "e"—(that meaning is always both differential, lacking any independent positive value, and deferred, open-ended until some impossible finality is attained); "supplement" (that privileged terms necessarily rely upon marginalized terms making the question of their relative importance undecidable); "iterability" (that the original meaning or truth of a statement can never be reproduced since every repetition is necessarily different from its predecessor in context); "dissemination" (that meanings are polysemic, endlessly escaping finality by inviting new readings and the production of new meanings).

Having provoked a crisis of positivism within the Structuralist tradition, can Derrida be said to have resolved it? François Dosse thinks not, characterizing Derrida's critical practice of "deconstruction"—close readings of texts that reveal immanent contradictions between what a text "wants" to say and what it is actually compelled to say—as a kind of "hyperstructuralism" marking the culmination of logically continuous process of self-destruction.[14] Structuralism, which began as a realist investigation of the deep structure of cultural practices, concludes that cultural practices keep the deep structure of reality permanently beyond our grasp. By claiming "there is no outside to the text"—where text implies all possible referents, all structures called "real" (economic, historical, social)—Derrida seems to have abolished the distinction between science and ideology, philosophical and literary practice, and to have projected the aporias of representation onto "reality" itself.

Or does he? Derrida implies something very close to these positions in many places, to be sure, and many of his American followers have used deconstruction enthusiastically to embrace radical relativism and a "postmodern" world view. Yet other commentators, Christopher Norris perhaps most forcefully, have pointed out that Derrida explicitly rejects radical relativism, the fictionalizing of philosophy, and the notion that any reading is as good as any another.[15] Therefore, Derrida's work is best described as a sublation of Structuralism, transcending and preserving its rational practice of ideology-critique, while negating its logocentric naiveté.

For Norris, Derrida is a rationalist critic of vulgar or "metaphysical" realism—the kind of realism that deludes itself into believing it knows more than it can possibly know. Derrida neither denies the existence of reality nor asserts that its structure is differential, he simply rejects "ideologies of representation" that ignore their internal limits in order to impose a single, ultimate meaning on reality. Derrida rejects the notion that deconstruction can dispense with rules of logic, existing knowledges, concepts, and theoretical constructions and somehow leap outside or beyond them and land with both feet securely on some alternative ground. We have no choice but to use the philosophical language that we have; there is no other available to us: "the irreplaceable, insurmountable, imperial grandeur of the rational order . . . is such that we cannot argue against it except by using it, we cannot protest reason without reason."[16] Thus Derrida sees no value in simply reversing the logocentric privilege of philosophical rationality over literary imagination for in doing so we simply exchange one metaphysics (vulgar realism) for another (vulgar relativism).

I find the idea of a rational tain behind the skeptical mirror of undecidability, the notion that a realist faith animates Derrida's critique of logocentrism, persuasive. Not only is a commitment to rationalism and realism consistent with what Derrida himself says in his interviews, but without it deconstruction is simply too frivolous for a serious philosopher to have dedicated his professional life to.[17] Unfortunately, and here I must disagree with Norris, the fact that Derrida is a rational critic of reason, a realist probing the limits of realism, does not in any way resolve the crisis of Structuralism. Deconstruction remains a negative philosophy: the existence of a reality beyond interpretation is assumed, but no positive statements about its nature are permitted. While Derrida does not foreclose the possibility of correspondence between representation and reality, he cannot defend it. If only negative knowledge is possible, if every positive knowledge is contaminated by logocentrism, if the highest achievement of philosophy is undecidability then why bother? Deconstruction seemingly ends in a philosophical impasse from which not even Norris suggests a plausible exit.

Philosophical deadlock threatens political deadlock. How can we move from philosophical undecidability to political decision? Attempts to formulate a political practice from deconstruction fall into one of two categories, either neoliberal pessimism or ethical utopianism. By the terms of a neoliberal, pessimistic reading, Derrida might be seen as rejecting what Peter Starr calls the "specular logic" of "revolutionary opposition" whose final eruption was the events of May, 1968.[18] According to Starr, the project of revolutionary opposition always fails to bring about liberation because the revolution and the regime become mirror images of each other. Liberation necessarily falls victim either to "repetition" (the revolution is victorious but at the price of becoming authoritarian and oppressive itself) or "recuperation" (the regime survives and emerges even stronger for having defeated or assimilated the revolutionary challenge). It is Starr's view that revolutionary opposition is a form of mental illness: obsessionally Manichean in its world view, paranoid in its projections of evil onto the regime, narcissistic in its uncompromising aggression against any opposition, and psychotically delusional in light of the collapse of Communism and its theoretical credibility. New, healthy tactics are called for: "complicitous subversion" (undermining prevailing ideologies through academically respectable criticism) and "political dissidence" (engaging in transgressive but restrained political and cultural acts of confrontation).

Any interpretation of Derrida linking him to the anti-Marxist reaction that made Paris the heartland of neoliberal philocapitalism by the late 1970s is discredited by his explicit refusal to endorse it. Nevertheless, it must be admitted that Derrida's reflections on Marxism manifest a deep ambivalence, expressing both solidarity with a Marxist criticism of contemporary capitalism and fear of the oppressive potential of any revolutionary attempt to actualize an anticapitalist alternative. Marxism is commendable as a "specter" haunting capitalist society, but not as blueprint for a revolutionary alternative. Predictably both critics on the Left and the Right are dissatisfied: Lacanian Marxist Slavoj Zizek chides Derrida for a lack of political nerve, while self-styled "postmodern, bourgeois liberal" Richard Rorty likens him to a modern Pontius Pilate, publicly washing his hands of political responsibility in order to preserve his personal and philosophical purity.[19] Disregarding the ad hominem nature of these polemics, it is difficult to disagree with their conclusions—for whatever reasons, a neoliberal pessimistic interpretation of Derrida's politics leaves them fully as ambivalent as his philosophy.

Simon Critchley proposes a "political supplement" to deconstruction in the form of a defense of ethical utopianism.[20] For Critchley, Derrida's defense of difference is also a critique of the logocentric ideology that the truth has already arrived, that the future is all used up. Derrida's rejection of closure, Critchley argues, must be seen as extending into the future and toward the possibility that the things might be radically different and better than they are now. On the other side of the critique of "presence"—the notion that the entire truth of a state of affairs can be represented—is the possibility of transcendence to which Derrida stubbornly clings.

Derrida's analytic practice reduces logocentrism to a state of undecidability with regard to the single truth it is attempting to describe. Critchley attempts to negotiate the move from philosophical undecidability to political decision via Emmanuel Levinas's concepts of alterity and ethical responsibility. The basis of all ethics, for Levinas, is a sense of responsibility toward the Other, a spontaneous openness to his or her alterity. Ethics stems from the fact that the Other is irreducibly different from me and cannot be adequately conceptualized as an abstract, impersonal "sameness" defined by me. Critchley argues that ethical responsibility—direct, personal and open interaction with the Other—leads to political responsibility—the need to rethink the binary relation between the Other and myself in terms of all others and thus in terms of ternary relations between individuals and a general, communal law that nevertheless refuses to eliminate individual difference. Working from Lefort's idea that democracy is a political form with an absent center of power (no king, or Leader), Critchley argues for an open political community that refuses to constitute itself as a positive entity and constantly questions its own legitimacy. Like deconstruction, democratic politics must not be founded upon science, knowledge, or wisdom, but rather upon avoiding the "tyranny of truth" by actively maintaining its own lack of truth. Grounded on alterity, democracy can never be finished or perfected according to a pre-existing plan; democracy cannot exist as an essence, it can only exist as an infinite task.

Critchley believes that democracy is the political supplement of deconstruction. However, it seems to me that his ethical utopianism has merely translated an empty philosophical formalism into an equally empty political formalism. Critchley recalls Kierkegaard's insight that the moment of decision is always a leap into uncertainty, a terrifying experience of freedom and responsibility, but nowhere does he add to the existentialist experience of freedom a Sartrean concept of "facticity"—that I am free only in relation to this world, this personal history, these social relations. I suspect Critchley would be even less inclined to follow Sartre toward an acceptance of Marxism as the objective knowledge of our facticity, but without some such knowledge aren't we leaping blindly from one uncertainty into another?

As for Lefort's oft-cited notion that democracy has no center of power, it is profoundly misleading insofar as it implies that politics floats freely above or beyond any economic conditions of existence. The existence of capitalism—economic inequality, predatory individualism, and corporate domination that extends from the economic through the cultural to the political—is conveniently ignored so as more effectively to trumpet the danger of totalitarian "egocrats" striving to fill the void of democracy with the force of their personality. Admittedly Critchley's ever self-questioning democracy is the antithesis of an identification with the Leader (and the Truth of Our Group be it nation, race, religion or political ideology), but it also lacks the powerful psychological and economic satisfactions provided by the latter: feelings of cultural security and self-worth that accompany identification with Our Group and the material benefits that accrue to each of Us when we organize against everyone of Them. Ethical platitudes and formalist concepts without positive benefits grounded in material conditions of existence are scarcely able to compete with Christian extremism, middle-class resentment, and imperial police actions as satisfying responses to the vicissitudes of unfettered global capitalism. Critchley's otherwise commendable notion that things might be radically different and better is undercut by his "undecidability" with respect to knowledge of how and why things actually are and thus any knowledge of what must changed. A politics of ethical utopianism may be more attractive than a politics of neoliberal pessimism but it is no less deadlocked.

ALTHUSSER AND THE CRISIS OF STRUCTURALISM

Easily the most overlooked aspect of the local context shaping Althusser's theoretical development is the crisis of Structuralism initiated by Derrida. In 1967 Althusser responded to this crisis by making a dramatic, "poststructuralist" change to his own epistemological position. Initially Althusser had distinguished between Marx's science of social formations (historical materialism) and Marxist philosophy (dialectical materialism). Marxist philosophy was posited originally as a "science of science," or in Althusser's notorious phrase, a "Theory of theoretical practice." However, as we have seen, Derrida had undermined such logocentric hubris by insisting that Structuralists could not escape the conventionality of their own knowledge and the fact that their own discourse is no more scientific than any other. Althusser could hardly have been unaware of his friend Derrida's work and it almost certainly figured in the rejection of his own "theoreticism" or epistemological scientism.[21] Althusser responded to the intellectual crisis of Structuralism by abandoning the notion of Marxist philosophy as the arbiter of science and by redefining it as a battleground, the site of a continuous struggle between science and ideology whose ultimate stake is the category of science itself. Marxist philosophy is "class struggle in theory," the philosophical defense of the knowledges produced by historical materialism.

In order to defend historical materialism (and the category of science), however, Marxist philosophy could no longer claim to know the Truth about scientific truth. What it could claim may be summarized by the following positions:[22]

- *Knowledge as historical production.* Historical materialism can say something about the history, if not the truth, of a given science since the production of knowledge is a social practice with a means of production and a labor process. Althusser describes the production of knowledge in terms of three degrees of "generality" (levels or thresholds of theoretical development): (a) "Generalities I" consist of concepts, facts, and observations that are the raw materials of theoretical labor; (b) "Generalities II" refer to theoretical frameworks or "problematics" consisting of rules of method, evidence and proof that are applied to the raw materials of Generalities I; (c) "Generalities III" are the new knowledges (and new questions) produced. Generalities I are never truly "raw" materials since they are always already worked up to some degree; Generalities II and III can never be independently guaranteed.
- *Realist epistemology.* As a science of social formations, historical materialism is justified in producing a history of sciences as social practices, but neither historical materialism nor Marxist philosophy can legitimately pronounce judgment on the validity of the knowl-

edges a given science has produced. However, where Derrida refuses to mount a positive defense of the very categories of rationality and realism upon which he continues to rely, Althusser not only does so, but takes Derrida's criticism of logocentrism into account in the process.

Althusser admits the conventionalist distinction between referents and concepts: every science produces knowledge by means of conventions, the application of a theoretical problematic to a "theoretical object" defined by the science itself. However, a scientific problematic must also "submit to the test of its object" and demonstrate its explanatory power by producing knowledge of it. Althusser defends objective validity of such knowledge in the form of three "materialist theses": (a) concepts of things are not identical to real things; (b) real things exist prior to and independently of concepts of them; (c) the primacy of the second thesis over the first. In short, Althusser responds to Derrida's criticism of Structuralism—that Structuralism's own discourse is no less conventional than those it purports to explain—by englobing conventionalism within a more basic realism.

Unlike Derrida, Althusser begins not with a negative critique of discourse but from the positive fact that discourses (including so-called scientific discourses) actually exist. Conceding the conventionalist thesis that it is impossible to demonstrate the truth of any discourse directly (since we can only demonstrate its truth by means of the very language, concepts, theories we seek to verify), Althusser insists we can defend the truth of our knowledge indirectly. Since not even Derrida denies that so-called sciences exist or that they actually work, the salient question is this: "What must the world be like for a science to exist and to work?" Well, first of all, the world must actually exist, and secondly, it must be ordered and regular rather than disordered and random. Furthermore, for a science to work, its concepts about the world must correspond more or less to the world itself.

- *The distinction between science and ideology.* Where Derrida stubbornly refuses to collapse philosophy into literature, Lévi-Strauss blandly refuses to distinguish Structuralist anthropology from mythology. According to Lévi-Strauss, "Myths signify the mind that evolves them by making use of the world of which it is a part."[23] Thus, Lévi-Strauss' interpretations of myth can be read as mythical themselves: because it is part of nature, the mind repeats nature in myth and the Structuralist method repeats the operations of the myths it studies.[24] Both myth and science are grounded in material reality, yet there is no way to distinguish one from the other or decide between the explanations they provide. Lévi-Strauss posits a transcendental matrix or "combinatory" of mental elements and ways of structuring them from which all myths (and all theories about myths) emerge for empirically contingent (and causally uninteresting) reasons. As a result, boundaries between science and ideology, or between anthropology and myth, are impossible to maintain.

Althusser also begins from the fact that mind is brain and brain is matter. He also agrees that all human explanations, mythic and scientific, are ultimately grounded in material reality. However, unlike Lévi-Strauss, Althusser defends a conceptual difference between science and ideology based on Spinoza's distinction between more and less adequate ideas grounded in the same material reality. For Althusser, more adequate ideas are produced by degrees of formalization (Generalities I, II, III) that distance them from personal motivations and interests (although never entirely). Scientific discourses, in other words, are concerned with explaining how things work, while ideological discourses are concerned with the meanings of things for a subject in relation to his or her lived experience. This is not necessarily a true-false distinction: an ideology may be true, but its truth is incidental; a science may be wrong, but if so it very much matters. Science is about rational belief; ideology is about psychological enjoyment or material interest. Science is about wanting to know; ideology is about wanting not to know, what Sartre calls "self-deception."

- *What is at stake in philosophy?* Philosophy is not a science, much less a science of science; it is a *Kampfplatz* where reason defends knowledges (produced elsewhere by the sciences) against hostile ideological meanings and interests: at stake in this struggle is the survival of knowledge itself. Although the victory of knowledge over ideology is possible, it is never certain and can never be final. Because ideology is a category of subjective meanings, interests and desires (at bottom our sense of identity) there can be no "end of ideology" in a final triumph of reason. Even after a science breaks with ideological discourse (by means of a rigorous conceptual framework) it continues necessarily to "swim in ideology" where, in stormy weather, it may at any time drown.

ON THE STRUCTURED SUBJECT
OF POLITICAL PRACTICE

Like other Structuralists, Althusser finds social subjects and their consciousness to be of less explanatory power than the structures that produce them. Althusser calls the practices that transform human beings into social subjects with identities, meanings, roles and functions the "ideological instance," and their material organizational forms, "ideological apparatuses." The political implications of Althusser's theory of ideology may be summarized in the following themes and concepts.

- *Ideological interpellation and social practice.* For Althusser there is no practice without a subject, and no subject without ideology. Unlike classical Structuralists, Althusser conceptualizes the ideological instance as contradictory: first, ideology not only subjugates individuals, it also enables them to act within a social formation; second, like other instances, the field of ideology is neither undifferentiated nor perfectly coordinated. We are socialized or "interpellated" (hailed by authority) in a variety of groups (families, churches, schools, political parties, professional organizations, and work places) in a variety of ways that are not easily reconciled. Our identities are structurally overdetermined, as complex and contradictory as the social formation that produces us.

  Given the enormous power and interest at work to insure social conformity, the ideological field is relatively stable and conventional social behavior predominates, but occasionally a destabilizing conflict of identities cannot be suppressed or assimilated and the "natural" rightness of the status quo is shaken. Social practices may transform as well as reproduce their conditions of existence. Furthermore, as conscious beings we cannot avoid the "lived experience" of freedom, of choosing our course of action. We know from our textbook introductions to brain physiology that we are totally determined beings, but we cannot consciously experience our determination for the simple reason that we are that determined consciousness. The phenomenological fact that we experience ourselves as free, however, means we are "free" to choose knowledge over ideology (in Sartrean terms, rational belief over blind faith). This is why Althusser gives such importance to ideology and to philosophy as "class struggle in theory."

- *History as a process without a subject or goal.* Althusser rejects both the pessimistic "posthistorical" tendency of classical Structuralism and the teleological optimism of classical historicism and Marxism. From the proverbial "God's eye" view of the world the outcome of history may be known in advance, but from the aspectual perspective of any merely human knowledge such omniscience is impossible. For Althusser, history is a process without a subject or goal. Social subjects may "choose" to reproduce rather than transform society, but the opposite choice is also a possibility. Althusser can conceptualize the possibility of positive transformation—not an end of ideology, of course—but at least the possibility of a less oppressive society with a less dehumanizing dominant ideology. Yet explanation is not the same thing as motivation.

- *The Communist party as the revolutionary organization of the working class.* And thus we return to the decisive political fact of Althusser's commitment to revolutionary Communism. While he was able to overcome the weaknesses of Structuralist social theory while creatively applying and developing its strengths in the service of Marxist social theory and philosophy, Althusser had absolutely no success in his attempts to influence the political course of the PCF. Althusser was widely recognized as a left-wing critic of French Communism, sympathetic to Maoism, yet as a member of the PCF, deeply involved in the working-class movement. However modishly fashionable his reconstruction of Marxism appeared to non- or even anti-Communist French intellectuals, Althusser himself remained stubbornly convinced that a Communist movement was the only possibility for a successful anticapitalist revolution and that the PCF was the only possibility of organizing the French working class in support of such a revolution. The PCF was the ideological apparatus of the working class and the organization through which it struggled politically. Without such a class-based organization, Althusser believed, the working class would disintegrate into atomized individuals, easy targets for ideological and political manipulation by bourgeois parties and powerless victims of capitalist employers free to lower wages by playing workers off against each other. After more than three uninterrupted decades of successful capitalist attacks on labor (and with no end in sight), who is to say that Althusser was wrong? Right or wrong, the local context of Althusser's project cannot be adequately understood in isolation from the politics of the PCF.

THE FAILURE OF COMMUNISM (1): THE PCF AND KHRUSHCHEV'S "BUNGLED DESTALINIZATION"

That capitalism could not be overthrown without a Communist movement did not by any means guarantee that it would be overthrown merely by the presence of one. Indeed, as Perry Anderson reminds us, the history of "Western" Marxism is a history of defeat and failure.[25] Among the most basic causes of these defeats and failures was the ongoing subordination of the European Communist parties to the Soviet Union long after a Leninist dictatorship of the proletariat had become a Stalinist dictatorship over the proletariat. For French Communism the complex process of "destalinization" came too late and proceeded too slowly. The PCF waited far too long before establishing its independence from the Soviet Union. It never abolished its top-down bureaucratic organization and it utterly failed to live up to its self-proclaimed role as the revolutionary party of the working class.

The process began with Khrushchev's revelations about the nature of Stalin's rule at the 20th Party Congress of the CPSU in 1956. It is difficult to exaggerate their disruptive effect; for many party members everything seemed suddenly chaotic and confused. The PCF leadership responded ambiguously, accepting the new direction of Khrushchev's reforms (a "new road to communism" at home and "peaceful coexistance" abroad), while ignoring the questions of organizational reform and the Party's continued subservience to the Soviet Union. Althusser welcomed the end of Stalinist orthodoxy, but he could not endorse the PCF's sudden embrace of reformism and humanism ("everything for Man" as one Party slogan proclaimed). Althusser attacked Stalin for abandoning the revolutionary heritage of Marx and Lenin, but it seemed to him that Khrushchev's speech amounted to a right-wing criticism of Stalinism that portended a right-wing direction for the international Communist movement. "I would have written nothing," Althusser later claimed, "if it had not been for the 20th Congress . . . and the subsequent liberalization." Khrushchev's reforms were "a bungled destalinization" that traded "a poor man's Hegelianism" [economism] for "a rich man's evolutionism" [humanism], while replacing Marxist concepts with bourgeois ideology.[26] In France, revolutionary goals were being abandoned as the PCF pursued a futile effort to forge a popular front alliance with the reformist socialist party and the radical democrats—callously sacrificing the economic interests of the working class to the political interests of the Party's bureaucratic elite. To curry favor with its potential allies, the PCF was disgracefully slow and ambivalent in its support for the Algerian revolution (resulting in a fateful alienation of the Communists from the powerful pro-Algerian student movement).

This rightward drift was the local context of Althusser's opposition to the Marxist-humanist thesis "man makes history" being espoused not only by left-wing anti-Communist intellectuals but by the Communist parties of Third International as well! It is also the source of Althusser's attraction to Maoism during the 1960s: Maoism claimed, both at home and abroad, to reject top-down bureaucratic Communism in the name of an alliance with the oppressed masses and in support of revolutionary change from below. From the Sino-Soviet split in 1960 and the withering criticism of Soviet "revisionism" by the Chinese to the beginning of the Chinese Cultural Revolution of the late 1960s, China seemed to many militant intellectuals to have replaced Russia as the ideological leader of the global Communist movement. Althusser was among the most prominent of many who invested their hopes for equalitarian, revolutionary Communism in Maoism (and in Third World struggles for liberation). The fact that such hopes were based on almost complete ignorance of the grim side of the Cultural Revolution does not by itself discredit the ideal itself nor gainsay the basic accuracy of the Chinese assessment of the antirevolutionary, bureaucratic character of the Soviet Union—and by extension its European parties such as the PCF.

THE FAILURE OF COMMUNISM (2):
THE EVENTS OF MAY 1968

Although the events of May 1968 owed nothing either to Structuralism or the PCF, they had profound consequences for both. Structuralism was roundly condemned by student radicals who derisively proclaimed,

"Structures don't take to the streets!"[27] The uprising produced a political-ideological crisis for classical Structuralism comparable to the intellectual crisis inaugurated by Derrida a year earlier. Le Monde went so far as to ask, "Has Structuralism been Killed by May '68?"[28] For Lévi-Strauss the uprising was an unmitigated disaster, reinforcing his posthistorical conviction that history was a process of degeneration. At the opposite extreme, Foucault strongly supported the militant students: "they are not making the revolution, they are the revolution."[29] For Foucault personally, the Events of May signified a dramatic political shift from a post-Communist reformism to a confrontational, neoanarchist *gauchisme*. Althusser, despite his theoretical insistence on the predominance of social contradictions and the possibility of their "condensation" into precisely the kind of revolutionary rupture that May, 1968 seemed to be, was scorned by the *groupuscules* for his association with Structuralism and the "reactionary" PCF. To his critics the uprising seemed a decisive victory of the young Marx over the scientific Marx championed by Althusser. Althusser became a target for *gauchiste* ex-disciples whose graffiti declaimed, "Althusser does not serve the people" [*Althus ser[t] pas le peuple*] and "Althusser is useless" [*Althus ser[t] á rien*].[30]

Paradoxically, the national strikes and student protests resulted in an institutional victory for Structuralism as student protests against the centralized and elitist structure of higher education merged with the Structuralists' battle against the predominance of classical humanism in the Sorbonne. Structuralists received most of the new university chairs created by the post-May reform of the educational system. Such institutional victories, in addition to the crushing defeat of the uprising itself, managed to restore some of Structuralism's intellectual prestige. Politically and ideologically, however, classical Structuralism remained moribund. The antistructuralist radicalism of May lived on after the defeat, much of it in the form of an eclectic synthesis of Althusserian and Lacanian theory and Maoist politics represented by *Tel Quel*, the most prominent literary journal of the day.[31] Althusser and Lacan seemed to promise an explanation of the defeat while pandering to the radical chic of former leaders of the May movement who were now prominent among the French cultural elite.

From 1969 to 1974 Althusser was fashionable again. But not only did he continue to develop his own "poststructuralist" framework by means of "self-criticism" and new conceptualizations of ideology and philosophy, he engaged in an increasingly explicit commentary and criticism of Communist politics as well. Uninvolved personally in the May uprising (he had checked into a psychiatric clinic in April), Althusser's earliest comments were written some ten months after the events. In these remarks, he insists on the potentially revolutionary significance of the massive general strike by French workers for which the student rebellion was a spark.[32] While noting that many workers were initially unprepared for a revolutionary struggle and that the Party had lost touch with revolutionary students and young intellectuals, Althusser generally avoids outright criticism of the PCF's decidedly antirevolutionary actions. Years later, however, in his autobiography, Althusser ruthlessly excoriates the PCF's lack of revolutionary leadership.[33] The Party did not allow, much less direct a merger of the working class and the students, and thus utterly failed to take political advantage of a virtual collapse of government authority. The PCF "did everything it could . . . to prevent a coming together of the student battalions and the fervent masses of workers who were conducting the longest strike action ever in world history."[34] Althusser contends that a revolutionary situation existed in 1968: "In May and June 1968 a lot of workers in a lot of factories believed that revolution was possible, expected it and were simply waiting for the Party to give its orders in order to bring it about."[35] Citing Lenin, Althusser argues "when your opponent really believes the game is up, when things are finished at the top, and the masses are going on to the offensive in the streets, then not only is a revolution "in the cards" but a revolutionary situation actually exists."[36] The PCF leadership, however, "utterly failed to grasp what was happening" and thus "missed the chance to change the course of history in a revolutionary manner."[37]

Leaving aside the question of whether a revolutionary situation did or did not exist, it is impossible to deny the desire of the Communists (the CGT and the PCF) to control events and to channel the strike wave into a traditional economic confrontation, albeit on a massive scale.[38] Instead of pressing the offensive, the PCF forced the militant rank and file to accept a settlement (admittedly a generous one) to end the general strike. The Party had been pursuing a reformist "Left unity" strategy throughout the 1960s—with itself in the power position—and its top-down, bureaucratic structure was threatened by the militancy of not only the *gauchistes,* but of its own rank and file. The PCF operated "out of fear of the masses," Althusser writes, "and fear of losing control (reflecting its permanent obsession with the primacy of organization over popular movements."[39] Forced to choose between a revolutionary struggle it did not want involving alliances it could not control and the survival of a Gaullist regime desperately anxious to trade economic concessions for political peace, the PCF embraced De Gaulle's call for an electoral solution. During the ensuing campaign, the Right was able to fall back on cold war politics as usual—a vote for the Left being a vote for "totalitarian" Communism—even as the PCF sought to demonstrate its "Republican" credentials by disavowing revolution. De Gaulle relied not only on the petty bourgeoisie of the countryside to remain in power, but on the indirect complicity of the PCF as well.[40] Without denying the "unprecedented" economic gains obtained from the government by the PCF, Althusser insists they be weighed against even greater political losses, the debilitating effect of "a revolutionary defeat the like of which had not been seen since the Commune."[41]

THE FAILURE OF COMMUNISM (3): EUROCOMMUNISM AND THE "UNION OF THE LEFT"

Eurocommunism signaled a posthumous victory of the Second over the Third International. Emphasizing civil liberties, personal rights, plural political parties, parliamentary institutions, and rejecting any sudden or violent rupture with capitalism, it marked the official embrace of "the constitutional path" by the Communist parties of Western Europe and their formal separation from the control of the Soviet Union. By the early 1970s the PCF was openly committed to Eurocommunism.[42] It signed a "Common Program" program with the Socialist Party (PS) in 1972 and the resulting Union of the Left immediately began to achieve electoral success in 1973, taking advantage of the end of the postwar economic boom and the onset of stagflation, "austerity" measures, and rising unemployment. From the point of view of the PCFs, the goal of the Union was the same goal it had been pursuing for decades: build a national electoral majority within which the PCF would predominate over the PS, forcing the latter to move further to the Left and leaving the PCF in control of the state. In 1976 the PCF officially abandoned the concept of the "dictatorship of proletariat" and other Bolshevik theories of the state and the revolutionary path to socialism. The French road to Communism would begin with a struggle against "state monopoly capitalism" (STAMOCAP) necessary to achieve popular democracy—only then could the parliamentary struggle for Communism begin.

The PCF attempted to transform itself from a class-based, cadre party into a mass-based electoral party aiming to appeal to the so-called "new class" of white collar, technical workers. Unfortunately, it made no corresponding effort to reform its authoritarian bureaucratic organization or to encourage popular participation in decision making within the party. The Communist trade unions of the *Confédération Générale du Travail* (CGT) shifted from an emphasis on union activity focused on economic issues to an emphasis on a political-electoral solution to the worsening economic situation of the working class. However the CGT's shift to a political strategy caused it to lose influence among the rank and file to its major rival on the Left, the independent CFDT (*Confederation Française Démocratique du Travail*). The CFDT capitalized on increasing militancy at the local level and pursued a more radical course—confrontation at the local level focused on concrete, specific, economic issues and the broader goal of worker control or *autogestion* in the work place. The CFDT refused to support the Union of Left, claiming it was too reformist, even as the CGT stubbornly clung to its "all or nothing" national-electoral strategy and defense of the Union. Not only did the CGT alienate some of its own members, it built high expectations in anticipation of electoral victory (and thus the risk of great anger and demoralization in the event of failure). Electoral defeat would also mean more austerity measures from the government with workers being in an even weaker position to resist.

The municipal elections of 1977 produced a clear majority for the Union and great expectations of another victory in the upcoming general elections in 1978. However, electoral success led to a confrontation between the PCF and the PS over the exact meaning of Common Program. The central issue was the extent of proposed nationalizations of insurance companies and the biggest industrial groups, but other issues of income redistribution and defense spending were also divisive. In September of 1977 talks collapsed, with each side blaming the other, but with the public blaming the PCF. Ultimately the cause of the split was the failure of the PCF's Eurocommunist strategy. The electoral success of the Union since 1972 had overwhelmingly benefited the PS, which as a result, had refused to succumb to PCF pressure to move to the Left. In fact, Mitterand had been working assiduously to further weaken PCF power within the Union while expanding the autonomy of the PS. What was really at stake in 1977, then, was the balance of forces within the Union of the Left and what the Union actually stood for. The PCF found itself in a lose/lose situation: if it remained in the Union and the latter emerged victorious, it would be subordinated to the PS and compelled to move to the Right and support programs it disagreed with; if it left the Union the PCF would surely be blamed for sabotaging an almost certain electoral victory of the Left. In 1968 moderation had put the PCF in a similar lose-lose position that it now faced as a result of its radicalism. Again the Party chose the defeat of the Left over the loss of its predominance within the Left.

THE FAILURE OF COMMUNISM AND THE TRIUMPH OF POSTMODERN NEOLIBERALISM

Althusser's dilemma was whether to stay with the PCF, despite his objections to its leadership, or to leave the party and lose his connection to working-class politics. He chose to remain, but as an internal critic always hoping to push the party in a more revolutionary, equalitarian direction. The compromise became ever more difficult. From Althusser's perspective the PCF had failed completely as a revolutionary party in 1968. During the shift to Eurocommunism, Althusser publicly criticized the PCF's "obsession" with a Common Program. Abandoning the phrase "dictatorship of the proletariat" might facilitate an alliance with the PS, he argued, but it blithely ignored the fact that "socialism" was not the ultimate goal but simply a transitional period of struggle leading either to a regression back toward capitalism or a progression toward Communism.[43] The PCF seemed to have forgotten that the class character of the existing state, the "dictatorship of the bourgeoisie," had to be eliminated and new "organizations of the masses" created. Althusser also criticized the ongoing lack of participatory democracy within the PCF itself: three levels of indirect elections to the Party's National Congress effectively excluded debate at the top while the top-down flow of decisions severely restrictive spontaneity and creativity from rank and file party members. Nevertheless, perhaps self-servingly, Althusser continued to believe that the PCF was the organization of the working class and that only Party members could obtain "real knowledge" of political practice—knowledge of what was possible, what was being done, and what it was necessary to change within the party itself.

Even more dramatically the entire ideological culture of France changed between 1975 and 1980. "Ultra-leftism" evaporated almost overnight. The Union of the Left provoked a rabid campaign against the dangers of Communism that launched the careers of the so-called "New Philosophers," a coterie of ex-Maoist, neoliberal agitators and media celebrities.[44] However, a much larger number of the radical intellectuals of the generation of Marx and Coca Cola gravitated from *gauchisme* toward the "modern" reformism of the PS (soon to betray the aspirations of its supporters for an end to hierarchical domination in the work place and the state upon assuming power in 1981). The PCF had become, in effect, a specter of its own revolutionary, anticapitalist past, a past long dead and buried. By dropping economic struggle at the local level, by diluting its revolutionary anticapitalist ideology, and by staking its future on an electoral alliance with the anti-Communist Left, the PCF helped to discredit any Marxist analysis or response to the concrete political situation. On the other hand, despite its own thoroughgoing reformism and disavowal of the Soviet Union, the PCF continued to perform the function of totalitarian bogeyman for opponents and "allies" alike. The PCF's final break with the Soviet Union took too long and was pursued too ambiguously to have any beneficial effect. From Khrushchev's revelations concerning Stalin's rule and the Soviet invasion of Hungary in 1956, through the invasion of Czechoslovakia in 1968, to the belated awareness of the dark side of the Cultural Revolution and the atrocities of Cambodia in the 1970s the ideal of Bolshevik-type revolutions had suffered irretrievable damage. The sensational success of Solzhenitsyn's books (published in France in 1974) both reflected and further contributed to the PCF's declining prestige.

Too often ignored, however, is the fact that throughout these years the Soviet influence on the PCF was counterrevolutionary, determined by a Russian foreign policy of "peaceful coexistence" with the West. To this legacy the PCF remained faithful even after its break with the Soviet Union. The Party had failed to act as an independent revolutionary party in 1968 and its embrace of anti-Soviet Eurocommunism seemed like a belated capitulation to the reformist ideology already staked out by the PS. Once global capitalism was accepted by both parties of the Left (albeit not yet at the symbolic level), all that remained for the Left and Right to fight over politically were "cultural values." When political leaders and intellectuals of the Left avoid the issue of class power, inequality, and conflict in order to focus exclusively on "humanist" issues (however worthy), they give implicit support to the predations of capital at home and abroad and virtually concede the votes of the economically exploited and discontented to the Right (using "wedge" issues such as patriotism, ethnocentrism, or religious revivalism to channel popular discontents away from the ruling class and capitalism). Simply put, the political Left suffers the kind of dramatic ideological reversal that by the 1980s had become global.[45]

Like religions, political ideologies trade in beliefs and hopes. While religions sell salvation (or more accurately the promise of salvation) by claiming a monopoly on the means to attain it, political ideologies sell a better life in this world with similar promises. The psychology of such belief is fragile. The more people who believe, the more credible the cause appears to be and the more converts it will attract. However, once belief is discredited (for whatever reason) exactly the opposite effect kicks in and an ideology can disappear as fast as a bull market. Justifiably or not the Soviet Union was widely believed by supporters and enemies alike to be the arrival of the political Promised Land. Many who believed in such a Promised Land were prone to identify with the Soviet Union and this identification gradually permeated the entirety of their political consciousness. When the Soviet Union was discredited the effect was devastating. Added to the socioeconomic anxiety and resentment attending the globalization of a now untrammeled capitalism, the collapse of socialism—the hope for an alternative to capitalism based on social justice and equality—has produced a profound ideological anomie. In the absence of any rational alternative to a postmodern, neoliberal "end of history," it is hardly surprising that so many have fallen prey to vicious, authoritarian, cynically manipulative yet emotionally resonant caricatures of older forms of social solidarity such as religion, family, and fatherland.[46] Behind them all, absurd and obscene, is the relentless pressure of what Horkheimer and Adorno call the "dialectic of enlightenment"[47]—the fanatical faith that with only a bit more authoritarian discipline, a bit more capitalist dehumanization and exploitation, a bit more "rational" domination of nature and a bit more encouragement of the predatory and paranoid aspects of human nature, the world will find happiness.

NOTES

1. Subject to fits of profound depression, Althusser was diagnosed as manic-depressive and he was in and out of psychiatric institutions with increasing frequency from 1946 onward. Suffering the full range of psychiatric treatments from drugs to shock therapy, Althusser lost his battle with mental illness in November of 1980 when he strangled his wife Hélène in their apartment at ENS. In the opinion of his closest friends, this act was the culmination of a steadily worsening crisis provoked by the political events of the late 1970s. With brutal candor Althusser shares the self-understanding he

achieved after years of analysis and reflection following the death of his wife in *Louis Althusser, The Future Lasts Forever: A Memoir* (New York: New Press, 1994).

2. The best history of Structuralism, to which I am much indebted, is François Dosse, *History of Structuralism*, 2 vols. (Minneapolis: University of Minnesota Press, 1997). Other useful accounts focusing on political as well as theoretical issues are Perry Anderson, *In the Tracks of Historical Materialism* (Chicago: University of Chicago Press, 1984); J. G. Merquior, *From Prague to Paris* (London: Verso, 1986).

3. I draw extensively on my own *Althusser and the Renewal of Marxist Social Theory* (Berkeley: University of California Press, 1992). See also Gregory Elliott, *Althusser: The Detour of Theory* (London: Verso, 1987).

4. Cited in Merquior, *From Prague to Paris*, 208.

5. Anderson, *In the Tracks of Historical Materialism*, 6.

6. Dosse goes so far as to posit Structuralism's success as the outcome of the crisis of Marxism in the 1950s. Dosse, *History of Structuralism*, Vol. 1, 162.

7. Ibid., Chapter 22.

8. Ibid., 207.

9. Ibid., 333.

10. Ibid., 352ff.

11. Quoted in Anderson, *In the Tracks of Historical Materialism*, 51, fn 32.

12. For much more detailed discussion see Resch, *Althusser and the Renewal of Marxist Social Theory*.

13. Once we accept the fact that subjective experience and objective knowledge can never coincide we can dispense with the pointless debate over their relative importance. This in turn allows us to recognize a complementary relationship between the approaches of phenomenology (being the subject) and Structural Marxism (explaining the subject). For a pioneering effort to see such a relationship between Sartre and Althusser see Mark Poster, *Existential Marxism in Postwar France: From Sartre to Althusser* (Princeton, NJ: Princeton University Press, 1975).

14. Dosse, *History of Structuralism*, Vol. 2, 17–31.

15. Michael Ryan, *Marxism and Deconstruction* (Baltimore: Johns Hopkins University Press, 1982); Christopher Norris, *Derrida* (Cambridge: Harvard University Press, 1987). My argument here is heavily indebted to Norris' excellent discussion.

16. Quoted in Dosse, *History of Structuralism*, Vol. 2, 24.

17. For an attempt to defend the silliness anyway see Geoffrey Bennington, *Legislations: The Politics of Deconstruction* (London: Verso, 1994).

18. Peter Starr, *Logics of Failed Revolt: French Theory after May '68* (Stanford, CA: Stanford University Press, 1995). Starr's exemplary figure is Lacan rather than Derrida, but the argument fits the latter as well as the former.

19. For a discussion of Zizek's critique, see Robert Paul Resch, "The Sound of Sci(l)ence: Zizek's Concept of Ideology-Critique." *Journal for the Psychoanalysis of Culture and Society* 6, no. 1 (Spring, 2001), 17–18; Norris discusses Rorty's critique in Derrida, 150–160.

20. Simon Critchley, *The Ethics of Deconstruction* (Oxford: Blackwell, 1992).

21. Although Derrida claims he and Althusser rarely discussed philosophical problems at length, they demonstrated a remarkable sensitivity toward and general knowledge of their respective positions. See "Politics and Friendship: An Interview with Jacques Derrida," in E. Ann Kaplan and Michael Sprinker, eds., *The Althusserian Legacy* (London: Verso, 1993), 183–231.

22. It should be noted that Althusser's response to the poststructuralist challenge differs fundamentally from that of the so-called "Post-Althusserian school" that emerged in Great Britain around Barry Hindess, Paul Hirst, Ernesto

Laclau and others and that continues to inflect the work of Slavoj Zizek and his followers. This body of work emphasizes the absolute autonomy of ideology, and the unity of extreme voluntarism in politics with extreme relativism in theory. See Resch, *Althusser and the Renewal of Marxiest Social Theory*, 99–105.

23. Cited in Anderson, *In the Tracks of Historical Materialism*, 52.
24. Ibid.
25. Ibid., 15–30.
26. Althusser quoted in Gregory Elliott, "Althusser's Solitude," in Kaplan and Sprinker, eds., *Althusserian Legacy* (London: Verso, 1993), 21–2.
27. On the effects of May, 1968 on Structuralism, see Dosse, *History of Structuralism*, Vol. 2, 116.
28. Ibid., 116.
29. Ibid., 120.
30. Ibid., 119.
31. Danielle Marx-Scouras persuasively argues that Tel Quel consistently defended a radical and elitist aestheticism and that its dramatic political shifts inevitably followed from calculations of benefits to the literary avant-garde. See *The Cultural Politics of Tel Quel* (University Park: Pennsylvania State University Press, 1996). For many French intellectuals Maoism was a way station on the journey from anti-stalinism to philocapitalism—a cynical professional path initially marked out by the ex-Trotskyist "New York Intellectuals" in the 1950s.
32. Althusser's comments were included in a letter to his friend Maria Macciocchi dated August 21, 1968; see Maria Antonietta Macciocchi, *Letters from Inside the Italian Communist Party to Louis Althusser* (London: New Left Books, 1973), 301–320.
33. Louis Althusser, *The Future Lasts Forever: A Memoir*.
34. Ibid., 230.
35. Ibid., 230.
36. Ibid., 230–231.
37. It is too often forgotten in the aftermath of the triumph of reaction that the events of May, 1968, in France were part of an intense and truly international eruption of revolutionary discontents directed against capitalist domination, alienation and imperialism—but also against the oppressive bureaucratic domination of the Soviet Union over the world Communist movement. Is it really idiotic to speculate that the failure of the former is deeply connected to the existence of the latter? On the international connections of the uprisings, see George Katsiaficas, *The Imagination of the New Left: A Global Analysis of 1968* (Boston: South End Press, 1987).
38. My remarks on May 1968 are based on Daniel Singer, *Prelude to Revolution: France in May 1968* (New York: Hill and Wang, 1970) and on George Ross, *Workers and Communists in France* (Berkeley: University of California Press, 1982).
39. Althusser, *The Future Lasts Forever: A Memoir*, 230.
40. Singer points out that the costs of a decade of Gaullist economic modernization had been borne by the industrial working class, while the agricultural sector continued to benefit from protectionism. The lack of economic discontent, coupled with susceptibility to the "Great Fear" fomented by the Right, was sufficient to ensure electoral victory for the regime. See Singer, *Prelude to Revolution*, 223–231.
41. Althusser, *The Future Lasts Forever: A Memoir*, 231.
42. In this section I rely heavily on Ross, *Workers and Communists in France*.

43. See Louis Althusser, "The Historic Significance of the 22nd Congress," in Etienne Balibar, *On the Dictatorship of the Proletariat* (London: New Left Books, 1977).

44. On the New Philosophers see Dominique Lecourt's withering *Mediocracy: French Philosophy since the Mid-1970s* (London: Verso, 2001). Included in the English edition is Lecourt's "Dissidence or Revolution" which deals with earlier developments.

45. Little did anyone realize that the collapse of Communism with an inhuman face would entail the collapse of capitalism with a human face as well. Ironically the fate of Mitterrand's regime bears out the truth of Althusser's gloomy prognostications even more than the rise of Reagan and Thatcher. For an excellent analysis see Daniel Singer's *Is Socialism Doomed? The Meaning of Mitterrand* (New York: Oxford University Press, 1988).

46. Bertholt Brecht always insisted that realism was on the side of the Left, a lesson postmodernists have forgotten—and as a result turned themselves into defenseless punching bags for the New Right. Putting postmodernism to work, the New Right has fashioned a powerful ideological synthesis extending from the Bible to free-market capitalism by way of the rigidly gendered family. For a chilling assessment of the damage, see Thomas Frank, *One Market under God: Extreme Capitalism, Market Populism, and the End of Economic Democracy* (New York: Anchor Books, 2000); Linda Kintz, *Between Jesus and the Market: The Emotions that Matter in Right-Wing America* (Durham, NC: Duke University Press, 1997).

47. If ever two books were overdue for an appreciative re-evaluation, they are the classic works of the Frankfurt School: Max Horkheimer and Theodor W. Adorno, *Dialectic of Enlightenment* (New York: Seabury Press, 1972); T. W. Adorno et al., *The Authoritarian Personality* (New York: Harper, 1950). Together these works demonstrate—my apologies to Horkheimer—that those who don't want to talk about capitalism should be silent about fascism (as well as communism, the New Right, postmodernism, gender, race, and alas, terrorism).

5 Hammer without a Master
French Phenomenology and the Origins of Deconstruction
(Or, How Derrida Read Heidegger)

Peter Eli Gordon

My democracy is not of this world.—René Char

How did the young Derrida's readings in phenomenology lead to the method known as deconstruction? What lessons did Derrida derive from his earliest studies of Husserl, and what were the local codes, both philosophical and political, that conditioned this reception? Was Derrida an "apologist" for Heidegger or his antagonist? Or, if we assume the answer must be more complex, how did Derrida's critical appropriation of Heidegger's philosophy move beyond such an opposition? My goal in what follows is to sketch a rudimentary background for answering these questions. Most specifically, I want to characterize the critical stance, beyond both Marxism and humanism that allowed Derrida's work to play a pivotal role in the French reception of phenomenology.[1]

To anticipate, my argument is that *deconstruction precedes postmodernism*. Notwithstanding the importance ascribed to Derrida's deconstructive method under the auspices of literary criticism, the method itself needs to be understood historically as originating out of a distinctively philosophical controversy surrounding the French reception of Husserlian and Heideggerian phenomenology in the period from *circa* 1945 to the early 1960s. But this controversy precedes a self-consciously "postmodern" or "poststructuralist" movement in philosophy, literary studies, or social thought. And notwithstanding claims by Luc Ferry and Alain Renault in their book, *La Pensée 68*, the core philosophical themes of Derridean deconstruction clearly antedate the events and values associated with May, 1968. Rather, they first emerged as a revisionist response to the post-war debate over the meaning of phenomenology, a debate to which Derrida wished to provide an anti-authoritarian solution.[2] If Derrida's distinctive role in these debates has been largely obscured in the English-speaking world, this is chiefly due to the fact that phenomenology has suffered an effective if not absolute exclusion from academic philosophy in both the United States and the United Kingdom (though less so in Canada, which retains stronger ties to the European, specifically French, philosophical curriculum).

The narrowness of the Anglo-American philosophical establishment may therefore help to explain why Derrida did not make his initial debut outside France as a philosopher.[3]

Most importantly, I would like to suggest that Derrida's stance in relation to Heidegger's philosophy was from the beginning *critical* and *non-apologetic*. Scholars have frequently wished to discredit deconstruction as a quietistic or aestheticist theory that must be dispensed with in the name of political responsibility. But this betrays a serious misunderstanding of Derrida's purposes. Deconstruction was born in the 1950s and early 1960s as an internal but expressly anti-authoritarian critique of Husserlian and Heideggerian themes that had themselves become authoritative in French philosophy. The chief aim of this critique was to mobilize those very methods in a creative and open-ended fashion by taking up Heidegger's "destruction of metaphysics" against phenomenology itself. Eventually, by the late 1960s, this turn of phenomenology against its own foundations drew a further stimulus from Nietzsche, whose *Twilight of the Idols* taught "how one philosophizes with a hammer."[4] But Derrida's philosophical practice was from the start animated by an emancipatory ideal—he later called it "*democratie à venir*" or "democracy-to-come"—which guided his dissent both from the French reverence for Heidegger as a "master-thinker" (*maître-penseur*) and from the doctrinaire Marxism of the French Communist Party.[5] Indeed, it is one of the more unhappy ironies in the reception of deconstruction that even today its self-professed "democratic" critics will often repeat charges that orthodox (and highly undemocratic) Communists in the 1940s and 50s first directed against the phenomenological movement as a whole and in the early 1970s revived in their effort to discredit Derrida himself.

A "hammer without a master": the phrase—*Le Marteau sans Maître*—is the title for a 1934 anthology of poems by René Char, whose "revolutionary convictions" won him early praise from the French Surrealists. An activist in the French Resistance, Char later forged an association with Heidegger.[6] (The same title was also given to a 1954 musical composition by Pierre Boulez.)[7] I have borrowed the phrase here to describe Derrida's position within French post-war debates over phenomenology, and to recollect the themes of mastery and unmastering that first opened the way to deconstruction. Jerrold Seigel has astutely observed that deconstruction drew political stimulus from the French Surrealists and their mood of "anti-authoritarian cultural revolt."[8] But deconstruction was in origin neither an attitude nor an aesthetic; nor can it be easily ranged among the various artistic and literary assaults on high modernism that Hal Foster termed the "anti-aesthetic."[9] As I shall explain below, *deconstruction was born from a context of local disputes within phenomenology well before it came into alignment with postmodernism.*

PHENOMENOLOGY IN DISPUTE, 1945–1960

In 1946, Jan Potočka, the Czech philosopher who had studied in 1933 at Freiburg with both Husserl and Heidegger, wrote from Prague to his old university friend Eugen Fink (Husserl's former student): "Phenomenology these days, as you might well imagine, is anything but popular here, and a phenomenologist finds himself in none too comfortable a position (especially as [a follower of] a German philosophical movement, and especially because of Heidegger)." But, Potocka hastened to add, "interest for phenomenology has grown quite high, as it seems to be the case in France...."[10] Potocka's conflicted sentiments are typical of the early post-war attitude toward the phenomenological movement. Edmund Husserl, the teacher of orthodox or "transcendental" phenomenology, had died in his Prague exile in the spring of 1939 even before the outbreak of war, though students continued to revere him as the founder of their movement. Yet a growing share among them turned to the revisionist or "existential" phenomenology fashioned in the twenties by the master's most famous apprentice, Martin Heidegger. Emmanuel Lévinas, who had studied with Husserl and Heidegger in Freiburg in 1928–29, later wrote that "I had gone to see Husserl...[l]ike a youth approaching a great master [*grand maître*]." But "[t]he main thing I discovered was the manner by which Husserl's path had been prolonged and transfigured by Heidegger." Such admiration remained strong well after the events of the war: "I will indeed never forget," wrote Lévinas, "Heidegger's relation to Hitler." "But the works of Heidegger, the manner in which he practiced phenomenology in *Being and Time*—I knew early on that this is one of the greatest philosophers in history."[11] Such comments testify to the German philosopher's continued prestige in the eyes of even his most vehement critics.

Phenomenology, as Paul Ricoeur has observed, was "both the sum of Husserl's work and the heresies issuing from it."[12] This may be especially true for France, where Husserl and Heidegger came into vogue nearly simultaneously.[13] Husserl came on the French scene, in Herbert Spiegelberg's words, "less as a central figure of the phenomenological movement than as its outdated founder."[14] Heidegger alone was the true beneficiary of this belated reception. Lévinas' 1930 monograph, *The Theory of Intuition in the Phenomenology of Husserl* (one of the earliest French studies of Husserl), announces his shift of allegiance toward Heidegger as both improvement and rebellion: "The intense philosophical life which runs through Heidegger's philosophy [wrote Lévinas]...permits us to sharpen the outline of Husserl's philosophy by accentuating certain aporias,...making certain views more precise, or opposing others."[15]

The tension between Husserlian transcendentalism and Heideggerian existentialism was to remain a defining feature of French phenomenology

for many decades to come. It furnishes the theme for the classic opening to
Merleau-Ponty's *Phenomenology of Perception* (1945):

> What is phenomenology? It may seem strange that this question has
> still to be asked a half century after the first works of Husserl. The fact
> remains that it has by no means been answered. Phenomenology is the
> study of essences...But [it] is also a philosophy which puts essences
> back into existence. ...It is a transcendental philosophy ...but it is also
> [one] for which the world is 'already there' before reflection begins...It
> is...a 'rigorous science,' but it also offers an account of space, time, and
> the world as we 'live' them. One may try to do away with these con-
> tradictions by making a distinction between Husserl's and Heidegger's
> phenomenologies; yet the whole of *Sein und Zeit* springs from an indi-
> cation given by Husserl and...which [he] towards the end of his life,
> identified as the central theme of phenomenology...with the result that
> the contradiction reappears in Husserl's own philosophy.[16]

While Merleau-Ponty wished to reconcile these divergent tendencies, this
was chiefly done by appealing to Husserl's later, unpublished writings—
a strategy, however, which courted charges that Merleau-Ponty had not
grasped the true significance of Heidegger's anti-subjectivistic critique of
the founder's doctrine. Whereas Heidegger claimed that "the world" (in
the phenomenological sense) has a grounding deeper than reason, Merleau-
Ponty continued to insist with Husserl that the world is not only "the cradle
of meanings" but is also "the native abode of all rationality."[17] In a 1946
rejoinder to Merleau-Ponty's public address, "The Primacy of Perception,"
the Heidegger-scholar Jean Beaufret pointedly asked "whether phenomenology, fully developed, does not require the abandonment of subjectivity and the vocabulary of subjective idealism, as, beginning with Husserl,
Heidegger has done."[18]

At stake was a basic quarrel, originating with Heidegger and Husserl
themselves, as to how much authority to grant consciousness over the constitution of experience. Merleau-Ponty cited with admiration a line from
Husserl's unpublished writings that "phenomenology...rests on itself, or
rather, provides its own foundations."[19] Though Merleau-Ponty would
remain mostly aloof from the controversy, the view that phenomenology
was "self-foundational" furnished a key to the debates that followed: The
question was not merely whether the phenomenological ego enjoys mastery over its own intentional sphere. This seemed to capture far broader
concerns about the status of philosophy as such: Is philosophy capable of
achieving a transcendental priority over history and culture? What does
confidence in such a priority say about the confidence of modernity itself? Is
philosophy—especially Husserlian, "rational" phenomenology"—correct
in its assumption of self-foundational control? Or is such mastery merely
a "bourgeois" fiction and hence vulnerable to the same criticism Marxism

leveled against bourgeois ideology? These were to be defining questions of the1940s and 1950s, not only for the early disputes that engulfed French existentialism, but also for Derrida's first, critical interventions in the debate over Husserl's legacy. To understand the significance of Derrida's role therefore requires a brief detour.

EXISTENTIALISM, MARXISM, HUMANISM

Jean Wahl's 1947 book, *A Little History of Existentialism*, begins: "This question of existentialism, it occupies New York...like Paris. Sartre wrote an article in *Vogue*; *Mademoiselle*, the magazine of seventeen-year old girls, a friend tells me, has devoted an article to existentialist literature; meanwhile, Marvin Farber has written...that Heidegger constitutes an international danger. Existentialism has become, not only a European problem, but a world problem."[20] In the immediate post-war years, while reports concerning Heidegger's wartime support for Nazism were still coming to light, Heidegger's philosophy itself came to enjoy a kind of second-life in France and abroad. Sartre's own journal *Les Temps Modernes* played a prominent role in the "Heidegger Affair" with a series of essays, both critical and defensive, assessing Heidegger's political record as well as his philosophical legacy.[21] Wahl's contributions to the Heidegger-reception are especially instructive since his career spans the decades from existentialism to deconstruction. A close associate of Lévinas and an important contributor, alongside Kojéve and Hippolyte, to the rediscovery of Hegelianism in France, Wahl had studied with Heidegger at Freiburg in 1928–29. Although as a Jew he was forced from his professorship by the Vichy government and suffered abuse by the Gestapo, Wahl remained a strong exponent of Heidegger's work. Exiled during the war to the United States, he returned to Paris after Liberation and in 1946 taught a course, "Introduction to the Thought of Heidegger," at the Sorbonne.

The lectures bespeak Wahl's conviction that Heidegger's revision marked an indispensable advance beyond Husserlian phenomenology. Although Wahl's own reading of Heidegger remained largely humanistic—he was influenced by both American pragmatism and Sartrean existentialism—the lectures also signal his dissent from the so-called "humanist" reception. Acknowledging the political disputes surrounding Heidegger's work, Wahl took care to distinguish it from what he called an "irrationalist philosophy." Its key theme, Wahl explained, was *Geworfenheit* (thrownness), i.e., the principle that "one is thrown in" ("*être jeté dans*") the world without the possibility of mastery over one's experience. Wahl complained that Heidegger's French translators risked a serious distortion when they attempted to graft the German philosopher's categories onto humanistic or Cartesian foundations. Alphonse de Waehlens's translation of *Geworfenheit* as "*déréliction*," for example, implied that the human subject is "abandoned by" some external support. But this privation only made sense if one first granted the split between human subjectivity and the external world that Heidegger wished to reject. Wahl deplored this error and further noted that it built upon Henri Corbin's influential yet "inexact" translation of key Heideggerian terms into French. The mistranslation was deceptive. As Wahl explained, "*être jeté*" meant simply that "man does not possess himself." To grasp one's thrownness in the Heideggerian sense was therefore to acknowledge such dispossession as a constitutive feature of life: "Human reality [*la réalité humaine*]," Wahl concluded, "is not master of its origins [*maîtresse de ses origines*]."[22]

The conflict between thrownness and mastery, though a mere parenthesis in Wahl's lectures, was soon to furnish the centerpiece for the so-called "humanism debate" between Heidegger and Sartre. Sartre had first learned of Husserl and Heidegger as early as 1932: it was apparently Raymond Aron who first roused Sartre's hope that even an apricot cocktail could be the object of rigorous description. But Sartre first learned about the details of the phenomenological method by reading Lévinas' monograph on Husserl, after which he pursued a year-long study of phenomenology in Berlin. Yet Sartre's own relation to Husserl was not without complications. Much like Lévinas, Sartre's conception of phenomenology already bore signs of Heidegger's revision: Jean-Marc Mouillie has termed it "*un apprentissage contestataire.*"[23] In his *Carnets*, Sartre wrote that he would criticize Husserl, "just as much as a disciple can in writing against his master [*tout autant qu'un disciple peut écrire contre son maître*]." Sartre's 1943 masterpiece, *Being and Nothingness*, subtitled, "An essay in phenomenological ontology," was crafted "entirely with phenomenological and existential techniques."[24] But the instability of this project was soon apparent, and Sartre concluded that his own work resembled "neither the Husserlian philosophy, nor that of Heidegger."[25]

If the basic character of existentialism in *Being and Nothingness* was voluntarist, this did not prevent those on the French left—especially orthodox Marxists—from branding Sartre a philosopher of despair. As Mark Poster has shown, French Communist intellectuals such as Henri Lefebvre, Henri Mougin, and Jean Kanapa subjected Sartre to unsparing criticism.[26] This hostility was doubtless fortified by existentialism's perceived affinities with Kierkegaard, Dostoyevsky, and contemporary religious thinkers such as the French-Catholic Gabriel Marcel. More ominous, however, was the presence of Heidegger himself, who most CP members were ready to dismiss as a fascist ideologue. The Communist theoretician Roger Garaudy, in an essay "A False Prophet: Jean-Paul Sartre" for the Communist journal *Les Lettres françaises*, went so far as to brand Sartre's existentialism an "illness."[27] He further faulted its indifference to historical conditions: "*Uprooted from history, freedom is nothing but an ineffective ersatz.*"[28] Sartre's philosophy, Garaudy concluded, could sustain only a "formless freedom."[29] Meanwhile, Lefebvre let fly a full arsenal of abuse: Sartre's existentialism was "bourgeois." It bespoke an "irrationalism" like that of the French surrealists and promoted merely "a metaphysics of shit."[30]

Wounded by these attacks, Sartre launched a defensive campaign; between 1944 and 1948 he published no less than three essays on the relation between existentialism and politics. The earliest response, published in the Communist paper, *Action*, drew a critical distinction between Heidegger's egregious behavior during the Third Reich as against the enduring merits of his work: "Heidegger was a philosopher well before he was a Nazi," Sartre wrote. "His adherence to Hitlerism, caused by fear, perhaps opportunism, and surely conformism, is not pretty....But is this sufficient to confirm the reasoning that 'since Heidegger is a member of the [Nazis] then his philosophy must be a Nazi philosophy?' This is not the case."[31] To be sure, the distinction between Heidegger's politics and his philosophy was strongly contested. For many readers, Communist and non-Communist alike, Heidegger's Nazism appeared as the "immediate implication" of his thought.[32] Sartre's attempt to draw a line between them staked out a moderate position in a debate that was to remain sharply polarized between a Heideggerian "orthodoxy" and its Marxist critics throughout the next half-century.

Sartre's most celebrated rejoinder to his Communist critics, "Existentialism is a Humanism," was first presented in late October, 1945.[33] "I would like to defend existentialism," Sartre began, "against a certain number of reproaches." It has been called a doctrine of "quietism and despair," or, a "bourgeois philosophy" that promotes merely "luxurious contemplation," and that conceives of "action in this world" as "totally impossible."[34] But Sartre insisted such charges were mistaken: "There is no doctrine more optimistic," he claimed. For existentialism holds that "the fate of man lies always with himself."[35] Its foundations are therefore strictly atheistic. Beginning always with "the subjectivity of the individual," it burdens man alone with absolute responsibility for his choices. Existentialism is accordingly a humanism, since "we recall to man that there is no other legislator besides man himself."[36]

The response from Heidegger was swift. Prompted by a written invitation from Jean Beaufret (then teaching philosophy in Paris), Heidegger drafted the "Letter on Humanism," which he sent to Beaufret in the autumn of 1946 for publication the following year.[37] Beaufret's letter had posed the question: "*Comment redonner un sens au mot 'Humanisme'?*" ("How can we restore sense to the world 'humanism'?"). This afforded Heidegger a welcome opportunity both to re-introduce the lineaments of his own work to post-war French readers who might otherwise have shunned an erstwhile champion of the Third Reich, and to dissociate his work from what he considered Sartre's humanist and voluntarist misappropriation.

The dispute casts an instructive light on the quarrel concerning transcendental mastery. On Heidegger's view, Sartre had transformed "phenomenological ontology" into a theoretical groundwork for human action. He had placed human "existence" before "essence" only in order to intensify the message that humanity is alone without God and so must bear complete and unconditioned responsibility for its own choices. But, Heidegger objected, the truly ontological question, or *Seinsfrage* (question of Being), was essentially contemplative and eschewed the radical freedom pervading Sartre's work. The task of philosophy was merely to "think" the meaning of Being. And such a task, "neither theoretical nor practical," stood in stark contrast to Sartre's belief in the sovereignty of the human subject: "But does such thinking...still allow itself to be described as humanism? Certainly not so far as humanism thinks metaphysically. Certainly not if humanism is existentialism and is represented by what Sartre expresses: *précisément nous sommes sur un plan où il y a seulement des hommes.* [We are precisely in a situation where there are only human beings] (*Existentialism is a Humanism...*) Thought from *Being and Time*, this should say instead: *précisement nous sommes sur un plan où il y a principalement l'Être* [We are precisely in a situation where principally there is being]."[38] With this shift of emphasis—from voluntarism to receptivity—Heidegger had dismissed the animating premise of Sartre's work. In *Being and Nothingness*, Sartre had claimed: "Consciousness is its own foundation [*La conscience est son propre fondement*]."[39] But in Heidegger's view this merely affirmed that Sartrean existentialism was still trapped in the metaphysics of subjectivity that the "existential" revision of phenomenology had meant to demolish. "Every humanism is either grounded in a metaphysics or is itself made to be the ground of one," Heidegger warned. And if being one's own "proper" foundation was the prerequisite for humanism, he reasoned, then humanism, too, must be rejected. In Heidegger's memorable image: "The human being is not the master of beings [*Herr des Seienden*]. The human being is the shepherd of being [*der Hirt des Seins*]." And for his French readers: "*L'homme n'est pas le maître de l'étant..., il est le voisin de l'Être.*"[40] Not a master, but a neighbor.

The humanism debate proved a decisive moment in the French reception of phenomenology. While Sartre remained prominent in French intellectual life well beyond 1946, Heidegger's assault on Sartre's subjectivism signaled the beginning of the end of the vogue for existentialist philosophy. The multidisciplinary rise of structuralism, e.g., in anthropology (Lévi-Strauss) as well as Marxism (Althusser), helped to reinforce the growing sense that existential "humanism" was in eclipse. To be sure, the symbolic appeal of humanist discourse remained strong, especially during the Nuremburg war-trials (beginning November, 1945) when former Nazis faced prosecution under the new juridical category of "crimes against humanity."[41] But the Cold War era saw the emergence of new, transnational alliances within Europe and new struggles against Europe's domination in its colonies overseas. And even while the United Nations passed the Universal Declaration of Human Rights in 1948, the very promise of applying humanist principles with greater "universality" also worked to destabilize the authority of an earlier humanism that had been confined to Europe alone. In 1947, Merleau-Ponty, excoriating the facile anti-Communism of Arthur Koestler's, *Darkness at Noon*, wrote: "In its own eyes Western humanism appears as the love of humanity, but for the rest of men it is only the custom and institution of a group of men, their password and occasionally their battle cry."[42] And, in 1951, the Vietnamese philosopher and Communist, Trân-Duc-Thao, wrote *Phenomenology and Dialectical Materialism* as a Marxist "corrective" to Husserlian phenomenology. Meanwhile, Roger Garaudy continued his campaign to discredit existentialism as "bourgeois" and out of step with the Communist movement.[43] But the prestige of orthodox Marxism itself proved vulnerable to historical events, especially following the Soviets' brutal response to the 1956 Hungarian uprising. Sartre, though increasingly isolated in philosophy as well as politics, persisted in his defense of humanism as the prerequisite for intellectual responsibility: "We concern ourselves with human beings," he admonished Garaudy, "and I fear that you will not have forgotten them."[44]

The early French debate over phenomenology provides a necessary context for understanding the early rise of deconstruction. But the connection was also institutional. Many who were later dubbed "postmodernists" received their education at the École Normale Superieur in the 1940s and 50s.[45] Pierre Bourdieu, a classmate at the ENS with Derrida in the early 1950s, studied not only with Louis Althusser and Michel Foucault, but also gained rigorous instruction in phenomenology under Merleau-Ponty. Jean-François Lyotard, better known for his 1979 manifesto, *La condition postmoderne,* wrote an introductory work, *La Phénoménologie*, in 1954 for the series, *Que sais-je?*[46] And Gilles Deleuze, who was only nineteen at the Liberation when he began studies under Hippolyte and Sartre at the Sorbonne, would later contribute a laudatory essay to a 1964 volume, *For Sartre*, in which he lamented "the melancholy of generations without a master-thinker [*sans maître-penseur*]":

> At the moment when we have come of age, our masters were those who struck us with a radical newness, ...who knew how to invent a new technique, artistic or literary, and who found a manner of thinking that corresponds to our modernity. Sartre was that for us (for the generation 20 years old at the liberation)....We speak of Sartre as though he belonged to a bygone era. Alas, we are the ones who in today's conformist moral order are bygone. That is why Sartre remains my master. [*C'est pourquoi Sartre reste notre maître*].[47]

THE YOUNG DERRIDA: READING HUSSERL

"One day," the legend goes, "the young *normalien* Jacques Derrida dazzled the 'caïman' of philosophy at the École, Louis Althusser, during a presentation, by finding seven layers of successive meaning in a text by Husserl. Something which didn't prevent him from failing the *agrégation* the first time. A reversal which, as was the word in that era, did not judge the candidate a flunk, but rather 'condemns a system.'"[48] True or not, the story captures quite well not only the interpretative acuity for which Derrida would later become famous, but also the peculiar sense that the rigorous exploration of philosophical texts was itself an emancipatory act. Just why this would have seemed the case requires closer examination.

In 1949, the young Algerian Jew Jacques Derrida arrived in France, first as a boarding student at the lycée Louis-le-Grand in Paris, where he immersed himself in French philosophy (e.g., Sartre, Marcel, Merleau-Ponty) and began preparations for the entrance exam to the ENS. Failing the first time, withdrawing the second time due to nervous collapse, he was eventually admitted in 1952 at age twenty-two, and commenced rigorous training in philosophy under Maurice de Gandillac, Louis Althusser, Jean Hippolyte, and others.[49] Derrida devoted his energies chiefly to Husserl, and over the course of his second year (1953–54), after research at the Husserl archives in Louvain, wrote his *mémoire* for the "diplôme d'études supérieurs" on the topic, "The Problem of Genesis in Husserl's Philosophy."[50] Notwithstanding encouragement from Hippolyte, it remained unpublished in France until 1990.[51] In the French preface, he confessed to his difficulty in re-reading from such a late vantage his very first formal venture into philosophy, an experience he likened to watching "an old roll of film." The remark may seem disingenuous. Although there can be no doubt this is an early work by a still-developing student, it displays all the brilliance of an original if controversial mind. The notoriously self-subverting style is already there. (Indeed, the English translator Marion Hobson refers to a warning from Althusser, written on the back of one of Derrida's early papers, that the student's twisted prose violated academic convention.)[52] But it is the content itself that merits closer scrutiny.

The preface announces Derrida's ambition to investigate the status of "genesis" in all of Husserl's work. But he immediately defeated expectations that the term could admit of simple definition. For "genesis" displayed the "irreducibility" of a "dialectic" at the heart of Husserlian phenomenology, because it united in one term two contradictory meanings, origin and becoming. On the one hand, genesis means "autonomy in relation to something other than itself." Genesis is thus "birth," "radicalness" or "creation." On the other hand, "every genetic product is produced by something other than itself, it is carried by a past, called forth and oriented by a future." Genesis is thus also "an inclusion, an immanence." Accordingly, genesis signals a tension "between a transcendence and an immanence, as its sense and direction. It is given at first both as ontologically and temporally indefinite and as absolute beginning, as continuity and discontinuity, identity and alterity, etc. [*à la fois la possibilité d'une continuité de la continuité et de la discontinuité, d'une identité de l'identité et de l'altérité, etc.*]."[53] "[T]his infinite contradiction would be at the same time the motivation and the final sense of the phenomenological enterprise."[54] But if genesis therefore stands "at the center" of Husserl's work, it therefore does so "in a double-way." Derrida provisionally calls this a "dialectic" although it promises no clear resolution: "Does Husserlian phenomenology offer us the real possibility of going beyond this alternative? Is it not on the contrary, just a constant oscillation between these two poles?"[55] This indeterminacy "puts in question the relations between philosophy and history" and "seems to disappoint every claim to an objectivity which is absolute, to a foundation which is autonomous [*l'autonomie d'un fondement*]."[56]

The analysis is familiar. It owes everything to the interpretative debates of the later 1940s over the conflicted status of phenomenological method.[57] And it raises again the controversial claim that phenomenology can serve as "its own proper foundation." Derrida had staked out a position that challenged both Merleau-Ponty and Sartre at the grounding premises of their thought. The "autonomy" of phenomenology was itself in jeopardy, and signaled the conflict between philosophy and history. The conflicted meaning of genesis was accordingly a sign that transcendental phenomenology would not succeed in bracketing its own historical conditions.[58] The idea of "genesis" now seemed to betray the fact that the transcendental ego—the very foundation of Husserlian doctrine—was thrown into a temporality it could not master.

Why did Derrida pursue such a strategy? What benefit was derived, and why did Derrida *want* to catch philosophy in a self-contradiction? The answer may lie in the curious use of the term "dialectic." The term is misleading, especially since Derrida's larger aim was to show how Husserlian phenomenology remained in a "constant oscillation" between foundation and becoming—a contradiction, then, which displays no pattern of elaboration toward a larger, more effective rationality.[59] In fact, the term is a relic of its political time: throughout the monograph, Derrida cited one contemporary piece of scholarship more frequently than any other: the "dialectical" critique of Husserl's work by the Vietnamese-Marxist, Trân-Duc-Thao, *Phénoménologie et matérialisme dialectique* (1951).[60] As he later confessed in his 1990 preface, the term "dialectic" served as "a kind of road sign" within "a philosophical and *political* map" according to which "a student of philosophy tried to find his bearings in 1950s France."[61]

With this "map" in view, we might better appreciate the strategic merit of Derrida's unusual position within the local context of post-war French thought. By undoing the authority of the Husserlian ego in favor of history, Derrida could align himself with the Marxist strategy of unmasking bourgeois ideology, but without submitting to the demands of Marxism itself. It is worth noting that while a student at the ENS, Derrida was affiliated with what he later called "noncommunist far-left groups."[62] Like Merleau-Ponty, Derrida was ready to expose the seeming universalism of European philosophy as an imperialist myth. Hence his scorn for Husserl's claim that philosophy had its "genesis" in "Europe" alone: "If the idea of philosophy as infinite *telos*, if the *eidos* Europe have [each] been brought into the world, and if this birth can be situated and dated, it can be asked what might have preceded and surrounded it. Does the establishing of philosophy divide humanity in its geographical and historical extension into two families, of which one would be limited to an empirical group, comprising on the one hand the European who preceded the spiritual advent of Europe, on the other hand, the non-Europeans? The hypothesis is laughable."[63] Derrida remained external to Marxism but shared its critique of humanist claims to universality. He could therefore pursue his own critique of Husserlian phenomenology while remaining free of what he called the "difficulties" of a "materialist" or orthodox-Marxist standpoint, without, however, retreating to the Sartrean position that the Marxists had dismissed as ideological.

For this task Heidegger's criticism of "metaphysics" served as a welcome instrument by which to disarm both camps at once. The materialists, Derrida announced, were no less guilty of metaphysical presumption than Sartre's existentialist humanism. Derrida's own solution, though here termed a "dialectic," was "not the one Trân-Duc-Thao speaks of." For the latter remains "prisoner of a metaphysics [*prisonniere d'une métaphysique*]."[64] A "dialectical philosophy," Derrida concluded, "has no right to proclaim itself a first philosophy."[65] "It is clear that we need to do everything to go beyond a 'worldly' dialectic. Hence we shall have to reject the conclusions of Trân-Duc-Thao [...] In going beyond [them] we will be faithful to the letter of Husserlianism. We do not claim to be so except in spirit, when we defend an explicitly dialectic conception in the face of its classical interpreters."[66] As this passage suggests, the as-yet-unnamed critical practice of deconstruction was already taking shape, as a form of ideology-critique "beyond" the dogmas of what Derrida called "first philosophy" (i.e., metaphysics). Derrida had now staked out a position that was both loyal to phenomenology *and* critical of the Communist opposition, without repeating the errors of the French phenomenological reception. As Vincent Descombes observed (writing in 1979), Derrida "remains, in a certain fashion, faithful to phenomenology."[67] But this fidelity pointed toward a critical disposition surpassing both humanism and Marxism alike.[68]

FROM *DESTRUKTION* TO *DÉCONSTRUCTION*

By the end of the 1950s, Derrida's writings on Husserl bore clear signs of Heidegger's influence. In *Being and Time*, Heidegger had called for a careful re-examination of the basic metaphysical models inherited from the canons of Western ontology, the premises of which were rooted so deeply in both our philosophical as well as our everyday understanding that they now passed as self-evident, whereas in fact their hold on our thinking was merely that of a "baleful prejudice." Heidegger thus called for a "rethinking" of what had been until now largely forgotten, in order to show that philosophers throughout the tradition—from Plato to Kant—had remained in thrall to a single ontological model, or "understanding of Being," which was itself founded upon a restricted understanding of time as the "present," or *Gegenwart*. The very Being of reality itself and the entities within the world were thereby grasped only in their "presence" (*Anwesenheit*), a "metaphysical" understanding that Heidegger termed "ontological oblivion" (*Seinsvergessenheit*). To undo this oblivion and to restore philosophy to a more "genuine" understanding of Being, Heidegger planned to undertake a so-called "destruction" (*Destruktion*) of the history of ontology.

Heidegger never fulfilled this ambition. That the second part for *Being and Time* remained unwritten (except for the separately-published *Kant and the Problem of Metaphysics* in 1929) may be partly due to the political events of the 1930s as well as the concomitant "turning" in Heidegger's work away from the rigors of phenomenological method and toward themes of poetry, art, and language.[69] Whatever Heidegger's reasons for abandoning the "destruction," it would not be wrong to see in Derrida's "deconstruction" an unexpected (and, in some respects, unfaithful) realization of Heidegger's plan. The French term *"deconstruction,"* as Derrida explained, is an explicit homage to the Heideggerian terms, *Destruktion* and *Abbau*, which captures the indeterminacy of the German combination, *Ab-Bau*, or, "to build-down."[70] Not surprisingly, it is Husserl's work which, as the privileged figure of "philosophy" as such, became the constant object of Derrida's first "deconstructive" efforts.

The 1959 presentation, "'Genesis and Structure' and Phenomenology" (published in 1965), announces Derrida's belief that any further study of Husserlian phenomenology would have to be carried out in the manner of Heidegger's destruction of the metaphysical tradition. Derrida now suggested that the very foundation of phenomenology must be "radically put in question."[71] For phenomenology is built upon a "principle of principles," i.e., the thesis that consciousness stands open to *"the original self-evidence and presence of the thing itself in person."*[72] But how could such self-evidence be proven? The answer, Derrida claimed, could be found in Husserl's belief that meaning can be wholly recuperated within the temporal present: "genesis" is not for Husserl a receptivity that opens out upon something other than reason itself. Rather, it signifies an Idea, or telos, thereby securing the self-foundation of phenomenology in a purely eternal "present." Reason, therefore, "unveils itself": "Reason, Husserl says, is the *logos* which is produced in history. It traverses Being with itself in sight, in sight of appearing to itself, that is, to state itself and hear itself as *logos*. It is speech as auto-affection: hearing oneself speak. It emerges from itself in order to take hold of itself within itself, in the "living present" of its self-presence. [...] Which amounts to saying that in criticizing classical metaphysics, phenomenology accomplishes the most profound project of metaphysics."[73] Notwithstanding the density of this passage, the link to Heidegger is obvious. Derrida's point is that Husserlian phenomenology presupposes the rational recuperation of the historical past. It transforms every "genesis" into "meaning" and it sees in "history" only the path by which "reason" can come to be wholly self-identical, or "present." But phenomenology is therefore—Derrida only implies this without naming Heidegger—the privileged paradigm for the metaphysics of presence.

Similar arguments were revisited and elaborated upon in Derrida's later writings on Husserl in the 1960s. Both of the major texts—the *Introduction to Edmund Husserl's "The Origin of Geometry"* (1962) and *Speech and Phenomena: Introduction to the Problem of the Sign in Husserl's Phenomenology* (1967)[74]—sought to show that Husserl's project is unfeasible and that its failure holds a larger, more "exemplary" significance.[75] What phenomenology had unwittingly revealed was an "impossibility" at the core of all philosophy: "the impossibility of resting in the simple maintenance [nowness] of a Living Present," and "the inability to live enclosed in the innocent undividedness of the primordial Absolute."[76] What Derrida saw in Husserl's philosophy (and in "philosophy" *tout court*) was the same error Heidegger had discerned in Sartre's existentialism. For no subjectivity could furnish its own foundation. Indeed, any theory that tried to place a sovereign subject at the foundation of meaning was trapped in a metaphysical humanism that proved itself upon analysis to be unstable. The theme was familiar, except that Derrida had now turned Heidegger's critique back upon Husserl—the student against the master. Merleau-Ponty, in his 1959–60 lectures on Husserl and Heidegger at the *Collège de France*, had called it "the law of parricide Socrates-Parmenides." As he observed: "one learns also from one's masters [*maîtres*] to do an other thing, which is the same thing."[77]

By the early 1960s, the rudiments of deconstruction were largely in place. The essays in Derrida's *Speech and Phenomena* (1967) reveal a shift more in emphasis than argument.[78] Derrida now examined Husserl's theory of signs as encapsulating Husserl's general theory of meaning and claimed it stood as a "privileged example" for the illusion of "metaphysical assurance" animating all of phenomenology.[79] Husserl had assumed that it must be possible for meaning to persist in its identity over time and across plural reiterations. Meaning must therefore be "ideal," for only "ideality"—as Derrida explained—could secure the self-identity of meaning and a "presence to consciousness can be indefinitely repeated." Ideality, Derrida concluded, was therefore Husserl's attempt to guarantee the "mastery of presence in repetition [*la maîtrise de la présence dans la répétition*]."[80] The primacy granted to the voice, Derrida concluded, was accordingly far more than a simple idiosyncrasy of Husserl's work. For phenomenology to sustain its cardinal belief in the sovereignty of consciousness, it must locate meaning in an ideality prior to the sign—in the "phenomenological voice"—to which Husserl awarded the highest philosophical virtues: presence, transparency, immediacy, etc. The attempt to locate voice before writing, Derrida concludes, is "implied by the whole history of metaphysics."[81]

Derrida's debt to Heidegger was now apparent. Derrida even followed the German philosopher's warnings about the metaphysical dangers of an industrialist paradigm (in, e.g., "The Question Concerning Technology," and "The Age of the World Picture"). The metaphysical critique of "phonocentrism" now implied a wholesale indictment of instrumental reason: The "power of the voice," explained Derrida, was symptomatic of the broader "determination of being as presence" which now constituted "the epoch of speech as *technical* mastery of objective being [*l'époch de la voix comme maîtrise technique de l'être-object*].[82] Aligning Heidegger's critique with his own, Derrida explained that the Greek-modernist faith in "*techné*" was the logical correlate to the phenomenological emphasis on "*phoné*." "History," Derrida concluded, "has never meant anything but the presentation (*Gegenwärtigung*) of Being, the production and recollection of beings in presence, as knowledge and mastery [*comme savoir et maîtrise*]."[83]

METAPHYSICS AFTER METAPHYSICS:
DERRIDA'S CRITIQUE OF HEIDEGGER

In a June 1971 interview, Derrida noted that Heidegger's philosophical accomplishment "is extremely important to me" and "constitutes a novel, irreversible advance all of whose critical resources we are far from having exploited." Yet he added: "what I write does not...*resemble* a text of Heideggerian filiation." "I have marked quite explicitly, in *all* the essays I have published...a *departure* from the Heideggerian problematic."[84]

How loyal was Derrida to Heidegger? As discussed above, Heidegger's critique of humanist mastery proved indispensable for the early Derrida as he charted a path beyond the postwar stalemate between the metaphysical anthropocentrism of French phenomenology and the "metaphysical" materialism of the French Marxists. But did Heidegger stand for Derrida as a *maître-penseur* (master thinker)? For others besides Derrida this was doubtless so. As Tom Rockmore and Ethan Kleinberg have demonstrated, a significant portion of the French post-war intellectual milieu seemed ready to grant Heidegger an elevated and perhaps even unchallenged status in the pantheon of great philosophers. Heidegger himself declared that "when the French begin to think, they think in German."[85] But Derrida's case is more complex. Renaut and Ferry were surely rash to classify Derrida as a mere epigone of "French Heideggerianism" whose philosophical originality—in their words—was an "illusion."[86] As Derrida explained to his interviewers in 1971, his own writing was both an elaboration upon Heidegger's philosophy *and* a departure from it.

Three texts, all originating in 1968, provide clear evidence of this conflicted bond. The first and most famous is "Différance," which Derrida, by then a *maître-assistant* at the ENS, presented at the Sorbonne to a Saturday assembly of the *Société française de Philosophie* on January 27, 1968.[87] The paper is a classic statement of Derrida's theoretical premises. But it is also an epitaph for Heidegger: "And thereby let us anticipate the delineation of a site, the familial residence and tomb of the proper [*le propre*], in which is produced, by *différance*, the *economy of death*. This stone—provided that one knows how to decipher its inscription—is not far from announcing the death of the tyrant."[88] The reference is apparently to Creon, who refuses Antigone's request that she be permitted to bury her brother Polynices. But the phrase "tomb of the proper" is a sign that Derrida wanted to direct his criticism against Heidegger's philosophy itself and most specifically against the metaphysical humanism which remains alive in *Being and Time* in its concept of *authenticity*. The French term, as rendered by Alphonse de Wae-hlens and Rudolf Boehm in their 1964 translation (of paragraphs 1–44 only) is "*propriété*. Heidegger had explained (§9) that the basic structure of human existence—or "Dasein"—is always directed toward its "ownmost possibility" ("*sa possibilité la plus propre*"). But this means that Dasein can either "lose" or "find" its own "proper" being, a distinction that obliged Heidegger to divide his labor between the analysis of Dasein in its "fallen" condition and Dasein in its "modified" condition of "authenticity."

All of Derrida's writing on Heidegger in one fashion or another aimed to expose the metaphysical humanism, and, by implication, the political authoritarianism, that are implied in Heidegger's attempt to sustain this kind of normative distinction—between proper and improper, original and derivative, and so forth. But Derrida's suspicions were roused not only by Heidegger's seemingly moralistic and anthropological categories. Derrida was also wary of the illicitly metaphysical assumptions that appeared to motivate Heidegger in privileging what was ostensibly most "genuine" or "original" in human experience, language or history.

Derrida's aim was to develop a conceptual instrument that could sustain the force of Heidegger's criticism without itself appealing to a stable origin or ground. The term "différance"—a neologism that combines the French verbs, "to differ" and "to defer" and which, because of the "a," exists only in writing but cannot be heard—served as this instrument. But it would be defined only in its absence from "presence," i.e., as an event of deferral *from* any stable site of meaning, including meaning as produced in history: "*Différance* is the non-full, non-simple, structured and differentiating origin of differences. Thus, the name 'origin' no longer suits it...we will designate as *différance* the movement according to which language, or any code, any system of referral in general, is constituted 'historically' as a weave of difference. 'Is constituted,' 'is produced,' 'is created,' 'movement,' 'historically,' etc., necessarily being understood beyond the metaphysical language."[89] *Différance* was therefore a "strategy without finality," and it ran through all structures of meaning without ever appealing to "a transcendent truth" that might "command theologically the totality of the field."[90]

The challenges of this argument were legion. Derrida admitted that *différance* is "neither a world nor a concept." But he claimed that it could sustain only a "strategic" meaning if it was to serve as an instrument with which "to think, if not to master" what is most irreducible about our 'era.'"[91] The phrasing closely echoed Heidegger's criticism of Sartre in the "Letter on Humanism." Like Heidegger, Derrida suggested that the task of thinking is what is most crucial: to "think" is emancipatory in itself, because thinking without a dogmatic conclusion may be the only means of recalling "the limits of mastery [*les limites structurelles de la maîtrise*]."

The argument bore comparison to the later Heidegger's criticism of ontotheology.[92] On Heidegger's account, ontotheology arose partly thanks to a "forgetting" what he called the "ontological difference"—i.e., the difference between revealed 'beings' and the partly-concealed "being" that was their condition. Similarly, Derrida's *différance* was an "absence" that conditioned "presence," without itself coming into view. But while Derrida repeatedly invoked Heidegger's example, he was also troubled by Heidegger's belief that philosophy could recollect and make whole what has been forgotten. For if meaning was *always* differential in Derrida's sense, it followed that the "meaning" or "truth" of Being were just "intrametaphysical effects" of *différance*.[93] Accordingly, there would be "no unique name, even if it were the name of Being. And, Derrida concluded, "we must think this without *nostalgia*, that is, outside the myth of a purely material or paternal language, a lost native country of thought."[94]

The impromptu responses to Derrida's paper from assembled members of the *Société* shed further light on his argument. Jean Wahl opened with a friendly jibe: "One has said that one cannot speak of différance with an *a*, and despite all this, one has spoken for more than an hour, and passionately, about différance with an *a*."[95] Another auditor seemed unhappy with Derrida's style: "I think that this use of language has been introduced into the French language under the German influence."[96] More serious was a query as to whether Derrida saw a relation between his own attempts to overcome metaphysical humanism and Michel Foucault's recent announcement that history was nearing "the disappearance of man" (a reference, apparently, to *Les Mots et Les Choses*, 1966).[97] But Derrida resisted efforts to historicize his work:

> I have never said that *différance* would *express* our epoque…But it is immediately obvious that what I have said of the subject, which Heidegger, above all, was the first to have said concerning the bond between metaphysics and humanism, theology and humanism, this fact that everything in my presentation depends upon Heideggerian overtures would also imply this 'disappearance' of man. [So] I would

fundamentally agree with Michel Foucault from the Heideggerian point of view that I indicated. But this does not prevent us, this being hardly a simple matter, from thinking that *The Letter on Humanism* remains or restores, against a certain humanism, a profound humanism.[98]

Between Foucault and Derrida there was a crucial difference. The former conceived of a path entirely beyond humanism, whereas Derrida had come to believe that just as there was no prelapsarian era before the forgetting of Being, so, too, Heidegger's own entrapment within humanism proved the vanity of hoping for the advent of an historical era entirely "beyond" metaphysical contamination. Ultimately, and perhaps most intriguingly, Derrida's response seemed to imply a principled antipathy to historicist categories: For if différance was always a deferral and difference from *any* stabilized horizon of meaning, then conventional habits of historical periodization (even the periodization of deconstruction itself) were rendered inoperable. Deconstruction, although born in history, seemed to exemplify a mode of thinking that resisted its own historicization within anything like a "local context" or "epoch."

Derrida further turned these anti-metaphysical arguments against Heidegger in the two early essays, "*Ousia and Grammé:* Note on a Note from *Being and Time*" and "The Ends of Man," both from 1968.[99] The first, published in an honorary volume for the Heidegger-scholar Jean Beaufret, offers a comparative analysis of Heidegger's remarks on "presence" against the background of conceptions of time from philosophical tradition. Derrida's challenge to Heidegger was now explicit: He wished to expose and "undo" what he called "*today, in France,* a profound complicity [between]… the camp of Heideggerian devotion and the camp of anti-Heideggerianism." For both groups were trying to clresistance" served as an "alibi" for "philosophical resistance."[100] The failure to take the philosopher seriously united those who rejected Heidegger and those who were faithful to him. Derrida now wished to pursue "a direction not opened by Heidegger's meditation."[101] Heidegger was perhaps right, Derrida granted, that as far back as the Greeks the understanding of Being as presence had blocked the more "primordial" understanding of temporality. But, he asked, "is not the opposition of the *primordial* and the *derivative* still metaphysical?"[102] Every time one poses a question of *meaning,* claimed Derrida, "it must be posed within the closure of metaphysics."[103] The difficulty in seeking to escape such metaphysical structures was that they were always at work in whatever languages one might wield against them. Language itself bore the indelible trace of metaphysical commitment, a complicity that could not be undone. As Derrida claimed: "difference is older than Being itself."[104]

Still, even while metaphysical commitments were intrinsic to any "system" of meaning, any such system was also intrinsically unstable. The repeated use of deconstructive analysis relied upon yet worked also to destabilize the authority of philosophy itself: "It is true," Derrida explained, "that the pleasure one might have in doing so...ultimately cannot be called to appear before the tribunal of any law. It is precisely the limit of such a tribunal—philosophy—that is in question here."[105] The analysis of such metaphysical "traces" in language was, Derrida concluded, already political in its effects. For a trace could never be brought under the control of any philosophical principle: "No philosopheme is prepared to master it. And it (is) that which must elude mastery" [*Aucun philosophème n'est paré pour la maîtriser. Et elle (est) cela même qui dois se dérober à la maîtrise*].[106]

Derrida's final lecture on Heidegger's legacy, "The Ends of Man," was first presented as a lecture in New York, at a 1968 colloquium on the topic "Philosophy and Anthropology."[107] A confession of both devotion to and dissatisfaction with Heidegger's accomplishment, the lecture also registers Derrida's sensitivity to the relation between metaphysics and politics, and his growing sense that humanism—as Merleau-Ponty had warned—had come to serve as an ideological weapon for the maintenance of European power.

To document this complicity, Derrida turned back to the earlier, "humanist" or "anthropologistic," reception of Heidegger in France, that began with Corbin's decision to translate *Dasein* as "human reality" (*réalité humaine*). This "monstrous translation," Derrida noted, which had determined "the reading or the nonreading of Heidegger during this period."[108] But even while Derrida wished to register his dissent from the humanistic interpretation, he was quick to note that Heidegger's philosophy itself remained trapped in the metaphysics of subjectivity it claimed to reject. This was not only due to Heidegger's constant appeals to the value of the "proper [*propre*] in man." The entire structure of the existential analytic in *Being and Time* presupposed a collective singular—the "we"—as its methodological and metaphysical premise.[109] "Dasein," wrote Derrida, "though *not* man, is nevertheless *nothing other than* man," an ambiguity that allowed Heidegger a subtle return to "the essence of man" and to a still-authoritative anthropologism that lay even prior to "the metaphysical concepts of *humanitas*." Sartre, Corbin, Merleau-Ponty, and the others, therefore, had not misread Heidegger, they had read him all too well.[110] The "name of man," explained Derrida "remains the link or the paleonymic guiding thread which ties the analytic of Dasein to the totality of metaphysics' traditional discourse."[111] In setting the existential analytic to work, Heidegger had been compelled to assume a certain unity to human experience, a unity untroubled by dislocation or violence, and distinguished *a priori* by its intimate understanding of Being. The "we" was thus hardly a neutral foundation for Heidegger's phenomenology. Implied in that beginning were all of the assumptions that joined Heidegger's thinking to a kind of political conservatism and "an entire metaphorics of proximity, of simple and immediate presence, a metaphorics associating the proximity of Being with the values of neighboring, shelter, house, service, guard, voice, and listening."[112]

This argument bore a discernable relation to contemporary politics—both to the recent colonial struggle against the French in Derrida's native Algeria (independent as of 1962, which prompted Derrida to move his family to the Metropole) and to the United States' involvement in formerly-French Indochina. In fact, Derrida opened his lecture with explicit reference to Vietnam and the student demonstrations in Paris. What was needed was somehow to destabilize the relations that reinforced European hegemony without appealing to a predetermined discourse of humanistic freedom. "A radical trembling can only come from the *outside*," Derrida explained. "This trembling is played out in a violent relationship of the whole of the West to its other."[113] Yet he was characteristically suspicious of quick resolutions or appeals to revolutionary violence. Although Derrida did not name the writers who backed such liberationist strategies, he might have mentioned Frantz Fanon, whose work on behalf of Algerian independence had not only drawn the admiration of Sartre, but whose theoretical writings were founded upon Kojéve's Hegelian dialectic of "master and slave" [*maître et de l'esclave*]. "It is precisely the force and the efficiency of the system," Derrida warned, "that regularly change transgressions into 'false exits.'"[114]

Derrida looked forward to the promise of "a new writing" that would challenge the solidaristic logic of the humanist "we" and disrupt the hegemony of the West without simply opposing it with an equally solidaristic "we" of nationalist liberation. One could not effect a simple "change of terrain." He proposed instead that "one must speak several languages and produce several texts at once." Two modes of deconstruction would have to be realized simultaneously, the first drawing inspiration from the philosophical writings of Heidegger, the second from the "style" and the "laughter" of a German thinker whose name had not often appeared in Derrida's previous texts—Nietzsche: "His laughter [of the *Übermensch*] will then burst out, directed toward a return which no longer will have the form of the metaphysical repetition of humanism, nor doubtless, 'beyond' metaphysics, the form of a memorial or a guarding of the meaning of Being, the form of the house and of the truth of Being.... No doubt that Nietzsche called for an active forgetting of Being: it would not have the metaphysical form imputed to it by Heidegger."[115] With the announcement in Derrida's 1968 texts of a Nietzschean style and a so-called "second" deconstruction, the privileged (if always contested) status of Heidegger as *maître-penseur* seems to have arrived at a new plateau. Derrida was now perhaps more than ever before directly critical both of the anthropocentric metaphysics *and* of the authoritarian politics implicit in Heidegger's thought.[116]

COMRADE MALLARMÉ: A CONCLUSION

In September of 1969, the Communist paper *L'Humanité* published a brief essay entitled, "Le camarade 'Mallarmé.'"[117] To the uninitiated it might have seemed an innocent summary of the literary-political afterlife of the French Symbolist poet Mallarmé. But it was in fact a polemic, directed against Derrida and his associates at the Marxist literary journal *Tel Quel* with which Derrida had been an affiliate since 1965. The essay was ingenious if somewhat impressionistic. It charted the three waves of historical "misfortune" visited upon Mallarmé by his readers; first, the *fin-de-siécle* "decadents"; second, the Weimar-era George Circle (a "narrow and closed" group, seemingly apolitical but in reality diffusing "the worst of predispositions amongst the pre-Nazi youth"); and third, the contemporary reception, dubbed here *"le malheur 'Heideggerien.'"*

What was the "Heideggerian misfortune?" The target was unmistakable. Mallarmé, the essayist explained, was now in the hands of ideologues who, though claiming to speak for linguistic and social "revolution," had in fact derived their theory of language from Heidegger's philosophy, for which, incidentally, Marxism served merely as a symptom for the "abjection" of the technological age and the forgetting of Being. But this was not surprising, because the Heideggerian "schema" of a "regressive history" had been traced, "word for word, from Kriek, the absurd Nazi ideologue." And now, the essayist concluded, the French public could witness the latest ideology, borrowing the same scheme, and claiming that all of history involved the "humiliation" of writing and its repression by speech, as if there were a "revolution of return to writing, the reprisal of the Nietzschean myth of return." Against such seemingly fantastic theories the essayist declared: "There is a revolution that had transformed the world, by means of technological transformations and the materials of labor."[118] There followed a quote from Lenin's *Notebooks on the Dialectic*: "the world does not satisfy man, and man decides, by his action, to change it."

The author of this polemic was Jean-Pierre Faye, a distinguished author, poet, and literary critic, who would move on to publish the first volume of his *Totalitarian Languages* in 1972, to be followed in later years by studies of anti-Semitism as well as a book entitled *The Trap: Heideggerian Philosophy and National Socialism*. A committed Marxist, Faye had also been a member of the *Tel Quel* editorial board for more than four years.[119] The immediate provocation for his essay may have been a special issue of *Tel Quel*, which included essays by Barthes, Foucault, and Derrida, and opened with an unlikely juxtaposition of quotations by Mallarmé and Marx.[120]

Faye's indictment, all the more wounding since it seemed an act of betrayal against his own colleagues, provoked an immediate response. A week later *L'Humanité* published a rejoinder by the novelist and *Tel Quel* founder Philippe Sollers, who wrote that Faye's essay had passed beyond censure to "insinuating defamation," but which, published in a Communist press, seemed falsely invested with "political authority." Faye's attempt to portray this intellectual history, wrote Sollers, exhibited "a stupefying unreality." He reminded readers that *Tel Quel* "declares openly that it means to develop itself on Marxist-Leninist foundations." Politically, its analyses were "in agreement with the French Communist Party," and had caused it to be "attacked violently by the bourgeois press." Faye had gone too far: "by making allusion to a theory of writing that we consider to be scientifically founded by the inaugural book of Jacques Derrida, *De la grammatologie* (1967), M. Faye, who incidentally retains of that work little but a quite fragmentary aspect, interpreted against sense, affirms peremptorily that it concerns the continuation of a Nazi ideology. This proposal is extremely grave. Not only does Derrida criticize Heidegger in several locations, but to insinuate that this work would have the least point in common with Nazism is defamation."[121]

A second rejoinder followed from Claude Prévost (a member of the editorial board for *La Nouvelle Critique*), who wrote that Faye had crafted "a simplified intellectual-historical lineage for Nazi ideology" that reduced "Heideggerian interpretation by association to more extremist and committed Nazi ideologues." And "obviously, though he proceeds by allusion, M. Faye is seizing upon the works of Jacques Derrida."[122] Faye then wrote a riposte in *L'Humanité*, reaffirming both his "esteem and admiration" for Derrida, and claiming he had "simply wanted to show how a language of the German extreme right could displace itself without anyone's being aware of it, and could introduce itself into the Parisian left."[123] The *Tel Quel* editors responded: "We would like to show...something entirely different, how a defamation against the left, and more precisely against *Tel Quel*, could slip, under the cover of the 'Parisian left' which M. Faye would like to represent, and *in plain sight of everyone*, into *L'Humanité*."[124] In the following issue (1970), they issued the *coup-de-grâce*: "M. Faye seems to us fundamentally a Social Democrat."[125]

The story of the Heidegger reception in France does not end here. Derrida's interpretation of Heidegger's philosophy spans the history of deconstruction, from the early analysis of metaphysics and writing (*Of Grammatology*, 1967) to the later reflections on one's own "proper" or "authentic" death (*Aporias*, 1993). The "Heidegger Affair" saw a second reprisal in France with the publication of Victor Farias' book (*Heidegger et le Nazisme*, 1987), which itself provoked a storm of new interpretations, including Derrida's *De l'esprit: Heidegger et la Question* (1987), Lacoue-Labarthe's *La Fiction du Politique* (1987), Jean-François Lyotard's *Heidegger et "les juifs"* (1988), and Pierre Bourdieu's *L'Ontologie politique de Martin Heidegger* (1988). This second phase has been discussed elsewhere and has generated a new round of frequently-bitter debate in Europe as well as North America.[126] Here it may suffice to note that Derrida's own views of Heidegger remained largely constant: *Of Spirit*, for example, attempts to marshal *historical* evidence for the claim that Heidegger's Nazism was hardly continuous with his philosophy but rather a symptom of his momentary lapse into the rhetoric of "spiritual," i.e., metaphysical, humanism.

What is striking in so many of these debates is the underlying methodological premise that political origins remain alive and unchanged despite all the metamorphoses of intellectual reception. Faye's charge—that Derrida had unknowingly betrayed his allies by opening an ideological passage through history from the German right to the French left—rests upon the controversial notion that the ideological markings of an idea are always identifiable, notwithstanding its interpretive movement across time and space, as if present-day interpreters must be held in some fashion responsible for its ideological beginnings. The assumption is dubious at best. It bespeaks a strange materialism, as if thoughts were fixed and definable in their properties; yet also a strange Platonism, as if those very thoughts, once born, were eternal in their meaning.

The controversies surrounding the Heidegger reception, in France and elsewhere, seem unable to dispel this belief. Even today, some of the most perspicacious scholars have been tempted to collapse reception into origin, as if the facts and contexts that may help us toward a better historical understanding of Heidegger's loathsome political choices could also grant us the authority to question the political pedigree of those who draw instruction from his work today. But are origins in this sense ever sufficiently powerful to "master" and contain philosophical meaning? The question itself underscores the paradox (which this essay, too, hasn't avoided) of attempting to contextualize a movement that wanted to resist full-blown contextualism in the name of intellectual freedom. For this reason, conventions of historical nomenclature and periodization are from a deconstuctivist perspective always suspect: they are attempts to delimit, fix, and ultimately put a stop to critical reflection. Indeed, one of the most intriguing implications of Derrida's legacy is that the critical impulse is never to be wholly mastered by the local context of meaning from which it is born. While history in general may furnish the preconditions for meaning, the suggestion that any *particular* historical context is therefore capable of imposing an ultimate limit upon meaning would seem to recapitulate the metaphysics of presence that deconstruction has urged us to challenge.

NOTES

1. For their comments on an earlier draft of this essay I would like to thank: Mark Bevir, Martin Jay, Judith Surkis, Samuel Moyn, Jill Hargis, Sara Rushing, and Ed Baring.
2. On the reception of Heidegger and Nietzsche in France, see Alan Schrift, *Nietzsche's French Legacy: A Genealogy of Poststructuralism* (New York: 1995); Tom Rockmore, *Heidegger and French Philosophy: Humanism, Antihumanism, and Being* (New York, 1995); Luc Ferry and Alain Renaut, *Heidegger and Modernity*, Franklin Philip, trans. (Chicago, 1990); Luc Ferry and Alain Renaut, *Why We are Not Nietzscheans*, Robert de Loaiza, trans. (Chicago, 1997); and Luc Ferry and Alain Renaut, *French Philosophy of the Sixties: An Essay on Antihumanism*, Mary Cattani, trans. (Amherst: University of Massachusetts Press, 1990). Fine general studies are: Vincent Descombes, *Le Même et l'Autre. Quarante-Cinq Ans de Philosophie Française* (1933–1978) (Paris: Minuit, 1979); and Gary Gutting, *French Philosophy in the Twentieth Century* (New York: Cambridge UP, 2001).

3. Recent studies on Derrida's early readings of both Husserl and Heidegger have begun to redress this distortion; but their philosophical work deserves supplementary contributions that pay closer attention to historical context. See, e.g., Leonard Lawlor, *Derrida and Husserl: The Basic Problem of Phenomenology* (Bloomington: Indiana UP, 2002); and Paola Marrati, *Genesis And Trace: Derrida Reading Husserl And Heidegger* (Palo Alto, CA: Stanford UP, 2005). Also see Tilottama Rajan, *Deconstruction and the Remainders of Phenomenology: Sartre, Derrida, Foucault, Braudrillard* (Stanford, CA: Stanford University Press, 2002).
4. Friedrich Nietzsche, *Twilight of the Idols, or, How one Philosophizes with a Hammer*, R.J. Hollingdale, trans. (London: Penguine Books, 1989), pp. 29–122.
5. On the theme "democracy to come" see Derrida, *Voyous* (Paris: Galilée, 2003).
6. André Breton, Letter to Rolland de Renéville. *Nouvelle revue française* (Juillet, 1932), cited in "Avant-Propos" by Marie-Claude Char, in Réne Char, *Le Marteau sans maître* (Paris: Gallimard, 2002), 9.
7. For comments on Boulez and "Le Marteau," see David Schiff, "Unconstructed Modernist: How Does One Account for the Fall of Pierre Boulez the Composer and the Rise of Pierre Boulez the Conductor?" *The Atlantic Monthly*, Vol. 276, September 1995.
8. Jerrold Seigel, *The Idea of the Self: Thought and Experience in Western Europe since the Seventeenth Century* (New York: Cambridge UP, 2005), 649.
9. Hal Foster, ed., *The Anti-Aesthetic: Essays on Postmodern Culture* (New York: New Press, 1998).
10. Brief J. Patočka and Eugen Fink vom 2. 5. 1946. Brief 13. In Eugen Fink und Jan Patočka, *Briefe und Dokumente, 1933–1977*, Michael Heitz and Bernard Nessler, eds. (München/Frieburg: Verlag Karl Alber, 1999), 47–49.
11. François Poirié, *Emmanuel Lévinas, Qui êtes-vous?* (Lyons: La Manufacture, 1987), 74.
12. Paul Ricoeur, *Husserl: An Analysis of His Phenomenology*, Edward G. Ballard and Lester E. Embree, trans. (Evanston, IL: Northwestern UP, 1967), 3.
13. For a summary, see Jean Hering, "La Phénomenologie il y a trente ans" in *Revue Internationale de Philosophie I* (1939).
14. Herbert Spiegelberg, *The Phenomenological Movement*, Vol. II. (The Hague: Martinus Nijhoff, 1960), 404.
15. Lévinas, *The Theory of Intuition in Husserl's Phenomenology*, André Orianne, trans. (Evanston, IL: Northwestern UP, 1973), xxxiv.
16. Maurice Merleau-Ponty, *Phénoménologie de la Perception* (Paris: Gallimard, 1945); in English as *Phenomenology of Perception*, Colin Smith, trans. (London: Routledge and Kegan Paul, 1962), vii.
17. Merleau-Ponty, Phenomenology of Perception, 430. On the concept of "world" in phenomenology, see my essay "Realism, Science, and the Deworlding of the World," in *The Blackwell Companion to Phenomenology and Existentialism*, Mark Wrathall and Hubert Dreyfus, eds. (Blackwell, 2005).
18. Merleau-Ponty, "The Primacy of Perception," in *The Primacy of Perception and Other Essays on Phenomenological Psychology, the Philosophy of Art, History, and Politics* (Evanston, IL: Northwestern UP, 1964), 12–42; 42.
19. Merleau-Ponty, *Phenomenology of Perception*, xx–xxi.
20. Jean Wahl, *Petit Histoire de L'Existentialisme* (Paris: Éditions Club Maintenant, 1947).

21. The details of that early controversy and especially its political dimensions are discussed at length in Ethan Kleinberg, *Generation Existential: Heidegger's Philosophy in France, 1927–1961* (Ithaca, NY: Cornell UP, 2005).

22. Jean Wahl, *Petit Histoire de L'Existentialisme* (Paris: Éditions Club Maintenant, 1947), 180–1; 198.

23. Jean-Marc Mouillie, "Presentation: Sartre et la phénoménologie" in *Sartre et la phénoménologie*. Jean-Marc Mouillie, ed. (Fontenay-aux-Roses: ENS Éditions, 2000), 15.

24. Jean-Paul Sartre, *Lettres au Castor*, II, 21, as quoted in Mouillie, "Presentation."

25. Ibid., II, 51.

26. Mark Poster, *Existential Marxism in Postwar France: from Sartre to Althusser* (Princeton, NJ: Princeton UP, 1975), esp. Ch. 4.

27. "Un faux prophét: Jean-Paul Sartre," *Les Lettres françaises* (No. 88, 28 decembre, 1945).

28. Ibid.

29. R. Garaudy, *Literature of the Graveyard* (International Publishers, 1948), 9; also see David Drake, *Intellectuals and Politics in Post-War France* (New York: Palgrave, 2002), for an account of Garaudy's attack on Sartre, 30–31.

30. Poster, 116.

31. Jean-Paul Sartre, "A propose de l'existentialisme: mis au point." *Action*, No. 17, December 29, 1944.

32. See, e.g., Karl Löwith's essay, "Les implications politiques de la philosophie de l'existence chez Heidegger," in *Les Temps modernes*, 14 (Novembre, 1946). On Löwith's interpretation, see Kleinberg, *Generation Existential*, esp. Ch. 4.

33. Sartre, "A propos de l'existentialisme: Mise au point;" *L'existentialisme est une humanisme* (Nagel, 1946); "Jean-Paul Sartre répond à ses détracteurs: L'existentialisme et la politique," in Colette Audry, ed., *Pour et contre l'existentialisme* (Editions Atlas, 1948), 181–90.

34. Jean-Paul Sartre, *L'existentialisme est une humanisme* (Paris: Gallimard, 1996), 21.

35. Ibid., 56

36. Ibid., 76.

37. Martin Heidegger, *Brief über den Humanismus* (Bern: A. Francke, 1947; Frankfurt: Klostermann, 1949), in English as "Letter on Humanism" in *Pathmarks*, William McNeill, ed. (Cambridge: Cambridge UP, 1998), 239–276. The "Letter" was first published in France in *Fontaine*, No. 58, 1947. On the association between Beaufret and Heidegger, see Kleinberg, *Generation Existential*.

38. Heidegger, "Letter on Humanism," *Pathmarks*, 260.

39. Sartre, *L'être et le néant. Essai d'ontologie phénonménolique* (Paris: Éditions Gallimard, 1943), 118.

40. Martin Heidegger, *Lettre sur l'humanisme*, Roger Munier, trans. (Paris: Aubier, 1964); Brief über den "Humanismus" in *Wegmarken* (Frankfurt: Klostermann, 1967), 313–364.

41. On the French debate over human rights see Martin Jay, "Lafayette's Children: The American Reception of French Liberalism," in *Refractions of Violence* (New York: Routledge, 2003), 149–162.

42. Maurice Merleau-Ponty, Humanism and Terror, *An Essay on the Communist Problem*, John O'Neill, trans. (Boston: Beacon Press, 1969), 176. Originally published 1947.

43. Trân-Duc-Thao, *Phénoménologie et matérialisme dialectique* (Paris, 1951).

44. Garaudy, *Perspectives*, 110–113. Sartre, "Marxisme et philosophie de l'existence," in Roger Garaudy, *Perspectives de L'Homme. Existentialisme, Pensée Catholique, Marxisme*, 2ime. ed. (Paris: PUF, 1960).

45. On the rise of structuralism and Sartre's eclipse by the end of the 60s, see Mouillie, "Presentation," 16.

46. Jean-François Lyotard, *La Phénoménologie* (Paris: Collection Que sais-je?, 1954).

47. Gilles Deleuze, "He was my Teacher," originally published as "Il a été mon maître" in Arts, Oct. 28–Nov. 3, 1964, 8–9; reprinted in Jean-Jacques Bochier, *Pour Sartre* (Paris: Éditions Jean-Claude Lattès, 1995), 82–88, in English as "He was my Teacher," in *Desert Islands, and Other Texts, 1953–1974* (Los Angeles: Semiotext(e), 2004), 77–80.

48. From: François Dufay, *Les Normaliens: de Charles Péguy à Bernard-Henri Lévy un siècle d'histoire* (Paris : J.-C. Lattès, 1993). On Derrida's relationship with Althusser, see "Politics and Friendship: An Interview with Jacques Derrida," in *The Althusserian Legacy*, E. Ann Kaplan and Michael Sprinker, eds. (London: Verso, 1993), 183–232.

49. Biographical information from Geoffrey Bennington and Jacques Derrida, *Jacques Derrida*. Geoffrey Bennington, trans. (Chicago: University of Chicago Press, 1993).

50. Jacques Derrida, *Le problème de la genèse dans la philosophie de Husserl* (Paris: PUF, 1990); translated in English as: *The Problem of Genesis in Husserl's Philosophy*, Marian Hobson, trans. (Chicago: University of Chicago Press, 2003).

51. Derrida, Preface to the 1990 edition, *The Problem of Genesis in Husserl's Philosophy*, xiv.

52. Marian Hobson, "Translator's Note" in *The Problem of Genesis in Husserl's Philosophy*, ix.

53. Ibid., 8.

54. Ibid., xxi–ii.

55. Ibid., xxvii.

56. Ibid., xviii.

57. See the remarks repeating Merleau-Ponty's arguments, in *The Problem of Genesis in Husserl's Philosophy*, xviii.

58. Ibid., xxvii.

59. Ibid., xxvii.

60. Trân-Duc-Thao, *Phénoménologie et matérialisme dialectique* (Paris, 1951). Derrida's further comments can be found in "The Time of a Thesis: Punctuations," in *Philosophy in France Today*, Alan Montefiore, ed. (Cambridge, UK: Cambridge UP, 1983), 34–50.

61. Derrida, Preface to the 1990 edition, *The Problem of Genesis in Husserl's Philosophy*, xv–xvi. For a summary of Thao's symbolic significance for Derrida, see the insightful essay by Tim Herrick, "A book which is no longer discussed today": Than Duc Thao, Jacques Derrida, and Maurice Merleau-Ponty," in *The Journal of the History of Ideas* (2005), 113–131.

62. Geoffrey Bennington and Jacques Derrida, Jacques Derrida, Geoffrey Bennington, trans. (Chicago: University of Chicago Press, 1993), 329.

63. Derrida, *The Problem of Genesis in Husserl's Philosophy*, 157.

64. Derrida, *Le problème de la genèse dans la philosophie de Husserl*, 257, n. 8. My translation.

65. Derrida, *The Problem of Genesis in Husserl's Philosophy*, xli.

66. Ibid., xlii.

67. Vincent Descombes, *Le Même et L'Autre: Quarante Cinq Ans de Philosophie Française (1933–1978)* (Paris: Les Éditions de Minuit, 1979), 166.

68. In the 1990 preface, Derrida notes the continuity between the mémoire and his more recent work. See his preface to the 1990 edition in *The Problem of Genesis in Husserl's Philosophy*, xiv–xv.

69. J. Habermas, *The Philosophical Discourse of Modernity*, Frederick Lawrence, trans. (Cambridge, MA: MIT Press, 1987), 131–160.

70. Derrida, "Lettre à un ami japonais" in *Psyché – Invention de l'autre* (Paris: Galilée, 1987), 387–393; in English as "Letter to a Japanese Friend" in *Derrida and Différance*, Robert Bernasconi and David Wood, eds. (Evanston, IL: Northwestern UP, 1988).

71. Derrida, "'Genesis and Structure' and Phenomenology," in *Writing and Difference*, Alan Bass, trans. (Chicago: University of Chicago Press, 1968), 164.

72. Ibid., 164.

73. Ibid., 166.

74. Derrida, *Edmund Husserl's Origin of Geometry: An Introduction*, J.P. Leavey Jr., trans. (Lincoln and London: University of Nebraska Press, 1989); originally published in French as *Introduction à L'Origine de la geometrie de Husserl* (Paris: Presses Universitaries de France, 1962).

75. The ending passage from the 1962 *Introduction à L'Origine de la geometrie de Husserl* appears to be the birthplace for Derrida's concept introduced in 1968 as "différance." See English edition preface, 153.

76. Ibid., 153.

77. Notes by Franck Robert to Merleau-Ponty's course, "Husserl aux Limites de la Phénoménologie. 1960," Merleau-Ponty, *Notes de Cours sur "L'Origine de la Géométrie de Husserl," suivi de Recherches sur la phénoménologie de Merleau-Ponty*, (Paris: PUF, 1998), 11–92, 13.

78. Jacques Derrida, *La Voix et le phénomène. Introduction au problème du signe dans la phénoménologie de Husserl* (Paris: PUF, 1967). In English (with additional essays), as *Speech and Phenomena, and Other Essays on Husserl's Theory of Signs*, David B. Allison, trans. (Evanston, IL: Northwestern UP, 1973).

79. Derrida, *Speech and Phenomena, and Other Essays on Husserl's Theory of Signs*, 5.

80. Ibid., 10.

81. Ibid., 16.

82. Ibid., 75; French, 84.

83. Ibid., 102; French, 115.

84. *Positions*, 54. "Interview with Jean-Louis Houdebine and Guy Scarpetta," (June 17, 1971).

85. *Antwort. Martin Heidegger im Gespräch*. Günther Neske und E. Ketterinig, eds. (Pfüllingen: Neske, 1988).

86. Ferry and Renault, *French Philosophy of the Sixties*, 122.

87. Derrida, "La Différance." Séance du samedi 27 janvier 1968. *Bulletin de la Société française de Philosophie*, LXIII, 1968: 73–120; republished in *Théorie d'ensemble*, coll. Tel Quel (Paris: Éditions du Seuil, 1968), and in *Speech and Phenomena, and Other Essays on Husserl's Theory of Signs*, David Allison, trans. (Evanston: Northwestern, 1973), 129–160; hereafter, "Différance."

88. Derrida, "Différance," 4.

89. Ibid., 11–12.

90. Ibid., 7.

91. Ibid., 7.

92. Specifically, "Différance" seems to invoke two texts by Heidegger, "The Principle of Identity," and "The Onto-Theological Constitution of Metaphysics," (published together in German in *Identität und Differenz*, in 1957).
93. Derrida, "Différance," 22.
94. Ibid., 37.
95. Ibid., 101.
96. Mlle J. Hersch, response, in "Différance," 107.
97. Ibid., 105. The reference is to Michel Foucault, *The Order of Things* (New York: Vintage, 1973), 387.
98. Ibid., 105.
99. Derrida, "Ousia and Grammé: Note on a Note from Being and Time" originally published in *L'endurance de la pensée: Pour saluer Jean Beaufret* (Paris: Plon, 1968), 29–67.
100. Ibid., 62.
101. Ibid., 34.
102. Ibid., 63.
103. Ibid., 51.
104. Ibid., 67.
105. Ibid., 39.
106. Derrida, "Ousia et Grammé," French version, 257.
107. Derrida, "The Ends of Man," first in French in *Marges de la Philosophie* (1972), from a lecture in New York, 1968, at an international colloquium on the theme, "Philosophy and Anthropology." In English as "The Ends of Man," in *Margins of Philosophy*, Alan Bass, trans. (Chicago: University of Chicago Press, 1982), 109–136.
108. Derrida, "The Ends of Man," 115.
109. Ibid., 123–24.
110. Ibid., 127.
111. Ibid., 127.
112. Ibid., 130.
113. Ibid., 115.
114. Ibid., 135.
115. Ibid., 136.
116. Derrida pursues a similar strategy—i.e., reading Nietzsche contra Heidegger—in *De la Grammatologie* (Paris: Editions de Minuit, 1967). In English as *Of Grammatology*, Gayatri Spivak, trans. (Baltimore: Johns Hopkins, 1974; corrected 1997), esp. 18–26.
117. Jean-Pierre Faye, "Le camarade 'Mallarmé'" in *L'Humanité* (Sept. 12, 1969), 9.
118. Ibid.
119. Jean-Pierre Faye, *Langages totalitaires* (Paris: Hermann, 1972).
120. "Theorie de l'ensemble," in Tel Quel, *Théorie d'ensemble* (Paris: Editions du Seuil, 1968).
121. Philippe Sollers, "'Camarade" et Camarade' in *L'Humanité* (Sept. 19, 1969), 9.
122. Prévost, "Sur 'Le Camarade Mallarmé'" *L'Humanité*, 9.
123. *L'Humanité* (Oct.10, 1969).
124. Tel Quel, 39 (Autumn, 1969).
125. Tel Quel, 40 (Autumn, 1970), "Conclusions," 103–104.
126. See, e.g., Richard Wolin, "French Heidegger Wars," in *The Heidegger Controversy, A Critical Reader*, R. Wolin, ed. (Cambridge, MA: MIT Press, 1993), 272–300. The first edition of this volume (New York : Columbia University Press, 1991) includes an illuminating interview with Derrida (omitted from the MIT reprint).

6 "A Kind of Radicality"

The Avant-Garde Legacy in Postmodern Ethics

Mark Bevir

INTRODUCTION

Jean Baudrillard, a leading postmodernist, once told an interviewer, "I was very, very attracted by Situationism," and "even if today Situationism is past, there remains a kind of radicality to which I have always been faithful."[1] Jean-Francois Lyotard, another prominent postmodernist, invoked a similar radicalism when he championed "the activity of the [avant-garde] artist and the critical philosopher, 'republican' politics—any inventive step which, on the path of the unknown, of the unacceptable, breaks with constituted norms, shatters consensus, and revives the meaning of the *différend*."[2]

The radical avant-garde—Dada, surrealism, and situationism—wanted to disrupt, and even overturn, bourgeois society. However, they also emphasized the difficulties of avoiding entrapment within that society, and the ability of that society to tame radical gestures, and even to reshape them for its own ends. They promoted a range of subversive sites and strategies that they hoped would prove immune to such recuperation. These sites and strategies included the body and desire, play and excess, aesthetic self-creation and stylized transgression. Collectively they constitute "a kind of radicality" which later continued to appeal not only to Baudrillard and Lyotard but also to poststructuralists such as Roland Barthes and Michel Foucault.

This chapter explores the avant-garde background to postmodern radicalism. It also offers a genealogical critique of themes in at least this strand of postmodern ethics and politics. It suggests that postmodern radicals such as Baudrillard, Foucault, and Lyotard remained wedded to avant-garde sites and strategies in a way that no longer made sense once they had rejected the "real." It thereby explains theoretical difficulties that are rightly thought to beset postmodern theory, but it does so in a way that might lead us to go beyond them.

POSTSTRUCTURALIST ETHICS

The structuralist movement in France fell apart in the late 1960s. It collapsed intellectually following Jacques Derrida's critique of its scientific pretensions. When Derrida extended his critique of the myth of presence from phenomenology to Ferdinand de Saussure's linguistic theory and the anthropology of Claude Levi-Strauss, he implied that structuralism was just one more example of a pernicious logocentrism that was so in thrall to certainty and so self-confident that it failed to recognize the indeterminate and unstable nature of meaning and language. While the structuralists were far from convinced by Derrida's own claims for deconstruction, they generally acknowledged, at least implicitly, that structures were unstable, conventional, and bound-up with language. Of course, several structuralists had long acknowledged themes very close to those now urged upon them by Derrida, so we should be wary of too sharp a contrast between structuralism and post-structuralism. Nonetheless, Derrida's critique of structuralism does appear to have marked something of a break. In the first place, structuralism lost much of its allure. As Richard Wolin suggests in his chapter, the younger generation of French intellectuals often moved toward a more liberal, human rights agenda. In the second place, structuralists who had shown little earlier sympathy for ideas such as instability and undecidability now began to do so. As Robert Resch suggests in his chapter, Louis Althusser opened his philosophy up to such themes even as he continued to defend structuralism as a method. And in the third place, structuralists who had paid some homage to these themes began to do so in a noticeably more forthright and sustained manner. It is this third group, which includes Barthes and Foucault, who are most often identified, along with Derrida, as poststructuralists. They emphatically rejected the very stable meanings and hidden structures or epistemes to which they had earlier seemed to appeal. They placed a greater emphasis—perhaps even a novel one—on the indeterminacy and superficiality of meaning. In doing so, moreover, they raised ethical issues that they then answered in ways which drew on the avant-garde tradition and which find parallels in the work of other postmodernists such as Baudrillard and Lyotard

Barthes and Foucault now echoed Derrida in relating the indeterminate and superficial nature of meaning to terms like play, fragment, and excess. Barthes began to argue that meaning arose from the open-ended play of signifiers and codes across the surface of texts. He suggested that each text is the product of the fragments or traces of other texts leaping across its pages so as to create a plurality or excess of meanings. Barthes wanted readers to approach texts in an equally playful spirit. In his view, because meanings do not derive from authorial intentions, systems of rules, or anything of the sort, readers need not worry about reducing the text to something else. Instead readers can enjoy tracing a fluid textuality of unfolding signifiers; they can lose themselves in the allusions one text makes to another; they can take pleasure in exploring a text in relation to other texts and thereby create yet more texts; they can follow the blending and clashing of texts across the one they are reading. Barthes provided an example of just such a reading in his lengthy study of Balzac's novella, *Sarrasine*.[3] He divided the novella into lexias, or segments, which illustrated how various codes played across the text to produce an excess of meaning: the lexias and codes, far from constituting a structure, break away from one another and from themselves, so as to fragment the text in ways that facilitate plural, and even contradictory, readings.

The collapse of structuralism was exasperated by the events of May 1968. The student radicals drew attention to a pessimistic determinism in structuralist thought, as in their depreciating slogan, "structures don't take to the streets." Structuralism was suffering from a political crisis as much as a philosophical one. It had lost the status of a scientific theory capable of critically unmasking the distortions of capitalist society. And yet it also lacked the ability to inspire and mobilize people in any kind of revolutionary praxis. Some critics complained that the poststructuralists' emphasis on play, fragmentation, and excess was less a response to this political impasse than a retreat from politics. They complained, for example, that Barthes, the scientific structuralist, had become a bourgeois man of letters; the sharp critic who had attacked bourgeois society and its literary institutions had developed a more literary, less political voice, which spoke of enjoying classic texts for their form and language. Such complaints touched on a more abstract issue. Structuralism had offered some the promise of a critical theory based on a scientific method that stripped away superficial, ideological appearances to reveal a hidden reality of exploitation and power. If poststructuralists rejected the very idea of hidden structures, the questions arose: for what purpose, did they criticize, and how would they justify such a purpose?

Barthes himself justified his reading of Balzac's novella in terms of pleasure, and he sought to locate pleasure in the body. He related the arbitrariness of the signifier by way of the play of textuality to an ethic of pleasure. Semiology is, he now suggested, an entertainment in which we read texts in terms of other texts so as to create yet more texts, for the end of criticism is not objective interpretation but enjoyment of the text conceived as a decentred object. Barthes read by skipping ahead, dipping in and out, and sampling texts. He savored texts not for their unity, but for "the abrasions I impose on the fine surface."[4] He even told one interviewer that his enjoyment of "the fragment" meant that he was "starting to have trouble writing texts of a certain length and continuity."[5] In his opinion, the most intense pleasure is the bliss that comes from encountering texts that extend indefinitely the play of codes. These texts refuse to allow us to settle on a clear interpretation. They unsettle us by denying us the security of an illusory stability. Bliss derives, in this view, not from grasping meanings but from absorption in textuality. Barthes equated such textuality with the surface of texts. He even suggested that such surfaces were somehow material. In doing so, he identified absorption in textuality as a material pleasure of the body. For Barthes, intellectual and physical enjoyment merge with reading, giving us erotic, bodily sensations.

Why, we might ask, does Barthes seem so anxious to equate textuality with materiality and bodily pleasure? The answer appears to lie in the way in which ethical questions pressed upon poststructuralists. Because poststructuralists remained hostile to humanist concepts of the subject, because they separated meaning and action from intentionality and choice, they could not properly justify any ethical claims they might seem to make by means of an appeal to some kind of free or authentic subjectivity. Barthes appealed to the body in an attempt to justify his ethics without mention of just such subjectivity. He even argued for a distinction between body and subjectivity in which the body is defined as an empty vessel capable of experiencing pleasure even in the absence of the consciousness that is necessary to give meaning to its experiences, and in which consciousness is defined as a subjectivity that arises form the historical biography of the body.[6] According to Barthes, if we examine our enjoyment of a text, we find not only a pleasure that reflects our subjectivity, but also a pleasure of the body. The distinction between body and subjectivity enabled Barthes to defend his ethics of pleasure while still insisting that the subject is a false unity.

The distinction between body and subjectivity played a similar role in some of Foucault's writings. In the 1950s and 1960s Foucault had applied his archaeological approach to medicine, the human sciences, and, in *Madness and Civilisation*, to the changing constructions of madness in Europe from the Renaissance to the late nineteenth century. Foucault argued that Enlightenment rationality relies on the exclusion and repression of modes of thinking that escape its boundaries; the mad are, for example, locked up within asylums. These other modes of thinking, including madness, thus provided him with sites of an alternate consciousness that he could use to speak out against bourgeois reason. Foucault sought to capture the reality and even freedom of madness conceived as authentic truth— "an undifferentiated experience, a not yet divided experience of division itself."[7] When Derrida extended his criticisms of Saussure to Foucault, he challenged just this aspect of *Madness and Civilisation*. He argued in particular that the very act of writing a history of madness ineluctably entails the imposition of language, order, and reason upon it: any attempt to give voice to madness is inevitably just another instance of its repression.[8] Although Foucault replied to Derrida, arguing against the reduction of practices to texts, he seems to have accepted this particular aspect of Derrida's criticism.[9]

Soon Foucault began to associate resistance with other sites, such as the body, and other strategies, such as self-creation and transgression. In so far as he continued to reject any concept of the subject prior to its discursive construction, he suggested that the body does not constitute a human nature to be liberated so much as a space at which power inscribes various human natures. Nonetheless, Foucault now championed the body as a site that refuses to be pinned down by discourse and power, arguing that freedom consists not in realizing a natural self but in resisting all ascriptions of identity. Just as Barthes distinguished the body from subjectivity, so Foucault now distinguished the body, which experiences pleasure, from the soul, which is the identity one acquires as an effect of discourse and power. On the one hand, he insisted not only that the soul arises as power imposes an identity on the body and so turns it into a subject, but also that prior to power going to work in this way, we do not possess the stability needed to constitute ourselves as subjects: "nothing in man—not even his body—is sufficiently stable to serve as a basis for self-recognition."[10] On the other hand, he implied that the body might act as a site from which to reject all ascribed identities: "once power produces this effect, there inevitably emerge the responding claims and affirmations, those of one's own body against power."[11]

THE AVANT-GARDE

The avant-garde provided post-structuralists, and other postmodernists, with concepts such as body and desire.[12] Indeed, it is probable that one reason why Barthes and Foucault moved easily from a broadly structuralist position to a poststructuralist one lay in their prior sympathy for an avant-garde that had long deployed concepts such as play, fragment, and excess in order to capture the indeterminacy and lack of depth that they ascribed to all meaning. Maybe Barthes, Foucault, and also Jacques Lacan, always were sensitive to these avant-garde themes in a way that placed them at odds with the scientific pretensions of other structuralists. Maybe Derrida's critique of structuralism acted as little more than an encouragement to them to draw on these avant-garde themes more than the high structuralism of Althusser.

We might trace these avant-garde themes back to the aesthetes of the late nineteenth-century. Many romantics had invoked a real harmony, which they defined in contrast to what they regarded as the alienated world of modern Europe. Typically they believed, at least in their more optimistic moments, that art was capable of giving expression to such harmony and so perhaps of contributing to a realization of the real. By the late nineteenth-century, however, the aesthetes were increasingly worried by the totalizing nature of bourgeois society. The romantic idyll of individuals living in harmony with themselves, one another, and nature gave way originally to *fin de siecle* decadence and then to avant-garde radicalism. The aesthetes, such as Oscar Wilde in Britain and Charles Baudelaire in France, turned to decadence and the baroque in part because they gave up on the idea of a natural or pre-social harmony. All that they had left was a belief in individual self-expression as a mode of aesthetic creation in the face of bourgeois society, and a hope that acts of transgression might contribute to the fall of bourgeois society and so the creation of a real or authentic alternative.

The avant-garde interpreted the First World War as further evidence of the corruption of bourgeois society, and its remarkable ability to absorb attempts at subversion. Whatever their differences, Dada, surrealism, and situationism all set out to repudiate the whole rational and moral ethos of European civilization. Because they believed that the world of art was implicated in the very bourgeois society that had produced the War, they challenged established ideas of originality, artistic form, and genius, turning instead to accounts of the opacity and limits of meaning, reason, and even the self. Because they emphasized the totalizing nature of bourgeois society, they sought locations beyond reason, such as the body and desire, or the impossible and the unknowable, from which they might launch their assaults upon just that society. And because they emphasized the recuperative powers of bourgeois society, they turned to subversive strategies that had a transitory or situational quality, strategies such as self-creation and transgression.

Dada exemplifies the avant-garde's simultaneous debt to and distance from *fin de siecle* decadence. Its work looked back to the aesthetes while instantiating an even greater rejection of bourgeois civilization conceived as a totalizing whole. On the one hand, Dada too sought to overturn existing social relations and conventional artistic practices. Marcel Janco recalled, "we began by shocking the bourgeoisie, demolishing his idea of art, attacking common sense, public opinion, institutions, museums, good taste, in short, the whole prevailing order."[13] On the other hand, its greater concern with the totalizing effects and recuperative powers of bourgeois society meant its practitioners went to great lengths in order to avoid evoking an alternative that might be absorbed by just that society. Sometimes they implied that their anarchic rejection of all codes precluded their postulating any new social relations. At other times they described their alternative vision as irrational so as to indicate its impossible relation to bourgeois society; they talked, for example, of our transgressing "the reasonable descriptions of man" in order to "recover the natural and unreasonable order."[14]

Although Dada declared itself "anti-art," it was, therefore, opposed to the bourgeois relations in which art conveyed meanings, not to the creation of art or meaning as such: its talk of a non-art or the impossible indicated only the force with which it rejected bourgeois norms and its determination that its alternative should not be absorbed by that society. Indeed, Dada art ran contrary to the prevalent notions of form and value precisely in order to create meanings that revealed a more natural mode of being, albeit one that they claimed probably would seem unnatural in the distorted world of today. So, for example, although Hugo Ball used his phonetic poems to renounce a language that had been corrupted, he did so with the intention of thereby returning to a truer language of immediate experience, that is, a language that supposedly had not been debased by being implicated within alienated social relations.

It has become a cliché to describe surrealism, which emerged in Paris in the 1920s, as an attempt to negate the Dada negation. Although the leading surrealists, including Louis Aragon and André Breton, initially sympathized with Dada, they came to believe that it precluded all efforts to create alternative, constructive artistic and political practices. The surrealists certainly adopted many of the sites and strategies that Dada had deployed to disrupt bourgeois society: they too explored the body and the erotic, and myth and the irrational, and they too believed in transgression, play, and fragmentation. However, in their view, Dada's use of these strategies made little sense in the absence of a constructive ideal. Hence they attempted to introduce such a constructive aspect to Dada's critique by appealing to an ideal of total unity. As their Second Manifesto explained, "it is vain to search for any other motive in surrealist activity than the hope of discovering that point . . . [where] life and death, the real and imaginary, the past and the future, the communicable and the incommunicable, the high and the low, cease to be perceived as contradictory."[15] They drew on sources such as romanticism, Hegelian philosophy, and hermetic alchemy to argue for a complementarity of opposites, including subject and object, reason and imagination, and life and death. The surrealists combined their ideal of unity with Dada's strategies by arguing that bourgeois society obstructed our vision of unity, and that Dada's strategies offered us the means of disrupting that society so as to access unity. The surrealists found intimations of unity in myth, the unconscious, the taboo, and the erotic. And they sought to access unity by way of play, festival, transgression, and, for that matter, fantastic images, automatic writing, and other experimental artistic techniques.

The work of Georges Bataille, the surrealist to whom the poststructuralists most often appealed, exemplifies the fusion of a vision of Dada's strategies with an ideal of unity. Bataille associated unity with a continuous element of being, which appeared as sovereignty, in contrast to a discontinuous element of being, which appeared as solidity. He associated sovereignty with an acknowledgement of the ambivalent and developing nature of the world, and so a transformative knowledge that promises "a voyage to the end of the possible of man." [16] He associated solidity, in contrast, with the attempts of bourgeois reason and orthodox science to postulate isolated and stable objects that then could be studied with detachment. According to Bataille, capitalism and solidity allow us to exist only as alienated and isolated beings within a homogenous, rational order devoid of activities such as festival, play, and sacrifice. In contrast, he wanted to promote both sovereignty and transformative knowledge by way of just such activities. He wanted to counter bourgeois reason with a new myth based on organic insights, a myth that would unite the individual with society by developing new possibilities for heterogeneity and new opportunities to abandon our selves to the sacred. He hoped for a new myth that would encourage us to suspend subjectivity by sacrificing self to other.

The constructive vision of Bataille and the other surrealists is perhaps at odds with one rationale for Dada's strategies. Dada adopted these strategies in no small measure because their situational and transitory qualities were supposed to make them immune to absorption within a totalizing bourgeois society. In so far as the surrealists tied such strategies to a constructive ideal that had determinate content—unity, sovereignty, transformative knowledge, sacrifice—they seemed to run the risk of having their ideal taken over by bourgeois society. To some extent, the surrealists tried to minimize this risk precisely by associating their visions of unity with sites beyond reason, such as myth, the irrational, and the unconscious. In addition they sometimes implied that their vision lacked all content so it could not be taken over. As Bataille explained, "we find the *human quality* not in some definite state but in the necessarily undecided battle of the one who refuses *the given*, whatever that may be, providing it is *the given*."[17] Elsewhere Bataille suggested that sovereignty was a type of unknowing or nonknowledge, a suggestion which echoes the ways in which other surrealists so often conceived of the marvelous. For Bataille, the sovereign moment consisted not only in the cancellation of bourgeois knowledge but also the suspension of any other knowledge; it consisted in the exhaustion of thought, the absence of meaning, silence. At one time he went so far as to relate his concepts of sovereignty and the sacred to a "new theology" which "has only the unknown as object."[18]

The avant-garde juggled the rival claims of strategies of resistance, which might be taken over by bourgeois society, and the avoidance of political decisions through an appeal to "the unknown" and even a kind of negative theology. These rival claims reappeared in the debate between Derrida and Foucault over the latter's history of madness. Derrida's complaint that Foucault could not reclaim an authentic madness without adopting a repressive metaphysics of presence echoes the avant-garde concern that if sites and strategies of resistance have content they can be taken over by bourgeois society. Foucault responded in a manner that echoed not only the surrealists but also, as we shall see, situationism.

When Derrida complained that Foucault's appeals to specific sites and strategies risked ascribing determinate content to them, Foucault replied that Derrida's retreat from such sites and strategies to a quasi-metaphysics neglected questions of power and politics. While Foucault accepted Derrida's suggestion that the very act of writing a history of madness entails the imposition of reason upon it, he nonetheless argued strongly against what he took to be Derrida's reduction of practices to texts. Foucault complained that when Derrida read texts so as to expose the conditions of possibility of language and thought as such, he failed to allow properly for their status as "events" located in particular relations of power. According to Foucault, Derrida's concern with textual traces neglects the extra-textual world of social relations. At least one commentator has claimed that Foucault himself shifted, around 1977, from an avant-garde position, which approached social and moral problems by way of a concern with language and attempts to go beyond its limits, to a position that approached language and reason by way of a concern with historical relations of power.[19] However, while there is little doubt that Foucault's position altered, we should not underestimate the extent to which avant-garde movements had concerned themselves with relations of power. We have seen that Dada and surrealism adopted sites and strategies with which to promote an unalienated alternative to bourgeois society. Furthermore, other avant-garde movements, notably the situationists, had distanced themselves from surrealism in a way that foreshadowed Foucault's response to Derrida: they had consciously focused their critical activities on social relations, not language.

The Situationist International was formed in 1957. Its members argued that their avant-garde predecessors had been too preoccupied with cultural values, when really a new culture could emerge only following "the triumph of the revolutionary movement."[20] They drew on Marxist themes in an attempt to overcome what they took to be the limitations of Dada and surrealism. Guy Debord gave the concept of the spectacle a prominent place in situationist theory.[21] The spectacle referred principally to the symbolic order of images and signs found in art, the media, and consumer society. Debord suggested that the alienation associated with capitalist production permeated the whole of bourgeois society. In his view, capitalist society embodied false concepts of labour and need such that people work and consume inauthentic commodities in processes that remove them from the immediate, playful world of true desire. The spectacle thus reduces individuals to passive observers whose only options are the inauthentic ones held out to them by the spectacle itself; while consumer society appears to offer numerous opportunities—goods, activities, and entertainments—it actually allows such things to appear only in the commodity form so people can not make an authentic choice—they can not choose the real. As Debord explained, "it is only inasmuch as individual reality *is not* that it is allowed to appear."[22]

Debord and other situtationists followed the avant-garde tradition in stressing the ubiquity and recuperative power of the spectacle. They ascribed to the spectacle the ability to absorb radical gestures: it could colonise subversive acts, turning them from fragments of authenticity into spectacles to be witnessed; it could remove their radical import, and even reproduce them as commodities and pre-patterned lifestyles. Equally, however, the situationists insisted, as had Dada and the surrealists, on the possibility of our advocating and even establishing an alternative, authentic society. They argued, for instance, that people always could find a point from which to oppose the spectacle since capitalism itself actually required people to have some awareness of the authentic reality that it distorted. Raoul Vaneigem even suggested that the spectacle was rapidly approaching a crisis from which a new, better society of radical subjectivity and true pleasure would at last emerge.[23]

The situationists defended the possibility of an authentic society in large part by tying alienation and recuperation to the process of commodification. In their view, if we just destroy the commodity form, we will allow the individual to have an unmediated relation to objects, and so we will thereby create an unalienated society characterized by total integration: they allowed that the resistance of the world still would generate divisions and challenges, but they added that people would confront these divisions and challenges directly, as opposed to through the alienated form of the commodity. Finally, the situationists argued, as had Dada and the surrealists, that the danger of recuperation meant that revolutionaries had to rely on spontaneous interventions of a situational nature to disrupt the spectacle. They hoped to attain glimpses of a truer reality by means of playful performances that bring fantasy into ordinary life, by means of transgressions that fragment bourgeois norms, and also by means of eruptions of the extraordinary in the everyday. In their view, the people who make such interventions thereby will begin to take direct control of their lives and so experience moments of authenticity, while those who witness such interventions might experience a shock that could loosen the hold of the spectacle upon them and so lead them to similar moments of authenticity.

POSTMODERN RADICALISM

Foucault's response to Derrida saw him promote avant-garde strategies by which to disrupt relations of power: he invoked Bataille's idea of transgression, and he associated his ideal of an aesthetics of existence with the example of Baudelaire.[24] The same can be said, moreover, of other postmodern radicals, including Baudrillard and Lyotard. Baudrillard drew, in his *For a Critique of the Political Economy of the Sign*, upon Debord's analysis of the impact of commodification on signification.[25] He later championed Bataille's notion of aesthetic excess for being able to avoid the structures it criticizes in a way Marxism cannot.[26] Lyotard explicitly defended an avant-garde aesthetic of the sublime.[27] Quite apart from these intellectual debts, postmodernists often had been involved in avant-garde organizations. Lyotard and Baudrillard were involved, alongside Debord, in *Socialisme ou Barbarie*, a journal that was associated with situationism.

Baudrillard, Foucault, and Lyotard continued to appeal to the sites and strategies that the avant-garde had tried to use in order to subvert bourgeois society. They continued to appeal to play and excess, the body and desire, and aesthetic self-creation and stylized transgression. To begin, the postmodern radicals followed the avant-garde in looking to the body and desire as sites of pleasure or authenticity that stand apart from bourgeois society and the patterns of subjectivity it defines for us. We have seen how

Barthes and Foucault tried to do so by sharply distinguishing the body from conscious subjectivity. Lyotard similarly rejected the idea of a natural self, while arguing that capitalism and instrumental reasoning construct egos that assert a reality principle and thereby thwart the flow of libidinal energy; he thereby introduced desire or libidinal energy as a site of unchannelled existence from which one might challenge bourgeois society.[28] The postmodern radicals could appeal to the body and desire as sites of resistance to domination only because they deprived them of all substantive content: after all, if the body had such content, it would constitute a subject, a determination of consciousness, which would involve its being in collusion with power.

This denial of substantive content also characterizes the appeals of the postmodern radicals to other avant-garde sites of resistance, such as the sublime. The postmodern radicals could appeal to these sites too only by suggesting that they are outside of discourse or consciousness and so lack any content that we might represent. Lyotard defined the sublime, for example, as that which "puts forward the unpresentable in presentation itself; that which denies the solace of good forms, the consensus of a taste which would make it possible to share collectively the nostalgia for the unattainable; that which searches for new presentations, not in order to enjoy them but in order to impart a stronger sense of the unpresentable."[29]

Postmodern radicals also reiterated avant-garde strategies for disrupting the spectacle while avoiding being absorbed by it. They too appealed to singularity, self-creation, and transgression. Sometimes the postmodern radicals associated subversion and even freedom with the singular or unrepeatable. Baudrillard evoked "the poetic singularity of the analysis," suggesting that only a singular event that remains outside the generalizing discourse of reason can avoid being integrated into the spectacle.[30] Lyotard similarly championed forms of knowledge that respect the singularity of an event rather than incorporating it within some general scheme. At other times the postmodern radicals suggested that aesthetic self-creation possesses an authenticity and power of subversion because its blatant artificiality is such a contrast to the veneer of naturalness with which bourgeois norms cloak themselves. Baudrillard wanted to "accentuate the false transparency of the world to spread a terroristic confusion about it, or the germs or viruses of a radical illusion—in other words, a radical disillusioning of the real."[31] He thought that we might unsettle the spectacle by an excessive and ridiculous embrace of it; we might push the system into a hyperlogic if we say, "you want us to consume—O.K., let's consume always more, and anything whatsoever; for any useless and absurd purpose."[32] At yet other times postmodern radicals advocated transgression of current limits while arguing that the content of these transgressions should vary with time and place. Foucault even suggested that Bataille's concept of transgression might act as the master-concept for a new era of the unthought. He wrote that transgression will "seem as decisive for our culture, as much a part of its soil, as the experience of contradiction was at an earlier time for dialectical thought."[33] Lyotard argued that the sublime and the just arise from perpetual transgressions that negate established norms. He wrote that justice "consists in working at the limits of what the rules permit, in order to invent new moves, perhaps new rules and therefore new games."[34]

Although Baudrillard and other postmodernists remained "faithful" to the sites and strategies of situationism, they came to think that its time was "past" for reasons which echo Derrida's critique of Foucault. The postmodern radicals complained that the situationists had never explained satisfactorily how we could possibly have any authentic experiences given the all-pervasive nature of the spectacle. They suspected that because representation always obscures reality, we cannot ever get behind the representations in order to identify "the real" or an authentic experience. Again, they suspected that if alienation is ubiquitous under the spectacle, then we cannot adopt a revolutionary standpoint that avoids entrapment in the spectacle or current relations of power. These suspicions appear to have inspired Lyotard's break with *Socialisme ou Barbarie* as early as 1964. Yet, despite this early appearance of such suspicions, they clearly gained piquancy from the impact of Derrida and, at least as importantly, from the events of May 1968. The idea that revolutionary groups protected their position from the disruptive voices of the rebels reinforced the suggestion that all theories of revolutionary praxis were merely more exercises of power rather than expressions of authenticity—theory seemed inevitably to quiet difference. Likewise, the idea that the rebels challenged hierarchies in sexual relations and football teams as well as industrial relations and politics reinforced the suggestion that the spectacle lacked a hidden, monolithic source—power seemed to function differently on the surface of various practices.

It was in the wake of May 1968, as well as Derrida's early work, that Foucault voiced the postmodern critique of situationism. He argued that situationism did not actually "liberate difference" so much as "guarantee that it [difference] will always be recuperated"; "you think you are seeing the subversion of the other declaring itself, but in secret, contradiction is working for the salvation of the identical."[35] Although the avant-garde emphasized the totalizing nature and recuperative power of bourgeois society, they continued to believe that it could be challenged and even overturned on behalf of a real, authentic alternative, perhaps a post-revolutionary society free of alienation. Postmodernists were emphatic in their rejection of the real so conceived. For them, there was only a transparent, superficial world of representation, modern consumer society, or power. For them, it did not make sense to appeal to an authentic reality beyond or beneath such things, nor even to describe such things as alienated in a way that would presuppose a contrast between them and a "real" world beyond or beneath them.

We already have encountered some of the ways in which Foucault expressed a rejection of the real and a related insistence that there is only the transparent surface of things. After he gave up on the possibility of recovering authentic or real experience in domains such as madness, he began to appeal to the body, defined in clear contrast to the subject. More generally, he began to develop his now famous concept of power as ubiquitous rather than a distortion beyond or beneath which we might glimpse the real. He appealed to Nietzsche's suggestion that "each society has its regime of truth, its 'general politics' of truth; that is, the types of discourse which it accepts and makes function as true."[36] In this view, truth and the subject are not sights of authenticity, but functions of a will to power. For Foucault, the ubiquity of power rendered fatuous attempts to locate its "condition of possibility" in "a central point" beyond or beneath it; rather, "states of power...are always local and unstable."[37]

Other postmodernists shared Foucault's rejection of the real. Baudrillard's concept of the hyperreal and Lyotard's of a terror of truth resemble his concept of a regime of power in that they depict the spectacle as all that there is. Baudrillard was somewhat ambiguous about the philosophical status of the real. He wrote about the ways in which objects function as pure signs in modern consumer societies, thereby leaving it unclear whether there have been (or might be) other societies in which the real is distinct from its representations. According to Baudrillard, the proliferation of signs has created a hyperreality devoid of real meaning and value: the world is an effect of the sign, for "the process of signification is, at bottom, nothing but a gigantic simulation model of meaning."[38] He argued that today there are no originals behind the constantly proliferating images; everything is just a copy of a copy, a simulation of a simulation, a representation of a representation. Baudrillard also suggested that the absence of originals behind the copies of copies undermines metaphors of depth and so concepts such as alienation. He rejected "the sign of alienation," and the "society of the spectacle," in favor of a postmodern perspective in which "there is no longer a scene [for] everything becomes inexorably transparent."[39]

Lyotard similarly defined the postmodern as an "incredulity towards metanarratives"—truths that underlie a civilization and purport to be universal.[40] He argued that all claims to knowledge are valid only within specific language-games that are tied to particular places and times. For him, all knowledge takes its validity from language-games that "define what has the right to be said and done in the culture in question," and that can be supported only by self-referential appeals to themselves.[41] Hence he concluded that any appeal to the real involves a terror of truth in which a particular narrative seeks to destroy others by claiming it is true. He asked radicals: "where do you criticise from? Don't you see that criticising is still knowing, knowing better? That the critical relation still falls within the sphere of knowledge, of realisation and thus of the assumption of power?"[42]

The postmodern radicalism of Baudrillard, Foucault, and Lyotard consisted to a notable degree of their appeals to sites and strategies long championed by the avant-garde. Postmodern radicalism takes from the avant-garde a concern to be absolutely modern (or postmodern) and yet to change the world (or perhaps the ways in which we talk about the world). Moreover, the relevant changes are still intended to take us away from the bourgeois subject, stable meanings, fixed forms, and the like, towards worlds and texts characterized by the playful and the erotic, the heterogeneous and the transgressive. However, the postmodern radicals also broke with the avant-garde in that they rejected the very idea of the real: they denied any possibility of a harmonious or unalienated society. Typically, they did so for reasons that echo Derrida's critique of structuralism; they take the very act of representation to be infused by things such as difference and power.

It seems to me that this postmodern radicalism confronts all sorts of problems because the avant-garde sites and strategies to which it remains attached make sense only in the context of that idea of the real that it repudiates. I have in mind here two aporias that are often said to bedevil postmodern radicals. The first aporia is that their rejection of the real leads them to challenge all claims to knowledge in a way that then precludes them properly justifying their own positions. If all reason is an illegitimate product of the spectacle, how can they defend their theories? Surely their promotion of self-creation and transgression, and their calls for constant novelty and blatant simulation, must be products of regimes of power/knowledge or particular language games just as much as must any other ethic? The second aporia is that their rejection of the real leads them to define subjectivity as produced by the spectacle in a way that precludes the possibility of the subject having any authentic experience. If the subject cannot break out of the spectacle, what is the point of transgression, self-creation, or constant novelty? Surely any apparent transgression or novelty actually must be a feature of the spectacle itself rather than a moment of authenticity or even of resistance? Once we recognize that postmodern radicalism exhibits a simultaneous debt to and distance from the avant-garde, we can grasp why it runs into these aporias. Because the postmodern radicals reject the real, they undermine the very avant-garde positions they continue to articulate. Because they reject the possibility of reason and freedom, they leave themselves devoid of reasons they might give us for adopting their theories and their ethics.

The polarity between a rejection of the real and an adherence to avant-garde sites and strategies also governs the most common reactions to postmodernism. On the one hand, there are radicals who retain a faith in the real, that is, something akin to the romantic ideal of harmony or the avant-garde ideal of an unalienated existence. From their radical perspective, postmodernism is a conservative doctrine tied to a narcissistic ethic at the expense of a proper concern with social and political reform.[43] On the other hand, there are those conservatives who deride radical ideas of a harmonious, unalienated existence as utopian. Like the postmodernists, they see difference and conflict as inherent within society. Unlike the postmodernists, however, they accept authority and hierarchy as essential to overcome difference, resolve conflict, and so create and maintain a precious social order. From their conservative perspective, postmodernism is a nihilistic doctrine that promotes a narcissistic hedonism and an irrationalist relativism to the neglect of a proper concern with social duty and intellectual standards.[44]

CONCLUSION

We can avoid the aporias that beset the postmodern radicals, and so pose new problems for their critics, only if we think through the implications that the rejection of the real has for the viability of appeals to avant-garde sites and strategies. By way of a conclusion, I want briefly to ask how we might do this. One way to broach this question is by exploring the implications of a rejection of the real for our concept of subjectivity. Postmodern radicals insisted on the location of the subject in a social world composed of things such as power-relations. They maintained that individuals are unable to have experiences, to reason, to adopt beliefs, and to act unaffected by social forces or structures. They thus rejected the very possibility of the unalienated subject held up as a constructive ideal by the avant-garde. In their view, the ways in which people experience the world necessarily depend on the action upon them of social forces such as power/knowledge, so they cannot have authentic or immediate experiences of the sort in which the avant-garde placed their faith. However, to deny that subjects can escape from all social influences is not to deny that they might be able to act creatively for reasons that make sense to them. A rejection of autonomy need not entail a rejection of agency. To the contrary, we must allow for such agency if only because we can not individuate beliefs or actions solely by reference to social contexts: because different people adopt different beliefs and perform different actions against the background of the same social context, there must be an undecided space in front of these structures where individuals decide what beliefs to hold and what actions to perform. Hence we might allow that the subject is an agent, though not an autonomous one. What is more, while a rejection of the ideal of autonomy would preclude our postulating any neutral or universal reason, an adoption of a concept of agency might enable us also to adopt a concept such as local or contextual reasoning; indeed a concern with consistency—a concern to organize one's beliefs in accord with one's own notion of best belief—can appear to be a necessary feature of all bodies of belief. We can allow that the subject is an agent who possesses a capacity for reasoning about a problem or belief within the context of the other beliefs she holds. In short, the postmodern radicals were so disillusioned with the real that they did not point out the more limited possibilities open to us: they focused so intensely on the impossibility of autonomy and universal reason that they barely allowed for the rather different possibilities of agency and local reasoning.[45]

Once we allow properly for agency and local reasoning, we might reconsider the viability of the avant-garde sites and strategies to which the postmodern radicals remained so attached. It seems to me, for example, that we should perhaps relocate the authentic realm not in the vestiges of an allegedly immediate experience, but in the possibility of choices based on local reasoning; we should broaden the concept of a desire so as to recognize that such choices might properly be based on any of a reason, desire, emotion, or need; we should renounce the odd privilege given to the choices associated with aesthetes; and we should cease to valorize transgression, since an authentic choice might be to participate in existing social organizations. At the very least, once we reject the real, we ought to question the avant-garde legacy that lurks within postmodern radicalism. An anti-foundationalist (perhaps postmodern) ethic could build instead on the possibilities of agency and local reasoning.

NOTES

1. J. Williamson, "An Interview with Jean Baudrillard," *Block* 15 (1989), 18.
2. J-F. Lyotard and J. Rogozinski, "The Thought Police," *Art and Text* 26 (1987), 30.
3. R. Barthes, *S/Z*, trans. R. Miller (London: Jonathan Cape, 1975).
4. R. Barthes, *The Pleasure of the Text*, trans. R. Miller (New York: Hill and Wang, 1975), 11–12.
5. R. Barthes, "Of What Use is an Intellectual?" in R. Barthes, *The Grain of the Voice: Interviews 1962–1980*, trans. L. Coverdale (London: Jonathan Cape, 1985), 276.
6. This is a point Barthes was particularly keen to make. The main source of his views is Barthes, *Pleasure*. There is also a useful discussion in R. Barthes, "The Adjective is the 'Statement of Desire'," *Grain*, 172–176.
7. M. Foucault, *Madness and Civilisation: A History of Insanity in the Age of Reason*, trans. Rol. Howard (London: Tavistock, 1965), xi.
8. J. Derrida, "Cogito and the History of Madness," in *Writing and Difference*, trans. A. Bass (London: Routledge and Kegan Paul, 1978).
9. M. Foucault, "My Body, This Paper, This Fire," *Oxford Literary Review* 4 (1979): 9–28.
10. M. Foucault, "Nietzsche, Genealogy, History," in *The Foucault Reader*, ed. P. Rabinow (Harmondsworth, UK: Penguin Books, 1984), 87–88.
11. M. Foucualt, "Body/Power," in *Power/Knowledge: Selected Interviews and Other Writings 1972–1977*, ed. C. Gordon (Brighton, U.K.: Harvester Press, 1980), 56.
12. Postmodern concepts of the body and desire clearly owe much to Freud and especially to the way Lacan read Freud. However, the way Lacan, and the postmodernists I am considering, read Freud, and so the content they gave to these concepts clearly owes much to the way Freud, Hegel, and other thinkers were brought together by Bataille and other surrealists during the 1930s and 40s.

13. M. Janco, "Dada at Two Speeds," in L. Lippard, ed., *Dadas on Art* (Englewood Cliffs, NJ: Prentice-Hall, 1971), 36.

14. H. Arp, "Dadaland," in Lippard, ed., *Dadas on Art*, 28.

15. A. Breton, "Second Manifesto of Surrealism," in *Manifestos of Surrealism* (Ann Arbor: University of Michigan Press, 1972), 123–124.

16. G. Bataille, *Inner Experience*, trans. L. Boldt (Albany: State University of New York Press, 1988), 7.

17. G. Bataille, *The Accursed Share, Vol. 2: Sovereignty*, trans. R. Hurley (New York: Zone Books, 1988), 343.

18. Bataille, *Inner Experience*, 102.

19. J. Rajchman, *Michel Foucault: The Freedom of Philosophy* (New York: Columbia University Press, 1985).

20. Canjuers and G. Debord, "Preliminaries Toward Defining a Unitary Revolutionary Programme," in K. Knabb, ed., *Situationist International Anthology* (Berkeley, CA: Bureau of Public Secrets, 1981), 309.

21. G. Debord, *The Society of the Spectacle* (Detroit: Black and Red, 1977). Later he suggested a sinister, shadowy group controlled the spectacle: G. Debord, *Comments on the Society of the Spectacle* (Sheffield, UK: Pirate, 1988).

22. Debord, *Society of the Spectacle*, #17.

23. R. Vaneigem, *The Revolution of Everyday Life*, trans. J. Fullerton and P. Siveking (London: Rising Free Collective, 1979).

24. M. Foucault, "A Preface to Transgression," in *Language, Counter-Memory, Practice* (Oxford: Basil Blackwell, 1977), 29–52; M. Foucault, "What is Enlightenment?" in *Foucault Reader*, 32–50.

25. J. Baudrillard, *For a Critique of the Political Economy of the Sign*, trans. C. Levin (St. Louis, MO: Telos Press, 1972).

26. J. Baudrillard, *The Mirror of Production* (St. Louis, MO: Telos Press, 1975).

27. J-F. Lyotard, "The Sublime and the Avant-Garde," *Art Forum* 22 (1984), 36–43.

28. J-F. Lyotard, *Libidinal Economy*, trans. I. Grant (Bloomington: Indiana University Press, 1993).

29. J-F. Lyotard, *The Postmodern Condition: A Report on Knowledge* (Minneapolis: University of Minnesota Press, 1984), 340.

30. J. Baudrillard, *The Perfect Crime*, trans. C. Turner (London: Verso, 1996), 103.

31. Ibid., 104.

32. J. Baudrillard, *In the Shadow of the Silent Majorities: or, the End of the Social and Other Essays* (New York: Semiotext(e), 1983), 46.

33. Foucault, "Preface to Transgression," 33. Also see M. Foucault, *The Order of Things: An Archaeology of the Human Sciences* (London: Tavistock Publishers, 1970), chap. 9.

34. J-F. Lyotard with J-L. Thébaud, *Just Gaming* (Minneapolis: University of Minnesota Press, 1985), 100.

35. M. Foucault, "Theatrum Philosophicum," *Critique* 26 (1970), 889.

36. M. Foucault, "Truth and Power," in *Power/Knowledge*, 131.

37. M. Foucault, *The History of Sexuality, Vol. 1: An Introduction*, trans. R. Hurley (New York: Pantheon Books, 1978), 93.

38. Baudrillard, *Political Economy of the Sign*, 91.

39. J. Baudrillard, *Fatal Strategies* (New York: Semiotext[e], 1990), 67.

40. Lyotard, *Postmodern Condition*, xxiv.

41. Ibid., 23.

42. J-F. Lyotard, "Adrift," in *Driftworks* (New York: Semiotext[e], 1984), 13.

43. See J. Habermas, *Philosophical Discourse of Modernity*; and, for a different example of the radical perspective, D. Kuspit, *The Cult of the Avant-Garde Artist* (Cambridge: Cambridge University Press, 1993).

44. See A. Bloom, *The Closing of the American Mind* (New York: Simon and Schuster, 1987); and, for a different example of the conservative perspective, D. Bell, *The Cultural Contradictions of Capitalism* (London: Heinemann, 1976).

45. Of course, there is considerable debate as to whether Foucault did belatedly try to allow for such agency in his final work, though if he did, it remains how this later work can be reconciled (if it can at all) with his earlier archaeologies and genealogies which seem so vehemently opposed to even limited forms of agency. For my own attempt to explore how Foucualt's work might appear if we tried to infuse it with a concept of agency see M. Bevir, "Foucault and Critique: Deploying Agency against Autonomy," *Political Theory* 27 (1999), 65–84.

7 Derrida's Engagement with Political Philosophy

Paul Patton

Opinion remains divided over the value of Derrida's contribution to political philosophy. Does his work provide important challenges to established ways of thinking about politics or does it amount to no more than hypercritical posturing that adds nothing to political thought? In part, the difficulty of answering this question may be attributed to local differences in the vocabulary, style and concerns of political philosophy. In Derrida's case, the difficulty is exacerbated by his apparent reluctance to engage with specifically political philosophy during the early part of his career. My aim in this chapter is, first, to replace Derrida's thought in its context of origin and to suggest how the transition from avoidance to engagement with political concepts might be understood in relation to developments in French thought during this period. Second, I will outline the different kinds of conceptual analysis undertaken during the period of so-called "affirmative deconstruction" since the mid-1980s, in order to clarify the nature of his engagement with political philosophy and specifically his analyses of democracy and "democracy to come." Finally, I will argue that there is more common ground than is often realized between his deconstructive analyses of democracy and some tendencies within contemporary liberal political thought. I conclude that both deconstructive and liberal normative approaches to political philosophy would benefit from further constructive engagement.

For much of the first two decades of deconstruction, Derrida did not write about politics or political concepts. In the absence of explicit connections between the conceptual politics of deconstruction and recognizably political issues or concepts, critics on both the left and right argued that it amounted to a form of nihilism, obscurantism and irrationalism that served no useful political purpose. He was accused of frivolity for his focus on questions of textual interpretation and for his apparent refusal to address real world political issues. Critics argued that his emphasis on *différance* and the undecidability of a-conceptual figures such as the *pharmakon*, supplement, mark or trace either led to indecision and a refusal to take sides or to a decisionism that rendered all political judgment arbitrary. The deconstruction of the accepted bases of moral or political judgment was widely perceived to be a purely negative procedure that provided no grounds for effective political action. Richard Wolin summarizes this criticism in the following terms: "since deconstruction qua political discourse seems to privilege the 'negative' moments of 'destabilization' and 'dismantling,' how might it counter the suspicion that it remains constitutionally incapable of fostering political solidarity: the democratic ideal of politics as an equitable and just framework for realizing collective goals and projects."[1]

Derrida's reluctance to engage with political concepts and issues began to evaporate towards the end of the 1970s. A lecture given at the University of Virginia in 1976 and subsequently published as "Declarations of Independence" presents itself as an experimental application to this exemplary political document of concepts and questions "that have been developed elsewhere on an apparently less political corpus."[2] A series of texts published during the 1980s show the evolution of his efforts to address political concepts, culminating in his assertion in "Force of Law" that the very idea of justice in contrast to law is bound up with the possibility of deconstruction.[3] Since then, he has developed detailed analyses of ethical and political concepts such as hospitality, forgiveness, friendship, equality, and democracy. He has written about Europe, the ideals of the Enlightenment and the changes underway in the international political system such as the prospects for a cosmopolitan global political order and the future of state sovereignty. He has also campaigned against apartheid, spoken out in defense of imprisoned intellectuals and writers and taken increasingly forceful positions on issues such as the treatment of illegal immigrants, the politics of reconciliation, the death penalty and the behavior of rogue states.

In 1993, in the face of the widespread belief in the death of Marxism as a political force, he aligned deconstruction with a radicalization of the spirit of Marxism and advocated a "New International" to extend the operation of international law to include social and economic conditions of life within sovereign states while simultaneously pursuing a radical critique of "the state of international law, the concepts of State and nation."[4] In the immediate aftermath of September 11, 2001, Derrida recorded a long interview in which he gave his most overtly political definition of the present task of philosophy: to analyze and draw "the practical and effective consequences of the relationship between our philosophical heritage and the structure of the still dominant juridico-political system that is so clearly undergoing mutation."[5]

Derrida has always resisted the suggestion that there was a political or an ethical turn in his work, most recently in *Rogues* where he insisted that "there never was in the 1980s or 1990s, as has sometimes been claimed, a *political turn* or an *ethical turn* in 'deconstruction,' at least not as I experience it. The thinking of the political has always been a thinking of différance and the thinking of différance always a thinking *of* the political."[6] His denial that there is any fundamental theoretical discontinuity between the ontological and stylistic concerns of his early work and the increasingly political focus of his later work is endorsed by many commentators.

Richard Kearney suggests that the interest in Levinas's ethics of alterity that had been present in Derrida's work from the outset became a renewed focus during the 1980s at the expense of his earlier preoccupation with the deconstruction of metaphysics.[7] John Caputo agrees that there is nothing like a Derrida I and a Derrida II but rather "a progression in which this originally ethical and political motif in his work, deeply Levinasian in tone, has worked its way more and more to the front of his concerns in the writings of the 1980s and 1990s."[8] In this volume, Peter Gordon points to the anti-authoritarian "emancipatory ideal" that animated even Derrida's earliest work on Husserl and identifies some of the politically motivated terminology in those essays.[9]

The latter part of the remark from *Rogues* cited above raises at least as many questions as it answers. What does the thinking of the political mean for Derrida? What is the thinking of *différance*? What is the relation between the thinking of the political and the thinking of *différance*? These questions are further complicated by the apparent distinction, marked by italicization, between a genitive "of" in "thinking of the political" and "of *différance*," and a nominative "of" in "thinking *of* the political." On one reading, Derrida says here that political thinking has always been differential thinking, in the double sense implied by the concept of *différance* and that, for this reason, his efforts to think *différance* were also efforts to think the political. In other words, the space of *différance* is also, or in some sense the same as, the space of the political. I will return to this claim in discussing the intellectual strategy of Derrida's analyses of political concepts below.

Over and above these questions of ethico-political and conceptual continuity between Derrida's earlier and later work, there remains the historical question of the external circumstances that allowed or impelled him to take up more overtly political questions during the 1980s. One obvious candidate is the political storm that erupted around the political affiliations of deconstruction, especially its close engagement with the philosophy of Heidegger at the end of the 1980s. Ferry and Renaut's *La Pensée 68*, published in 1986, argued that the Heideggerian influenced anti-humanism of Derrida and others of his generation was incapable of providing a coherent account of the "the status of subjectivity in a democracy."[10] The following year saw the publication of Farias's *Heidegger et le nazisme* and beginnings of "the Heidegger affair," as well as the discovery of Paul De Man's wartime writings for a Nazi controlled Belgian newspaper.[11] Some commentators suggest that the increasingly prominent role assumed by questions of justice and the concept of democracy in his writings may be seen as a response to successive attempts to tarnish deconstruction by association with De Man and Heidegger. John McCormick suggests that Derrida's "Force of Law" is an apologia cast in the mould of the trial of Socrates and a response to critics in the midst of the attacks on deconstruction provoked by the De Man affair.[12] Geoffrey Bennington concurs that "it is perhaps not coincidental that most of Derrida's more explicit political reflections have appeared since that time."[13]

While there is no denying Derrida's involvement in the polemics surrounding these affairs, it seems unnecessarily reductive to identify them as the cause of the undoubted shifts of emphasis and tone in his work during this period. On the one hand, there is evidence to suggest a longstanding commitment to democratic politics. In an interview with Michael Sprinker recorded in 1989, Derrida explained his earlier reluctance to join the French Communist Party by reference to its Stalinism and its incompatibility with "the democratic left to which I have always wished to remain loyal."[14] On the other hand, his increasing engagement in public political activity pre-dates the Heidegger and De Man affairs. A recent biography links this increased activity to the election of the French socialist government in 1981.[15] Later that year, Derrida was arrested in Prague in the course of efforts to support dissident Czech intellectuals. He served as the first elected director of the *Collège Internationale de Philosophie* in 1983. He wrote for an exhibition of "Art Against Apartheid" and published an essay in praise of Nelson Mandela's admiration for the rule of law, parliamentary democracy and its potential to give birth to "a society without class and without private property."[16] His seminars at the EHESS during this decade were often devoted to political thinkers and political questions. The work undertaken for these seminars provided the material for his political philosophical texts of the early 1990s: *Specters of Marx* and *Politics of Friendship*. In the light of this evidence, perhaps the historical question to be asked is not so much what impelled Derrida to engage with political philosophical issues at this point in his career, but rather what prevented him from doing so much earlier. Perhaps the reasons for his earlier reticence to engage with political philosophy should be sought in his relationship with the French intellectual left and the local context in which his thought developed during the 1960s.

DECONSTRUCTION AND MARXISM

The question of the politics of deconstruction accompanied Derrida's work from its beginnings. He always endorsed the view, shared by many French philosophers of his generation, that philosophy is by nature a form of political activity.[17] Thus, in response to leftist critics in 1971, he insisted that deconstruction "is not *neutral*. It *intervenes*."[18] In common with others on the intellectual left during this period, he sought to intervene on the side of difference against identity and in favor of openness against closure. He intervened against dogmatism in whatever field by exposing the limits of all attempts to provide secure metaphysical foundations or final vocabularies. The movement of *différance* and the permanent possibility of citation or iteration served to ensure that the possibility of reinterpretation and transformation within established institutions of thought and society always remained open.

In the intellectual atmosphere that prevailed in France during the latter half of the twentieth century, the question of the politics of any given project inevitably turned around its relationship to Marxism. This was especially so during the highly politicized decades immediately before and after 1968.[19] Explicit or implicit references to Marx appeared in several of Derrida's key texts from the 1960s and 1970s.[20] Throughout much of this period, he worked at one of the most important intellectual institutions of French Marxism, the *École Normale Supérieure* in Paris, where he had been a student from 1952 until 1956. In 1964, he returned as a director of study in philosophy and remained there for twenty years before moving to the *École des Hautes Études en Sciences Sociales* in 1984. He taught alongside Althusser during the years in which the seminars that gave rise to *For Marx* and *Reading Capital* dominated the intellectual life of the *École Normale*. He was familiar with many of those involved in these seminars and with the issues raised by their efforts to redefine Marx's philosophy and his materialist theory of history. Nevertheless, despite this proximity and despite his own commitment to the political left, he remained apart from the ensuing debates. Throughout this period, he refrained from raising deconstructive questions about Marxism, while at the same time insisting on the importance of Marxism, the heterogeneity of Marx's own texts and the necessity of one day subjecting them to the kind of critical reading that he willingly pursued in relation to other philosophies.[21]

In his 1989 interview with Sprinker, Derrida elaborates on some of his concerns about the Althusserian reading of Marx according to which an "epistemological break" separated the early writings from the anti-humanist problematic that emerged in his scientific analyses of capital. He explains that his deep involvement in the philosophies of Husserl and Heidegger during the 1960s raised questions about the historical character of the concepts of objectivity, scientificity and history on which Althusser and his followers relied.[22] While some of these concerns were implicitly raised by Althusserian epistemology, they were not pursued with sufficient radicality or rigor: "I believed, and I still believe now, that one must pose many historical or 'historial' questions about the idea of theory, about the idea of objectivity. Where does it come from? How is objectivity's value constituted? How is theory's order or authority constituted? How did theory become prevalent in the history of European philosophy? etc. And I did not see these genealogical questions, so to speak, on science, objectivity, etc. being posed by the Althusserian discourse, or at least not in a manner that seemed satisfactory to me."[23] In hindsight, Derrida saw the lack of attention to the philosophical history of key concepts such as "history," "ideology," "production" and the thesis of determination "in the last instance" as both a philosophical and political weakness of the Althusserian project.[24]

However, he refrained from raising such questions in public for reasons that were both micropolitical and macropolitical. Within the cloistered atmosphere of the *École Normale Supérieure*, the intellectual hegemony of the Althusserians was accompanied by an element of intimidation. While in the public arena, any criticism of their efforts to challenge the intellectual orthodoxy of the Communist Party might have played into the hands of its Stalinist leadership.[25]

Not until the publication of *Specters of Marx* in 1993 did he devote an entire essay to the legacy of Marxism. *Specters* remained faithful to his earlier philosophical reticence, by pursuing a deconstructive analysis of Marx's ambivalent relationship to the theme of spectrality that haunts his writing, and by maintaining a deconstructive skepticism with regard to fundamental concepts of his philosophy of history such as labour, mode of production and social class. However, in the intervening years much had changed with respect to the political and intellectual status of Marxism in France and in the world: the collapse of Eastern European socialism and the reunification of Germany appeared to many to signal the death of Marxism as a political force. Derrida freely admitted the appeal of being out of step with the times in speaking up for Marxism.[26] In addition, he suggested that fidelity to the spirit of Marxism was a responsibility especially incumbent on those who, over the preceding decades, had endeavored both to resist the hegemony of Marxist dogma and to challenge all forms of reaction or conservatism in politics or in philosophy.[27] In full awareness of the checkered history that Marxism has inspired and conscious of the contradiction at the heart of the injunction to remain faithful to the heritage of a revolutionary tradition, he insisted that his primary concern was to reiterate his longstanding commitment to a principle of "radical and interminable critique" that can also be found in Marx. Deconstruction, he insisted, "would have been impossible and unthinkable in a pre-Marxist space. Deconstruction has never had any sense or interest, in my view at least, except as a radicalization, which is to say also *in the tradition* of a certain Marxism, in a certain *spirit of Marxism*."[28]

THE RECONCEPTUALIZATION OF POLITICS

While Derrida often insisted that there had always been a moral and political dimension to his work, on other occasions, notably in his 1989 interview with Sprinker, he recognized that it was "too easy an answer" to say that deconstruction has always been a political enterprise.[29] He went on to suggest that an articulation between deconstruction and politics "must imply a radical re-elaboration of the concept of politics in general circulation."[30] By the "re-elaboration" of accepted ways of understanding politics he does not mean the invention of a wholly new concept but rather the reworking of existing concepts or "philosophemes" in terms of which politics has been thought within the European tradition. In the essays devoted to political concepts, he pursues two distinct intellectual strategies for transforming established ways of thinking about politics. The first undertakes genea-logical enquiries into the origins of a given concept, its history, interpreta-tions, and the interconnections it has to other concepts or philosophemes, in order to identify elements of the present concept that we might want to reconsider or even abandon altogether. The second involves a redescription of existing concepts, which reproduces in each case a distinction between a contingent or conditioned form of the concept and an absolute or uncondi-tioned form. Let us consider each of these strategies in turn.

In the interview cited above, Derrida goes on to suggest that, in order to achieve the re-elaboration of our understanding of politics, it would be necessary to undertake "a series of genealogical deconstructions of par-ticular philosophemes such as democracy and friendship."[31] Democracy and friendship were the topics of his 1989 seminar, which he describes as oriented towards a "deconstruction of what is called the *given concept of democracy*" and the elaboration of an understanding of democracy "for which the current concepts that serve to define democracy are insuf-ficient."[32] In similar fashion, his discussion of law and justice in "Force of Law" alluded to the need for an historical genealogy of different concepts of law, right, justice and the manner in which these are bound up with other concepts such as responsibility and the network of concepts related to this: property, intentionality, will, freedom, conscience, consciousness and so on.[33] The purpose of such genealogical enquiries into the origins, history, interpretations and interconnections that a given concept has to other concepts or philosophemes is to identify elements that we might want to reconsider or even abandon altogether.

Derrida undertook a partial genealogy of the concept of democracy in the book that resulted from his 1989 seminar, *Politics of Friendship*. On one level, it is not democracy but friendship that appears to be the primary concern. He retraces the long history of citation of the remark attributed to Aristotle, "O my friends, there is no friend," from Diogenes Laertius, Florian, Montaigne, Kant and Nietzsche to Blanchot. At the end of a series of meditations on the treatment of friendship in the works of these writ-ers, he reveals the syntactic ambiguity of the phrase, not in order to cor-rect the successive misinterpretations of its meaning but to demonstrate the principle of iterability according to which sentences are always inter-preted in a given context but also, by virtue of their status as sentences, endowed with the capacity to break with a given context and be reinscribed in new contexts. On another level, the text is centrally concerned with the concept of democracy and its relation, throughout the history of political philosophy, to friendship and the network of related concepts such as kin, family, masculinity, love and enmity or hostility. Derrida takes his point of departure from Aristotle's characterization of democracy as a form of association modeled on the friendship between brothers. He analyses the aporia contained in the concept of friendship in order to demonstrate that the same tensions contaminate and delimit our inherited concept of democracy: tensions between individuality and universality, between inclusion and exclusion, and between a social or civic relationship and a naturalized, ethnocentric or familial one. His point is not simply to criticize much less to abandon the democratic tradition but to open up the possibility of a different way of understanding this peculiar manner of living together with others. In this manner, he asks whether it might be possible to envisage a form of democracy finally and completely dissociated from all the historical residues of fraternal friendship that have excluded women and made it an association of men: "is it possible to think and to implement democracy, that which would keep the old name 'democracy', while uprooting from it all those figures of friendship (philosophical and religious) which prescribe fraternity: the family and the androcentric ethnic group? Is it possible, in assuming a certain faithful memory of democratic reason and reason *tout court*...not to found, where it is no longer a matter of *founding*, but to open out to the future, or rather to the 'to come', of a certain democracy?"[34]

Derrida's second intellectual strategy for transforming established ways of thinking about politics involves the redescription of existing concepts in order to distinguish between a contingent or conditioned form of the concept and an absolute or unconditioned form. In "Psyche: Invention of the Other," first presented as a series of lectures in 1984, he addressed the widespread criticism of his work by asking in what sense can the movement of deconstruction, "far from being limited to the negative or destructuring forms that are often naively attributed to it, be inventive in itself, or at least be the signal of an inventiveness at work in a sociohistorical field?"[35] While his unequivocal answer was that deconstruction "is inventive or it is nothing at all," he immediately added that, in order for this to be true, deconstruction must call into question the traditional concept of invention.[36] The manner in which it does so establishes a pattern that will be repeated throughout his subsequent analyses of political concepts. Traditionally, an invention involved the coming about of something new, something that would be "other" to what has gone before. In order for an invention to be recognized as such it must be capable of being received in accordance with the rules and procedures of some pre-existing practice or institution. It follows that an invention would not break entirely with existing institutions, laws or procedures but would only make explicit that which was already possible within "the economy of the same."[37] On this basis, he argued, an invention "would be in conformity with its concept...only insofar as, paradoxically, invention invents nothing, when in invention the other does not come."[38] But this appears to contradict other elements of the concept of invention, namely that it should break with existing institutional procedures or that it should involve the advent of something truly "other." From this perspective, an invention properly so called appears to require the coming about of something that did not fall within the existing space of the possible, something that, strictly speaking, therefore would be impossible. Derrida calls this "absolute" or "pure" invention and affirms that it is in this sense that he wants to say that deconstruction is inventive. Deconstructive "invention" serves a political function to the extent that it assists in opening up the present in order to "let the other come."[39]

In other writings since the 1980s, he offers parallel analyses of concepts of the gift, justice, responsible decision, democracy and the cosmopolitan right of hospitality. For example, hospitality as it is practiced in particular contexts is always conditional in the sense that it is offered to certain determinate others, endowed with a particular social status and subject to certain reciprocal duties in relation to the rights of the host. But since the conditional practice of hospitality derives its meaning from a concept of absolute or unconditional hospitality—which would welcome the other in the absence of any conditions such as knowledge of name, status or provenance, and without any restrictions with regard to their movements or behavior while in the domain of the host—it is always possible to criticize the existing conditional forms by reference to the unconditional.[40] In each case, affirmative deconstruction invents or reinvents the structure of the distinction between two poles or ways of understanding the concept in question in order to argue, first, that the difference between these two poles is irreducible, and second, that the ever-present possibility of invention, reconfiguration or transformation in our existing, historically conditioned and contingent ways of understanding the phenomenon in question is guaranteed by the existence of the pure or absolute form of the concept.

In this manner, "Force of Law" contrasts law and justice in order to argue that the law is deconstructible precisely by reference to the unconditioned concept of justice. Derrida's point is not that the unconditioned concept provides extra-legal, transcendent, or mystical content to an idea of justice as such. On the contrary, he argues that the concept of justice is inherently aporetic or "impossible" because it includes contradictory demands. For example, justice requires both that we address the specificity of a particular case and that we treat all cases equally in conformity with a universal law. It requires that we deliberate and calculate the merits of a particular case in accordance with the relevant principles *and* that we put an arbitrary end to such deliberation by making a decision. It follows that a just act or decision will unavoidably pass through a moment of indetermination or "undecidability," but equally that it is only by means of its determination in particular acts, decisions or laws that justice is ever realized. Finally, it follows that the irreducible gap between justice and law is what calls for decision in particular cases, but also what enables us to criticize particular decisions or particular laws as unjust and in need of reform.

In these terms, for example, he suggests that we can "inspire" new forms of forgiveness by reference to the paradoxical idea of the unforgivable or that the idea of unconditional hospitality underpins the possibility of improvement or progress in the existing conditional forms of welcome extended to foreigners: "It is a question of knowing how to transform and improve the law, and of knowing if this improvement is possible within an historical space which takes place *between* the Law of an unconditional hospitality, offered *a priori* to every other, to all newcomers, *whoever they may be*, and *the* conditional laws of a right to hospitality, without which *The* unconditional Law of hospitality would be in danger of remaining a pious and irresponsible desire, without form and without potency, and even of being perverted at any moment."[41] Since the same irreducible gap opens up in each case between the conditioned and unconditioned form of other normative concepts, there is always scope for political negotiation between these two poles. It is because changes in the actual institutional forms of the political virtue in question always take place within the differential space between the conditional and the unconditional that Derrida can say that the thinking of *différance* was always a thinking of the political.

Whenever the question of the purpose or the politics of deconstruction is raised, Derrida points to the undesirability of having a "good conscience" about established ways of acting and thinking.[42] In other words, he points to the desirability of being willing to question and challenge what is currently accepted as self-evident in our ways of thinking and acting, while at the same time refusing to specify how we should think or act otherwise. In *Specters of Marx*, he describes this as a form of critique that "belongs to the movement of an experience open to the absolute future of what is coming."[43] In this respect, his deconstructive analyses of political concepts resemble the open-ended critical strategy found in other post-structuralist thinkers such as Foucault and Deleuze and Guattari.[44] Like them, he wants to provide reasons for thinking that criticism of the present is not only possible but desirable, but in a way that does not rely on some implicit teleological or utopian vision of the future. Formulating the different figures of the unconditioned or "undeconstructible" is one way to insist upon the relation to an open but non-teleological future.

DEMOCRACY TO COME

Derrida's 2001 interview, "Autoimmunity: Real and Symbolic Suicides," along with the two essays published in *Rogues*, provides the most detailed account of what he considers to be the most important questions in contemporary political philosophy, namely the nature of democracy in domestic as well as international arenas and its connection with both the sovereignty of the responsible individual and that of the state. In these essays, he pursues the dual strategy outlined above of investigating the history of the concept of democracy and drawing a distinction between its past and present forms and its potential future. His distinction between actual democracies and a "democracy to come" shares many of the characteristics of his earlier contrasts between conditioned and unconditioned concepts of hospitality, forgiveness, and so on. His excursions into the history of philosophical characterizations of democracy, from Plato and Aristotle to Rousseau and Tocqueville, serve to highlight the complex and contradictory character of the concept that we have inherited from this tradition.

Towards the end of the longest essay in *Rogues*, "The Reason of the Strongest (Are there Rogue States?)," Derrida revisits the various contexts in which he has employed the term "democracy to come" in order to summarize and clarify the distinguishing features of this aporetic concept. First, he points out that "democracy to come" does not refer to a determinate future form of democracy because the "to come" in this phrase does not refer to a future that will one day become present but to a structural future that will never be actualized in any present. Rather than a future present it refers to the absolute future of pure invention, the unforeseeable and wholly other. "Democracy to come" is not something that is in principle possible yet deferred but rather of the order of the "im-possible." For this reason, it is not a regulative Idea, either in the strict Kantian sense or in the less strict but common sense of the term. It does not belong to the architectonic and conceptual apparatus that sustains Kant's concept of regulative as opposed to constitutive Ideas of Reason. Nor does it regulate in the sense of providing a rule to be followed or a single, consistent set of norms to be applied.[45]

Second, "democracy to come" does not refer to a determinate form of democracy because of the complexity of the process by which we derive our contemporary concept of democracy from the historical tradition. We "inherit" ideas of democracy from that tradition, but this is always selective and involves rejecting as well as endorsing aspects of the past. Since the history of democratic thought is already riven by tensions and contradictions, it is not surprising that the possible futures of democracy should involve paradox. The contradictory demands at the heart of the received concept of democracy include the tension between the sovereign power or force of the people and the absence of force signified by the rule of law. This points to the aporia between force and law already discussed in "Force of Law." In addition, there is the tension between the incalculable singularity of the individual and the calculable, exchangeable equality of all citizens, and that between democracy's commitment to inclusivity and to exclusivity. The latter tension emerges in political argument over who the people are who make up the sovereign and the conditions by which membership is determined: "One will never be able to 'prove' that there is more democracy in granting or in refusing the right to vote to immigrants."[46]

Finally, there is the aporia that in its specific form depends on the place of freedom in a democracy: "must a democracy leave free and in a position to exercise power those who risk mounting an assault on democratic freedoms."[47] A democratic state may either allow enemies of democracy to seize power by democratic means or, alternatively, it may seek to prevent this by interrupting or suspending democratic procedures. Either way the outcome is dangerous for democracy. In its general form, Derrida suggests that this aporia amounts to the susceptibility of democracy to the logic of autoimmunity, by which he means a body's suppression of the very immune system which protects it against internal or external threats.[48] The suspension of democratic procedures to protect democracy or the suspension of civil liberties to protect the freedom of citizens are examples of this logic of autoimmunity in the political sphere.

In addition to these negative determinations of the concept, there are a number of ways in which "democracy to come" is defined positively. Foremost among these is the manner in which, like a promise already uttered in the past, it intervenes in or structures the action of agents in the present by reference to a future event. In this sense, as Derrida suggested in *The Other Heading*, and as he reiterates in *Rogues*, "democracy to come" must have "the structure of a promise—*and thus the memory of that which carries the future, the to-come, here and now.*"[49] As this reference to the here and now suggests, the concept of "democracy to come" is supposed to play an immediate and active role in the present. It calls for and sustains "a militant and interminable political critique."[50] In effect, the phrase is not simply constative but also performative: it functions both as an open-ended descriptive function and as an imperative or a demand for more democracy. Here, as in *Specters of Marx* and *Politics of Friendship*, "democracy to come" is linked to justice, as opposed to law, in the sense that justice orients the improvement of the law.[51] In turn, as in the case of the appeal to unconditioned concepts of hospitality, forgiveness or gift, the concept of "democracy to come" opens up a space for the renegotiation or reconfiguration of present determinate forms of democracy. In this manner, Derrida relies on the concept of "democracy to come" to provide a reason to think that existing democracies or so-called democracies "remain inadequate to the democratic demand."[52]

DECONSTRUCTION, COSMOPOLITANISM, AND CONTEMPORARY LIBERALISM

Derrida's discussion of "democracy to come" overlaps with some themes of contemporary cosmopolitan political theory. Consider, for example, the manner in which his contrast between existing democracies and democracy to come converges with Archibugi's understanding of democracy as a process towards an unattained and unattainable ideal: "As a journey, the democratic process is not only unfinished but also endless."[53] It is true that, unlike many liberal critics of present forms of intra- and inter-state democracy, Derrida draws attention to the aporetic character of the concept, but like them he speaks and writes throughout as a friend of democracy. A striking example of this in *Rogues* occurs in his discussion of the Islamic other to liberal democracy when he affirms the need to join forces with those in the Islamic world who fight for "the secularization of the political" and for an interpretation of the Koranic heritage that privileges the "democratic virtualities" it contains.[54] A further feature in common with contemporary liberal cosmopolitanism is the manner in which, from *Specters of Marx* onwards, Derrida ties the future of democracy to the question of international order. In *Rogues* he suggests that the question of an international, interstate or trans-state democracy is "one of the possible horizons of the expression 'democracy to come.'"[55] On this issue, he clearly aligns himself with those who advocate a more democratic international order that would encompass reform of the United Nations and in particular the role of the Security Council: "To put it in the most cut and dried terms, I would say that the fate of the democracy to come, in its relation to world order, depends on what will become of this strange and supposedly all-powerful institution called the Security Council."[56]

Other features of Derrida's genealogical and analytic approach to political concepts resonate with Richard Rorty's "historicist and antiuniversalist" version of political liberalism.[57] Rorty famously argued that deconstruction has no bearing on the public political culture of contemporary liberal democracies and that its significance is confined to the private pursuit of self-transformation. He condemned the entire tradition that extends from Hegel and Nietzsche to Foucault and Derrida as "largely irrelevant to public life and to political questions."[58] Not only is this claim impossible to sustain in the light of Derrida's work since the 1980s, but in fact there is considerable common ground between them. Derrida is an ironist in the sense that Rorty uses the term to differentiate himself from metaphysicians who believe that there are real essences and an intrinsic nature of things, which it is the task of philosophy to discover.[59] Rorty's ironists are nominalists who believe that nothing has an intrinsic nature or real essence. Derrida's concept of democracy is ironic in precisely this sense. He denies that there is, even in the Greek tradition from which it derives, "a proper, stable, and univocal meaning of the democratic itself...perhaps it is a question here of an essence without essence."[60] Rawls's political liberalism is similarly ironic in the sense that it is committed to both the plurality of reasonable conceptions of the good and their peaceful cohabitation in a well-ordered society on the basis of practical rather than theoretical reason. The truth or falsity of moral or political judgments is not at issue.

Like Rorty and the later Rawls, Derrida is an historicist in the sense that he affirms the essential historicity of the concept, precisely because there is no essence or idea (*eidos*) of democracy.[61] In common with Rorty's ironist he believes that all our descriptions of events and states of affairs are couched in particular vocabularies that are subject to change. As such, the ironist is aware of the contingency of his or her own "final vocabulary" and also aware that such vocabularies can neither be justified nor refuted by argument but only replaced by other vocabularies. With reference to his discussion of the issue of the name of democracy in *Politics of Friendship*, he raises the paradoxical prospect of one day abandoning the name of democracy, albeit in the name of features of democracy that we have inherited from the tradition.[62] Like Rorty, Derrida abandons the task of providing philosophical foundations for liberal democratic political concepts. As we noted above, he has always insisted that deconstruction is pragmatic in the sense that it seeks to intervene in order to change things or at least to intensify transformations already underway.[63] He and Rorty part company, it is true, over the role that philosophy can play in relation to these social and political transformations. Rorty prefers the efforts of artists and journalists to change the sensibilities of people, thereby awakening them to hitherto unnoticed or unappreciated harms, violations of right or limitations of democratic principles. Artists and journalists are better equipped than philosophers to ensure that liberal democratic institutions are as widely entrenched and as inclusive as possible.[64] While Derrida insists that the kinds of conceptual analysis he undertakes can play a positive role, Rorty is skeptical to the point of suggesting that "Western social and political thought may have had the last *conceptual* revolution it needs."[65]

If the points of convergence between Derrida's way of thinking about democracy and aspects of contemporary "postmodern" liberalism in the English-speaking world suggest the possibility of dialogue between them, their differences suggest that such engagement would be fruitful for both traditions. Derrida's aporetic analysis of democracy and his willingness to question fundamental presuppositions of its current forms undoubtedly serve to differentiate him from less critical and more complacent versions of liberalism. However, it also leaves a number of questions unanswered. As he has admitted, there is a kind of formalism about his aporetic analysis that leaves it somewhat disengaged from both the objects of political concern and the terms in which criticism can effectively engage with present institutions, policies and practices of government.[66] For example, when he invokes the critical function of "democracy to come" and suggests that it underwrites the criticism of "what remains inadequate to the democratic ideal," he refers to the plight of those who suffer from "malnutrition, disease and humiliation" and who are deprived not only of bread and water but also equality, freedom and "the rights of all."[67] In doing so, he appeals to certain determinate conceptions of equality, rights and entitlement, but does not spell out how these relate to what he has elsewhere characterized as the variable and paradoxical resources of the democratic tradition. What precisely is the content of the "democratic demand" that is not met by the condition of those who suffer and how is it anchored in the democratic tradition? Given the historicity and variability of the concept, what in the present allows us to present it as a "demand" of the democratic ideal? There is a rich and wide-ranging debate within contemporary liberal political theory over the basis of rights, kinds of equality and their relationship to the concept of democracy that Derrida does not mention much less engage. The interest and force of his political-conceptual analyses would be enhanced if he had done so.

Further questions are raised by the manner in which his aporetic analysis of democracy relies on a rather simple and anachronistic concept of democracy. There is nothing extraordinary in the suggestion that the contemporary form and concept of democracy might be transformed in the future, as it has been in the past. The essential lack of essence and the resultant historicity of the concept already implies this possibility. Derrida is not the first philosopher to draw attention to the fact that, at least in its pure form, democracy includes the principle that all principles of public reason, including this one, are open to criticism: "Democracy is the only system, the only constitutional paradigm, in which, in principle, one has or assumes the right to criticize everything publicly, including the idea of democracy, its concept, its history, and its name."[68] This feature of unqualified democracy gives rise to the aporia implied in the logic of autoimmunity. It amounts to the potentially suicidal character of democracy. Derrida attributes this antinomy to the role of freedom in the concept of democracy, in particular as this was defined by Aristotle. He represents Aristotle's definition in terms of two pairs of concepts: freedom and equality, and equality of number as opposed to equality of worth. Democracy is founded upon the freedom of individuals to think and act as they choose. This freedom extends to all, so that no individual's choices are more worthy than another's. In turn, this implies that the governing principle is equality of number: the decision of the majority is the final arbiter of justice. But this acceptance of equality of number rather than worth leads to the destruction of both equality and freedom, since it leaves open the possibility that an anti-democratic party might attain the majority. In this manner, "In the name of one couple, the couple made up of freedom and equality, one agrees to a law of numbers (equality according to number) that ends up destroying both couples; both the couple made up of the two equalities (equality according to worth and equality according to number) and the couple equality-freedom."[69]

This antinomy arguably exposes a limitation of Derrida's discussion as much as it does of the concept of democracy. In order to formalize the aporia of autoimmunity, he relies on a very limited textual base and an anachronistic concept of democracy by contemporary standards. Had he taken into account more recent theorists of liberal democracy, he would have confronted a more complex axiomatic in which considerations of value do play an important role. For many modern theorists, the value of freedom is considered to set limits to the operation of the democratic principle of equality of number. The freedom of each is of such value that neither individuals nor the numerical majority are allowed to infringe upon it. This idea is embodied in Kant's universal principle of public right, in Mill's harm principle and in the first principle of Rawls's theory of justice. In each case the freedom of each to live as he or she chooses does not extend to impinging on the freedom of others to do likewise. In effect, these philosophers add further axioms to those set down in Aristotle's definition, thereby providing more complex concepts of democratic freedom and justice. They privilege equality of worth (the value of freedom for each member of the society) over equality of number (the value of majority decision). This kind of autolimitation on the freedom enjoyed in democratic society serves to immunize liberal democracy against those forms of exercise of freedom that might undermine the freedom of others. However, it leaves open the question of permissible responses to breaches of this principle, some of which might undermine that very freedom. It would be helpful to show how the logic of autoimmunity can arise in these more complex axiomatizations of liberal democracy.

These limitations show the importance of extending the textual base of Derrida's arguments, in order to bring his conceptual analyses to bear on a broader range of contemporary democratic theorists, if his contribution to political philosophy is to have a future. At the same time, consideration of his work might open up new perspectives within contemporary liberal thought. Consider the manner in which he draws upon his earlier work to introduce into the discussion of cosmopolitan democracy elements of his critique of the autonomous subject, or "ipseity," and to relate this to the problem of sovereignty. By "ipseity" he means the idea of a sovereign self that possesses the power to give itself "its own law, its force of law, its self-representation, the sovereign and reappropriating gathering of self in the simultaneity of an assemblage or assembly."[70] The present international order of sovereign states shows us that, so long as democracy incorporates this idea of sovereignty, it cannot but ensure that the reason of the strongest will prevail. Derrida concludes that it is imperative to dissociate democracy from the principle of sovereignty. He contrasts the unconditionality of sovereignty with the unconditionality of "democracy to come" in order to argue for limits to sovereignty, for example by constitutional measures that might ensure that it is shared among different parties and that might regulate the manner in which it can be employed. A sovereignty that is no longer indivisible and unconditional but divisible and subject to conditions in this way is no longer sovereignty in the traditional sense of the term.

This is an important and far-reaching challenge, not only to the existing order of sovereign states but to the traditional concept of democracy insofar as this is defined in terms of the autonomy and self-legislating power of a people. Moreover, since this challenge to the traditional concept of democracy is carried out in the name of democracy and at the level of principles, it also has implications for the domestic sphere. As Derrida remarks, "it is a question of separating democracy and autonomy."[71] This is an almost unimaginable thought that takes a path diametrically opposed to that taken in recent years by much egalitarian liberal theory, and by much neo-liberal public policy, where there has been a tendency to rely ever more strongly on concepts of autonomy and responsibility in the elaboration of principles of equality and justice. We see this, for example, in the principle associated with Rawls, Dworkin, and others that individuals are responsible for the inequalities that result from their own choices, but entitled to compensation for inequalities brought about through no fault of their own. What would be the implications for political theory and public policy of a democracy without autonomy? The difficulty of answering this question perhaps illustrates what Derrida means when he suggests that democracy is an "ultrapolitical" as well as a political concept.[72] Developing the implications of this and other ultrapolitical and unconditional concepts and bringing them to bear on the terms of public political reason in contemporary liberal democracies would be a novel and important contribution. Derrida's final political essays suggest that it is too soon to judge the value of deconstructive political philosophy.

ACKNOWLEDGMENT

I am grateful to Miriam Bankovsky and Sam Haddad for helpful comments on earlier versions of this paper, and to the editors of this volume for their encouragement and guidance in developing the final version.

NOTES

1. Richard Wolin, *The Seduction of Unreason* (Princeton, NJ: Princeton University Press, 2004), 233. For accounts of these and other criticisms of Derridean politics, see Richard Bernstein, "Serious Play: The Ethical-Political Horizon of Derrida" in *The New Constellation: The Ethical-Political Horizons of Modernity/Postmodernity* (Cambridge: MIT Press, 1992), 172–198; Nancy Fraser, "The French Derrideans: Politicizing Deconstruction or Deconstructing the Political," in G. Madison, ed., *Working Through Derrida* (Evanston, IL: Northwestern University Press, 1993), 51–76; Geoffrey Bennington "Derrida and Politics," in T. Cohen, ed., *Jacques Derrida and the Humanities: A Critical Reader* (Cambridge: Cambridge University Press, 2001), 193–212.
2. Jacques Derrida, "Declarations of Independence," in *Negotiations: Interventions and Interviews 1971–2001*, edited, translated and with an Introduction by Elizabeth Rottenberg (Stanford, CA: Stanford University Press, 2002), 47. This text was first published in French in *Otobiographies: L'enseignement de Nietzsche et la politique du nom proper* (Paris: Galilée, 1984), 13–32.
3. Jacques Derrida, "Force of Law: The 'Mystical Foundation of Authority,'" in Drucilla Cornell et al eds., *Deconstruction and the Possibility of Justice* (New York: Routledge, 1992), 15. This text was first published in *Cardozo Law Review*, 11 (5–6), 1990, 920–1045. Other texts in this series include, "No Apocalypse, Not Now (Full Speed Ahead, Seven Missiles, Seven Missives)," delivered at a colloquium at Cornell University in 1984 and first published in *Diacritics*, translated by Catherine Porter and Philip Lewis, 14 (2), 1984, 20–31; "Racism's Last Word," which first appeared as a catalogue essay for an exhibition entitled "Artists of the World Against Apartheid" in 1983 and subsequently in *Critical Inquiry*, translated by P. Kamuf, 12, 1985,

290–299; "Admiration de Nelson Mandela: ou les lois de la réflexion," first published in J. Derrida and M. Tlili eds., *Pour Nelson Mandela* (Paris: Gallimard, 1986) and translated as "The Laws of Reflection: Nelson Mandela, in Admiration," in J. Derrida and M. Tlili, eds., *For Nelson Mandela* (New York: Seaver Books, 1987), 13–42.

4. Jacques Derrida, *Specters of Marx*, translated by Peggy Kamuf (New York: Routledge, 1994), 86.

5. Jacques Derrida, "Autoimmunity: Real and Symbolic Suicides," in G. Borradori, ed., *Philosophy in a Time of Terror* (Chicago: University of Chicago Press, 2003), 106.

6. Jacques Derrida, *Rogues: Two Essays on Reason*, translated by Pascale-Anne Brault and Michael Naas (Stanford, CA: Stanford University Press, 2005), 39. Similar denials occur in M. Payne and J. Schad, eds., life.after.theory (New York: Continuum, 2003), 26, where he says: "I would be presumptuous enough to say that you wouldn't find discontinuity in my theoretical discourse. There are a lot of changes in terms of emphasis, or displacements, but there is no systematic discontinuity"; and in *Paper Machine*, translated by Rachel Bowlby (Stanford, CA: Stanford University Press, 2005), 89, where he offers the following qualification: "What I am putting forward here is not the outline of some 'ethical turn,' as it has been described, any more than the previous allusions to responsibility, hospitality, the gift, forgiveness, witnessing, etc. I am simply trying to pursue with some consistency a thinking that has been engaged around the same aporias for a long time."

7. Kearney writes, "what is different about Derrida's thinking here and in other texts after 1972, is that another dimension—the ethical—is added to the ontologico-epistemological concerns dominating his early writings." R. Kearney, "Derrida's Ethical Re-Turn," in G. B. Madison, ed., *Working Through Derrida* (Evanston, IL: Northwestern University Press, 1993), 29.

8. John D. Caputo, *Deconstruction in a Nutshell* (New York: Fordham University Press, 1997), 127.

9. See Chapter 5, page 104 of this volume.

10. L. Ferry and A. Renaut, *French Philosophy of the Sixties: An Essay on Anti-humanism*, translated by Mary S. Cattani (Amherst: University of Massachusetts Press, 1990), xxviii. Elisabeth Roudinesco sums up this book as an attempt "to prove that this entire philosophical generation was hostile to democracy," in Derrida and Roudinesco, *For What Tomorrow... A Dialogue*, Jeff Fort trans. (Stanford, CA: Stanford University Press, 2004), 15.

11. See Richard Wolin, *The Heidegger Controversy* (New York: Columbia University Press 1991); Hamacher, W., Hertz, N. and Keenan, T., eds., *Paul de Man: Wartime Journalism 1939–45* (Lincoln: University of Nebraska Press, 1988) and *Responses: On Paul de Man's Wartime Journalism* (Lincoln: University of Nebraska Press, 1989).

12. John P. McCormick, "Derrida on Law: Or, Poststructuralism Gets Serious," *Political Theory* 29, no. 3, (2001): 395–423.

13. Bennington, "Derrida and Politics," 194.

14. Jacques Derrida, "Politics and Friendship," in *Negotiations: Interventions and Interviews 1971–2001*, edited, translated and with an Introduction by Elizabeth Rottenberg (Stanford, CA: Stanford University Press, 2002), 163. This interview was first published in E. Ann Kaplan and M. Sprinker eds., *The Althusserian Legacy* (New York: Verso, 1993), 183–231.

15. Jason Powell, *Jacques Derrida: A Biography* (New York: Continuum, 2006), 150–158.

16. Jacques Derrida, "The Laws of Reflection: Nelson Mandela, in Admiration," 25.

17. A passing remark in *Specters of Marx* refers to "political philosophy which structures implicitly all philosophy or all thought on the subject of philosophy." Specters, 92.

18. Derrida, *Positions* (Chicago: The University of Chicago Press, 1981), 93.

19. Although he was not an active "soixante huitard" at the time, Derrida subsequently became aware of the profound impact that the "seismic jolt" of May 1968 had on his own work and on French university culture in general. He described it as a philosophical event that, whether one is aware or approves of it or not, "changes things in philosophy." See *Points: Interviews 1974–1994*, translated by P. Kamuf (Stanford, CA: Stanford University Press, 1995), 349.

20. For example, during the discussion after his presentation of "Différance" to the Société Française de Philosophie in January of 1968, Lucien Goldmann described his reaction to the paper as that of "listening to a mixture of eighty percent Marx and twenty percent Althusser and Foucault, which I find hard to accept." Derrida did not respond to the details of what it was that Goldmann found acceptably Marxist in his presentation, but he did take up the implied criticism of the anti-humanism of Althusser and Foucault by affirming that between what Goldman classed as eighty percent of his paper and what he classed as twenty percent "there is a certain systematic relation about which I care a great deal." See "The Original Discussion of 'Différance' (1968)," in David Wood and Robert Bernasconi eds., *Derrida and Différance* (Evanston, IL: Northwestern University Press, 1988), 93.

21. Derrida, *Positions*, 62–63.

22. Derrida repeatedly insists on the importance of Husserl's phenomenology, and the critical questions opened up by Heidegger, for his own practice of deconstructing the concepts and oppositions that inhabit and structure metaphysical discourse. His translation and Introduction to Husserl's *The Origin of Geometry* was published in 1962. *Voice and Phenomena* appeared in 1967. In relation to his doubts about the Althusserian critique of historicism, see also his comments on the need to ask further questions about the historicity of history and its relationship to the history of essence and the meaning of *Being in Positions*, 58–59.

23. Derrida, "Politics and Friendship," 161–162.

24. Ibid., 174.

25. Ibid., 163.

26. In the 1989 interview with Sprinker, he comments that "today, when in France any reference to Marx has become forbidden, impossible, immediately catalogued, I have a real desire to speak about Marx, to teach Marx—and I will if I can." See "Politics and Friendship," 166. Similarly sentiments are expressed in 1993 when he affirms: "I believe in the political virtue of the contretemps." *Specters*, 88.

27. Derrida, *Specters*, 90.

28. Ibid., 92.

29. Derrida, "Politics and Friendship," 178.

30. Ibid., 177.

31. Ibid., 178.

32. Ibid.

33. Derrida, "Force of Law," 20.

34. Jacques Derrida, *Politics of Friendship*, translated by George Collins (New York: Verso, 1997), 306.

35. Jacques Derrida, "Psyche: Invention of the Other," *Acts of Literature*, Derek Attridge, ed. (New York: Routledge, 1992), 335–356.

36. Derrida, "Psyche," 337.

37. Ibid., 341.

38. Ibid.

39. In this manner, he argues that deconstruction "can consist only in opening, uncloseting, destabilizing foreclusionary structures so as to allow for the passage towards the other." "Psyche," 341.

40. Jacques Derrida, *Of Hospitality: Anne Dufourmantelle Invites Jacques Derrida to Respond* (Stanford, CA: Stanford University Press, 2000); *On Cosmopolitanism and Forgiveness*, translated by Mark Dooley and Michael Hughes, with a preface by Simon Critchley and Richard Kearney (New York: Routledge, 2001); "Affirmative Deconstruction," in Paul Patton and Terry Smith, eds., *Jacques Derrida: Deconstruction Engaged* (Sydney: Power Publications, 2001), 57–104.

41. Derrida, *On Cosmopolitanism and Forgiveness*, 22–23.

42. In "Force of Law," he insists that deconstruction's commitment to the interrogation of the origins, grounds and limits of the conceptual apparatus in terms of which we think and practice justice leads it to denounce "not only theoretical limits but also concrete injustices, with the most palpable effects, in the good conscience that dogmatically stops before any inherited determination of justice." "Force of Law," 20. See also Derrida, *The Other Heading: Reflections on Today's Europe*, translated by Pascale-Anne Brault and Michael Naas (Bloomington and Indianapolis: Indiana University Press, 1992), 81.

43. Derrida, *Specters*, 90.

44. See Paul Patton, "Future Politics," in Patton and Protevi, eds., *Between Deleuze and Derrida* (New York: Continuum, 2003), 15–29, and "After the Linguistic Turn: Poststructuralist and Pragmatist Political Theory," in John Dryzek, Bonnie Honig and Anne Phillips, eds., *The Oxford Handbook of Political Theory* (Oxford: Oxford University Press, 2006), 125–141.

45. Derrida, *Rogues*, 85.

46. Ibid., 36.

47. Ibid., 34.

48. Derrida, "Autoimmunity: Real and Symbolic Suicides," 94.

49. Derrida, *The Other Heading*, 78; *Rogues*, 85–86.

50. Derrida, *Rogues*, 86.

51. In Specters, he distinguishes "an idea of justice—which we distinguish from any law or right or even human rights—and an idea of democracy which we distinguish from its current concepts and from its determined predicates today." *Specters*, 59.

52. Derrida, *Rogues*, 86.

53. Daniel Archibugi, "Principles of Cosmopolitan Democracy," in Archibugi, D., Held, D., and Köhler, M., *Re-imagining Political Community: Studies in Cosmopolitan Democracy* (London: Polity, 1998), 200.

54. Derrida, *Rogues*, 33.

55. Ibid., 81.

56. Ibid., 98.

57. Rorty uses this phrase to describe Rawls's liberalism in "The Priority of Democracy to Philosophy," *Philosophical Papers Volume 1: Objectivity, relativism and truth* (Cambridge: Cambridge University Press, 1990), 180.

58. Richard Rorty, *Contingency, Irony, and Solidarity* (Cambridge: Cambridge University Press, 1989), 83. Simon Stow comments on Rorty's efforts to distance himself from Derridean deconstruction, and Derrida's responses to some of his characterizations, infra chapter 9, 199–201.
59. Rorty, *Contingency, Irony, and Solidarity*, 73–95.
60. Derrida, *Rogues*, 32.
61. Ibid., 37.
62. Ibid., 89–90.
63. Derrida, "Force of Law," 8–9.
64. Richard Rorty, "Human Rights, Rationality and Sentimentality," *Philosophical Papers Volume 3: Truth and Progress* (Cambridge: Cambridge University Press, 1998), 167–185.
65. Rorty, Contingency, *Irony, and Solidarity*, 63.
66. In his discussion of European cultural identity and the aporia to which this is subject, Derrida writes: "We have, we must have, only the thankless aridity of an abstract axiom, namely that the experience and experiment of identity or of cultural identification can only be the endurance of these antinomies." *The Other Heading*, 71.
67. Derrida, *Rogues*, 86.
68. Ibid., 87.
69. Ibid., 34.
70. Ibid., 11.
71. Ibid., 84.
72. Ibid., 39.

8 From the "Death of Man" to Human Rights

The Paradigm Change in French Intellectual Life

Richard Wolin

THE STRUCTURALIST MOMENT

An assault on humanism was one of French structuralism's hallmarks, an orientation that in many respects set the tone for the more radical, post-structuralist doctrines that followed. As one critic has aptly remarked, "Structuralism was...a movement that in large measure *reversed* the eighteenth-century celebration of Reason, the credo of the *Lumières*."[1]

It was in this spirit that one of the movement's founders, Claude Lévi-Strauss, sought to make anthropology useful for the ends of cultural criticism. Lévi-Strauss famously laid responsibility for the twentieth century's horrors—total war, genocide, colonialism, as well as the threat of nuclear annihilation—at the doorstep of Western humanism. As he remarked in a 1979 interview: "All the tragedies we have lived through, first with colonialism, then with fascism, finally the concentration camps, all this has taken shape not in opposition to or in contradiction with so-called humanism...but I would say almost as *its natural continuation*."[2] Anticipating the poststructuralist credo, Lévi-Strauss went on to proclaim that the goal of the human sciences "was not to constitute, *but to dissolve man*."[3] From here it is but a short step to Foucault's celebrated, neo-Nietzschean adage concerning the "death of man" in *The Order of Things*.[4]

For Lévi-Strauss "human rights" were integrally related to the ideology of Western humanism, and therefore ethically untenable. He embraced a full-blown cultural relativism ("every culture has made a 'choice' that must be respected") and argued vociferously against cross-cultural communication. Such a ban was the only way, he felt, to preserve the plurality and diversity of indigenous cultures.[5] His strictures against cultural mixing are eerily reminiscent of the positions espoused by the "father of European racism," Comte Arthur de Gobineau. In *The Inequality of Human Races* (1853-55) the French aristocrat claimed that miscegenation was the root cause of European decline. The ease with which an anti-racism predicated on cultural relativism can devolve into its opposite—an unwitting defense of racial separatism—was one of the lessons that French intellectuals learned during the 1980s in the course of combating the ideology of Jean-Marie Le Pen's National Front.[6]

Lévi-Strauss's polemical critique of Western humanism represents a partial throwback to J. G. Herder's impassioned defense of cultural particularism at the dawn of the Counter-Enlightenment in *Yet Another Philosophy of History* (1774). For Herder, a dedicated foe of universal Reason's leveling gaze, it was self-evident that "Each form of human perfection is...national and time-bound and...individual.... Each nation has its center of happiness within itself, just as every sphere has its center of gravity."[7] While Herder's standpoint may be viewed as a useful corrective to certain strands of Enlightenment thought (e.g., the mechanistic materialism of the High Enlightenment; La Mettrie, after all, sought to view "man as a machine"), in retrospect his concerted defense of cultural relativism ceded too much ground vis-à-vis the political status quo. In order to achieve their ends, the advocates of political emancipation required a more radical and uncompromising idiom. Unsurprisingly, they found it in the maxims of modern natural right as purveyed by *philosophes* such as Voltaire, Rousseau, Diderot, and Condorcet.

During the 1960s, among many French intellectuals cultural relativism came to supplant the liberal virtue of "tolerance"—a precept that remained tied to norms mandating a fundamental respect for human integrity. When combined with an anti-humanist-inspired Western self-hatred, ethical relativism engendered an uncritical Third Worldism, an orientation that climaxed in Foucault's enthusiastic endorsement of Iran's Islamic Revolution.[8] Since the "dictatorship of the mullahs" was anti-modern, anti-Western, and anti-liberal, it satisfied *ex negativo* many of the political criteria that Third Worldists had come to view as "progressive." Similarly, Lévi-Strauss's unwillingness to differentiate between the progressive and regressive strands of political modernity—e.g., between democracy and fascism—suggests one of the perils of the structuralist approach. By preferring the "view from afar," or the "*longue durée*," the structuralists, like the anti-*philosophes* of yore, denigrated the human capacities of consciousness and will. Instead, in their optic, history appeared as a senseless fate, devoid of rhyme or reason, consigned a priori to the realm of unintelligibility.[9]

The parallels between the core ideas of Counter-Enlightenment and post-war French thought have been shrewdly analyzed in a recent study of Joseph de Maistre's intellectual legacy. With tact and discernment, the author phrases the problem as follows: "Maistre's absence from current debates is a yet much greater surprise given the uncanny resemblance between his work and the dormant trends in recent French thought. Bataille on the sacred as the defining feature of human existence...Blanchot on the...violence of all speech and writing; Foucault on the social function of punishment in pre-Revolutionary Europe; Derrida on violence and difference...— all of these themes...were anticipated and extensively elaborated in Maistre's writing."[10]

In the concluding pages of *Madness and Civilization*, Foucault praised the "sovereign enterprise of Unreason," forever irreducible to practices that can be "cured." Foucault's contrast between the exclusionary practices of the modern scientific worldview, whose rise was coincident with Descartes's *Discourse on Method*, and the non-conformist potentials of "madness" qua "other" of reason, would help to redefine the theoretical agenda for an entire generation of French intellectuals. Even in the case of Derrida, who formulated a powerful critique of Foucault's arguments, there was little disagreement with the latter's central contention that Reason is essentially a mechanism of oppression that proceeds by way of exclusions, constraints, and prohibitions. Derrida's own indictment of "logocentrism," or the tyranny of reason, purveys a kindred sentiment: since the time of Plato, Western thought has displayed a systematic intolerance vis-à-vis difference, otherness, and heterogeneity. Following the precedents established by Nietzsche and Heidegger, deconstruction arose in order to overturn and dismantle Reason's purported life-denying, unitary prejudices.

In a similar vein, Jean-François Lyotard attained notoriety for his controversial equation of "consensus" with "terror." The idea of an uncoerced, rational accord, argues Lyotard, is a fantasy. Underlying the veneer of mutual agreement lurks force. This endemic cynicism about adjudicating disputes linguistically is another one of poststructuralism's hallmarks. Yet, one cannot help but wonder how Lyotard expects to convince readers of the rectitude of his position if not via recourse to time-honored discursive means: the marshaling of supporting evidence and the force of the better argument. If, as Lyotard insinuates, "force" is all there is, on what grounds might we prefer one position to another? One cannot help but suspect that, ultimately, there is something deeply unsatisfying about the attempt by Lyotard and his fellow poststructuralists to replace the precepts of argumentation with rhetoric, aesthetics, or agonistics.[11]

THE FRENCH HEIDEGGER REVIVAL

The point of departure for French antihumanism was the momentous reception of Heidegger's 1947 "Letter on Humanism." Certainly one of the more baffling developments of modern European intellectual history concerns the rebirth of Heideggerianism in post-war France, at a time when the philosopher's career in Germany had reached its nadir. For in 1946 Heidegger was dismissed from his position at the University of Freiburg for having, in the words of a university denazification commission, "in the fateful year of 1933 consciously placed the great prestige of his scholarly reputation... in the service of the National Socialist Revolution, thereby [making] an essential contribution to the legitimation of this revolution in the eyes of educated Germans."[12] In the aftermath of the university commission's stern findings, Heidegger suffered a nervous breakdown that required two months of hospitalization. He was only reinstated some five years later, at a time when the political situation in Germany had stabilized.

We now know that, in the aftermath of this setback, Heidegger consciously set out to find among a French philosophical public the vindication that had been denied him in his own country. The first gambit in this strategy of rehabilitation was the publication of his 1947 "Letter on Humanism." This text was a fifty-page response to an epistolary inquiry by the French philosopher, Jean Beaufret. Beaufret's two essential questions concerned: (1) a clarification of the relationship between fundamental ontology and "ethics"; and (2) the contemporary prospects for revivifying the concept of "humanism."[13]

Heidegger, refusing to deviate from the position he had established at the time of the publication of *Being and Time* (1927), argued that ontology—the "question of Being"—had rendered an independent ethical theory superfluous. Every attempt to formulate an ethics, he explained, risked "elevating man to the center of beings."[14] In this respect, such attempts courted the dangers of a relapse into an *anthropocentric* mode of philosophical questioning. For Heidegger, such subject-centered approaches to philosophy represented the essence of the traditional metaphysics from which the Freiburg sage had desperately sought to free himself (especially in the *later* philosophy, of which the "Letter" constitutes, as it were, the ideal type).

To Beaufret's other query concerning the contemporary status of "humanism" ("How can we restore meaning to the word 'humanism'?"), Heidegger responds: "I wonder whether that is necessary." For a restoration of humanism similarly risked succumbing to the fatal lures of "metaphysical subjectivism."

In his response to this question, Heidegger also took the occasion to differentiate his philosophy of Being from the existentialism of Jean-Paul Sartre. This move was a strategic imperative given the considerable prominence Sartrian existentialism had come to enjoy after the war. Moreover, Sartre had just come out with the short, but highly influential, existentialist primer, "Existentialism is a Humanism."[15] The painstaking detail of Heidegger's "Letter" allowed him to put to rest all doubts that there might exist significant affinities between the two variants of *Existenzphilosophie*.

In "Existentialism is a Humanism," Sartre had maintained: "We are precisely in a situation where there are only human beings"; a statement that in many ways merely echoed his well known characterization of existentialism in terms of the priority of "existence" over "essence." In the "Letter on Humanism," conversely, Heidegger seeks to reverse the terms on his French rival by claiming the direct obverse: "We are precisely in a situation where principally there is Being."[16]

To be sure, the reversal (or "*Kehre*") of the relationship between "Being" and "human being" that Heidegger sought to effect was critically motivated. For Heidegger himself became convinced that the "planetary" devastation of the Second World War was of *metaphysical provenance*: it was a direct result of the philosophical paradigm of "metaphysical subjectivism" or the "will to will," which, from Descartes to Nietzsche, had singularly determined the manner in which "man" allows "beings" to "come to presence" in the modern world. The terrible consequence of this mode of disclosing the world, according to Heidegger, was a frenzy of *technological nihilism*, whose catastrophic results were transparent for all to see. Thus, to criticize this paradigm, to advocate its reversal, signified a crucial step in the reestablishment of a radically different, more harmonious relationship between "man" and "Being."

There are other fascinating "strategic" aspects of Heidegger's text. Although to discuss them fully would take us far afield from the inquiry at hand, it should at least be noted that the "Letter" includes uncharacteristically rhapsodic discussions of both Marxism and the Soviet Union. With reference to the author of *Das Kapital,* Heidegger at one point observes: "Because Marx by experiencing estrangement attains an essential dimension of history, the Marxist view of history is superior to that of other historical accounts." The "inferior" views of history he goes on to reject are those of Husserl and Sartre, neither of which, according to Heidegger, "recognizes the importance of the historical in Being."[17] With respect to the "doctrines of communism," Heidegger goes out of his way to note: "from the point of view of the history of Being it is certain that an elemental experience of what is world-historical speaks out in it."[18]

These peculiar asides can be explained in terms of the precariousness of the current world political situation. The Cold War had begun, but at this point no one knew which camp would triumph. Heidegger had already been mistreated by the occupying French troops: classifying him as a "*Nazi-typique*," they had proceeded to confiscate his house as well as his invaluable personal library. Clearly, Heidegger did not wish to burn his bridges to the other side, just in case.[19] Moreover, as Anson Rabinbach has pointed out, the precise fate of Heidegger's two sons, who were reported as "missing" on the eastern front, was still very much uncertain.[20] The favorable allusions to Marxism and communism in this dense philosophical text, therefore, can only be explained as a result of a number of pressing circumstantial concerns.

Yet, because in the "Letter" the relationship between the ends of "humanity" and those of "Being" are so prejudicially formulated, a fatal precedent was established for post-war French thought. For it is safe to say that Heidegger drew the *wrong* conclusions from his involvement with Nazism in the 1930s. Instead of rejecting a specific type of politics, the politics of totalitarianism that had led to the "German catastrophe" of 1933–45, the later Heidegger appeared to reject human "praxis" *in toto*. From the ethereal standpoint of his later philosophy of Being, there were no "essential" differences between communism, fascism, and world democracy. All three were "essentially" equivalent insofar as all three represented instances of technological nihilism. As he remarks in 1945, "Today every-thing stands under this reality, whether it is called communism, fascism, or world democracy."[21]

In the philosophy of the early Heidegger, Dasein, or human reality, played an essential role in the disclosure of Being. As he remarks in *Being and Time*: "Only so long as Dasein *is*—that is, the ontic possibility of the understanding of Being—'is there' Being."[22] In the later Heidegger, how-ever, it is as if humanity itself comes to represent little more than an *impedi-ment* to the quasi-holy "sendings" (*Schickungen*) of Being. And thus, in the Nietzsche lectures, Heidegger affirms that the "essence of nihilism is *not at all the affair of man,* but a matter of Being itself";[23] and that "The History of Being is neither the history of man and of humanity, nor the history of human relation to beings and to Being. *The history of Being is Being itself, and only Being.*"[24] In "Overcoming Metaphysics," Heidegger delivers, as it were, a final indictment of the possibilities of meaningful human action in the world: "No mere action will change the state of the world, because Being as effectiveness and effecting [*Wirksamkeit und Wirken*] closes all beings off in the face of the Event [*das Ereignis*]."[25] And if we return to the 1947 "Letter on Humanism," we find the following specification of the relationship between "Being" and "man": "Man does not decide whether and how beings appear, whether and how God and the gods or history and nature come forward into the clearing of Being, come to presence and depart. *The advent of beings lies in the destiny of Being.... Man is the shep-herd of Being.*"[26] The foregoing depictions of the possibilities for human action in the world come to a focal point in Heidegger's oft-cited remarks in the 1966 *Spiegel* interview. In Heidegger's view, so forlorn and remote are the prospects of human betterment in the here and now that, "Only a god can save us!"[27]

The full story of the reception of Heidegger's thought in post-war France merits an independent treatment.[28] In the context at hand—that is, with a view to understanding its impact on French anti-humanism—I seek to pro-vide only the main outlines. It is important to note that Heidegger's main champion in France, Jean Beaufret—the addressee of the "Letter"—was both an ex-*résistant* and a Marxist. For Heidegger, it was Beaufret's status as a *résistant* that was crucial: it functioned as an important prophylac-tic against attempts to link him or his thought in the *après guerre* with Nazism. At the same time, it is less obvious what Beaufret, qua Marxist, saw of value in the later Heidegger's philosophy of Being.

The answer to this question pertains to the intellectual politics of the period. This was the era of existentialism's great vogue. The names of Sar-tre, de Beauvoir, Merleau-Ponty, and Camus (who in the late 1940s had not yet broken with Sartre) were on everyone's lips. With his novellas and short stories of the pre-war period (e.g., *Nausea* and "The Wall") Sartre had established himself as a *littérateur* of the highest order. Yet, by the *après guerre*, he had risen to become France's most celebrated philosopher, one of the nation's leading dramatists and political commentators, as well as the founding editor of one of the world's most prestigious intellectual organs, *Les Temps modernes*.[29] One of the primary tasks of the *marxisant* intellectuals of the period, therefore, was to put a damper on this rising tide of existential humanism as purveyed by Sartre and company, which was viewed as a direct philosophical challenge to the worldview of dialectical materialism.

Enter Beaufret qua champion of the later Heidegger. For insofar as the ex-*résistant* was able to show that, as a philosopher of existentialism, Sartre was essentially *an impostor*—that is, that his "existential humanism" had virtually nothing to do with the real item—Beaufret believed he possessed the theoretical leverage necessary to disqualify the formidable humanistic challenge to communism posed by Sartre and his disciples. Thus, Beaufret was able to invoke Heidegger's "Letter"—which, as we have seen, amounted to an extensive denigration of Sartre's position on the relation between humanism and existentialism—as an important piece of evidence in his attempts to unmask the inauthenticity of Sartre's philosophical credentials.

Moreover, as Rabinbach points out, "what led Beaufret to Heidegger [was] his essentially correct intuition that the perspective of a history of Being *ipso facto* sanctions not merely violence and 'resolve' in the face of 'nihilism,' but Marxism's account of the violence of human history."[30] That is, there existed significant intellectual affinities between Marxism and the Heideggerian "history of Being" insofar as both doctrines displayed an a priori mistrust of Western humanism. The thinking of Marx and Heidegger thus converged in the conviction that humanism merely provided a veil of ideological respectability for the exploitation and mass conformity characteristic of bourgeois society. By virtue of the calculated paeans to the virtues of Marxism that Heidegger sprinkled throughout his influential 1947 "epistle," he had managed to meet Beaufret halfway, as it were. Even though Heidegger himself remained a virulent anti-communist after the war,[31] his remarks about Marx in the "Letter," coupled with his devastating critique of the "planetary" dominance of modern technology (*das Gestell*), made his thought *salonfähig* for an entire generation of French left-wing intellectuals—to the point where one would be justified in speaking of a "left Heideggerianism."

Heidegger's "Letter" became one of the foundational texts for French post-war theoretical discourse. In a large measure it came to occupy this niche of honor owing to its exemplary articulation of the position of philosophical anti-humanism. As Vincent Descombes remarks, "After Heidegger's intervention [in the "Letter on Humanism"], the word 'humanism' ceased to be the flag which it had been such a point of honor to defend." He continues: "Marxists condemning the bourgeois ideology of 'Man'; Nietzscheans despising the doctrine of resentment born in the spent intelligence of the 'last man'; structuralists of a purist persuasion announcing with

Lévi-Strauss the program of the 'dissolution of man'—all these contended with one another in their antihumanism. 'Humanist' became a term of ridicule, an abusive epithet, to be entered among the collection of derided 'isms' (vitalism, spiritualism, etc.)."[32]

Yet, the question remains: can one recoup a notion of moral responsibility once the capacities of human agency are so thoroughly denigrated as a species of "metaphysical illusion"?

"STRUCTURES DO NOT GO OUT INTO THE STREETS"

In France, structuralism's death can be dated with a fair amount of precision: the evening of May 10/11, 1968—the famous "night of the barricades" that was one of the highlights of the legendary "May Movement." Lucien Goldmann, author of *The Hidden God* and other works, conceived a memorable *bon mot* to describe this watershed. Ever since, it has served as structuralism's unofficial epitaph: "*structures do not go out into the street to make a revolution.*" Thereby, Goldmann served notice that structuralist proclamations concerning "the end of history" had been distinctly premature.

For nearly two decades, structuralism, borrowing a page from Alexandre Kojève's celebrated Hegel lectures, had dismissed the idea of progressive historical change as one of the primary delusions of modern consciousness. "Events"—in the sense of *événements*—ceased to exist. Change was a deception. It operated at the level of "appearance." It served to conceal long-term continuities that, in the last analysis, were determined by deep structures. Whether one examines Lévi-Strauss's theory of kinship, Lacan's view of the unconscious, Althusser's conception of "science," or Foucault's quasi-fatalistic notion of the episteme—which purportedly defines with algorithmic precision the limits of "discursivity" (the regime of the "sayable" and "unsayable")—viewed formally, the results were the same. (Thus, in a well-known passage in *The Order of Things*, Foucault claims that, from a structuralist point of view, the differences between Marx and David Ricardo are trivial. They are part and parcel of the same episteme). Attempts at conscious historical transformation were decreed an illusion. What counted—to use the expression made famous by Fernand Braudel—was the *longue durée*. Subjectivity and politics were the *écume* or foam predestined to be subsumed by the undertow of deep structures.

May 1968 gave the lie to the truisms and pieties of two decades of French intellectual life. As one contemporary observer remarked, May 1968 was not merely a student revolt; it was "the death warrant of structuralism."[33]

Latin Quarter students staged an unforgettable month of cultural revolution and political theater. Conversely, the Left Bank's so-called *maître penseurs* (master thinkers)—the progenitors of "French Theory"—had egg all over their faces. A year later, de Gaulle, whose imperial presidency dated from 1958, was out of office. Wheels of change had been set in motion that left the cultural and political landscape of modern France permanently transformed. Out of the ashes of May emerged a plethora of vibrant contestatory social movements: Medecins Sans Frontieres (Doctors without Borders), the Mouvement Libération des femmes (MLF), the prison reform movement (GIP), gay rights (FHAR, led by the charismatic Guy Hocquenghem), as well as the *autogestionnaire*-oriented *"deuxième Gauche."* As subsequent research has shown, many of these groups developed directly out of the prolific, militant-dominated "Action Committees" of May 1968. To borrow nomenclature developed by Nanterre sociologist Alain Touraine: the self-production of civil society had begun. As one observer has astutely noted, "The many Action Committees that flourished in 1968 may have thought they were overturning capitalism, but in fact they were generating participatory democracy."[34] For a time at least, a variety of grass roots social movements and civic associations had effectively seized the reigns of "historicity" from the "state."

In *Democracy in America* Tocqueville famously observed that a vibrant and multi-layered associational life is the surest safeguard against the risks of a despotic-authoritarian usurpation of "the political." "Democratic peoples...are independent and weak," claimed Tocqueville. "They can do hardly anything for themselves, and none of them is in a position to force his fellows to help him. They would all therefore find themselves helpless if they did not learn to help each other voluntarily."[35] One of the best-documented gains of May 1968 has been the effective burgeoning of French civic and associational life. As Pierre Rosanvallon has shown in a recent book, *Le Modèle politique français: la société civile contre le jacobinisme de 1789 à nos jours*, since the May events participation in a wide range of engaged civic associations has expanded dramatically. During the 1950s, around 5,000 associations were created each year; in the 1960s around 10,000; in the 1970s, 25,000; in the 1980s, 40,000; and in the 1990s, 60,000. Today approximately 40 percent of the French adult population belongs to an association. All told, there are around 700,000 associations in a country of 60,000,000.[36] Many of these gains are directly attributable to the new confidence in the value and effectiveness of participatory democracy that has proven to be one of May 1968's most impressive and enduring legacies.

In sum, following years of stultifying Gaullist repression, with the student-worker insurrection France experienced an unprecedented explosion of *repressed subjectivity*.[37] Ironically, in philosophical terms, May was widely perceived as a vindication of Sartre's conception of the *pour-soi,* or self-positing subjectivity. The May revolt was populist and democratic. Conversely, structuralism and poststructuralism were perceived as a resolutely *mandarinate idiom*: the very cant of hierarchy and privilege against which the students were rebelling. *"Althusser is useless*!" proclaimed one of the most visible banners to appear on the walls of the University of Nanterre. Whereas both structuralists and poststructuralists had written off change in favor of underlying glacial, impersonal constants, Sartre's theory of subjectivity contained a voluntaristic optimism about progressive historical change that, in the eyes of many, had come to the fore during the May events. Whereas structuralists and poststructuralists freely embraced the dour and pessimistic "death of man" thesis, in many respects May 1968 appeared as a rousing vindication of Sartre's faith in the capacity of men and women to endow history with meaning. As François Dosse notes in *The History of Structuralism*: "Sartre's analysis of the alienation of individuals caught up in the practico-inert, and his insistence on the capacity of individuals to impose freedom by the actions of committed groups fused into a dialectic that made it possible to escape isolation and atomization, shed more light on May 1968 than did any structuralist position about structural chains, the subjected subject, or systems that reproduce or regulate themselves." Dosse appropriately titles his chapter devoted to the May revolt, "Jean-Paul Sartre's Revenge."[38] Similarly, in *Les Idées qui ont ébranlé la France* (*The Ideas that Shook France*), Didier Anzieu, alluding to Sartre's concept of the "group-in-fusion," writes: "[In essence,] the May student revolt tried out its own version of Sartre's formula, 'the group is the beginning of humanity.'" Thus, it is hardly an accident that, during May, Sartre was the only French intellectual permitted by student leaders to address the large rally at the Sorbonne.

In a perceptive article, François Furet identified the historical preconditions behind structuralism's rise. He suggested that the movement's endemic cynicism about historical change represented a theoretical corollary to the widely sensed impasse of Fifth Republic political culture. After all, following the brutal 1956 Soviet invasion of Hungary, the French Communist Party suffered irreparable damage as a credible source of political opposition. The French Socialist Party's luster was also permanently tarnished. For it was largely as a result of its policies—the senseless war in Algeria, for example—that the Fourth Republic had run aground, allowing de Gaulle to assume the role of political savior. Lastly, under the General's eleven-year quasi-benign, authoritarian reign, until May at least, all sense of political possibility seemed brusquely foreclosed. Little wonder, then, that among French intellectuals structuralism's apocalyptical "death of man" thesis found keen resonance.

One of the main ironies of poststructuralism's reception history, then, is that at the very moment its star began to fall precipitously in France, it gained a new lease on life across the Atlantic. Thus, as one oft-cited study of Derrida's work has shown, during the early 1980s, when articles devoted to his thought in France slowed to a trickle—at most, one or two a year—in North America, conversely, an academic cottage industry spawned translations of and commentaries on his texts.[39]

In sum and bluntly put: in the aftermath of May, a new generation of intellectuals perceived the structuralist/poststructuralist attack on the "subject" as counterproductive and self-defeating. For, according to the new consensus, the denegation of subjectivity manifestly stifled attempts to conceptualize problems of social change. Consequently, in May's wake there blossomed numerous, alternative competing theoretical paradigms that, unlike the structuralism/poststructuralism dyad, took the ideas of "practice" and "action" seriously.

One fruitful approach was developed by University of Nanterre sociologist Alain Touraine. In books like *The Voice and the Eye* and *The Return of the Actor,* Touraine sought to do justice to the rebirth of a vibrant and oppositional associational life both in France and throughout Europe. At a later point, Touraine would extend this "action-oriented" framework to cover the development of anti-nuclear and environmentalist citizen initiatives, not to mention Solidarity, the independent trade union movement in Poland.

These developments have led observers to speak of a new actor-centered "pragmatic turn" animating French social and political thought. It is in this vein that commentators have proclaimed "the birth of a new paradigm...: a communicative action that could represent both a real path of emancipation as a social project.... The pragmatic turn accords a central position to action endowed with meaning; it thereby rehabilitates intentionality."[40] Accordingly, the motivations and self-understanding of the actors themselves regain pride of place. Such considerations remained imperceptible from the standpoint of the previously dominant paradigm: a joyless and misanthropic "anti-humanism." The new theoretical approaches, conversely, stress the creativity and open-endedness of social action. In a neo-Kantian spirit, they unite in recognizing *the primacy of practical reason*. Recoiling from structuralism's languorous positivism as well as poststructuralism's inability to theorize "the social" (in the eyes of most critics, owing to its "linguistic idealism" or inordinate focus on questions of "textuality"), the new methods portend what might be called a *rehumanization of the social sciences*. Thus, in the eyes of one acute observer: with the emergence of the new, action-oriented analytical frameworks, "The social is no longer conceived as a thing; it is no longer an object of reification.... [Instead], the social fact is perceived as a semantic fact bearing meaning. Habermas's theory of communicative action...is mobilized to recapture social actions as facts at once psychological and physical...."[41]

One of the major casualties of the new stress on the value of intersubjectivity has been French Nietzscheanism: the intellectual lineage that extends from Georges Bataille and Pierre Klossowski in the 1930s to the post-war appropriations by Derrida, Deleuze, and Foucault. In the 1880s Nietzsche had famously proclaimed: "the one thing that counts is to give style to one's life existence [aesthetic]...there is only an aesthetic justification of existence." Ultimately, however, the aestheticist approach seemed suitable only to a socially indifferent elitism: an ethos conducive to hedonistically inclined *Übermenschen und –frauen*. At base, it seemed incompatible with the *esprit de sérieux* mandated by the imperatives of democratic self-transformation. May 1968 had demonstrated that society was open and susceptible to the constructive influence of democratic participation. In

May's aftermath a new interest emerged in what might be called "logics of justification." Men and women took stock of the fact that the virtues of "public reason" could be mobilized for purposes of constructive social change.

Even among former poststructuralists, the spirit of May proved infectious. Many began revising their theories accordingly. Thus, during the late 1970s, the "rebirth of the subject" became an omnipresent topos.[42] Roland Barthes published a semi-confessional, well-received autobiography, *Barthes par Barthes*. Foucault abruptly abandoned *The History of Sexuality* project in order to investigate the ideas of aesthetic self-fashioning—an "aesthetics of existence"—in ancient Greece and Rome as well as among modernists such as Baudelaire. Led by Philippe Sollers and Julia Kristeva, the *Tel Quel* group belatedly jumped aboard the bandwagon of Eastern European "dissidence." In 1978, to their disciples' chagrin, they announced—to anyone who was still listening—that in the upcoming parliamentary elections, they would be voting for Valéry Giscard d'Estaing's center-right UDF (Union de la démocratie française).[43] Proclamations concerning the "death of the author," once so fashionable, now seemed rash and outdated.

The May movement had effectively unmasked Marxism—at least in its official, orthodox variants—as an ideology of domination. As is well known, the 1974 translation of Solzhenitsyn's path-breaking exposé of the Soviet Gulag had a far-reaching impact in France. Chroniclers of French political life are fond of referring to the "Solzhenitsyn effect." Shamed by years of pro-Moscow fealty and embarrassed by a misguided *tiers-mondisme*, in which the frustrated revolutionary expectations of first world intellectuals were paternalistically projected upon the third world, since the mid-1970s French thinkers had begun a long term process of reassessing the forgotten virtues of democratic republicanism. Within a matter of years, political loyalties among French opinion leaders were dramatically transformed. French intellectuals vowed that never again would they allow blind allegiance to a political cause to stifle considerations of conscience. After a long post-war hiatus, "morality" once again became a legitimate topic of political discussion.

Seemingly overnight, the posters of Mao, Fidel, and Che were removed from Latin Quarter dormitory walls. The new exemplars of *moral politics* were a generation of Eastern European dissidents who had staked life and limb on "speaking truth to power": figures like Russia's Andrei Sakharov, Czechoslovakia's Vaclav Havel, and Poland's Adam Michnik. Among French intellectuals, the ethos of *droits de l'homme*—human rights—had been reborn. As an insightful observer has remarked: "The modern French left's heightened sensibility to the issues of human rights and civil liberties...and its tireless activism on behalf of these issues, is...one of the most important legacies of [May]."[44] In 1977, during a lavish state visit to the Elysée Palace by Soviet President Leonid Brezhnev, a number of media-savvy French intellectuals—led by Foucault, Sartre, and New Philosopher André Glucksmann—decided to stage a high-profile, rival soirée in honor of Soviet dissidents. Foucault, with characteristic eloquence and understatement, commented as follows: "This isn't a meeting...and above all it isn't a reception symmetrical with the one that is taking place at this very moment. We simply thought that, on the evening when M. Brezhnev is being received with pomp at the Elysée by M. Giscard d'Estaing, other French people could receive other Russians who are their friends."[45]

Twenty years earlier, Sartre, oblivious to "really existing socialism's" appalling political track record, had claimed that Marxism was the "unsurpassable horizon of our time." Conversely, for a subsequent generation of engaged intellectuals, human rights had become the incontestable benchmark—the alpha and omega—of any future politics.

As is often the case in a country where politics and intellectual life are intimately intertwined, major developments on the international political stage played a key role in solidifying this transformation:

1. Unspeakable revelations concerning the scope and extent of Cambodia's so-called "killing fields," where, within the space of a few years, approximately 1.5 million persons were brutally murdered. Moreover, as is well known, during the 1950s Khmer Rouge luminaries such as Pol Pot, Ieng Sary, and Khieu Samphan received their training in Marxism at the finest Parisian universities. As Ieng Sary's deputy, Suong Sikoeun, observed: "The French Revolution influenced me very strongly, above all Robespierre... Robespierre and Pol Pot: both men have the same quality of decisiveness and integrity."[46]
2. The perilous exodus, circa 1978, of Vietnamese "boat people" fleeing political persecution from a recently installed Marxist regime that, just a few years earlier, many left-leaning French intellectuals had cheered on to victory.
3. What in retrospect might be described as the coup de grâce for *marxisant* French intellectuals: the 1979 Soviet invasion of Afghanistan and ensuing twelve-year brutal occupation.

Little wonder, then, that within a few years time, the vote-totals of the PCF, historically one of Western Europe's most successful Communist parties, dwindled from over 20 percent to the low single digits.

MICHEL FOUCAULT: HUMAN RIGHTS ACTIVIST

Undoubtedly, in American academic culture the figure who has had the most far-ranging and pervasive influence on the development of "postmodernism" is Michel Foucault. It is therefore worth enquiring how the foregoing narrative—the retreat from structuralism's "end of history"/"death of man" hypothesis—affected Foucault's own intellectual and political development. For it is well known—and Foucault himself has avowed as much in interviews—that, for the author of *Discipline and Punish,* May 1968 represented something of a methodological and political watershed—despite the fact that, since Foucault himself was teaching in Tunisia at the time, he had no first-hand contact with the May events. Nevertheless, ample evidence suggests that during the 1970s Foucault developed a new understanding of politics that closely paralleled the political evolution of the sixty-eighters themselves. That evolution gradually abandoned the *gauchisme,* or "leftism," that in the post-May era had become the dominant political credo, and turned increasingly toward a politics of human rights.

We know that, for a time, Foucault worked closely with members of the post-May Gauche Prolétarienne (GP) on questions of prison reform. His work for the Prison Information Group (GIP) coincided with research on his most influential book, *Surveiller et Punir* (*Discipline and Punish*). Should one desire a measure of Foucault's own post-68 flirtations with an uncompromising *gauchisme,* one would do well to examine his 1972 "On Popular Justice: Dialogue with the Maoists." In the course of a conversation with GP leader Pierre Victor (nom de guerre of the late Benny Lévy), Foucault famously praised the 1792 September massacres—an important prologue to the so-called "Big Terror" of the Year II—as an *"approximation of...popular justice*; a response to oppression which was strategically useful and politically necessary."[47] He went on to observe that, by establishing revolutionary tribunals, the Committee of Public Safety, had erred on the side of "proceduralism." Instead, they should have allowed the thirst for popular vengeance—famously exemplified by the blood-soaked, revolutionary *journées* —to find a direct and unmediated outlet.

However, it is of interest to note that Foucault refrained from practicing what he preached. Later that same year, a working class girl was brutally murdered in the northern coal-mining village of Bruay-en-Artois. Frustrated by the authorities' unwillingness to prosecute a local notable, GP leaders tried to convene a popular tribunal to effect summary justice, i.e., to try and execute the suspected culprit. (At the time, Pierre Victor condemned the separation of trial and sentencing as an atavistic bourgeois encumbrance.) In this case, however, Foucault exercised a cautionary influence on the young *gépistes* (the members of the GP), urging them to abandon their irresponsible revolutionary theatrics. In fact, Foucault was slowly coming to the conclusion that there was no hard and fast line separating the penchant for violence on the part of the revolutionary left from the revolutionary right. In his introduction to Gilles Deleuze and Félix Guattari's *Anti-Oedipus,* he expressed this realization as follows: "How does one keep from being fascist, even (especially) when one believes oneself to be a revolutionary militant? How do we rid our speech and our acts, our hearts and our pleasures, of fascism? How do we ferret out the fascism that is ingrained in our behavior?"[48]

Foucault's partisanship for *droit de l'hommisme* first surfaced during the mid-1970s in his defense of so-called "New Philosophy." Writing in the pages of *le Nouvel observateur*, the philosopher penned a fulsome, three-page review essay of André Glucksmann's *Les Maîtres penseurs*. In retrospect, one might say that it was Foucault's review, rather than "New Philosophy" itself, that enunciated a sea-change in French intellectual politics: the movement away from Marxism and toward the paradigm of human rights. In many respects, New Philosophers like Glucksmann and Bernard-Henri Lévy were Foucault's bastard intellectual progeny. For Glucksmann's thesis in *Les Maîtres penseurs* overlapped with a Nietzschean standpoint that Foucault himself had helped to popularize: "la volonté de savoir" = "la volonté de pouvoir"; "the will to know" = "the will to power." Simply put: Western thought betrays a "will to domination" that culminates logically in the "totally administered world" of the Gulag.

> The whole of a certain left has attempted to explain the Gulag... in terms of the theory of history, or at least the history of theory. Yes, yes, there were massacres; but that was a terrible error. Just reread Marx or Lenin, compare them with Stalin and you will see where the latter went wrong. It is obvious that all those deaths could only result from a misreading. It was predictable: Stalinism-error was one of the principal agents behind the return to Marxism-truth, to Marxism-text which we saw in the 1960s. If you want to be against Stalin, don't listen to the victims; they will only recount their tortures. Reread the theoreticians; they will tell you the truth about the true.[49]

Although Foucault's disciples have often criticized his endorsement of Glucksmann's arguments—as is well known, his actions precipitated a major break with Gilles Deleuze, whom he had hired in the philosophy department at the University of Vincennes—in many ways the philosopher acted with admirable uprightness and consistency. Heretofore, the French left had vehemently denounced the totalitarianisms of the far right. By what right should it ignore the equally murderous totalitarianisms that had been established by left-wing regimes? Moreover, in a crypto-Trotskyist spirit, the French left had historically exonerated Marx and Marxism from any responsibility for the Gulag. (One especially egregious example of this failing was Sartre's declaration, following the Warsaw Pact invasion of Hungary, that the Soviet Union was still "objectively" a worker's state.) Yet, at this historical juncture, such denials seemed morally untenable—a pure and simple act of bad faith. It was Foucault, marching shoulder to shoulder with the New Philosophers, who helped precipitate this breach.

During the late 1970s, Foucault worked closely with France's leading left-liberal trade union, the CFDT (Confédération française et démocratique du travail). It was this organ that, by stressing theories of worker self-management or *autogestion*, laid the groundwork for the so-called "*deuxième gauche*" or "second left." By encouraging ideals of worker autonomy and democratic self-governance, the CFDT represented the authentic heir to the spirit of May.

In 1979 Foucault, once again in the company of Sartre and New Philosopher André Glucksmann, played a key role in calling attention to the plight of Vietnamese refugees—the so-called "boat people"—fleeing in droves from an oppressive Communist regime. Similarly, in December 1981, when Poland's General Jaruzelski declared martial law, thereby suppressing Soviet-dominated Eastern Europe's only independent trade union, Foucault was in the forefront of the protest against newly elected president François Mitterrand's de facto acquiescence in the face of this disheartening and tragic state of affairs. It was at this point, moreover, that a political friendship blossomed between Foucault and Bernard Kouchner, the founder of *Médecins sans Frontières* and France's most outspoken human rights advocate. During this period Foucault assembled a small group of journalists, activists, and intellectuals to closely monitor human rights abuses around the world.[50]

François Dosse has glossed Foucault's remarkable political metamorphosis as follows: "In the late seventies and early eighties, Foucault embraced the cause of human rights.... Slowly, under the influence of the profound changes of the day, [he] once again began acting like a universal intellectual cum defender of democratic values. As his thinking and practice changed, he drew closer to Sartre, to whom he had been completely opposed until then."[51]

By helping to popularize and affirm a human rights agenda, Foucault inherited Sartre's coveted mantle as France's leading public intellectual. Ironically, the thinker who once articulated a theory of the "specific intellectual" established himself as an eloquent spokesman for what has become, since the dark days of Auschwitz, the world's most valuable universalistic moral and political credo. At the time of Foucault's death in 1984, prominent observers noted with irony that the ex-structuralist and "death-of-man" prophet had played a pivotal role in facilitating French acceptance of political liberalism. As one commentator has aptly remarked, "As much as any figure of his generation, [Foucault] helped inspire a resurgent neo-liberalism in France in the 1980s."[52]

To be sure, there was always a tension between the later Foucault's theoretical pronouncements and his political practice. Having abandoned the *démarche* of *La Volonté de savoir*, according to which "power" was omnipresent and inescapable, in his later writings Foucault flirted with the trope of an "aesthetics of existence." He displayed an intense fascination with Baudelaire's dandyism as well as Nietzsche's famous maxim in the *Gay Science* concerning the preeminence of "style." In a similar vein, in the final pages of *The History of Sexuality*, as an antidote to the false promises of sexual emancipation—"*le roi sexe*"—Foucault counsels us to seek out a "different economy of bodies and pleasures."[53]

Yet, viewed according to another optic, these two antithetical political frames—"body politics" and "human rights"—prove complementary rather than mutually exclusive. As political thinkers from Kant to Rawls to Claude Lefort have suggested, liberal democracy provides an optimal framework for the ends of individual self-realization. Since, unlike communitarian approaches to politics, it is agnostic concerning the *summum bonum* or "the ultimate good," democracy is compatible with a dizzying plurality of *Lebensformen* or "forms of life." In this sense, democracy provides the ideal terrain for a Foucauldian "aesthetics of existence" to flourish. This would seem to be one of the undeniable lessons of the modernist aesthetic—as embodied by Rimbaud's immortal maxim: "Il faut être absolument moderne"—with which the later Foucault so profoundly identified.

However, were this hypothesis concerning the complementarity of "body politics" and political liberalism to be borne out, Foucault's reductive equation of "modernity" with "carceralism"—the normalizing practices of a disciplinary society—would stand in need of drastic revision. I would therefore like to suggest that, in his political involvements, Foucault gave the lie to his philosophy of history or "metatheory," which misleadingly conflated "norms" with "normalization." In this respect, later in life Foucault seems to have come to a conclusion analogous to the leading representatives of the Frankfurt School: "rule of law," or *Rechtsstaat,* provides a necessary and indispensable "magic wall" safeguarding civil society from the constant threat of authoritarian encroachments.[54]

The *Gauchistes* of the 1960s and early 1970s equated Gaullism with fascism. By the same token, they viewed themselves—mistakenly, as it turns out—as a new "resistance." (One might point out that, viewed sociologically, the conflation of Gaullism with fascism helps to explain the preponderance of Jews in Gauche Prolétarienne leadership positions.) But the 1970s taught the leftists—Foucault included—an important lesson: societies governed by the "rule of law" contain internal prospects for progressive social change. It is this fact that distinguishes them profoundly from political dictatorships. In the eyes of France's left-wing militants, the proliferation of new social movements that proceeded under the banner of "cultural revolution"—feminism, gay rights, environmentalism, citizen initiatives, and the so-called "second left"—drove this point home indelibly and irretrievably. Along with his fellow leftists, Foucault realized that to deny this fundamental normative insight would be both hypocritical and politically self-defeating. The theory of "soft totalitarianism," according to which Communist dictatorships and Western-type "disciplinary societies" are birds of a feather, was disingenuous. It masked the fact that constitutional democracies remain open to the transformative potentials of "public reason" in a way that sets them apart qualitatively from authoritarian regimes.

WHY "FRENCH THEORY"?

There remains the issue of the widespread and influential American academic reception of French theory, much of which has proceeded under the
banner of "postmodernism." This theme raises a number of complex questions. The reception rhythms of French theory have differed from discipline
to discipline. Initially, postmodernism seemed to harbor certain muted,
redemptory expectations, e.g., in influential works such as Lyotard's *The
Postmodern Condition*, a book that first appeared twenty-five years ago.
Suffice it to say that, at this point in time, these expectations have dimmed
significantly. The "left Heidegger" take on modernity as an incessant technological nightmare— "the devastation of the earth," the reduction of all
Being to "standing reserve"—has proved untenable.[55] It would seem that
modernity's emancipatory potentials merit a second look.

In 1976 Christopher Lasch published *The Culture of Narcissism*, an
important book on the demise of the 1960s as the highpoint of public
political engagement. According to Lasch, with the Vietnam War's end, the
already problematic counterculture maxim "the personal is the political"
was elevated to the status of an *idée fixe*. A movement-oriented politics of
active contestation had given way to a highly privatized lifestyle politics.
While neoconservatives began to regroup effectively following the debacle
of Nixon's presidency, ex-1960s radicals embarked on various New Age-
inspired voyages of personal discovery.[56] Significantly, these were also the
years when French Theory vogue began to take root in North American
universities. Viewed from the standpoint of the "sociology of knowledge,"
there seems to be a strong correlation between an age of depoliticization
and postmodernism's rise to academic prominence. One feels compelled
to enquire whether, to borrow a phrase from Foucault, the postmodern
"implantation" was not essentially an expression of political *displacement*
in the Freudian sense: a sublimation of *public sphere politics* in the direction of *cultural politics*. In describing academic trends of the 1970s and
1980s, given the paramount role played by French thinkers who prided
themselves on "difficulty" —to the point where *illisibilité* or "unreadabil-
ity" became a paradoxical virtue—it is common practice to refer to the
"detour of theory." What is worrisome in retrospect is that, bluntly put,
what began as a "detour" turned into a blind alley from which the devotees
of postmodernism failed to emerge. For if one surveys postmodernism's
reception history, one fact that stands out is its stark inability to make
inroads beyond the bloodless and antiseptic corridors of academe.

As an academic phenomenon, one of postmodernism's hallmarks was
an abiding obsession with things cultural. From a methodological standpoint, this meant a heady fusion of the Frankfurt School and Gramsci,
along with the high priests of Left Bank structuralism/poststructuralism.

There is little doubt that, compared with the pieties and clichés of orthodox Marxism, the "cultural turn" was a breath of fresh air. Yet, in the long run, it fell victim to its own reductive and dogmatic assumptions. The standard metaphors of poststructuralist discourse—"textuality," "episteme," and the seemingly omnipresent Lacanian "Symbolic"—were often stretched to the point of absurdity. We now know that attempts to understand domination from a strictly cultural standpoint can be severely limiting. Crushing poverty, "ethnic cleansing," and structural unemployment are not merely the by-products or effects of "discursivity." They contain an inexpungeable *empirical dimension* that culturalist paradigms have either overlooked or systematically downplayed. Paradoxically, the upshot of the academic left's culturalist obsessions has been a consequential neglect of traditional sources of power: political domination (e.g., as practiced by the Republicans from 1980–92) and expanding economic injustice. When one surveys the preoccupations of the cultural left, it seems that both of these concerns have fallen beneath the radar scope. Thus, it is far from happenstance that the 1990s, as an epoch of globalization, witnessed a timely return of the political economy paradigm.

For some time now overseas observers of the American academic scene have reacted with bemusement at the idiosyncratic manner in which French ideas have been received across the Atlantic. One frequent target of criticism has been the appropriation of poststructuralist thought for the ends of "identity politics"—a concept that the French, educated in the rigidly assimilationist civic republican tradition, have a difficult time comprehending. (Or, as a French friend remarked a few years back: "identity politics—that's what they had in Germany between 1933 and 1945.") In France, where, for generations the "immigrants-into-Frenchmen" model of citizenship has predominated, the hyphenated ethnicities that are integral to American melting pot lore—Irish-American, African-American, Japanese-American—are essentially unknown.

One of the most common objections concerns the way that, across the Atlantic, European scholarly discourses have been refashioned to suit the utilitarian needs of political groups in search of social advancement. French commentators have been taken aback at the way in which demanding theories and concepts have provided a glib epistemological warrant for the follies of American-style political correctness and multiculturalism. They are fond of pointing to the paradox that poststructuralist doctrines that are endemically suspicious of "meaning" and "subjectivity" have become a rallying cry for the political activism of "marginalized subjectivities." Thus, ironically, in North America French philosophers whose stock-in-trade has been a deconstruction of the "transcendental subject" have been turned into intellectual oracles or gurus, provoking an adulation bordering on hero-worship.[57]

NOTES

1. Translator's Preface, François Dosse, *History of Structuralism*, vol. I, trans., D. Glassman (Minneapolis: University of Minnesota Press, 1997), xiv.
2. Claude Lévi-Strauss, "Entretien avec Jean-Marie Benoist," *Le Monde* 21–22 January 1979, 14; emphasis added.
3. Claude Lévi-Strauss, *The Savage Mind* (Chicago: University of Chicago Press, 1966), 247; emphasis added.
4. Michel Foucault, *The Order of Things*, Alan Sheridan trans. (New York: Pantheon, 1994), xxiii. "It is comforting, however, and a source of profound relief to think that man is only a recent invention, a fixture not yet two centuries old, a new wrinkle in our knowledge, and that he will disappear again as soon as that knowledge has discovered a new form." See also Nietzsche's indictment of "the last man," in *Thus Spoke Zarathustra*, trans. R. J. Hollingdale (New York: Vintage, 1961), 45–47.
5. For an excellent exploration and critique of these elements of Lévi-Strauss's oeuvre, see Tzvetan Todorov, *On Human Diversity* (Cambridge, MA: Harvard University Press, 1992), 60–89.
6. Richard Wolin, "Designer Fascism," in *Fascism's Return: Scandal, Rivision and Ideology since 1980*, Richard J. Golsan, Ed. (Lincoln: Univeristy of Nebraska Press, 1998).
7. J. G. Herder on *Social and Political Culture,* ed. F. Barnard (Cambridge: Cambridge University Press, 1969), 184, 186.
8. For Foucault's positions, see "Inutile de se soulever?" *Le Monde* 10, 661 (May 11, 1979), 12; English translation: "Is it Useless to Revolt?" *Philosophy and Social Criticism*, VIII, 1 (Spring 1981), 1–9; "Iran: the Spirit of a World Without Spirit," in *Michel Foucault: Politics, Philosophy, Culture* (New York: Routledge, 1988), 211–226; "Una polveriera chiamata Islam," *Corriere della Sera*, 104, 36 (13 February 1979). See also Janet Afaray, "Sh'I Narratives of Karbala and Christian Rites of Penance: Michel Foucault and the Culture of the Iranian Revolution, 1978–1979," *Radical History Review* 86 (Spring 2003), 7–35.
9. See the conclusion to Lévi-Strauss, *Tristes Tropiques*, trans. J. and D. Weightman (New York: Penguin, 1992), 414, where, in opposition to the Enlightenment project, the anthropologist concludes with a paean to what he calls, "the great religion of non-knowledge."
10. Owen Bradley, *A Modern Maistre: The Social and Political Thought of Joseph de Maistre* (Lincoln: University of Nebraska Press, 1999), xi–xii. As Bradley goes on to observe: "Particularly contemporary is his belief that the key to the 'normal' functioning of society is to be sought in the 'abnormality' of social excess and that social theory must therefore consider not only moments of stability but also moments of transformation and transgression. Equally fashionable is his thesis that the moorings of order are found in the spheres of language, the imaginary, and the symbolic."
11. For more on the affinities between postmodernism and political agonistics, see Chantal Mouffe, "For an Agonistic Pluralism," in *The Return of the Political* (New York: Verso, 1993), 1–8; and Chantal Mouffe, "For an Agonistic Model of Democracy," in *The Democratic Paradox* (New York: Verso, 2000), 80–107.
12. September 1945 report of the Freiburg University de-nazification commission concerning Martin Heidegger. Cited by Hugo Ott, *Martin Heidegger: Unterwegs zu seiner Biographie* (Frankfurt: Campus, 1988), 305–306.

13. For the best discussion of the circumstance surrounding the French publication of Heidegger's "Letter," see Anson Rabinbach, "Heidegger 2: The Remake" (forthcoming in New German Critique).
14. Martin Heidegger, "Letter on Humanism," in *Basic Writings* (New York: Harper Row, 1977), 232.
15. Reprinted in *Sartre, Essays in Existentialism* (Seacaucus, N J: Citadel Press, 1965), 31–62.
16. Heidegger, "Letter on Humanism," 214.
17. Ibid., 219, 220.
18. Ibid., 220.
19. The details of this episode are recounted by Ott in *Martin Heidegger*, 294.
20. Rabinbach, "Heidegger 2"; Heidegger's sons eventually returned unharmed.
21. Martin Heidegger, *Das Rektorat, 1933–34: Tatsachen und Gedanken* (Frankfurt: Klostermann, 1983), 25.
22. Cited in Richard Wolin, *The Politics of Being: The Political Thought of Martin Heidegger* (New York: Columbia University Press, 1990), 148.
23. Martin Heidegger, *Nietzsche*, vol. 4 (New York: Harper Row, 1982), 221.
24. Ibid., 215, emphasis added.
25. Heidegger, "Overcoming Metaphysics," in *The End of Philosophy* (New York: Harper Row, 1973), 82.
26. Heidegger, "Letter on Humanism," 234.
27. See, Heidegger, "Only a God Can Save Us: The Spiegel Interview," in Richard Wolin, ed., *The Heidegger Controversy: A Critical Reader* (Cambridge, MA: MIT Press, 1992), 91–116.
28. See Dominique Janicaud, *Heidegger en France*, 2 vols. (Paris: Albin Michel, 2001).
29. For an informative, Bourdieu-inspired analysis of Sartre's role in the contemporary intellectual "field," see Anna Boschetti, *The Intellectual Enterprise: Sartre and Les Temps modernes* (Evanston, IL: Northwestern, 1988).
30. Rabinbach, "Heidegger 2," 24.
31. See Heidegger's remarks to Herbert Marcuse in a letter of 12 May 1948, where the philosopher observes that he made common cause with Nazism insofar as he "expected from National Socialism a spiritual renewal of life in its entirety, a reconciliation of social antagonisms, and a deliverance of Western Dasein from the danger of communism." Heidegger's letter may be found in Wolin, *The Heidegger Controversy*, 162–163.
32. Vincent Descombes, *Modern French Philosophy* (Cambridge: Cambridge University Press, 1980), 31.
33. Epistémon (alias Didier Anzieu), *Ces Idées qui ont ébranlé la France* (Paris: Fayard, 1968).
34. Julian Bourg, "May 1968 and the Institution of Civil Society," paper presented at the Columbia University conference on "Liberalism's Return," April 11–12, 2004.
35. Alexis de Tocqueville, *Democracy in America*, G. Lawrence trans. (New York: Harper and Row, 1966), 513, 516, 514.
36. See Pierre Rosanvallon, *Le Modèle politique français: la société civile contre le jacobinisme de 1789 à nos jours* (Paris: Seuil, 2004), 428. I thank Julian Bourg for providing this reference.
37. See the remarks of Michael Seidman, *The Imaginary Revolution: Parisian Students and Workers in 1968* (New York: Berghahn Books, 2004), 7: "May was significant since it gave protesters the opportunity to begin emancipating themselves from a traditional and conservative Gaullist regime."

38. François Dosse, *History of Structuralism*, vol. II, D. Silverman trans. (Minneapolis: University of Minnesota Press, 1967), 112–121.
39. See Michele Lamont, "How to Become a Dominant French Philosopher: the Case of Jacques Derrida," *American Journal of Sociology* 93, no.3 (1987), 607.
40. François Dosse, *The Empire of Meaning: The Humanization of the Social Sciences*, trans. H. Melehy (Minneapolis: University of Minnesota Press, 1999), xvi.
41. Ibid., xviii.
42. On this point, see Dosse, *History of Structuralism*, vol. II, chapter 31, "The Subject; or, The Return of the Repressed," 324–335.
43. See P. Forest, *L'Histoire de Tel Quel* (Paris: Minuit, 1992).
44. Ron Haas, "May '68 and French Cultural Revolution," paper presented at the meeting of the Society of French Historical Studies, Paris, June 18, 2004.
45. Cited in David Macey, *The Lives of Michel Foucault* (New York: Pantheon Press, 1993), 380.
46. Cited in Eric Weitz, *A Century of Genocide: Utopias of Race and Nation* (Princeton, NJ: Princeton University Press, 2003), 147. As Weitz observes: "Almost one-quarter of the one-hundred or so Cambodians sent to study in France in the late 1940s and 1950s, including Pol Pot, Ieng Sary, and Khieu Samphan, joined the French Communist Party, through which they again encountered French revolutionary republicanism but also, of course, Marxism-Leninism. In a study group, they read Marx, Lenin, [and] Stalin...Pol Pot's first published article, in 1953, 'Monarchy or Democracy?' tellingly cited the examples of the French, Russian, and Chinese revolutions, which had overthrown corrupt monarchies and replaced them with democratic regimes."
47. Michel Foucault, "On Popular Justice: A Discussion with Maoists," Translated by John Mepham, in *Power/Knowledge: Selected Interviews and Other Writings 1972–1977*, Colin Gordon, ed. (New York: Pantheon Books, 1980), 1–36.
48. Michel Foucault, *Preface to Gilles Deleuze and Félix Guattari, Anti-Oedipus: Capitalism and Schizophrenia* (New York: Pantheon, 1977).
49. Michel Foucault, "La Grande Colère des faits," *Le Nouvel Observateur*, May 9, 1977, 85.
50. See the discussion of these developments in James Miller, *The Passion of Michel Foucault* (New York: Simon and Schuster, 1993), 327.
51. Dosse, *History of Structuralism*, vol. II, 336.
52. Miller, *Michel Foucault*, 315.
53. Michel Foucault, *The History of Sexuality*, vol. 1, Robert Hurley, trans. (New York: Vintage Books, 1990), 159.
54. Franz Neumann, "The Rechtsstaat as Magic Wall," in *Rule of Law Under Siege*, W. Scheuerman, ed. (Berkeley: University of California Press, 1996), 243–265.
55. Heidegger, "Overcoming Metaphysics," in Wolin, *The Heidegger Controversy*, 67–90.
56. For an excellent account and critique of this situation, see Todd Gitlin, "The Anti-Political Populism of Cultural Studies," *Dissent* (Spring 1997).
57. See the remarks in François Cusset, *French Theory: Foucault, Derrida, Deleuze et Cie. Et les mutations de la vie intellectuelle aux États-Unis* (Paris: La Découverte, 2003), especially 293–296. See also Vincent Descombes, "Je m'en Foucault," *London Review of Books*, March 5, 1987; Descombes, too, stresses the extreme "décalage" or abyss between the American and French employments of French Theory.

9 "The Democratic Literature of the Future"

Richard Rorty, Postmodernism, and the American Poetic Tradition[1]

Simon Stow

Richard Rorty's relationship to postmodernism is a source of considerable controversy. For many, Rorty is the living embodiment of everything that is wrong with the postmodern academy: a promoter of relativism over objectivity; custom over Truth; rhetoric over Reason; art over science; and theory over practice. Susan Haack complains that there "could be no honest intellectual work in Rorty's post-epistemological utopia;"[2] Terry Eagleton scorns him for his elitism;[3] Richard Posner declares him "nostalgic, pessimistic, almost Spenglerian, cursory, and wholly without practical suggestions;"[4] and Norman Geras complains that Rorty's worldview "leads by the shortest possible route to the outlook of...[the]...persecutors and murderers" of the Third Reich.[5] It is a view in which, according to Simon Blackburn, "the cloven-hooved and triple-horned figure of Richard Rorty" leads "the danse macabre in the steps of Nietzsche, Lyotard and Derrida."[6] Equally, however, for many of those thinkers responsible for popularizing postmodernism in the Anglophone world, this same dancing-devil of postmodernism is a very much a reactionary figure, one opposed to both their intellectual and political outlook. Ernesto Laclau chides Rorty for his uncritical acceptance of liberalism;[7] Chantal Mouffe for his "complacency;"[8] and Jonathan Culler, writing in 1988, declared Rorty's work "altogether appropriate for the age of Reagan,"[9] a particularly galling criticism for anybody no doubt, but doubly so for a person such as Rorty raised in a Trotskyite household.

What then has Rorty done to engender such hostility from both the defenders of Truth with a capital "T" and the advocates of deconstruction with a small "d"? The simple answer is that he has told a story in which many of the ideas associated with postmodernism have been combined with a tradition of American pragmatic philosophy to support the political institutions of American-style liberalism. Rorty has collapsed many of the apparent distinctions between postmodernism and pragmatism to construct a seamless narrative in which both lead—albeit contingently and not inevitably—to the politics of twenty-first century America. As such, in Rorty's case, "historicizing postmodernism"—showing the ways in which the ideas associated with postmodernism have been incorporated into, and been transformed by their association with, local intellectual traditions—simply seems to require recounting his narrative and noting the ways in which Rorty has borrowed from postmodernism to bolster his pragmatist defense of liberalism. Nevertheless, once we start to do this, the vehement objections of both the pragmatists and the postmodernists to Rorty's characterizations of their work suggests that—as befits a self-confessed ironist such as Rorty—there is considerably more going on in his work than his simple story suggests. Indeed, paying close attention to these objections reveals often small but significant differences between Rorty and those whom he would regard as allies. It is these differences, along with Rorty's philosophical *style*, which suggest that his work belongs to neither pragmatism nor postmodernism, but rather to an indigenous tradition of artists, poets and thinkers concerned to provide a literary foundation for the American Republic by writing what Walt Whitman called "the democratic literature of the future."[10] Viewed from this perspective, Rorty's relationship to postmodernism becomes largely one of philosophical coincidence and poetic opportunism. Establishing this claim requires, of course, recounting Rorty's story about pragmatism and postmodernism; identifying the American political poetic tradition; locating Rorty's work within it; and finally showing how Rorty used and then abandoned the popular characterization of postmodernism in order to promote his own political agenda. First, however, it is necessary to say a word or two about terminology.

As the furor generated by Richard Rorty's work suggests, the term "postmodernism" is something of a shibboleth, dividing people according to their vastly differing perceptions of the word. Here the word "postmodernism," as well as its various derivations including "postmodern" and "postmodernist," is being used in the way it is currently used in common academic parlance—as Richard Rorty himself often seems to use it—as a label that is used to describe a worldview that is never clearly defined, but which is vaguely associated with stylistic irony, a rejection of objective Truth, intrinsic textual meaning, and philosophical foundations. Here it will be suggested that although Rorty holds many—though crucially not all—of the philosophical views identified as being associated with postmodernism in the introduction to this volume, he is often deliberately vague about his use of the term in order to advance his political agenda. Indeed, it will be argued that both of these aspects of his work—his deliberate vagueness and his opportunism—further help to locate him within a tradition of distinctly American political poetry. Nevertheless, such aspects are by themselves insufficient to connect Rorty to this tradition. The definition of tradition that is being employed here—borrowed from the work of Mark Bevir—demands not only a family resemblance amongst a core set of ideas, but also clear historical evidence of influence, shared understandings, and links between the thinkers in the tradition.[11] For this reason, Rorty's connection to this tradition will also be established by providing evidence of the manner in which Rorty has consciously sought not only to inherit this tradition, but also to transform it and pass it on.

PRIVATE IRONY AND PUBLIC HOPE: MERGING THE PRAGMATIC AND THE POSTMODERN

For many, Rorty's postmodernist hooves and horns first became evident in 1979 with the publication of *Philosophy and the Mirror of Nature*, a book in which he eschewed much of what passed for traditional philosophy.[12] Amongst other cornerstones of the discipline, Rorty rejected epistemology; the representational theory of truth; the conceptual dualisms of the mind-body and appearance-reality distinctions; as well as the suggestion that philosophy had any special insight with which to adjudicate the disputed claims of other disciplines. By way of an alternative, he sketched out an account of philosophy which focused on the more creative and problem-solving aspects of the discipline. As Rorty noted, however, *Philosophy and the Mirror of Nature* "got mostly bad reviews in all the philosophical journals, and it sold slowly at first. Very gradually, in the course of the 80's people started to read it, and eventually it did gain a certain momentum."[13] Not coincidentally, perhaps, during the period in which his book was gaining momentum, Rorty was surfing an emerging wave of French theory that was beginning to crash onto American academic shores.

According to his autobiographical essay "Trotsky and the Wild Orchids," Rorty first became aware of the then trickle of French theory into America at Princeton in about 1976. He did so via his then colleague, the literature professor Jonathan Arac.[14] A mere seven years later, in an article provocatively titled "Postmodernist bourgeois liberalism," Rorty identified the Hegelian heritage of his work and appeared explicitly to embrace the emerging theory. "I use 'postmodernist,'" he wrote, "in a sense given to this term by Jean-François Lyotard, who says that the postmodern attitude is that of a 'distrust of metanarratives,' narratives that describe or predict the activities of such entities as the noumenal self or the Absolute Spirit or the Proletariat."[15] Even here, however, Rorty was keen to tie the foreign import to an indigenous tradition. Referring to what he called John Dewey's "naturalized Hegelianism," he labeled the pragmatist "a postmodernist before his time."[16] It was, however, in 1989's *Contingency, Irony, and Solidarity* that Rorty most aggressively conflated postmodernism with American pragmatism.

"About two hundred years ago," wrote Rorty in the first chapter of that book, "the idea that truth was made rather than found began to take hold of the imagination of Europe."[17] The source of this idea was, he said, the French Revolution, which showed that "the whole vocabulary of social relations, and the whole spectrum of social institutions, could be replaced almost over night."[18] Freed from questions about the will of God and the nature of man, Rorty asserted, humanity was now free to make itself anew. It was aided in this quest, he suggested, by Charles Darwin, whose work made it possible to see all human behavior including the "fulfillment of the desire to know the unconditionally true and to do the unconditionally right—as continuous with animal behavior."[19] As such, he unfitted us, wrote Rorty, "for listening to transcendental stories" such as those of the Kant and his successors.[20] It was these purely contingent developments, Rorty asserted, that paved the way for postmodernism and pragmatism, both of which "made identical criticisms of Enlightenment and specifically Kantian attempts to view moral principles as the product of a special faculty called 'reason.' [Both]...thought that such attempts were disingenuous attempts to keep something like God alive in the midst of a secular culture."[21] Postmodernism and pragmatism were, he suggested, virtually synonymous, separated only by the names of their biggest advocates. "The great names of the first tradition," he asserted "include Heidegger, Sartre, Gadamer, Derrida and Foucault. The great names of the second...James, Dewey, Kuhn, Quine, Putnam and Davidson."[22]

Declaring that "existentialism, deconstructionism, holism, process philosophy, poststructuralism, postmodernism, Wittgensteinianism, anti-realism and hermeneutics" were all names associated with the same "anti-essentialistic, antimetaphysical movement" in philosophy, and that his own preferred term for the movement was "pragmatism,"[23] Rorty conflated a number of would-be distinct sets of claims. All, he suggested, were "ways of saying that we shall never be able to step outside language, never be able to grasp reality unmediated by linguistic description."[24] It was this recognition, he asserted, that created a new philosophical method, one that eschewed traditional argumentation. The method was, he wrote, "to redescribe lots and lots of things in new ways, until you have created a pattern of linguistic behavior which will tempt the rising generation to adopt it, thereby causing them to look for appropriate forms of nonlinguistic behavior."[25] Philosophy on this account became a kind of writing: collapsing many of the hitherto rigid distinctions between the disciplines of literature, philosophy, science and politics. As far as the latter was concerned, this method could not, said Rorty, provide any guidance for choosing between competing normative accounts of human existence. There were, he said, simply no such criteria to guide our choices. Seeking to fill this lacuna, Rorty offered his now infamous account of post-foundational liberalism.

Following Judith Shklar, Rorty suggested that liberals are simply people for whom "cruelty is the worst thing that we can do."[26] Citing Joseph Schumpeter's assertion that "[t]o realize the relative validity of one's convictions and yet stand for them unflinchingly, is what distinguishes a civilized man from a barbarian,"[27] Rorty suggested that there were no non-circular justifications for political values, and that convincing people of the need to avoid cruelty was not a matter for philosophy, but rather for "the novel, the movie and the TV program."[28] Drawing a firm public/private distinction,

Rorty argued that the pragmatic tradition—with its focus on piecemeal reforms and the here and now—would be a valuable source of insight for American public philosophy. The creativity and play that grew out of postmodernism—the sort of thing that Mark Bevir discusses in his essay in this volume—was, Rorty suggested, simply inappropriate for matters of public politics. Nevertheless, he asserted, a figure such as Derrida was entirely compatible with, and indeed essential to liberal society. Derrida's importance to postfoundational liberalism lay, he said, "in his having had the courage to give up the attempt to unite the private and the public, to stop trying to bring together a quest for private autonomy and an attempt at public resonance and utility."[29] Derrida, on Rorty's account, realized the uselessness of philosophy to politics, but nevertheless showed us that the Nietzschean quest for autonomy and self-creation was something that could still be practiced as long as it was confined to the *private* sphere. For Rorty, that is to say, liberalism was the perfect combination of postmodernist self-creation and American pragmatism: the triumph of private irony and public hope.

PUBLIC ACRIMONY AND PRIVATE ANNOYANCE: THE CRITICAL RESPONSE

If Richard Rorty felt that he was to be applauded for his efforts to conflate several would-be distinct sets of ideas—pragmatism and postmodernism among them—to offer a new justification for liberalism, he was to be sorely disappointed. "My *Contingency* book" he wrote, "got a couple of good reviews, but these were vastly outnumbered by reviews which said the book was frivolous, confused and irresponsible."[30] It was not, however, simply those knee-jerk traditionalists opposed to postmodernism—a group that Rorty characterized as "conservative know-nothings"[31]—who had a problem with Rorty's narrative; rather, it was a broad array of thinkers from many otherwise opposing traditions. Most notable among them were a number of American pragmatists who vehemently objected both to Rorty's characterization of their tradition, and to his attempts to locate himself within it.

Richard J. Bernstein spoke for many when he declared that: "when Rorty speaks of 'pragmatism' or 'we pragmatists' his meaning is so idiosyncratic that one can barely recognize any resemblance between what he says and any of the classical pragmatists."[32] Indeed, James Gouinlock objected to Rorty's reading of John Dewey, noting the former's tendency to identify a "good Dewey" with whom he agreed, and a "bad Dewey" to whom he ascribed those works—such as Dewey's *Logic: The Truth of Inquiry*—that did not fit his idiosyncratic interpretation.[33] It was an approach that not only misrepresented the pragmatist canon, Gouinlock asserted, but which also damaged its legacy. "Unwittingly but inexorably" he wrote, "Rorty threatens to undo Dewey's work, rather than carry it forward."[34] Rorty's response to Gouinlock is, however, highly revealing. "I think," he wrote, "that the letter of Dewey's teachings often become a stumbling block to a grasp of their spirit."[35] Rorty was, that is to say, largely unconcerned by the suggestion that he had somehow misread or misrepresented the work of others, be they pragmatists, neo-pragmatists, or simply those whom he chooses to characterize as such. In a footnote in *Contingency, Irony, and Solidarity*, for example, he similarly observed that "[Donald] Davidson cannot be held responsible for the interpretation I am putting on his views, nor for the further views I extrapolate from his;"[36] a suggestion with which Davidson was in wholehearted agreement.[37]

Verisimilitude in presenting the arguments of others, and precision in categorizing them, simply do not then appear to be a part of Rorty's intellectual agenda. Indeed, even when he is called to task over his readings of canonical works, his response seems to be a literal or figurative shrug of the shoulders. Facing, for example, an often hostile and sometimes scathing reaction to *Achieving Our Country* in a collection edited by John Pettigrew, Rorty offered a brief *mea culpa*—"Over and over again, in reading [these] essays, I have winced at my own ignorance of the figures, trends, and events they mention"[38]—before going on effectively to dismiss these criticisms with a brief "On the other hand," and a reiteration of his argument from the book in question. It is a strategy which explains not only why so many pragmatists are keen to disown him, but also why he does not necessarily belong to their tradition, especially given the definition of the term being employed here, one which demands clear shared-understandings between thinkers. Indeed, much about Rorty's approach suggests that he might more profitably be grouped with the postmodernists, at least as far as they are popularly understood. Nevertheless, they too seem reluctant to embrace him.

An explanation for Rorty's strong misreading of the pragmatic tradition, and further evidence for his apparently postmodernist bent seems to be found in his assertion, in *Consequences of Pragmatism*, that in reading, "the critic asks neither the author nor the text about their intention but simply beats the text into a shape that will serve his purpose. He does this by imposing a vocabulary...on the text which may have nothing to do with any vocabulary used by that text or its author."[39] Such a characterization of Rorty as a postmodernist seems, however, to find little favor with many of those figures associated with the label. Somewhat ironically perhaps, Jacques Derrida—himself often regarded as the most creative or irresponsible of the misreaders, depending on the perspective of the person doing the characterizing—seemed to object to Rorty's misreading of *his* work. Although he accepted that deconstruction "shares much" with pragmatism, and appeared to enjoy Rorty's characterization of him as a romantic utopian, Derrida baulked at Rorty's attempt to confine his work to the private sphere.[40] Similarly, Simon Critchley raised a number of what he called "critical questions about Rorty's understanding of deconstruction, particularly as this impinges on questions of ethics and politics."[41] Politically, too, many of the postmodernists objected to Rorty's attempts to associate himself with their approach. Laclau and Mouffe were joined in their objections to Rorty's complacency by Critchley, who argued that Rorty was blind to "the evidence of imperialism, racism and colonialism that have always accompanied—or perhaps has always been the reality behind the cynical veneer of a legitimating discourse—the expansionism of Western liberal democracy."[42]

Rorty appears then to be politically and philosophically friendless. As he himself noted: "If there is anything to the idea that the best intellectual position is one that is attacked with equal vigor from the political right and the political left, then I am in good shape."[43] Nevertheless, the considerable hostility generated by his narrative, and indeed, the manner in which Rorty seemed to revel in his pariah status should, perhaps, be our first clues as to how we might best characterize his relationship to postmodernism and how to place it within an indigenous American tradition. They are, however, intimately connected to a further such clue: Rorty's prevarication over his relationship to the postmodernist label.

"THAT IS NOT WHAT I MEANT AT ALL": RORTY AND POSTMODERNISM

Upon taking his current position in the Comparative Literature department at Stanford University, Rorty suggested that he be given the title "Transitory Professor of Trendy Studies." Alas, as he himself notes, "nobody liked the idea."[44] That Rorty should make such a suggestion—even perhaps as a joke—is indicative of an increasingly aggressive attempt to disassociate himself from the postmodernist label. Writing in 1998, Rorty declared that: "The word 'postmodern' has been rendered almost meaningless by being used to mean so many different things."[45] Elsewhere he has suggested that the word "never had any clear sense" and "should be dropped from our philosophical vocabulary."[46] Indeed, since the early 1990s Rorty has begun to suggest that his categorization as a postmodernist was something of a mistake, one usually forced on him by others. "Some postmodernists who initially took my enthusiasm for Derrida to mean that I must be on their political side," he wrote in 1992, "decided, after discovering that my politics were pretty much those of Hubert Humphrey, that I must have sold out."[47] Indeed, as the more recent Rorty describes it, his apparent flirtation with postmodernism was really something of a romantic misunderstanding, one in which his friendly overtures were mistaken for professions of devotion. It is, that is, as if he had never written an article entitled "Postmodernist bourgeois liberalism." And, although this later Rorty will still occasionally defend the postmodernists against their "conservative know-nothing" critics, much of what he has written since the early 1990s has been something of a "Dear Jacques" letter concerned to put as much distance as possible between his work and postmodernism as it is popularly understood. It is a letter in which Rorty seems to have three key criticisms of the postmodernists, two of which suggest that, despite the pragmatists' objections, he might still belong to their tradition, but a third which appears to put him firmly in the tradition of American public poetry concerned with writing "the democratic literature of the future."

In the first instance, Rorty objects to the way in which deconstruction's playful open-endedness has been turned into just another method. Derrida's Anglophone followers, he declared, "take him to have given us a method—the deconstructive method—of reading texts: a method which helps see what these texts are really about, what is really going on in them."[48] Such an approach is, he suggests, indicative of a metaphysical yearning. They think of Derrida "as providing new, improved tools for unmasking books and authors," but he notes that the quest for "unmasking" is the metaphysical desire to show things as they really are.[49] In the second, Rorty objects to the jargonized vocabulary the postmodernists have developed. "The contemporary academic left," he writes, "seems to think that the higher your level of abstraction, the more sweeping and novel your apparatus, the more radical your critique."[50] Such an approach is, he suggests, politically ineffective and often counter-productive.[51] Indeed, it is what he believes to be the inapplicability of much of what passes for postmodernism to practical politics that draws the greatest part of Rorty's ire. "After reading Jameson," he wrote about *The Cultural Logic of Late Capitalism*, "you have views on practically everything except what needs to be done."[52] It is, however, Rorty's third criticism of the postmodernists that is most revealing. They are, he suggests, "unpatriotic."[53]

"The left's hostility [to me]" wrote Rorty in "Trotsky and the Wild Orchids," "is partially explained by the fact that most people who admire Nietzsche, Heidegger and Derrida as much as I do—most of the people who either classify themselves as 'postmodernist' or (like me) find themselves thus classified willy-nilly—participate in what Jonathan Yardley has called the 'America Sucks Sweepstakes.' Participants in this event compete to find better, bitterer ways of describing the United States."[54] Lest he sound too much like those whom he dismisses as "conservative know-nothings," Rorty notes that he admires the work done by figures such as Noam Chomsky and the postmodernist-Left on the problem of America's foreign policy, and that as such, he is a proponent of a self-critical patriotism which suggests that the only way for America to move forward is to acknowledge her oftentimes shameful past.[55] Such patriotism is, he suggests, "compatible with remembering that we expanded our boundaries by massacring the tribes which blocked our way, that we broke the word we had pledged at the Treaty of Guadalupe Hidalgo, and that we caused the death of a million Vietnamese out of sheer macho arrogance."[56] It is an approach that seems to build on the theory of moral psychology outlined by Nietzsche in his *Genealogy of Morals*; or more prosaically, perhaps, on that generated by the more enlightened parents at Little League games. The theory suggests that it is only by recognizing and taking pride in one's strengths that one is able to acknowledge and seek to change one's weaknesses. It is this "Little League Psychology" that Rorty finds missing from the current American Left. "We now have," he writes, "among many American students and teachers, a spectatorial, disgusted, mocking Left rather than a Left which dreams of achieving our country."[57] It is, he says, a Left which prefers "knowledge to hope."[58]

It is the notion of "hope" that forms the basis for much of Rorty's criticism of the postmodernist Left, a group that he sees being entirely devoid of the stuff. By "hope" Rorty seems to mean some plan or vision of the future. "The academic Left has," he suggests, "no projects to propose to America, no vision of a country to be achieved by building a consensus on specific reforms."[59] This is not, however, simply the criticism of a pragmatist turned off by the abstraction of the postmodernist approach. It is, rather, evidence of a deeper commitment in Rorty's thought, one that is manifested in his celebration of works such as Andrew Delbanco's *The Real American Dream*.[60] The claim that the current academic Left lacks *hope* is, within Rorty's moral vocabulary, one of the worst charges that he could level against them, second only perhaps to the suggestion that they were guilty of cruelty. *Hope*, and its connection to *utopia*, is a perennial theme in Rorty's political work; and it is this—along with his hostility to metaphysics and abstraction—which suggests that we should connect him not the recent postmodernist school, but rather to an older, distinctly American poetic tradition concerned with writing the "democratic literature of the future." For although, as Sara Rushing points out in her essay in this volume, postmodernism is sometimes associated with a desire to find a kind of political utopian hope that is compatible with anti-positivism, there is a distinct ambivalence and decided reticence about such attempts that stands in stark contrast to the gusto with which Rorty embraces the idea. Indeed, unlike his postmodernist counterparts who continue to seek strategies of resistance in both language and politics, Rorty—like many of his fellow poets of American democracy—appears to see this utopian hope as trumping all other approaches.

AN AMERICAN POETIC TRADITION?

To many, perhaps, seeking to locate Rorty's work within a tradition of distinctly American poetry might seem like something of a quixotic mission. Since the founding of the Republic, a persistent theme of American letters has been the absence of any such tradition worthy of the name. "In the four quarters of the globe," asked Sydney Smith in 1820, "who reads an American book? or goes to an American play? or looks at an American picture or statue?"[61] It was a comment echoed by Alexis de Tocqueville in the Second Volume of *Democracy in America* published in 1840. "The inhabitants of the United States have, then," he wrote, "at present, properly speaking no literature."[62] What writers they did have, Tocqueville suggested, borrowed largely from Europe. "They paint with colors borrowed from foreign manners; and as they hardly ever represent the country they were born in as it really is, they are seldom popular there."[63] In this, Tocqueville echoed Ralph Waldo Emerson whose 1837 essay "The American Scholar" called for a distinctly American poetry. "Perhaps the time is already come," he declared, "when it ought to be, and will be something else; when the sluggard intellect of this continent will look from under its iron lids, and fill the postponed expectation of the world with something better than the exertions of mechanical skill."[64] It was a call that Emerson would make repeatedly, most famously of course in 1844's "The Poet."

As many of his friends and contemporaries later made clear, *Leaves of Grass* was Walt Whitman's attempt to meet Emerson's challenge.[65] Emerson himself was initially delighted by this effort, sending Whitman a letter of congratulation, the most famous excerpt from which—"I greet you at the beginning of a great career"—the ever self-promotional Whitman took to printing as an endorsement in subsequent editions of the text. It is, however, a less-famous extract from Emerson's letter that best captures the dominant motif of the American poetic tradition that connects both Whitman and Rorty. "It has," wrote Emerson of Whitman's epic poem, "the best merits, namely of fortifying & encouraging."[66] It is this commitment to fortifying and encouraging through a distinctly American literature that connects Whitman to Rorty, and Rorty to the American poetic tradition. It is, furthermore, a tradition with which Rorty has consciously sought to align himself, most notably in his later works where, in addition to citing Whitman's *Democratic Vistas* as an inspiration,[67] he has taken to quoting approvingly Whitman's suggestion that the "United States themselves are essentially the greatest poem."[68]

Two key aspects of this American poetic tradition are a concern with writing a distinctly American poetry for a specifically American audience, and for generating optimism and hope within that audience about the possibilities of America's democratic future. As Whitman declared in the preface to the first edition of *Leaves of Grass*: "The attitude of Great Poets is to cheer up slaves and horrify despots."[69] Underpinning these concerns is, however, an almost complete faith in the moral, political and emotional power of literature, not only to support the democratic institutions of the American Republic, but also to *create* the nation itself. Rorty's own belief in the power of literature is well documented. He describes literary criticism as the paradigmatic critical practice in contemporary society, suggesting that it does for thinkers such as himself "what the search for universal moral principles is supposed to do for metaphysicians."[70] In so doing, he echoes Whitman's own belief in the power of literature, that which he calls "the greatest art."[71] "Our fundamental want to-day in the United States," Whitman declared:

> with our closest, amplest reference to present conditions, and to the future, is of a class, and the clear idea of a class, of native authors, literatures far different, far higher in grade than any yet known, sacerdotal, modern, fit to cope with our occasions, lands, permeating the whole mass of American mentality, taste, belief, breathing into it a new breath of life, giving it decision, affecting politics far more than the popular superficial suffrage, with results inside and underneath the elections of Presidents or Congresses—radiating, begetting appropriate teachers, schools, manners, and, as its grandest result, accomplishing, (what neither the schools nor the churches and their clergy have hitherto accomplish'd, and without which this nation will no more stand, permanently, soundly, than a house will stand without a substratum) a religious and moral character beneath the political and productive and intellectual basis of the States.[72]

"Above all previous lands," Whitman continued, "a great original literature is surely to become the justification and reliance, (in some respects the sole reliance) of American democracy."[73] For Whitman then, as for Rorty, literature was to provide the basis for the American Republic. Sharing a mutual suspicion of metaphysics, both figures reject philosophy—political or otherwise—as a foundation for the nation. Indeed, Whitman declares that the writer of such poetry is "no arguer,"[74] and suggests that his effectiveness relies not on argument, but on results alone. "The proof of a poet is," he declares, "that his country absorbs him as affectionately as he has absorbed it."[75] The effect, that is to say, is performative. Such performativity—itself often associated with postmodernism—finds its echo in Rorty's work. "I am not," he writes, "going to offer arguments against the vocabulary I want to replace. Instead, I am going to make the vocabulary I favor look attractive by showing how it may be used to describe a variety of topics."[76] Indeed, both thinkers suggest that the value of literature lies precisely in its moral and emotive power. Whitman's assertion that the "true question to ask respecting a book, is, *has it help'd any human soul?*"[77] finds its echo in Rorty's suggestion that we "should see great works of literature as great because they have inspired many readers, not as having inspired many readers because they are great."[78]

Within this tradition, the job of the poet is to provide a vision of the American future towards which citizens can aspire. It is precisely this that Whitman seeks to provide in his *Democratic Vistas*. "I submit," he writes, "...that the fruition of democracy on aught like a grand scale, resides altogether in the future."[79] The poet must provide, he suggests, a vision of this future, what he calls "the fervid and tremendous IDEA, melting everything else with restless heat, and solving all lesser and definite distractions in vast, indefinite, spiritual, emotional power."[80] It is this aspect of Whitman's work that finds its echo in *Achieving Our Country* when Rorty asserts that "you cannot urge national political renewal on the basis of descriptions of fact. You have to describe the country in terms of what you passionately hope it will become, as well as in terms of what you know it to be now. You have to be loyal to a dream country rather than to one to which you wake up every morning. Unless such loyalty exists, the ideal has no chance of becoming actual."[81] Indeed, Rorty—following Whitman's own rejection of argument—suggests that "it is not much use pointing to the 'internal contradictions' of a social practice, or 'deconstructing' it unless one can come up with an alternative practice—unless one can at least sketch a utopia."[82] In stark contrast to Foucault's assertion that "to imagine another system is to extend our participation in the present system,"[83] Rorty's work is positively bursting with calls to and for utopia. In *Achieving Our Country*, for example, Rorty borrows from the American pragmatic tradition and approvingly cites William James's observation that: "Faiths and utopias are the noblest exercise of human reason."[84]

In borrowing from the American pragmatic tradition to make his case, Rorty is, once again, following the lead of Whitman who likewise borrowed from a variety of sources in fashioning his narrative. Rorty suggests that the poet's "job is to pick out useful strands from each and then weave a new, improved, narrative."[85] The current intellectual Left would, for example, do better he suggests, "if they emphasized the similarities rather than the differences between Malcolm X and Bayard Rustin, between Susan B. Anthony and Emma Goldman, between Catharine MacKinnon and Judith Butler."[86] Tellingly, Rorty sets out to do precisely that: to weave a narrative that will, he believes, produce a better outcome for America. It is a narrative that puts together such apparently contradictory figures as Trotsky and Eliot, Nabokov and Freud, Kant and Hegel, Nietzsche and Mill and, of course, the American pragmatists and the French postmodernists. In this, Rorty is simply following the lead of Whitman who, in a long footnote to *Democratic Vistas*, identifies various other kinds of literature, including the Old and New Testament, Plutarch, Homer, Milton, Cervantes and Shakespeare, of which he observes: "These, I say, are models, combined, adjusted to other standards than America's, but of priceless value to her and hers."[87] The poet's job is, he suggests, to make such material useful to America. "To him," he writes "the other continents arrive as contributions."[88] He is to do so by weaving a narrative out of the materials he has at hand, regardless of the relationships of these materials to each other. As Whitman declares in perhaps the most famous passage of his most famous work:

> Do I contradict myself?
> Very well then....I contradict myself;
> I am large....I contain multitudes.[89]

Whitman and Rorty both seek to create a narrative out of the conflicting voices of the American Republic, borrowing from wherever they can— even foreign traditions—to make their distinctly American poetry. It is an approach that depends entirely upon its *effect*: it is precisely for this reason that those criticisms of Rorty which focus on his readings, misreadings, or apparent *misunderstandings* of the thinkers whose work he draws from in his own narrative are so misplaced. Indeed, Rorty himself calls such critics "second rate": such critics misunderstand the purpose of the exercise, focusing on the *details* and not on the desired or actual *effects*.[90]

Central to achieving this poetic effect is the creation and aggrandizement of the figure of the poet-hero. The aim here is to underpin and enhance the force of the poet's words, and his effects, by presenting a vision of what Malcolm Cowley called "his idealized or dramatized self."[91] As Rorty memorably observed: "you cannot make a memorable character without thereby making a suggestion about how your reader should act."[92] As befits the weaver of a narrative that borrows from many, often conflicting, traditions, the creation of the poet-hero has many aspects. Most obviously in Whitman's case there is the daguerreotype of the author that graced the first edition of *Leaves of Grass*. Whitman is depicted with his shirt open-necked, hand on hip, and his hat and head jauntily cocked to one side. As Cowley continues: "The hero depicted in the frontispiece—this hero named 'I' or 'Walt Whitman' in the text should not be confused with the Whitman of daily life…he is put forward as an representative American workingman, but one who prefers to loaf and invite his soul."[93] It is an approach that finds its echo in the jaunty Richard Rorty depicted on the cover of *Contingency, Irony, and Solidarity*. The same open-necked shirt, head tilt and arm arrangement, combined with Rorty's engaging smile suggest, perhaps, a less-threatening approach to philosophy than the irascible, scowling James Coburn look-a-like Rorty depicted on the cover of Herbert Saatkamp's *Rorty & Pragmatism* collection.[94] Indeed, both Whitman and Rorty share an acute concern with the presentation and reception of their own work, not least because, in a very important way, the substance of their work relies on its *style*. It is a concern that manifests itself in Whitman's publication of Emerson's letter in subsequent editions of his poem; and in Whitman's penning—under various pseudonyms—the majority of the favorable reviews that his book received upon its publication.[95] We see the same thing in Richard Rorty's ongoing account of, and his reaction to, the popular reception of his books. Thus, when David L. Hall declares that Rorty "suffers…from 'the last infirmity of the noble mind'—the desire for fame,"[96] he captures something about Rorty's self-aggrandizement, but misses its broader political purpose. It is a publicly-oriented trope, one that finds its fullest expression in the never-ending call for a distinctly American poetry.

The call for an American poetry that will serve as a basis for the Republic has been around as long as the Republic itself, evident as much in Noah Webster's assertion that American art ought to be judged in and of itself and not against European standards, as in Charles Wilson's Peale's stated hope that his art and museum would "influence public opinions that republicanism would be highly promoted."[97] A key aspect of this tradition is, however, a call for an art or poetry just like the one being offered by the person making the call. We see this not only in the work of Webster, Peale, and Emerson, but also in that of Whitman and Rorty too. In the preface to the 1855 edition of *Leaves of Grass*, Whitman declares that America "awaits the gigantic and generous treatment worthy of it."[98] America is, he suggests, particularly fertile ground for such poets. "Of all nations the United States with veins full of poetical stuff most need poets and will doubtless have the greatest and use them the greatest."[99] It is a call for an American public poetry that he repeats several times more in *Democratic Vistas*. "Never was anything more wanted," he writes, "than, today, and here in the States, the poet of the modern is wanted, or the great literatus of the modern."[100] It is a call for a popular political poetry aimed at the masses. "I should demand" he continues, "a programme of culture, drawn out, not for a single class alone, or for the parlors or lecture-rooms, but with an eye to practical life, the west, the working-men, the facts of farms and jack-planes and engineers, and of the broad range of women also of the middle and working strata, and with reference to the perfect equality of women, and of a grand and powerful motherhood."[101] Whitman is, in effect, calling for a poetry just like his own and, in so doing, aggrandizing both himself and his work. We see the same trope in Richard Rorty's work. "We would like," he writes, "to be able to admire both Blake and Arnold, both Nietzsche and Mill...So we hope some critic will show us how these men's books can be put together to form a beautiful mosaic."[102] It is not coincidental that Rorty himself is such a critic, just as when he says: "It would be good to have a reformist text, one...which did not say that all things must be made new, or that justice can be attained only by the forcible overthrow of all existing social conditions. It would be as well to have a document which spelled out the details of a this-worldly utopia without assuring us that this utopia will emerge full-blown, and quickly, as soon as some single decisive change has occurred."[103] He is, that is to say, making a call for a text much like the one he has sought to provide in *Contingency, Irony, and Solidarity* or *Achieving Our Country*.

The American poetic tradition to which Rorty belongs is then one that valorizes the role of the poet and his role in the creation of the American Republic. It is a trope that we see as much in Whitman and Emerson's call for a distinctly American poetry as in Rorty's assertion that "the poet, in the generic sense of the maker of new words, the shaper of new languages, [is] the vanguard of the species."[104] For Rorty the poet is someone "who makes things new,"[105] one who invents new languages, and who can thereby change the world. "[C]hanging the way we talk," says Rorty, is a way of "changing what we do and what we think we are."[106] Such figures impose their will on the world through the sheer strength of their language, through the "method" of redescription. It is this which is, he says, "the 'method' of utopian politics;" most significantly it is, he suggests, *his* method.[107] Such figures, Rorty suggests, are what he calls "Strong Poets." Their function is to obliterate previous readings and meanings with the strength of their interpretations. As his predecessor observed in *Leaves of Grass*: "He most honors my style who learns under it to destroy the teacher."[108] It is a method that Rorty believes is common to scientists, poets and political thinkers.[109] In this sense, the term "poet" is all encompassing. Foreshadowing Rorty's later work on Thomas Kuhn, for example, Whitman observes that: "Exact science and its practical movement are no checks on the greatest poet but there is always encouragement and support."[110] Indeed, describing his method as "[w]hatever works" Rorty suggests that "[y]ou use whatever phrases the audience learned growing up and you apply them to the object at hand."[111] It is an approach that collapses the distinctions between disciplines and between high and low culture in the interests of achieving its effects. Just as Whitman borrowed from folk songs and Italian opera, Rorty declares that the job of binding people together is a task "for genres such as ethnography, the journalist's report, the comic book, the docudrama, and, especially, the novel."[112] The reference to journalism is, however, revealing of the tradition.

After having dismissed the existence of an American literary tradition in the second volume of his *Democracy in America*, Tocqueville observes: "The only authors whom I acknowledge as American are journalists. They indeed are great writers, but they speak the language of their country and make themselves heard."[113] As such, Tocqueville's failure to find an indigenous American literary tradition might be thought to arise not from the absence of such a tradition, but rather from Tocqueville's failure to recognize that the American tradition was somewhat different from the aristocratic European literary tradition that he was taking as his model. Indeed, the work of figures such as Noah Webster, Hugh Henry Brackenridge, and William Dunlap suggests that at the time of Tocqueville's writing there was a tradition of American writers, thinkers and artists who displayed a number of traits that we see in both Whitman and Rorty. All were concerned with using art and literature as a foundation for the Republic; an engagement with practical political matters; a willingness to borrow from European sources to fashion their own distinctive style; and a concern with self-aggrandizement and self-promotion that was linked to their broader nationalistic goals.[114] Indeed, Emerson's call for a national poetry was, in many ways, a response to what he perceived to be the failure of these socially-focused efforts. In his "Divinity School Address" and elsewhere, Emerson preached the value of the individual artist separate from society, advocating an artistic withdrawal in order to follow what he called "the highest Instinct." After Emerson, notes Joseph J. Ellis: "Alienation became the customary and most comfortable posture for American intellectuals; criticism rather than celebration of the dominant American institutions and attitudes became the accepted norm."[115] As such, it is unsurprising that the publicly focused Whitman should eventually draw Emerson's ire. In Rorty's work, however, we see the combination of both strands of this American poetic tradition. The connection to Whitman's public poetry is only the most dominant strand. In his focus on what he calls Nietzschean self-creation in liberalism, Rorty is also connected to the Emersonian, private aspects of the tradition. Indeed, Rorty describes Nietzsche as Emerson's "disciple," arguing that the latter's "America was not so much a community of fellow citizens as a clearing in which Godlike heroes could act out self-written dramas."[116] In advocating a vision of liberalism as the triumph of private irony and public hope, Rorty is weaving a new narrative out of the both these strands—Whitman *and* Emerson—combining both to offer a new vision for the American Republic, and in so doing, placing himself firmly in their American poetic tradition.

HISTORICIZING RORTY'S POSTMODERNISM

If we accept this characterization of Rorty as an American poet of democracy in the tradition of Walt Whitman, Ralph Waldo Emerson, as well as their precursors and successors, such as Noah Webster, William Carlos Williams, and, most recently, Cornel West—a figure who not only self-consciously embodies this tradition but who also explicitly acknowledges Rorty's influence[117]—then we might think of Rorty's relationship to the set of ideas known as postmodernism as one largely of contingency and philosophical coincidence. Rorty, like many of these American poets of democracy, holds a number of the philosophical views associated with postmodernism. Most obviously there is the belief in the power of language to shape the world, a view that corresponds to what the editors of this volume call linguistic antirepresentationalism. Similarly, the likes of Rorty, Whitman, and Webster all hold some version of epistemological antifoundationalism, a rejection of eternal principles or fixed perspectives.[118] Much the same can be said for ontological essentialism, with Rorty and his fellow writers having what appears to be a limitless belief in the plasticity of human beings to shape and be shaped by their circumstances. In their collapsing of disciplinary boundaries, and their embracing of both science *and* poetry, high *and* low culture, these writers in the American poetic tradition might also be thought to share postmodernism's conceptual anti-dualism. Similarly, stylistic irony is a constant across both approaches. Nevertheless, Rorty and his ilk are considerably less concerned with the questions of power that dominate the work of the postmodernists. They are, furthermore, certainly no anti-humanists in the way in which that term is understood to suggest a rejection of free agency and liberal autonomy. Indeed, Rorty's criticism of Foucault's failure to realize that "the selves shaped by modern liberal societies are better than the selves earlier societies created,"[119] captures the difference between the respective stances of the American poetic tradition and that of the postmodernists. As such, we might conclude that the connections between the American poetic tradition and the set of ideas known as postmodernism seem to be more generalized—and far less congruent—than the Bevirean concept of tradition would allow. This does not mean, of course, that Rorty has no connection to postmodernism. Indeed, it was the apparent similarities between his poetic tradition and the ideas associated with postmodernism which made Rorty's opportunistic use of the popular characterization of these ideas both so seamless, and so initially successful.

For Rorty then, postmodernism was very much a flag of convenience under which he sailed for a period in the 1980s and 1990s. He used the emerging interest in the concept to promote his own distinctly American, distinctly liberal-democratic agenda. Postmodernist texts—such as those penned by Derrida and Lyotard—were simply part of a vast body of literatures that Rorty appropriated for his own ends. They were further narrative material from which he sought to weave his own story in much the same way that Whitman, Webster and Dunlap appropriated European artistic traditions and adapted them to the American context for American purposes. That this older poetic tradition shares a number of important philosophical assumptions with the set of ideas known as postmodernism made this borrowing and weaving easier than it might otherwise have been, and, for a brief period at least, offered Rorty a number of potential allies in his quest to provide a new grounding for liberalism and the American polity in a postfoundational world. When it became apparent, however, that such an association was a hindrance rather than a help, Rorty—displaying the opportunism of the poet who weaves from whatever is at hand in order to achieve his desired effect—sought to disassociate himself from the postmodernists and to seek out new allies. As he himself suggests, there was nothing particularly *postmodern* about his approach. "Deconstruction," he wrote in 1989, "is not a novel procedure made possible by a recent philosophical discovery. Recontextualization in general, and inverting hierarchies is particular, has been around for a long time. Socrates recontextualized Homer; Augustine recontextualized the pagan virtues…and Hegel recontextualized Socrates and Augustine."[120] Rorty simply appropriated this method towards his own end, that which he, following James Baldwin, calls "Achieving Our Country."

DON'T LOOK BACK: THE DEMOCRATIC
LITERATURE OF THE FUTURE

In closing, it might be noted that this tradition of American poetry to which Rorty belongs is one that places great emphasis on the future. The vision of America towards which it seeks to inspire its citizens is always some way off, always to be strived for and never, perhaps, to be achieved. In this it might be argued, the tradition not only preempts the criticisms leveled against Rorty's work by the postmodernists, it may actually be better suited to achieving their goals. For Rorty, as for all his precursors within the tradition, the model of America is always a model of a better America, one in which her promises and benefits have been extended to all her citizens. As such, neither Rorty, nor the tradition to which he belongs, might be accused of complacency about America, liberalism or their values, except to the extent that they both see the values on which the nation was founded as being sufficient for her improvement. In this tradition, the future of America is always open. Rorty notes that his project would "regard the realization of utopias, and the envisaging of still further utopias, as an endless, proliferating realization of Freedom, rather than a convergence toward an already existing Truth."[121] More significantly, perhaps, in inviting all of her citizens to help write America—what Whitman called "the greatest poem"[122]—Rorty, and the tradition to which he belongs, offers hope for that democratic future, rather than a mere litany of criticism and failures in the manner of the great majority of the postmodernist Left. As Rorty notes, self-consciously following Whitman in this as in much else, "[t]he vista, not the endpoint, matters."[123]

NOTES

1. This work was completed with the assistance of a Faculty Summer Research Grant from The College of William and Mary. The author is grateful to the participants in the conference "Historicizing Postmodernism: The Untold Story of Ideas Some Call Postmodern," at the University of California, Berkeley, September 11–12th, 2004, especially Mark Bevir, Fred Dolan, Jill Hargis, Paul Rabinow, and Sara Rushing, for their comments.
2. Susan Haack, "Vulgar Pragmatism: An Unedifying Prospect," in *Rorty & Pragmatism: The Philosopher Responds to his Critics*, ed. Herman J. Saatkamp (Nashville, TN: Vanderbilt University Press, 1995), 139.
3. Terry Eagleton, *The Eagleton Reader*, ed. Stephen Regan (Oxford: Blackwell, 1998), 285.
4. Richard Posner, *Public Intellectuals: A Study of Decline* (Cambridge, MA: Harvard University Press, 2001), 340.
5. Norman Geras, *Solidarity in the Conversation of Humankind: The Ungroundable Liberalism of Richard Rorty* (London: Verso, 1995), 73.
6. Simon Blackburn, "Richard Rorty," *Prospect*, March 20, 2003.
7. Ernesto Laclau, "Deconstruction, Pragmatism, Hegemony," in *Deconstruction and Pragmatism*, ed. Chantal Mouffe (London: Routledge, 1996), 65.
8. Chantal Mouffe, "Deconstruction, Pragmatism and the Politics of Democracy," in *Deconstruction and Pragmatism*, 6, 10.
9. Jonathan Culler, *Framing the Sign: Criticism and Its Institutions* (Oklahoma City: Oklahoma University Press, 1988), 55.
10. Walt Whitman, "Democratic Vistas," in *Complete Poetry and Prose* (New York: The Library of America, 1982), 972.

11. Mark Bevir, *The Logic of the History of Ideas* (Cambridge: Cambridge University Press, 1999).
12. Richard Rorty, *Philosophy and The Mirror of Nature* (Princeton, NJ: Princeton University Press, 1979).
13. Richard Rorty, quoted in Derek Nystrom and Kent Puckett, *Against Bosses, Against Oligarchies: A Conversation with Richard Rorty* (Charlottesville, VA: Prickly Pear Pamphlets, 1998), 53.
14. Richard Rorty, "Trotsky and the Wild Orchids," in Richard Rorty, *Philosophy and Social Hope* (London: Penguin Books, 1999), 12.
15. Richard Rorty, "Postmodernist bourgeois liberalism," in Richard Rorty, *Objectivism, Relativism, and Truth: Philosophical Papers Volume 1* (Cambridge: Cambridge University Press, 1991), 198–199.
16. Rorty, "Postmodernist bourgeois liberalism," 201.
17. Richard Rorty, *Contingency, Irony, and Solidarity* (Cambridge: Cambridge University Press, 1989), 3.
18. Rorty, *Contingency, Irony, and Solidarity*, 3.
19. Richard Rorty, "A World Without Substances or Essences," in *Philosophy and Social Hope* (London: Penguin, 1999), 68.
20. Ibid.
21. Richard Rorty, "Introduction: Relativism: Finding and Making," in *Philosophy and Social Hope*, xxix.
22. Ibid., xix.
23. Rorty, "A World Without Substances or Essences," 47–48.
24. Ibid., 48.
25. Rorty, *Contingency, Irony, and Solidarity*, 9.
26. Judith Shklar, cited in Rorty, *Contingency, Irony, and Solidarity*, xv, 74.
27. Joseph Schumpeter, cited in Rorty, *Contingency, Irony, and Solidarity*, 46.
28. Rorty, *Contingency, Irony, and Solidarity*, xvi.
29. Ibid., 125.
30. Rorty, "Trotsky and the Wild Orchids," 14.
31. Richard Rorty, "Remarks on Deconstruction and Pragmatism," in *Deconstruction and Pragmatism*, 13.
32. Richard J. Bernstein, "American Pragmatism: The Conflict of Narratives," in *Rorty & Pragmatism*, 63.
33. James Gouinlock, "What is the Legacy of Instrumentalism? Rorty's Interpretation of Dewey," in *Rorty & Pragmatism*, 72. See also, Thelma Z. Lavine, "America and the Contestations of Modernity: Bentley, Dewey, Rorty," in the same collection, 37–49.
34. Gouinlock, 87.
35. Richard Rorty, "Response to Gouinlock," in *Rorty & Pragmatism*, 99.
36. Rorty, *Contingency, Irony, and Solidarity*, n.3, 10.
37. Donald Davidson, "A Coherence Theory of Truth" and "Afterthoughts, 1987," in *Reading Rorty*, ed. Alan Malachowski (Oxford: Blackwell, 1990), 139–155.
38. Richard Rorty, "Intellectual Historians and Pragmatist Philosophy," in *A Pragmatist's Progress? Richard Rorty and American Intellectual History* (New York: Roman and Littlefield, 2000), 207.
39. Richard Rorty, *Consequences of Pragmatism* (Minneapolis: University of Minnesota Press, 1982), 93.
40. "I obviously cannot accept the public/private distinction in the way he uses it in relation to my work." Jacques Derrida, "Remarks on Deconstruction and Pragmatism," in *Deconstruction and Pragmatism*, 78.

41. Simon Critchley, "Deconstruction and Pragmatism—Is Derrida a Private Ironist or a Public Liberal?" in *Deconstruction and Pragmatism*, 19.
42. Critchley, 23.
43. Rorty, "Trotsky and the Wild Orchids," 3.
44. Rorty, in *Nystrom and Puckett*, 55.
45. Richard Rorty, "Afterword: Pragmatism, Pluralism and Postmodernism," in *Philosophy and Social Hope*, 262.
46. Rorty, "Preface," *Philosophy and Social Hope*, xiv.
47. Rorty, "Trotsky and the Wild Orchids," 18.
48. Rorty, "Remarks on Deconstruction and Pragmatism," in *Deconstruction and Pragmatism*, 13.
49. Ibid., 14.
50. Richard Rorty, *Achieving Our Country: Leftist Thought in Twentieth-Century America* (Cambridge, MA: Harvard University Press), 92–93.
51. "The flurry of deconstructive activity seems to me to have added little to our understanding of literature and to have done little for leftist politics." Rorty, "Remarks on Deconstruction and Pragmatism," 15.
52. Rorty, *Achieving Our Country*, 78.
53. Richard Rorty, "The Unpatriotic Academy," in *Philosophy and Social Hope*, 252.
54. Rorty, "Trotsky and the Wild Orchids," 4.
55. "Jameson's side of the argument," he notes, "gets a lot of support among leftists in Latin America and Asia—people who have first hand knowledge of what the CIA can do to a poor nation's hopes for social justice." Rorty, *Achieving Our Country*, 57.
56. Ibid., 32.
57. Ibid., 35.
58. Ibid., 36.
59. Ibid., 15.
60. Andrew Delbanco, *The Real American Dream: A Meditation on Hope* (Cambridge, MA: Harvard University Press, 1999). See Richard Rorty, "I Hear America Sighing," *New York Times*, November 7, 1999.
61. Sydney Smith, *The Edinburgh Review*, XXIII (1820).
62. Alexis de Tocqueville, *Democracy in America*, Vol. 2. (New York: Vintage, 1990), 56.
63. Ibid., 56.
64. Ralph Waldo Emerson, "The American Scholar," in *The Portable Emerson*, ed. Carl Bode (New York: Penguin Books, 1981), 51.
65. See, for example, "Reminiscences of Walt Whitman," *The Atlantic Monthly*, Vol. 89 (2), 163–175. Whitman's friend John Townsend Trowbridge asserted that: "He freely admitted that he could never have written his poems if he had not first 'come to himself,' and that Emerson helped him to 'find himself.' I asked if he would have come to himself without that help. He said, 'Yes, but it would have taken longer.' And he used this characteristic expression: 'I was simmering, simmering, simmering; Emerson brought me to a boil.'"
66. The letter is reproduced in the Introduction to Walt Whitman, *Leaves of Grass. The First (1855) Edition*, ed. Malcolm Cowley (New York: Penguin Books, 1976), ix.
67. The first essay in Achieving Our Country is titled "American National Pride: Whitman and Dewey."
68. Walt Whitman, Leaves of Grass, quoted in Rorty, *Achieving Our Country*, 22.
69. Whitman, *Leaves of Grass*, 15.
70. Rorty, *Contingency, Irony, and Solidarity*, 80.

71. Whitman, "Democratic Vistas," 991.
72. Ibid., 932.
73. Ibid., 932–933.
74. Whitman, *Leaves of Grass*, 9.
75. Ibid., 24.
76. Rorty, *Contingency, Irony, and Solidarity*, 9.
77. Whitman, "Democratic Vistas," 987.
78. Rorty, *Achieving Our Country*, 136.
79. Whitman, "Democratic Vistas," 956.
80. Ibid., 935–936.
81. Rorty, Achieving Our Country, 101.
82. Richard Rorty, "Introduction," in *Objectivity, Relativism, and Truth*, 1991), 16.
83. Michel Foucault, *Language, Counter-Memory, Practice: Selected Essays and Interviews*, ed. Paul Rabinow (Ithaca, NY: Cornell University Press, 1990), 230.
84. William James, cited in Rorty, *Contingency, Irony, and Solidarity*, 9.
85. Richard Rorty, "Response to Bernstein," in *Rorty & Pragmatism*, 68.
86. Rorty, *Achieving Our Country*, 51.
87. Whitman, "Democratic Vistas," n. 959.
88. Whitman, *Leaves of Grass*, 6.
89. Ibid., 85.
90. Richard Rorty, "Posties," *The London Review of Books*, September 3, 1987, 11.
91. Malcolm Cowley, "Introduction," in *Leaves of Grass*, viii.
92. Rorty, *Contingency, Irony, and Solidarity*, 167.
93. Cowley, xv.
94. Indeed, a rule of thumb for evaluating the general tenor of a book's attitude to Rorty is the picture on the cover. Those that find him sympathetic offer us the smiling Rorty, those that do not, the scowling one.
95. Cowley, viii.
96. David L. Hall, *Richard Rorty: Prophet and Poet of the New Pragmatism* (Albany, NY: SUNY Press, 1994), 231.
97. Charles Wilson Peale, quoted in Joseph J. Ellis, *After the Revolution: Profiles of Early American Culture* (New York: W.W. Norton, 1979), 70.
98. Whitman, *Leaves of Grass*, 6.
99. Ibid., 8.
100. Whitman, "Democratic Vistas," 932.
101. Ibid., 962.
102. Rorty, *Contingency, Irony, and Solidarity* 81.
103. Rorty, "Failed Prophecies, Glorious Hopes," in *Philosophy and Social Hope*, 208.
104. Rorty, *Contingency, Irony, and Solidarity*, 20.
105. Ibid., 13.
106. Ibid., 20.
107. Ibid., 7.
108. Whitman, *Leaves of Grass*, 81.
109. Indeed, Rorty identifies three examples: "Galileo, Yeats, or Hegel." *Contingency, Irony, and Solidarity*, 12.
110. Whitman, Leaves of Grass, 14.
111. Rorty, in *Nystrom and Puckett*, 57.
112. Rorty, *Contingency, Irony, and Solidarity*, xvi.
113. Tocqueville, 56.

114. For an in-depth discussion see Joseph J. Ellis, *After the Revolution: Profiles of Early American Culture.*
115. Ellis, 221.
116. Rorty, "Truth Without Correspondence to Reality," in *Philosophy and Social Hope*, 25.
117. Cornel West, "On My Intellectual Vocation," in *The Cornel West Reader* (New York: Basic Books, 1999), 26–27.
118. "Webster's nationalism derived from the relativistic perspective now associated with cultural anthropology: namely, that cultures cannot be rated on some hypothetical scale, because no such scale exists; all cultures are inevitably expressions of particular social, economic, and historical circumstances." Ellis, 210.
119. Rorty, *Contingency, Irony, and Solidarity*, 63.
120. Ibid., 134.
121. Ibid., xvi.
122. Whitman, *Leaves of Grass*, 5.
123. Richard Rorty, "Truth without Correspondence to Reality," 28.

10 The Secular and the Post-Secular in the Thought of Edward Said

David Hawkes

SAID'S LATE STYLE

It is easy to forget, today, the shockingly radical impact made by Edward Said's *Orientalism* when it was first published in 1978. The book took issue with an entire scholarly discipline, charging the whole institutionalized study of "the Orient" with political reaction and cultural prejudice, as well as with intellectual dereliction. To make matters worse, its argument deployed the unfamiliar methodology of Michel Foucault and the French poststructuralists. Such innovations chimed harmoniously with the historical context. *Orientalism* was among the most timely books of the twentieth century, both facilitating and exploiting the transition from colonialist to post-colonial studies in the Western academy. Predictably enough, it was fiercely rejected by the established generation of Orientalists. Equally predictably, it was enthusiastically taken up by the coming generation of cultural theorists. Its canonization was thus only a matter of time, and Said's ideas were already quite mainstream by the late 1980s. Today, the basic assumptions of *Orientalism* are conventional, indeed axiomatic, in many areas of the humanities.

In one important respect, however, Said's progress from margin to center seems to have been reversed. Throughout his career, he laid heavy stress on the concept of the "secular." In *The World, the Text and the Critic* he wrote that criticism should be "skeptical, secular, reflectively open to its own failings," and he frequently advocated what he called the "politics of secular interpretation."[1] He used this term to describe the critical tradition in which he worked and, especially toward the end of his life, he also used it to designate an ethical and political goal. Unlike his criticism of Orientalism, Said's commitment to the secular was widely shared throughout the academy at the beginning of his career, and it seemed uncontroversial until quite recently. As John McLure pointed out in 1995, "in the academic literature of postmodernity and postmodernism the secularity of the moment is frequently simply assumed, and evidence to the contrary is not so much denied as disappeared through subtle and reiterated acts of selective attentiveness."[2]

In *Representations of the Intellectual,* Said unequivocally declared that the "true intellectual is a secular being."³ By that time, however, many observers were already beginning to argue that the new millennium would develop into a "post-secular" era. Throughout the post-colonial world, and also in the United States, the religious ideologies that secularism had assumed were obsolete were rapidly increasing their cultural and political influence. This has been reflected in the academy by the emergence of "post-secular" schools of thought in theology, philosophy, anthropology and literary criticism. Said's consistent advocacy of the secular, which hardened and deepened in response to the resurgence of religion, is beginning to appear tendentious, even quixotic. I would argue, however, that the idiosyncratic senses in which Said uses terms like "secular" and "religious" suggest that his ideas stand in a more complicated relation to the "post-secular" than simple opposition or denial. William Hart has recently written of "My surprise and bafflement at Said's cryptic, fugitive, but persistent references to the sacred, religious, theological, and Manichean. Why these religious references by a self-described secular critic, a thinker whose work, on first glance, seems indifferent if not irrelevant to religious matters? I contend that the presence of these references and others signals the persistence of religion as a Western conceptual category."⁴

Hart is correct to say that Said was perplexed and frustrated to find "signs everywhere of a 'return of the repressed'—an irruption, in ostensibly critical circles, of repressed religiosity."⁵ But he goes too far when he claims that "Said thinks of secularism as religion-abolished or as religion-strictly quarantined,"⁶ and claims that "for Said [religion] is an immoral and demonic force."⁷ In *Covering Islam* and elsewhere, Said takes considerable pains to defend monotheistic religion against the flippant and ignorant depictions of Western commentators.⁸ Hart finds it paradoxical that Said elsewhere seems to caricature "religion" in the same reckless and uninformed manner in which he castigates the Orientalists for treating Islam. But Said's use of the term "religion" can be deceptive, and insofar as Hart's characterizations are accurate they do not apply to religion in the conventional sense, but to "religion" in Said's unique and personal use of the term. In the Saidian context, "religion" usually designates certain tendencies in postmodern philosophy and aesthetics, rather than any overtly devotional or cultic practices.

The idea that discourses like philosophy or aesthetics have theological implications was hardly foreign to Said. Consider the relation between two texts that lay close to his heart: Adorno's *The Philosophy of Modern Music* and Thomas Mann's *Doctor Faustus.* Adorno argues that Schoenberg's twelve-tone system of composition buries the subjective personality of the composer beneath the formal logic of the music's progression. According to Adorno, Schoenberg's music thus corresponds to capitalist economics, which elevates the abstract representation of human activity that we know as "money" to dominance over the human subjects whose activity it represents. Furthermore, Schoenberg gives prominence to the tritone, histori-cally known as the "devil's interval" because of its systematic disruption of musical harmony, which was conceived as expressing God's harmonic ordering of the universe. This feature of Schoenberg expresses the dishar-monious and alienated condition of the subject in modernity.

Adorno's arguments are made entirely in the secular tradition, based on the solid ground of philosophy, economics, and musical theory. But Mann's novel provocatively extends the tradition of theological discourse into the twentieth century. It treats the supernatural, demonic significance of Schoenberg's music quite literally: the composer Adrian Leverkuhn really *has* sold his soul to Satan. To use Hegelian terminology, Mann repre-sents in religious "picture thinking" the forces that Adorno discusses using abstract, secular concepts. And yet the observations and conclusions of the two books are essentially identical in content, despite this difference in form. Said was surely aware that that the boundary between theology and philosophy is more terminological than substantive.

In his last years, suffering from leukemia, Said wrote movingly of the "late style" of such diverse figures as Adorno, Beethoven, Cavafy, and Lampedusa. This style, he claimed, was characterized by a willful embrace of the marginal, a determined rejection of fashion, an abandonment of the desire to please an audience. Referring to Adorno's reading of Beethoven, Said remarks that "late style" reveals "a moment when the artist who is fully in command of his medium nevertheless abandons communication with the established social order of which he is a part and achieves a con-tradictory, alienated relationship with it. His late works are a form of exile from his milieu."[9] It may seem that Said's strengthened commitment to the secular, at a time when political and intellectual developments threatened to render the concept otiose, represents his own form of "exile" from the post-secular milieu taking shape around him. It can even be argued that Said's late break with Yasser Arafat, and his rejection of a two-state solu-tion to the Israeli-Palestinian conflict, were political manifestations of his "late style," and the direct results of his devotion to the secular. Before we can raise these issues, however, we need to attempt the complicated task of deciding exactly what Said means by the this heavily-fraught term, the "secular."

THE PROBLEM OF THE SECULAR

Said employs the word "secular" in such disparate ways that the concept might seem beyond the reach of definition. Nevertheless, it is possible to discern certain continuities that unite the various significances acquired by the term in his work. An initial point to note is that Said always uses it to refer to his own critical method. Secularity is the essence that dis-tinguishes Said's preferred mode of thought from those of other thinkers.

Equally notable is his continuous insistence on the term's central importance. Aamir Mufti has called our attention to the paradoxical neglect of the concept by critical commentators:

> Edward Said has never left any doubt as to the significance he attaches to what he calls secular criticism. It is by this term, not *postcolonial criticism*, that he identifies his critical practice as a whole. The meaning of this term is a theme he has returned to repeatedly since first elaborating it at length in the introduction to *The World, the Text, and the Critic*. But this facet of the Saidian project has received nothing like the attention that, for instance, has been lavished upon the concept of Orientalism or the strategy of what he calls the contrapuntal reading. Nor does it seem to have been productive for younger scholars in quite the same way as these two latter conceptual constellations. There may even appear to be something odd about the persistence of this concern in Said's work, at least within the context of the Anglo-American academy.... Interpreters have often shied away from this aspect of Saidian criticism, despite its undeniable importance in the corpus of his work.[10]

A case can certainly be made that the "secular" is the pivotal concept in Said's work, and that many of his other central concepts are defined in relation to it. In informs, for example, his distinction between relations of "filiation," in which allegiance is determined "by birth, nationality, profession," and "affiliation," in which associations are made on the basis of "social and political conviction, economic and historical circumstances, voluntary effort and willed deliberation."[11] Said suggests that accepting the demands of filiation is irrational and superstitious, because involuntary, while the choice to affiliate is rational and secular. In "Reflections on Exile," the concept of the "secular" is enlisted to define Said's understanding of the "exile": "The exile knows that in a secular and contingent world, homes are always provisional...exile is irremediably secular and unbearably historical...."[12] And yet critics have paid much attention to Saidian terms like "affiliation" and "exile," while usually shying away from an engagement with his understanding of the "secular."

Part of this wariness may spring from the latent contradiction between Said's critique of orientalism and his advocacy of secularism. The West's claim to be the bearer of Enlightenment to the East, its pose as the rational vanquisher of tyrannical superstition, was a central tenet in the ideological justification of imperialism. As Peter van der Veer has pointed out, "the very distinction between religious and secular is a product of the Enlightenment that was used in orientalism to draw a sharp opposition between irrational, religious behavior of the Oriental and rational secularism, which enabled the westerner to rule the Oriental."[13] Secularism is an occidental concept, the argument runs, and Said displays the residual influence of colonialism when he seeks to recommend it as the preferred intellectual and political order for post-colonial societies, in which the cultural influence of religion runs deeper than it does in the West.

This argument seems to me unjust. Said does not use the word "secular" in the sense of "non-religious" that it has acquired in the modern context, but in a sense that reflects his profound knowledge of the term's traditional significance. The modern concept of the "secular" is absent from the Bible, as James Diamond has recently observed: "There really is no word in Biblical or rabbinic Hebrew that denotes the secular. The Hebrew words for the sacred or the holy are *kadosh* (adjective) or *kodesh* (substantive). The antonym for *kodesh* is *hol* which the revised *Jewish Publication Society Tanakh* translates as 'profane'.... The sacred and the profane here are cultic distinctions and criteria, not cultural or worldview or lifestyle signifiers."[14]

In the Biblical context the nearest equivalent to our concept of the "secular" effectively designates "gentile." Diamond goes on to point out that "the appropriation of the *kodesh* and *hol* binary by the rabbis for the liturgy of the *Havdalah* ceremony that marks the termination of *Shabbat* on Saturday night at dusk does not point to *hol* as denoting or connoting the secular but rather the 'ordinary' or the 'weekday.' 'Blessed are you, God, Sovereign of the world, who makes a distinction between the holy and the ordinary, between light and darkness, between Israel and the nations, between the seventh day and the six days of creating....'"[15]

Said's concept of the secular grows out of these ancient roots. He intends it to mean attention and allegiance to "the nations," rather than to a particular nation; hence Bruce Robbins argues that the "most crucial meaning of secular, in [Said's] usage, is as an opposing term not to religion but to nationalism."[16] But Mufti remarks that, while Robbins is correct to note the importance of anti-nationalism to Said's concept of the secular, the term can also designate affiliation with a group. He announces his intention to map out "...the meaning of secular criticism by arguing that a concern with minority culture and existence occupies a central place within it.... The Saidian critical position implies, I shall argue, not a contentless cosmopolitanism but a secularism imbued with the experience of minority – a secularism for which *minority* is not simply the name of a crisis."[17]

The terms "minority" and "majority" are, of course, mutually definitive, so that the presence of a minority in any culture reveals to the majority the contingency of its own identity; it proves that the self is the product of the other. Acknowledgment of the minority is thus a precondition for secular consciousness, in the Saidian sense that this involves a recognition of one's own contingency. The secular is thus associated with contingency itself and, in monotheist and Platonic thought, this taints it with the unsightly blemish of temporality. As Harvey Cox puts it: "From the very beginning of its usage, secular denoted something vaguely inferior. It meant 'this world' of change as opposed to the eternal 'religious world'.... It implies that the true religious world is timeless, changeless, and thus superior to the 'secular' world which was passing and transient...."[18]

In a similar argument, Daniel Philpott interprets secularism in the light of its binary opposition to "religion": "religion is a set of beliefs about the ultimate ground of existence, that which is unconditioned, not itself created or caused, and the communities and practices that form around these beliefs.... If this is religion, secularization is the decline of it."[19] If we define "religion" in opposition to contingency, then Said's use of "secular" certainly implies opposition to religion. That is by no means the only possible definition of "religion," however. In order to understand the true nature of Said's opposition between the "secular" and the "religious" traditions, we will need to examine its most influential sources, and this may provide us with a firmer grasp of what he intends these terms to designate.

THE INFLUENCE OF VICO, FOUCAULT AND LUKACS

The concepts of the contingent and the secular explicitly merge in Vico's idea of "gentile" history, which he elaborated in *The New Science* (1725). Vico argues that, after the flood, the history of the gentile nations diverged from that of the Hebrews. Whereas the course of latter was determined by divine Providence, the former was shaped and guided by human beings. Being of human manufacture, the history of the gentiles could be studied and known by human methods, and in this sphere, Vico claimed, the true (*verum*) is interchangeable with the made (*factum*). The most momentous consequence of this is that knowledge of human affairs is rendered contingent, rather than essential. Indeed, this is true not just of the object of knowledge, but also of the knowing self. As Giuseppe Mazzotta puts it, "For Vico there is no a priori essence for the self: one is what one makes of oneself, and one makes of oneself what one knows, so that being, knowledge, and making are ceaselessly interwoven in an endless recirculation."[20] This concept of identity as relational and contingent was vitally important to Said, and it determined his political positions quite as surely as his philosophical and aesthetic views.

Said takes up Vico's tradition in *The World, the Text and the Critic*. The introduction is entitled "Secular Criticism," the conclusion is called "Religious Criticism," and the opposition between these two modes informs the method of the whole book. Said delineates his understanding of this polarity with reference to Vico:

> There is a great difference between what in *The New Science* Vico described as the complex, heterogeneous and 'gentile' world of nations and what in contrast he designated as the domain of sacred history. The essence of that difference is that the former comes into being, develops in various directions, moves toward a number of culminations, collapses, and then begins again—all in ways that can be investigated because historians, or new scientists, are human and can know history

on the grounds that it was made by men and women.... As for sacred history, it is made by God and hence cannot really be known, although Vico understood perfectly well that in a priest-ridden age such as his, God had to be respected and loudly celebrated.[21]

Said describes his own work as deploying "secular criticism" to "de-idolize" the various pieties asserted by "religious criticism," by using "what a secular attitude enables—a sense of history and a healthy skepticism about the various official idols venerated by culture and by system...."[22] But he is clearly not using the term "religious" in any conventional sense here. Said cannot have been unaware that the most fundamental tenet, even the *raison d'etre,* of the monotheistic religions is, precisely, the elimination of "idols." Nor could he have been ignorant of the constant, frequently revolutionary, incursions into worldly affairs that have, in every epoch (and especially in our own) been carried out in the name of religion. He seems rather, as Hart notes,[23] to be using the term "religion" to designate what monotheistic religions call "idolatry," and he is aware that idolatry is not an exclusively "religious" phenomenon. In fact, it could be argued that Said is not using the term "religion" to refer to any faith or cult, but to certain tendencies within the local context of postmodern philosophy—that is to say, with a discourse that considers itself to be secular.

I would contend that what Said means by "religion" is in fact the exact opposite of what most people understand by that term. In the introduction to *The World, the Text and the Critic,* he associates "religious criticism" with the "principle of noninterference in...the world,"[24] and he identifies it, above all, with Derridean deconstruction: "As it is practiced in the American academy today, literary theory has for the most part isolated textuality from the circumstances, the events, the physical senses that made it possible...."[25] Said's notion of "secular" criticism here refers to historicist methods, and his countervailing concept of "religious" criticism refers to such ahistoricist methods as deconstruction. It is certainly true that deconstruction, as usually practiced, is vulnerable to the charge of ahistoricism. But only through a reversal of conventional terminology can it be described as "religious." The ultimate target of deconstructive critique is "logocentrism," the idea that meaning is ultimately determined by the *logos.* The term *logos* refers, in the Bible, to the "Word" of God, that is, to what Christianity figures as God's "son," so that any philosophy that seeks to undermine the determining power of the *logos* is *ipso facto* anti-religious. "Religion," in the traditional sense, is not the true opponent of Said's secularism. Rather, he is opposed to methods of interpretation that ignore the role of historical circumstances in the formation of meaning.

In a similar fashion, while Said's allied concept of "worldliness" is clearly meant to connote cosmopolitanism, as opposed to nationalism, he also wrests it into meaning an acceptance of historical contingency. "My position," he writes, "is that texts are worldly, to some degree they are events, and, even when they appear to deny it, they are nevertheless a part of the social world, human life, and of course the historical moments in which they are located and interpreted...."[26] Although texts may be "worldly," however, they are not necessarily, or at least not exclusively, material. It is easy to elide the distinction between historicism and materialism, but for Said the difference was vital. Part of the reason why his term "secular" is frequently understood in simple opposition to religion is that it is assumed that secularity must imply materialism. The strong influence on Said of the ultra-materialist Michel Foucault argues in favor of such a reading, but in fact Said took pains to distance himself from the reductive approach of his mentor.

The work of Foucault, arguably the greatest single influence on Said's methodology, is notable for its rhetorical commitment to "materialism," and Said sometimes echoes this rhetoric, happily associating himself with Raymond Williams' term "cultural materialism." Said's understanding of "materialism," however, is unconventional, and more nearly approximates to what is usually known as "historicism." He raises this issue himself: "But what do I mean by 'material' in this case? I mean the ways, for example, in which the text is a monument, a cultural object, sought after, fought over, possessed, rejected, or achieved in time."[27] Elsewhere, Said equates "idealism" with ahistoricism: "Every idea or system of ideas exists *somewhere,* it is mixed in with historical circumstances, it is part of what one may very simply call 'reality.' One of the enduring attributes of self-serving idealism, however, is the notion that ideas are just ideas and that they exist only in the realm of ideas."[28] Materialism, for Said, is historicist, and idealism is ahistoricist. But he does not exclude the possibility of an idealist historicism, and in fact this may be the most accurate philosophical characterization of Said's own critical method.

Said's notion of secularity certainly involves close attention to the realm of ideas. To understand how Said arrived at this position, we need to return to the secular tradition established by Vico. For Vico, attention to the "history of the gentiles" (what Said calls "secular history") is the very antithesis of materialism. The material world was made by God; what human beings have made is the world of ideas. As Vico puts it in *The New Science*:

> ...in the night of thick darkness enveloping the earliest antiquity, so remote from ourselves, there shines the eternal and never failing light of a truth beyond all question: that the world of civil society has certainly been made by men, and that its principles are therefore to be found within the modifications of our own human mind. Whoever reflects on this cannot but marvel that the philosophers should have bent all their energies to the study of the world of nature, which, since God made it, He alone knows; and that they should have neglected the study of the world of nations, or civil world, which, since men had made it, men could come to know. This aberration was a consequence of that infirmity of the human mind by which, immersed and buried in

the body, it naturally inclines to take notice of bodily things, and finds the effort to attend to itself too laborious; just as the bodily eye sees all objects outside itself but needs a mirror to see itself.[29]

Said's reading of Vico stresses his concern with the body, but also emphasizes its inseparability from the realm of ideas: "Vico is concerned with what happens to sense impressions in the mind given the overwhelming preponderance of the body. He associates intelligence with a sort of search-and-rescue operation, by which the mind gathers and holds on to something that does not fall under the senses, even though that 'something' could not come into being without the body and sense experience."[30] We are a long way here from the kind of militant materialism expressed in Foucault's absolute opposition to "the notion of 'spirit.'" For Said, contingency involved the recognition that binary oppositions are mutually definitive, and this was especially true of the polarity between matter and ideas. He had no interest in reducing one pole of the dichotomy to the other; his interest was in the relation between the two.

The imperative that material circumstances and ideas must be conceived as distinct, despite the fact they are ontologically inseparable, distances Said from the methodological and rhetorical commitment to "materialism" that currently dominates political literary criticism in America, western Europe, and even in large sectors of the postcolonial world. It arises, I think, from his reading of Georg Lukacs's concept of the "totality." Lukacs attacks materialism as "inverted Platonism," and describes both idealism and materialism as "reflection theories" that reflect the "reification" of consciousness: "In the theory of 'reflection' we find the theoretical embodiment of the duality of thought and existence, consciousness and reality, that is so intractable to the reified consciousness. And from that point of view it is immaterial whether things are to be regarded as reflections of concepts or whether concepts are reflections of things. In both cases the duality is firmly established."[31] Such dualities can be abolished, according to Lukacs, by adopting "the point of view of the totality,"[32] and this perspective is also an element of the Saidian "secular." In *The World, the Text and the Critic*, Said argues that this totalizing perspective enables Lukacs to break free from the constraining ideology of "reification": "Lukacs says, reification is the alienation of men from what they have produced, and it is the starkly uncompromising severity of his vision that he means by this all the products of human labor, children included, which are so completely separated from each other, atomized, and hence frozen into the category of ontological objects as to make even natural relationships virtually impossible."[33]

Lukacs views the antinomies of bourgeois thought as resulting from the alienation of mankind from what we have produced, and the consequent tendency to fetishize, or as Lukacs puts it, to "reify" what we have made. This is a very ancient idea. We find it in the Decalogue's prohibition of graven images, and in Isaiah's diagnosis of "idolatry" as the adoration of "the works of men's hands." For Vico, the essential task was to distinguish between "the works of men's hands" and the works of the Creator, and for Said the mistaking of culture for nature is the essence of "religious" criticism. To study human, "gentile" history as if it were "sacred" is to idolize our own works. We should note, however, that such an error does not constitute "religion" in the monotheistic sense but rather its opposite: idolatry. In fact, it is plausible to view Said as, in effect, a secular monotheist and to argue, with Hart, that what Said calls "religion" is more precisely known as "idolatry."[34] In *Culture and Imperialism,* Said traces the notion of the secular back to a long "tradition of humanistic learning that derived from that efflorescence for secular anthropology...we associate with the late eighteenth century and with such figures as Vico, Herder, Rousseau, and the brothers Schlegel. And underlying *their* work was the belief that mankind formed a marvelous, almost symphonic whole whose progress and formations, again as a whole, could be studied exclusively as a concerted and secular historical experience, not as an exemplification of the divine."[35]

This repeated insistence that secularism involves the study of society "as a whole," rather than in terms of isolated, micrological elements, sets Said's thought apart from the currently prevailing critical tendency to focus on the local and the particular. It also militates against any facile notion that Said's secularity is simply opposed to religion in the conventional sense. In fact, the technique of totalization, the belief that the parts can only be understood in relation to the whole, involves a translation of the divine into secular, philosophical terms. As Lukacs puts it: "God, the soul, etc.... are nothing but mythological expressions to denote the unified subject or, alternatively, the unified object of the totality of the objects of knowledge considered as perfect (and wholly known)."[36]

To find a genuinely "anti-divine" philosophy, we must turn again to poststructuralism and its denigration of "logocentric" and "totalizing" modes of thought. Poststructuralism is the paradigm of "religious criticism" for Said, and in *The World, the Text and the Critic* he follows Lukacs in connecting the loss of a totalizing perspective in recent criticism to the contemporary political context: "It is no accident that the emergence of so narrowly defined a philosophy of pure textuality and critical noninterference has coincided with the ascendancy of Reaganism...."[37] As the economy comes to appear more abstract and immaterial, so a philosophy based on the autonomy of pure representation will grow more plausible. It is only from the perspective of the totality that the postmodern economy and postmodernist philosophy can be perceived, not as reflections of each other, but as part of a greater whole. This ability to connect such things as "pure textuality" with such things as "Reaganism" is one of the powers Said attributes to secular criticism, but this by no means exhausts its political utility.

SECULARISM AND STATEHOOD

Towards the end of his life, as part of his "late style," Said brought his concept of secularity to bear on his immediate political concerns. It came to be the foundation of his complicated and subtle anti-Zionism. In *The Politics of Dispossession* he claimed that the state of Israel is characterized by "Judaism, in two dimensions, each, commonsensically, incompatible with the other: the universal (timeless) and the secular (temporal)."[38] It was the ahistorical, "timeless" and religious claims of Zionism, its ascription of privileged status on grounds of "filiation" rather than of "affiliation" to which he took exception. In the words of James Diamond: "In a sovereign Jewish state the abstraction of a secular national polity from out of the matrix of a pre-modern faith community has proved to be extremely difficult, if not impossible. The fact that there is no separation of religion and state in Israel tells us that secular Zionism, for all its early vigor and for all its hold upon the Israeli body politic, has been defeated by Orthodox, more precisely ultra-Orthodox, Judaism."[39]

At the end of his life, Said seems to have given up on the ultimate secular ambition: a better life in this world. Said's final rejection of the Palestinian Authority's commitment to partition, and his call instead for the "secularization" of Israel, lay well beyond the boundaries of mainstream debate, or of practical possibility. His position changed at a time when the policies of both Israel and the Arab world were increasingly directed by sectarian, religious concerns, and it reflected an idealistic defiance of the tide of history. Said was in no doubt about which way the tide was flowing; as he admitted in *The Politics of Dispossession*: "With every apparent consolidation of its national existence Israel seems more and more to represent not only the place apart of Judaism but also the concentrated actions of Judaism."[40] He sometimes seemed to acknowledge the world-wide, growing divergence between empirical reality and the conclusions of post-colonial theory: in 1998 he remarked on the election in India of "the BJP, which is the Hindu fundamentalist party, which says that India is a Hindu state, denying that which, for example, the early secular nationalists like Ghandi and Nehru asserted: that India is a diverse state and you can't call it Hindu because there are Muslims, Christians, Parses, and Sikhs. So in that political context, therefore, one has to call attention to the historical realities, rather than to some theoretical standpoint, either primitive or utopian and complex like hybridity itself."[41]

Said thus ended his life insisting on the primacy of local context over theoretical tradition. Shortly after the Palestinian National Council, of which he was a member, passed the declaration of statehood in 1988, Said composed a lengthy reflection on the process for *Social Text*. He recalled how the stated aim of the P.L.O. had initially been a single, democratic and secular state in Palestine, and how by 1974 this goal had been replaced by the partition of the territory into two separate states. Partition was the solution pushed by Yasser Arafat's Fatah faction, and any liberated territory would come under the control of the Palestinian National Authority, which was dominated by Fatah. Many Palestinians rejected this policy, but in 1988, impelled by the *intifada*, the PNC ratified the two-state solution.

Said voted for the measure, and even translated the official declaration of statehood into English at Arafat's request. But his article betrays considerable unease with the document, while also emphasizing its momentousness: "the PNC was asking of itself nothing less than emphatic transformation: from liberation movement to independence movement."[42] Said eventually came to see Arafat's acceptance of partition as springing from a base, personal ambition to rule a sovereign territory, and in his last years he argued passionately against the division of Palestine along sectarian lines. By 1999 he had concluded that "Palestinian self-determination in a separate state is unworkable," and that "The politics of separation can't work in the Middle East."[43] The partition of Palestine into ethnic or religious enclaves violated Said's stress on secularism at the deepest level. As he put it in *The Guardian*: "To be recognised at last by Israel and the US may mean personal fulfillment for some, but it doesn't necessarily answer Palestinian needs or solve the leadership crisis. Our struggle is about freedom and democracy; it is secular and for a long time—indeed up to the last couple of years—it was fairly democratic."[44]

In 1999, Said put "secular rights" at the head of his list of interests shared by Palestinians and Israelis, and in 2002 he was asked why, in an era of cultural and economic global homogenization, national and religious conflicts were growing more numerous and bitter. One explanation he offered was the "legacy of empires": "In the case of the British, whenever they were forced to leave a place, they divided it up. It happened in India. It happened in Palestine. It happened in Cyprus. It happened in Ireland. The idea of *partition* as a quick way of solving the problem of multiple nationalities. It's like someone telling you, 'Okay, the way to learn a musical piece is to divide it into tinier and tinier units, and then suddenly you can put it all together.' It doesn't work that way. When you divide something up, it's not so easy to put it back together."[45]

One of the most compelling arguments against the two-state solution was that it involved, at least in practical effect, abandoning the principle that exiled Palestinians had the right of return to their former homes in Israel. In Said's terms, Arafat's apparent willingness to take this step was facilitated by an essentialist understanding of identity as "filiation" rather than as "affiliation." The Palestinian National Charter, passed by the PNC in 1968, declared that "The Palestinian identity is a genuine, essential, and inherent characteristic; it is transmitted from parents to children." This definition played into the Israeli government's hands, enabling them to construct a competing version of an exclusive national identity. From Said's perspective, however, the Israeli-Palestinian dichotomy was, like all binary oppositions, mutually definitive: "The notion of separation...was in effect to quarantine the Palestinians into townships or Bantustans or whatever you want to call them, which falsifies the relationship between Palestinians and Israelis, which is really a very close one. Israelis can't be understood without Palestinians, and visa versa. So the one-state solution is really the only alternative now. In other words, the Palestinians and Israelis are so mixed, especially in the West Bank and Gaza but also inside Palestine, that the only solution is a multi-confessional, multi-ethnic, multi-cultural state."[46]

Said often used the term "secular" to designate this anti-essentialist and relational view of identity, as when he declared in 1999 that "There can be no reconciliation unless both peoples, two communities of suffering, resolve that their existence is a secular fact, and that it has to be dealt with as such."[47] In his last deployment of the secular, then, Said uses it to denote an acceptance that identity is relational, rather than essential. He presents the Israeli-Palestinian conflict as involving a mutually definitive binary opposition, and he protests against the idea that its poles can exist in isolation from each other. What is needed, rather, is an acknowledgment of the interdependence of its elements: that is to say, a "totalizing" perspective. Only from the point of view of the totality can we understand Israelis and Palestinians as *one* people, rather than two. Totalization is thus a precondition of "secularism" in Said's politics, as in his philosophy. But we should not forget that totalization is itself a form of secular monotheism, and that Said also deploys it as a weapon against the polytheistic idolatry of postmodernism. Paradoxical though it may appear, it is precisely Said's tenacious, defiant advocacy of the "secular" which will guarantee the continued pertinence of his thought to any "post-secular" era.

NOTES

1. Edward W. Said, *The World, the Text and the Critic* (Cambridge, MA: Harvard University Press, 1983), 26.
2. John McClure, "Postmodern/ Post-secular: Contemporary Fiction and Spirituality," *Modern Fiction Studies* 41.1 (1995) 141–163, at 143.
3. Edward W. Said, *Representations of the Intellectual* (New York: Pantheon Books, 1994), 120.
4. William D. Hart, *Edward Said and the Religious Effects of Culture* (Cambridge: Cambridge UP, 2000), 41.
5. Ibid., ix.
6. Ibid., 7.
7. Ibid., 10.
8. Edward W. Said, *Covering Islam: How the Media and the Experts Determine How We See the Rest of the World* (New York: Vintage, 1997).
9. Edward W. Said, "The Rage of the Old," *The Guardian*, August 1, 2004.
10. Aamir R. Mufti, "Auerbach in Istanbul: Edward Said, Secular Criticism, and the Question of Minority Culture," *Critical Inquiry* 25, (Autumn 1998), 95–125, at 95–96.
11. Said, *The World, the Text and the Critic*, 24–25.
12. Edward W. Said, "Reflections on Exile," *Granta* 13 (1984), 160.

13. Peter van der Veer, "The Foreign Hand: Orientalist Discourse in Sociology and Communalism," in *Orientalism and the Postcolonial Predicament: Perspectives on South Asia*, Carol A. Brekenridge and Peter van der Veer eds. (Philadelphia: University of Pennsylvania Press, 1993), 24.
14. James S. Diamond, "The Post-secular: a Jewish Perspective," *Cross-currents* (Winter, 2004), 1–2.
15. Ibid., 3–4.
16. Bruce Robbins, "Secularism, Elitism, Progress and Other Transgressions, On Edward Said's 'Voyage In,'" *Social Text*, 40 (1994), 25–37.
17. Mufti, "Auerbach in Istanbul: Edward Said, Secular Criticism, and the Question of Minority Culture," 96.
18. Harvey Cox, *The Secular City* (New York: Macmillan, 1965), 19.
19. Daniel Philpott, "The Challenge of September 11 to Secularism in International Relations," *World Politics* 55.1 (2002) 66–95, at 68.
20. Giuseppe Mazzotta, *The New Map of the World: The Poetic Philosophy of Giambattista Vico* (Princeton, NJ: Princeton University Press, 1998), 14.
21. Said, *The World, the Text and the Critic*, 290–291.
22. Ibid., 291.
23. Hart, *Edward Said and the Religious Effects of Culture*, 92.
24. Said, *The World, the Text and the Critic*, 2.
25. Ibid., 4.
26. Ibid.
27. Said, *The World, the Text and the Critic*, 339.
28. Edward Said, "Zionism from the Standpoint of its Victims" (1979), in *The Edward Said Reader*, Mustafa Bayoumi and Andrew Rubin, eds. (New York: Vintage, 2000), 55.
29. *The New Science of Giambattista Vico*, Thomas Goddard Bergin and Max Harold Fisch, trans. (Ithaca: Cornell University Press, 1984), 96
30. Edward Said, "Vico on the Discipline of Bodies and Texts," *Modern Language Notes* 91 (1976), 817–826, 823.
31. Georg Lukacs, *History and Class-consciousness*, Rodney Livingstone, trans. (Cambridge, MA: MIT Press, 1971), 200.
32. Ibid., 27.
33. Said, *The World, the Text and the Critic*, 16–17.
34. Hart, *Edward Said and the Religious Effects of Culture*, 92.
35. Edward W. Said, *Culture and Imperialism* (New York: Vintage, 1994), 44.
36. Lukacs, 115.
37. Said, *The World, the Text and the Critic*, 23.
38. Edward W. Said, *The Politics of Dispossession: The Struggle for Palestinian Self-Determination, 1969–1994* (New York: Vintage, 1995), 17.
39. James Diamond, "The Post-secular: a Jewish Perspective," 5.
40. Said, *The Politics of Dispossession*, 17.
41. Edward W. Said, Interview with *Al Jadid* magazine, Vol. 4, no. 22 (Winter 1998).
42. Edward W. Said, "Intifada and Independence," *Middle East Report*, May-June 1989, 12–26, 12–13.
43. Edward W. Said, Interview in *The Guardian*, September 11, 1999.
44. Edward W. Said, "Arafat's Gamble: the Lost Liberation," retrieved from http://www.radioislam.org/historia/zionism/esaid-arf.html, September 20, 2006.
45. Daniel Barenboim and Edward Said, *Parallels and Paradoxes: Explorations in Music and Society* (New York: Pantheon, 2002), 12.
46. Edward W. Said, Interview with *Al Jadid* magazine, Vol. 4, no. 22 (Winter 1998).
47. Edward W. Said, "Truth and Reconciliation," *Al-Ahram Weekly* Online (412, 12-20 January 1999).

11 Longing for a "Certain Kind of Future"

Drucilla Cornell, Sexual Difference, and the Imaginary Domain

Sara Rushing

INTRODUCTION

Drucilla Cornell and Judith Butler have frequently been grouped together under the name of postmodern feminism. Both have been vocal critics of this label. Butler has sharply called into question what she sees as "the effort to colonize and domesticate these theories under the sign of the same, to group them synthetically and masterfully under a single rubric;" and she has suggested that such crude schematizing loosely veils an "excuse not to read, and not to read closely."[1] Cornell has similarly noted that "'postmodern' has become a catch-all phrase that defines very different philosophical positions as giving a similar message."[2] As described in the introduction to this volume, these "very different philosophical positions," or the different traditions of thought that typically get conflated as postmodernism, range from Richard Rorty's neopragmatism to German philosophical hermeneutics, from Jacques Derrida's deconstruction and Michel Foucault's genealogical critique to Jacques Lacan's psychoanalytic thought. All of these traditions have been brought into certain local contexts as they have made their way in contemporary American scholarship. The overlapping themes associated with these traditions take on different meanings and implications not only within the different traditions themselves, but also within the specific individual interpretations of these particular themes. One can see this in the wide-ranging interpretations of "postmodernism," not to mention anti-humanism and anti-essentialism, within feminist theory. Thus as Cornell suggests, attempting to reduce postmodernism (and postmodern feminism) to any "similar message" is futile.

And yet, Cornell follows her critique of this reductive tendency by admitting that she uses the term "postmodernism" anyway, because "It indicates...a longing...that we not be fated to entrapment by the political and ethical concepts of feminism identified as modern."[3] In "feminism identified as modern," which both Cornell and Butler frequently associate with Catharine MacKinnon, gender hierarchy may be reversed (women may be put "on top") but gender never loses its ontological thrust or regulatory power. Instead, under the guise of liberation, new gender norms get established and naturalized. The meaning of "woman" may change, but it is still clear what it means to be woman and who is (and is not) represented by this term. In contrast to this position, Cornell suggests that "postmodern feminism" is best understood as the "project to demoralize gender,"[4] or to "denaturalize the narrow moral symbolism and mythologies through which masculinity and femininity are defined."[5] If Butler and Cornell can be seen as sharing a critical objective, demoralizing gender is an apt way to describe it.

However, they undertake this critical project in importantly different ways. Both Butler and Cornell aim to counter the positivist and programmatic impulse at work in MacKinnon's feminist theory, which seeks to control from within the present horizon more or less specifically what shape the future ought to take. In contrast, both Butler and Cornell figure the "incommensurability"—the gap—between the present and the future as a condition of futurity itself. But Butler and Cornell deal with this gap somewhat differently. For Butler, this gap is a temporal matter: she discusses possibility in terms of the time that is not yet, or the future. Yet Butler is concerned with how thinking and acting in the *present* can function to safeguard or foreclose the possibility of a certain kind of future's unfolding. Her emphasis is thus on performances or claims that have an insurgent effect in the present; performances (say, of "woman") or claims (say, for human rights) that invade and occupy just those categories that require for their stability certain constitutive exclusions. In this sense, Butler is focused on how those who are outsided, abjected others trouble current categories by inhabiting them.

Cornell shifts between talking about the realm of possibility in both temporal terms (the "not-yet-dreamed-of") and spatial terms ("the imaginary domain"). Where Butler is concerned with how excluded others can unravel social categories by demanding to inhabit them, by demanding *inclusion*, Cornell is interested in refiguring the "outside"—the place of the altogether Other—as a place of power and not merely debasement. This place of representational possibility beyond our existing categories functions to trouble and transform those categories *from the outside*. The idea of "the beyond," as both a space outside and a time ahead, is thus crucial for Cornell. Furthermore, in contrast to Butler, Cornell's idea of "the beyond" is explicitly utopian. This is an adjective that Butler does not embrace. She even uses the word "utopian" pejoratively in places, or at least distances herself from this project. Much hinges, however, on how one understands utopianism. By way of conclusion I will return to this point and suggest that Butler and Cornell exemplify a post-positivist utopianism that flows from and is consistent with their postmodernism.

Other differences between Butler and Cornell bear mentioning. Butler fills in the temporal gap between the here-and-now and the not-yet with ethical attitudes such as patience and humility, which increase the probability of our responding with a disposition of generosity to the uncertain moment that the present always is. Cornell, in contrast, fills in this gap with certain legal, moral and philosophical ideals. Cornell often appropriates, though refigures, typically liberal terms to describe these ideals, such as rights, the good, and self-representation. Butler is suspicious about the regulatory power of ideals, suspicious of representational projects, and suspicious of legal rights. Finally, though both Butler and Cornell draw on poststructuralist and psychoanalytic thought in order to critique modern feminist theory, they locate themselves differently within these broad traditions. Butler draws more on Michel Foucault, and thus focuses foremost on social-discursive factors and the normative effects of power on determining who counts as socially intelligible. While Jacques Lacan is a prominent figure in Butler's work, she is *as* critical of his insights about the relationship between the unconscious and the social as she is attuned to their significance. Cornell draws more thoroughly on Lacan and on Jacques Derrida, and thus focuses foremost on symbolic (psychic and linguistic) factors and the logical possibility of new representations of being, beyond the limits of representation in the present cultural order. These different influences matter for the question of whether patriarchal reality is engendered primarily by unconscious fantasies and the structure of language or by social norms. Between Cornell and Butler there is a distinct difference of emphasis, and thus a difference in where each focuses hopes for transformation (i.e., on psychic and cultural imaginaries or on normative social practices). This difference bears out in the critical frameworks within feminist theory that each adopts for analyzing the production and maintenance of sexuality. Though both Cornell and Butler seek to demoralize gender, Butler works to do so with a primary focus on gender (as she conceives it), while Cornell works with a primary focus on "sexual difference."

This essay examines this distinction in detail. I focus on how Cornell develops, defends, and *modifies* her understanding of "sexual difference" through her particular interpretations of Derrida, Lacan and Luce Irigaray, and in an on-going dialogue with Butler that persistently exposes the dilemmas attendant to aspects of poststructuralism, psychoanalytic thought and French feminism. As I show, Cornell brings a deep engagement with and pragmatic appropriation of these traditions into a local American legal feminist context. Within this context, theorists have disagreed both about how women should represent themselves to the law and how the law should regard women and represent them back to society. Should women be afforded equality because they are basically the same as men, or must true treatment as equals be predicated on recognition of the way the sexes are different? Are men and women really just "different," or is the difference affected through male (sexual) domination and female (sexual) subordination? When the law engages with and addresses these questions, for example, when it describes women and provides them with certain rights on the basis of that description, what effect does that have on either transforming or reinforcing specific cultural representations of women as a distinct social class? When women are treated by the law as a distinct social class, how does that presume and stabilize normative sexuality? In seeking rights from the law, how are women and gays and lesbians divided, or "class-ified," from each other? Though simplified here, these are nonetheless the crucial debates within the local contexts of feminist, feminist legal, and queer legal theory over the past decades. And it is these debates that Cornell seeks to move beyond but not disregard. Put differently, her aim is to resist the "urgency" of the prescriptive legalism associated with Catharine MacKinnon, but also the "hesitancy" that makes Derrida's futural politics appear to involve a retreat from politics, as Paul Patton describes in this volume. Her aim is to get beyond the problematic essentialist and relativist tendencies identified with Irigaray, Lacan and Derrida, so that the traditions these thinkers represent can be made useful for contemporary feminist dilemmas.

SEXUAL DIFFERENCE

In her 1994 article "Against Proper Objects," Judith Butler offers a critique of the way lesbian and gay studies and feminist theory have described their respective "objects" of investigation. Specifically, Butler exposes the confusion attendant to the conceptions of "sex" and "gender" posited in order to distinguish these two scholarly fields from each other. What is necessary, she asks, for the establishment of some foundational object of lesbian and gay studies, namely "sex," that is different from the foundational object of feminism, namely "gender"? What is necessary for the establishment of different conceptions of "sex" within gender studies and gay and lesbian studies? As Butler shows, conventional feminism assumes a concept of sex as biological dimorphism, which is often elided as it precedes and enables the socially constructed "gender," feminism's *proper* object. Lesbian and gay studies, in contrast, assumes a concept of sex as itself the proper object, an object that "would include not only questions of identity and attribute (female or male), but discourses of sensations, acts, and sexual practice as well," and thus would exceed the purview of feminism.[6] Butler argues that to maintain the distinction between feminism and gay and lesbian studies, the main methodological move that must take place is the reduction of feminism to an exclusive focus on gender. This is a reduction that does not jibe with the history of feminist theory and practice. A major theoretical framework engaged by contemporary feminist theorists is excluded, namely the framework of "sexual difference."

As Butler explains, gender is a sociological notion pertaining to men and women as social groups, regulated by social norms. In a conventional sociological account like the one that gender studies has purveyed, subjectivity is taken as innate, "sex" is taken as natural, biological, and objective, and masculine and feminine genders are understood as cultural constructions that pre-existing subjects get socialized to live in various ways. (To be clear, this is *not* Butler's conception of gender, which is cast rather as a matter of reiterative performances of certain social "scripts"; performances that effect—produce or "materialize"—sex and subjectivity within pre-existing social norms of recognition and legitimacy. Furthermore, the opposition between sociological versus psychoanalytic accounts that Butler provisionally posits in the above-mentioned essay is obviously not a clear one, and she is a good example of someone who looks to both sociological theory and psychoanalytic theory in order to explore questions of gender.)

Within conventional gender theory, as Butler describes it, men and women are seen as two unique positive entities that come to mean what they do independently of each other, based on biological differences onto which social characteristics are mapped. Sexual difference, in contrast, is a structuralist and poststructuralist notion pertaining to "the masculine" and "the feminine" as positions in the *symbolic* order of language and culture. Masculine and feminine are not regarded as traits embodied by actually existing men and women, but rather as differentially established positions in a symbolic order, within which each position takes on a different set of meanings. One key disagreement between those who start with sexual difference as a point of departure and those who start with gender as a point of departure concerns whether sociological or psychological factors take priority in the consideration of subjectivity. This is not to suggest that theorists must pick between one or the other—patriarchal culture as an effect *either* of relations in society *or* of unconscious processes like Freud's Oedipal and castration complexes. Clearly most contemporary feminist theorists believe that the lines between biology, culture, psychology and language are blurry. But an analysis of gender focuses on how men and women get formed as such because of social norms, where an analysis of sexual difference focuses on how men and women get formed as such because of certain psychic laws and the symbolic representations of sex that follow from them.

The question of sexual difference is the question of how these he-subjects and she-subjects get produced as such, and what they stand for—represent—in society and why, and thus how we must represent ourselves within existing cultural symbolizations in order to be recognizable masculine or feminine subjects. From a feminist perspective—from the perspective of analyzing and critiquing patriarchy and sexual subordination (the systematic *devaluing* of the feminine position within sexual difference)—the question of sexual difference is always also a question of social transformation. And unlike a conventional gender analysis, social transformation is not a matter of either valuing whatever traits are associated with women or of changing social practices and relations such that women have access to whatever has historically been men's (and thus valued). In so far as sexual difference is a product of the alchemy between the unconscious, language and culture, social transformation must originate at the level of the unconscious, the level of imaginary associations and fantasy projections. The question, then, is about how to change the way deeply ingrained notions of femininity are imposed upon women as the condition of their having a place within the social hierarchy that structures culture, identity and recognition.

As we shall see, the "imaginary" dimension of sexual difference is what attracted Cornell to this framework: she sought a way to talk about masculinity and femininity as meanings and associations—as *fictions*—independent from real men, real women, and assumptions of how they supposedly "are." Cornell is concerned with representationally limiting sexual stereotypes, but she approaches stereotypes not as myths that accrue from empirically observable social phenomena so much as unconscious fantasy projections that condition and enable our subjectivity. As we shall also see, despite being intrigued by the potential ontological slippage within sexual difference, Butler ultimately rejects this framework of analysis because she finds it conservative: all the representational expansiveness that Cornell seeks to secure cannot change the fact that a certain kind of sexual difference analysis finally preserves humanity in the order of the two, masculine and feminine.

THE LEGACY OF LACAN IN FEMINIST THEORY

From a psychoanalytic perspective, the subject is formed through sexuality, and sexuality is formed through the unconscious—through fantasies, wishes, repressed desires, forbidden identifications, and psychic laws governing all of the above. From a structuralist perspective, sexual difference is a matter of the relation between individual parts in a more complex order, or structure, where the individual parts (here the masculine and the feminine position) depend for their meaning on their relation to each other. As Elizabeth Grosz explains, in a structuralist theory of meaning, binary oppositions attain meaning in differential relation to each other: not "as contraries ('A' and 'B'), but as contradictories ('A' and 'not-A')...the one term generating a non-reciprocal definition of the other as its negative. The presence and absence of the *one* term defines *both* positions in the dichotomy."[7] As a theory of difference (versus, say, uniqueness), the focus of a sexual difference analysis is specifically on how the feminine is defined as that which is the not-masculine. This is a consequence, as we will see, of making the phallic signifier "the one term" that governs the system, thus making the masculine position the norm for which the feminine position is the other, or the deviation.

Though neither Freud nor Lacan focused on the term "sexual difference" itself, both were occupied with the question of what distinguished masculine and feminine sexuality, or what Freud called "the male and female dispositions."[8] And again, for both Freud and Lacan this was not a matter either of socialization (i.e., training) to specific roles or of straightforward biology; this was not a simple question of nature versus nurture. Rather, this was a matter of how unconscious processes and identifications, which complexly rely on embodiment and kinship structure, function to regulate our desire so that we can move from nature to culture. While Freud and Lacan were thus both concerned with how to "read" the contents of the unconscious, crucial distinctions between their accounts bear mentioning. First, Freud offered what could be considered a structural account of the mind, the parts of which included the ego, id, and super-ego, and the development of which relied on the kinship structure of father, mother, child. Lacan, drawing on the linguistic theory of Ferdinand de Saussure, offered a structural*ist* analysis of the mind: he sought to analyze the unconscious and conscious cultural order (and the relationship between the two) as if they were structured like a language, in which each part in a closed system gets its meaning as it is differentially related to other parts, and as they are all regulated by certain eternal laws. Second, Freud's account was at least partly biologistic—he was concerned to a certain extent with the penis as a tangible physical organ that, in the all-important castration complex, girls envied and boys feared the loss of.[9] In contrast, Lacan refigured the phallus as a *symbol* in a system of signification.[10]

To be clear then, Lacan argues that the phallus as he understands it is not connected to the penis. The phallus is a symbol, and what Lacan uses it to symbolize is desire. Desire is by definition unsatisfiable. That is, desire is always the desire for what we do not have: for the Other (the impossible realm of truth, the outside of language), what we lack, fullness and completeness, being the *center* of the world. For both Lacan and Freud, individuated subjectivity comes at the price of certain formative severings: for example, being cut off from the mother's body, perceiving the mother's penis to have been cut off, and, for Lacan, being othered from an ideal image of our self as it is reflected back at us in a mirror. Prior to the earliest division, when the infant is distinguished from the mother, the infant exists in an imaginary fantasy world where all is one—the infant is everything, and everything is (for the needs of) the infant. After this division, there is difference.

In short, for both Freud and Lacan the crucial unconscious processes we undergo en route to subjectivity involve a series of losses, which engender a primary understanding of having and lacking, of wholeness and unity versus incompleteness and insufficiency. The phallus, for Lacan, is a (nearly nostalgic) representation of this place where there is no lack, the place we desire to be (because there is no desire there, because all our needs are met) but can never access. In Grosz's words, the phallus functions "on an imaginary level to signify presence and absence or fullness and privation."[11] In Lacan's words, "one may, simply by reference to the function of the phallus, indicate the structures that will govern the relations between the sexes. Let us say that these relations will turn around a 'to be' and a 'to have', which, by referring to a signifier, the phallus, have the opposed effect, on the one hand, of giving reality to the subject in this signifier, and, on the other, to derealizing the relations to be signified."[12] What Lacan means here is that the phallus is the *privileged* signifier in the signifying system that is language, the order of culture. As such, the relation to the phallus is what differentiates the meaning (the position) of masculine and feminine subjects. It *is* one's relation to the phallus that determines one's subjectivity. And the two relationships available are being the phallus and having the phallus.

A thorough explanation of how Lacan arrived at this idea—"being" the phallus versus "having" the phallus—would require an in-depth journey through Freud's concepts of the phallic phase, the castration complex, and the Oedipal complex, and then through Lacan's specific modification of these concepts as he refigured them through the lens of Saussurian linguistics, which is to say symbolically. Such a journey is beyond the scope of this paper. What matters for our purpose (which, again, is to travel from Lacan to Irigaray, from Lacan to Derrida, and from Lacan, Irigaray and Derrida to Cornell and "the beyond") is to grasp the way woman comes to be signified within Lacan's account of sexual difference. Most crucially, Lacan's account of woman (the feminine position in language) and man (the masculine position in language) is, as Grosz begins to suggest above, a theory of their asymmetrical positioning. Not all feminist theorists agree; many have debated about whether Lacan offers a theory of patriarchy or what amounts to a patriarchal theory. As Grosz explains, feminist defenders of Lacan, such as Ellie Ragland-Sullivan and Juliet Mitchell, have denied that the privilege of the phallus as the crucial mark of difference means the theory is necessarily phallocentric (i.e., making men the "One" and women the "Other").[13] Grosz rejects this reading, arguing that "the phallic signifier is *not* a neutral 'third' term against which both sexes are analogously or symmetrically positioned."[14] In other words, Lacan's is not just a theory of differential meaning, but of differential value. Despite Lacan's claims, the phallus was not an arbitrary choice of symbolic image, and its connection to the penis is not particularly arbitrary either. In fact, in one explanation of why he chose to make the phallus the privileged signifier of difference, Lacan writes that "this signifier is chosen because it is the most tangible element in the real of sexual copulation, and also the most symbolic in the literal (typographical) sense of the term, since it is equivalent there to the (logical) copula. It might also be said that, by virtue of its turgidity, it is the image of the vital flow as it is transmitted in generation."[15] Indeed. The fact remains that in Lacan's account the feminine is signified as the not-masculine, and the masculine is signified in terms of a set of meanings that are clearly superior. Masculine is associated with fullness, with presence, with being active, with *being*; feminine is associated with lack, with absence, with being passive, with being *nothing*. In short, the masculine subject is a subject, while the feminine really amounts to an object. Thus the feminine is associated with being the phallus—the object of desire—and the masculine is associated with having the phallus—possessing the object of desire.

Furthermore, since desire is always a matter of fantasy projection, *as* object of desire woman has no particular agency in how she is figured, or represented. Sexual difference as it manifests in social relations, then, is an effect of psychically generated fantasies that get imposed by the active subject on the passive object, culturally intelligible in so far as she fits herself into one of the various impoverished symbolizations of her sex.

Not surprisingly, feminists have also debated about the implications of this theory of sexual difference for the possibility of social transformation. This is the debate that Cornell and Butler are smack in the middle of. As one scholar has explained, French psychoanalytic theory has had something of a "difficult reception" in the United States, in so far as it "is either celebrated for demonstrating that sexual difference is a 'symbolic' phenomenon (a 'contingent historical formation'), or else denounced as a form of 'biological essentialism,' a return to anatomical difference that is ultimately ahistorical, despite its notorious emphasis on language."[16] Cornell strives to figure sexual difference as neither essential nor totally contingent. Rather, in so far as sexual difference—sexed subjectivity—takes place in culture, in language, and at the level of the unconscious, it is a historical formation that is deeply implicated in our psyches and difficult to transform. Our current set of sexual symbolizations, fantasy-regulated stereotypes and images, *can* be transformed, but they cannot simply be ignored or superceded by the sheer force of will. Put differently, Cornell wants to engage with sexual difference without either reifying it or simply repudiating it. For while she agrees with feminist critics who decry the phallocentrism of Lacan's theory, she also admits that she remains "enough of a Lacanian to defend the idea that the masculine and the feminine are constrained by a system of representation that holds enormous sway in our culture. Even words that we all use are always already sexually represented."[17] Elsewhere Cornell argues that we cannot just "do away" with the psychoanalytic categories of "the masculine" and "the feminine," because there clearly *is* a symbolic cultural order that "polices and reinforces gender hierarchy and identity" along the lines of these categories.[18] Though the current configuration of sexual difference may not be necessary in any fundamental, essential sense, this is the configuration in which we find ourselves. Thus Cornell describes herself as working from Lacan's "very simple lesson that the entire order of patriarchal culture divides us into two sexes, male and female, in the form of a hierarchy that privileges the masculine."[19]

Of course, the way one reads this "simple lesson" makes a significant difference in whether and how one finds Lacan instructive for feminist purposes. Cornell works to read Lacan ethically. What she means by this is that his theory of the asymmetrical positioning of masculine and feminine subjects in our current cultural order should not be taken as a description of an inevitable reality. Rather, it should be interpreted as a diagnosis of an ethical dilemma, a diagnosis that ought to inspire a different attitude toward the (unrecognizable feminine) other, namely an attitude of *striving* toward the social good of recognition of the other. This is not to suggest that Lacan intended his theory as an ethical challenge to rigid gender hierarchy, which he almost certainly did not. This is not to read Lacan as *himself* an ethical feminist, as Cornell characterizes herself. But contrary to the many feminist theorists who suggest that Lacan is deeply phallocentric, and that this means he has nothing to offer feminist scholarship, Cornell argues that in fact his analysis is invaluable, because it helps us "explore the bar that feminism runs up against and therefore helps us think differently about what we are fighting."[20]

"What we are fighting" is the "dearth of symbolizations of the feminine within sexual difference," resulting from the imposition of certain psychical fantasies of Woman on women in the form of the existing gender hierarchy.[21] That is, what we are fighting as feminists is the impoverished symbolic field within which our "choice" is limited to two options. We can take up our position as women in society by accepting the limited ways women can be represented—ways limited through the imposition of fantasies that "simplistically divide actual women into two kinds, good girls, loving mothers, adoring and nonthreatening sisters on the one hand, and manipulative mistresses, suffocating mothers, man-hating lesbians, and psychotic drop-outs on the other."[22] Or, we can "reposition ourselves on the side of the masculine, appropriate the phallus, and thus become lawyers, doctors, professors, etc. But then we will not be able to express our power as feminine. The repudiation of femininity, therefore, is inevitable if we are to be allowed entrance into the boys' club."[23]

As suggested above, it is this apparent acceptance of the impoverished choice between reification and repudiation of the feminine that Cornell identifies with MacKinnon's feminism, and which she is seeking a way around, or, more accurately, *beyond*. As it stands, there is no "beyond" to the structure Lacan describes, within which "there cannot be a conception of a feminine subject of right, because within that schema all there is is the projection of Woman as an imaginary figure, in which women are the signifiers of men's desire, and in which their erasure and violation is not even commented on."[24] Without some sort of feminist translation, there remains only the Lacan who makes a dubious ally in the quest to analyze and transform rigid gender identity. There remains only an *understanding* of capture—of woman conceived to exist purely as she mirrors man and reflects his needs and desires—but not a way *out* of it. In her attempt to figure social transformation from within a theory of sexual difference—to retain what is instructive in Lacan while modifying what is problematic—Cornell looks to Derrida and Irigaray for help.

CORNELL AND DERRIDA

Derrida approaches sexual difference as one thread to follow in his deconstruction of "phallogocentrism," or the absolute priority in philosophy of the logos (the word as presence) and the phallus (the privileged symbol of masculine as presence).[25] Derrida takes up this question of sexual difference through close readings of certain canonical thinkers working in or against the grain of the phallogocentric tradition, to expose how these thinkers work either to stabilize some tidy binary opposition of male/female, or to neutralize (i.e., desexualize) sexual difference, to make it invisible by subordinating it to ontological difference. Derrida argues that efforts to binarize or neutralize sexual difference suggests the extent to which this difference is really a pivotal issue for these thinkers, and not some marginal question as many would have us believe. Derrida thus seeks to expose sexual difference as *the* difference installed, whether acknowledged or not, at the outset and as the condition of philosophy. For Derrida, then, "the woman question" is not a modern development but an ancient and persistent philosophical dilemma.

The exception to the generalization that Derrida offers is Nietzsche. In *Spurs*, Derrida reads Nietzsche's various encounters with the woman question as precisely not "figuring" her, but as allegorizing women in a way that challenges the very idea of the figure, in the sense of determinable identity or truth. Nietzsche allegorizes woman in various ways, some more palatable than others.[26] But Derrida argues that Nietzsche's ultimate point (which is Derrida's point) is that there is no truth of woman. That is, Nietzsche's many styles of talking about woman are meant to suggest the necessary failure of any hermeneutic project (determining the true meaning of Nietzsche's allegorical texts, *or* the true meaning of woman). In this sense, the multiplicity of woman is an allegory for the multiplicity of meaning itself. In Derrida's language, then, the dilemma confronted by phallogocentric philosophers can be understood in terms of the "undecidability" of the question of sexual difference. This is an undecidability that has been repressed and denied and continues to trouble "the whole of ontology, which is the effect of an inspection, appropriation, identification, and verification of identity."[27]

In the introduction to *Derrida and Feminism: Recasting the Question of Woman*, the authors cast Derrida in opposition to this tendency, arguing that he has reopened the question of woman in philosophy by *undeciding* a tradition inaugurated by Aristotle, "who decides the question of woman by placing her and figuring her in a way that continues to hold sway" (namely as "nourishing medium," as "the body, nature, or unformed and irrational matter," as "the other to man").[28] This "placing" and "figuring" of woman, this attempt to secure for her some determinate *location* and thus *meaning*, exemplifies what Derrida describes as a topological project. It aims to "map" parts of the whole into their proper place in the order of things. Derrida rejects this project, not only as undertaken toward implicitly misogynist ends but also as undertaken by "reactive" feminists (a term he cites Nietzsche as using, but also seems to be using himself, not merely citing) who seek to reverse the conventional conceptual privileging. From Derrida's perspective, this feminist reaction may seek to put women in a better place, but it nonetheless still seeks to determine the "truth" of Woman and place her accordingly. That is, it is still a project focused on "distributing sexual identity cards."[29]

In contrast, Derrida describes his own approach to sexual difference as "not antifeminist, far from it," but "not feminist either."[30] Derrida advances no agenda for women, but rather seeks to effect a *dis*placement of the concept of "Woman." Thus when asked in an interview how he would describe "woman's place" in light of the question of sexual difference, Derrida responds "Frankly, I do not know. I believe that I would not describe that place." He continues, "Why must there be a place for woman? And why only one, a single, completely essential place? This is a question that you could translate ironically by saying that in my view *there is no one place for woman*."[31] Similarly, when asked whether, in the wake of deconstructing the old sexual binary, Derrida had in mind any "'new' concept of woman," he responds "No, I do not believe that we have one, if indeed it is possible to *have* such a thing or if such a thing could exist or show promise of existing. Personally, I am not sure that I feel the lack of it."[32] In other words, a new concept of woman is not even particularly desirable. Finally, Derrida responds to this line of inquiry by saying, "I do not know if it is to a change in representation that we should entrust the future."[33] That is, what Derrida seeks in displacing the concept of woman is a "general deformation of logic"—of the phallocentric logic within which sexual difference is subordinated to difference and "the wholly other" is always already masculine.[34] He writes that, "The concept of the concept, along with the entire system that attends it, belongs to a prescriptive order. It is that order that a problematics of woman and a problematics of difference, as sexual difference, should disrupt along the way."[35]

In contrast to the prescriptive ordering he critiques, Derrida dreams of a "sexuality without number" that opens up a new dance of sexual difference, "beyond the opposition feminine-masculine, beyond bi-sexuality as well, beyond homosexuality and heterosexuality...."[36] But while this deconstruction of phallogocentrism sounds like a feminist-friendly project, the implications of this project have met with critical resistance. Some feminist theorists have read Derrida to mean that there is no place for woman. Margaret Whitford, for example, has argued that in deconstructing the masculine/feminine binary and "colonizing" women's space and voice, "Derrida is trivializing feminism, and, by extension, women's agency."[37] Rosi Braidotti has accused Derrida of *using* women by using "the metaphor of woman to question the status of truth, knowledge, and subjectivity at the expense of women's concrete social struggles."[38] Cornell, however, reads Derrida as operating in an ethical and utopian mode. It is the exposure of the "beyond" here—the exposure of "the limit of any system of ideality established as reality"—that Cornell heralds as the grounds for an alliance between deconstruction and feminism.[39] Cornell takes seriously Derrida's hope for a new dance of sexual difference (beyond, say, Fred and Ginger, tuxedo and heels), and she does not demand to know precisely what moves will constitute that dance and who the performers will be. For Cornell, it is this capacity of Derrida's work to give us "a way to approach the feminine as allegory rather than as fact" that is its selling point.[40]

This is not to suggest that "real women's suffering" doesn't matter. Rather, it is to suggest that working to secure a place for actual women from within the existing set of actual choices—what Cornell calls submitting to the "tyranny of established reality"—has tended in feminist thought to entail a repudiation of the feminine and a mere reversal of the oppositional hierarchy.[41] This project, Cornell argues, "seems to reset the trap of rigid gender identities."[42] In contrast, Cornell argues for allegorizing "the feminine" as separate from particular women. Highlighting the fictional and imaginary dimension of the feminine provides an alternative to "descriptions of the way women supposedly 'are.'"[43] It is the modern feminist reliance on descriptions of the way women supposedly are (even if only because the social reality of male domination has constructed them as such) that Cornell seeks to trouble. For MacKinnon, not unlike Nietzsche's "reactive" feminists, these descriptions of women constitute a distinctly hermeneutic project: through each woman's expression of her own experiential truth of domination a "new knowledge" of the social reality of women's sexual violation by men is generated.[44] This new knowledge (the epistemological foundation) produces a new mapping (the ontological foundation). MacKinnon has described this outcome in terms of "a systematic, systemic, organized, structured, newly coherent picture of the relations between men and women...."[45] While MacKinnon clearly believes that establishing this truth of women's collective experience on the bottom is a step in the direction of changing this reality, Cornell is skeptical about the emancipatory potential of such descriptive positivism. She is skeptical about the sexual self-representation that can occur within, to use Derrida's words, the prescriptive order of the concept of "woman."

What Cornell appropriates most thoroughly from Derrida, then, is, first, the deconstruction of the limit of any supposedly totalized system of meaning, second, his claim that conceptual oppositions cannot be simply reversed, denied or neutralized, and, third, his example of the potential for allegory to open up endless multiple interpretations (not "descriptions") of sexual difference.[46] And yet, as fruitful as these insights are, they are nonetheless insufficient for Cornell's purposes. While Derrida *acknowledges* the beyond, he ultimately fails to *venture* beyond the mere exposure of the limit of the sexual binary. That is, like Lacan, whose analysis ultimately "leaves us with no escape,"[47] Derrida does not provide a way of thinking "the feminine" beyond repudiation, because he so thoroughly refuses the question of a new concept of woman as a metaphysical lapse. For all his consideration of the relationship between difference and sexual difference, Derrida does not ultimately take off "from within sexual difference," or from an explicit grappling with the sexual binary.

In the above interview, Derrida poses this as a question to himself, saying "I do not know. Must one think 'difference' 'before' sexual difference or taking of 'from' it?" For Cornell this is *the* crucial question. And it is a question Derrida finally evades. In the face of Derrida's hesitation here, Cornell finds a tension "between the postmodern deconstruction of rigid identity structures and the very idea of identity itself, and the attempt to specify the feminine, even if only as a subversive force against the symbolic."[48] Thus Cornell describes her central disagreement with Derrida by saying, "as attractive and necessary as I think it is to keep dreaming the dream of a new choreography of sexual difference, I also want to argue that we should, indeed must, in the sense of ethical obligation, take off from within sexual difference."[49] Derrida may critique the phallogocentric tendency to make ontological difference prior to sexual difference, but in Cornell's opinion this is not the same as recognizing the priority of sexual difference—at least as a contingent but phenomenologically evident and psychically embedded social division that we cannot simply ignore or repudiate. That is, where Derrida denies that "it is to a change in representation that we should entrust the future," Cornell's point is that we are always already represented. Thus a change in how representation itself takes place, if not new specific representations of identity, will surely figure in transformation. In order to think "the feminine" beyond repudiation, and representation beyond ontology, Cornell turns to Irigaray.

CORNELL AND IRIGARAY

Cornell figures Irigaray as pursuing the distinctly feminist project of working to deconstruct "the *conceptualization* of femininity as the *truth* of feminine difference," and to affirm feminine sexual difference as *something*, not nothing.[50] She figures Irigaray as such in contrast to Lacan, who signifies woman as castrated, as lack, as the repressed, as a negative; in contrast to Derrida, who deconstructs the negation of the feminine and yet hesitates to offer anything non-negative in its wake; and in contrast to dominant strains of Anglo-American feminism, within which radical feminism repudiated all (devalued) things feminine, and cultural feminism embraced all (revalued) things feminine. Broadly conveyed, Irigaray's project involves exposing the extent to which phallogocentrism (particularly Western metaphysical philosophy, linguistics, and psychoanalytic thought as they converge in Lacan) renders feminine subjectivity impossible. Subjectivity *is* masculine subjectivity (and thus desire is masculine desire, pleasure is masculine pleasure, the feminine is the masculine understanding of feminine—if the cultural order revolves around the phallus, all is on/in masculine terms). Irigaray shows us, in Cornell's words, how "feminine difference cannot be expressed except as signified in the masculine imaginary or the masculine symbolic."[51] The illustrative comparison that Cornell makes is between MacKinnon's very literal (if thoroughly heterosexual) definition of woman as "fuckee" and Irigaray's metaphorical interpretation of the feminine imaginary body as an extended auto-erotic zone, the source of her own meaning, pleasure and desire. In contrast to MacKinnon, Irigaray's project is a symbolic, poetic, *evocative* project, aimed at woman's signifying herself, writing (and *righting*) herself on her own terms, which is to say "in the feminine."[52] Irigaray figures mimesis as a kind of representational act that heeds the "bipolar world of gender identity" that we are in, but does not merely repeat it.[53] In Cornell's words, mimesis "allows us to circle within the feminine in order to live sexual difference differently, because this time *mimicry* is affirmative. *Mimesis* implies an evaluation of the feminine" as worthy of an affirmative metaphor.[54]

Lest this calls to mind the essentialism of "different voice" theories like Carol Gilligan's, however, Cornell makes clear that the notion of feminine writing that Irigaray and French feminism proffered is not about embracing or "prizing" women's being how they are (and thus should be). Though it has been a point of continual contention within feminist theory, Cornell denies the essentialist and gender-moralizing reading of Irigaray. It is a mistake, she argues, to take Irigaray as trying to instate some new *identity* for women. In Cornell's account feminine writing, as an act of imaginative representation, embodies an ethical and utopian aspiration, not a normative one. Feminine writing is not about producing *descriptions* of feminine sexual difference aimed at the truth of woman, but about "opening up the possible through metaphoric transformation."[55] This project thus relies on allegories and myths that expand the possibility of recognition and identification with the other. Unlike descriptions, which tend to be rooted in and reaffirm the "real world," allegories and myths are before and beyond the "real world." As such, they have a disruptive, transformative, fantasy dimension that can work to challenge our current order.[56] In disrupting the very language of the present, disrupting the meaning of the categories we recognize and live in the here and now, allegorical representations of the feminine can displace our horizon of knowledge. They displace settled meaning, and this displacement functions to make *possible* meaning, *possible* presentations of ourselves, and *possible* relations to others, always ahead of us. In this sense, then, feminine writing is cast not only as ethical but also as futural.

Cornell brings Irigaray and Derrida together, affirming the feminine as a metaphor of undecidability. Cornell takes seriously Derrida's warnings about the prescriptive order of the concept—she does not want a new "definition" of woman or a new specific representation of woman. Rather, she wants to take the radical otherness customarily assigned to the feminine and remetaphorize that otherness as the invaluable site and condition of representational possibility itself. In the rigid gender hierarchy of the here and now, actually embodied women *and* actually embodied men are limited, by institutionalized meaning, in how they can represent themselves.

Within the dominant masculine imaginary, women have tended to get the short end of the stick, but *everyone* is limited in the intelligible cultural representations available to them. So it is for the sake of us all that Cornell seeks to protect the beyond *as* beyond; to transform the feminine as nowhere and nothing into the emancipatory "outside" to the limited, unfree reality of the here and now. Drawing on her engagements with Lacan, Derrida and Irigaray, Cornell ultimately *names* this space beyond "the feminine." To the extent that the masculine comes to mean presence for Lacan, the feminine comes to mean beyondness for Cornell. At least until Judith Butler comes along.

CORNELL AND BUTLER

It is not exactly the case that Butler just came along. She and Cornell have been critical interlocutors from early on. In 1993 Butler reviewed one of Cornell's first books for *Diacritics*, and many of the themes emergent there continued to inform their debates. In her review-essay, entitled "Poststructuralism and Postmarxism," Butler critiques Cornell's argument in *The Philosophy of the Limit* about the particular importance of safeguarding the gap between the present and the future. Butler describes this safeguarding as "holding out for what exceeds the cognitive and linguistic grasp of the present and, hence, the act by which an unmasterable future is secured," and she calls this safeguarding an "odd kind of activity."[57] In her essay, Butler also critiques Cornell's construction of ethics as a "failed striving" toward certain ideals of collective life such as recognition. While Butler would also come to figure ethics as predicated on the limits, or failure, of recognition, the particular kinds of ideals that Cornell posits, and the necessity of "striving," is something they continue to disagree on, as discussed below. Two other exchanges are of primary importance for the topic at hand: the 1995 "conversation" among Seyla Benhabib, Nancy Fraser, Butler, and Cornell published as *Feminist Contentions,* and a 1998 interview of Butler and Cornell by Elizabeth Grosz and Pheng Cheah about Irigaray, entitled "The Future of Sexual Difference."[58] *Feminist Contentions* is significant for its restatement of the tensions laid out in "Poststructuralism and Postmarxism" and its illumination of Butler and Cornell's different interpretations of Lacan and Irigaray. "The Future of Sexual Difference" is significant for its indication of the extent to which the previous exchanges functioned to move each thinker partly in the direction of the other, with Cornell's shift as the focus here.[59]

Despite her ultimate rejection of a sexual difference analysis, Butler does entertain the possibility that this approach could hold some potential in so far as "sexual difference registers ontologically in a way that is permanently difficult to determine. It is neither fully given nor fully constructed."[60] Here

Butler echoes Derrida's sentiment that what is attractive is the *problem* sexual difference persistently poses, which is the problem "of determining where the biological, the psychic, the discursive and the social begin and end."[61] If sexual difference is undecidable, if it is inherently problematizing, there is perhaps something fruitful there. Butler contends, however, that Lacan's theory of the symbolic effectively immobilizes this problem, by rendering the masculine and the feminine as more or less stable signifieds held in place by the transcendental signifier of the phallus, conceived as the fundamental marker of human difference. Furthermore, Butler argues, "To the extent that [Lacan's] symbolic encodes a set of idealizations, it is constituted by the imaginary that it claims to govern. In this sense, the symbolic is nothing other than the reification of a given imaginary."[62] Finally, Butler is critical of the extent to which Lacan's "claim that masculine and feminine are forever constituted in this particular asymmetry appears to reconsolidate the cultural presumption of heterosexist hegemony."[63] Lacan makes the masculine and the feminine, and the meanings they currently engender, into seemingly inevitable subject positions regulated by seemingly inalterable psychic laws. What this boils down to for Butler is that Lacan renders the symbolic static, presumptively heterosexual, and seemingly resistant to change. In other words, he *ontologizes* the symbolic and heteronormalizes us.

Regarding Lacan's ontologizing, Cornell and Butler are largely in agreement. As discussed above, Cornell recognizes the extent to which Lacan's unreconstructed theory of the symbolic has no escape hatch. Lacan runs aground, as Cornell explains it, because while he may acknowledge "the 'fiction' of sexual difference," he nonetheless "emphasizes the *truth of the economy* that allows this difference to *appear* both inevitable and true...."[64] Put differently: while the "the masculine" and "the feminine" may be fantasy projections, not things that exist in the real world, the economy of castration that the phallus anchors is treated by Lacan as the empirical truth of subject-formation. However, Cornell believes that certain insights of Irigaray and Derrida can help to loosen the ontological congealment at work in Lacan's theory. Irigaray's remetaphorization of "the feminine," as the site of something beyond instead of nothing here and now, turns Lacan on his head. Derrida's spotlight on the inconsistencies at work in Lacan's defense of the phallus as the marker of difference exposes the tears in the fabric of the symbolic. Derrida helps expose how the logic of that system of meaning and representation is disturbed by "sexuality that fails to mean what *it is supposed* to within phallogocentrism."[65] For if sexuality is the product of unconscious processes of signification, and signification is always broken up by the "very slippage of language," then the inevitability and stasis associated with Lacan's theory of linguistically produced sexual subject positions appears tenuous.[66] It may be the case that the feminine within Lacan's masculinist symbolic is signified as lack, as man's desire, and, consequently, as whatever man phantasmatically projects onto her. But the ethical implication of understanding that there is a limit to this symbolic is that the symbolic is vulnerable, and thus the feminine might be signified *otherwise*. Given this opening up of Lacan, Cornell is able to read him as saying that there can be "no fixed signified for Woman within the symbolic order" (or, in Derrida's language, "no one place for woman"). And Cornell is able to figure that instability as the condition of the logical possibility of social transformation.[67]

Thus where Butler ultimately rejects Lacan's theory of the symbolic because of what she sees as its limiting totalization, Cornell uses Derrida's exposure of the "failure of totalization" in Lacan's symbolic order, and Irigaray's idea of the beyond of this order, to undermine the ontological thrust of Lacan's theory. For again, Cornell argues that even when a system of ideals is established as "Reality," there is a limit to the prison of ontology that "seems to shut out all our other possibilities as 'unreal.'"[68] Beyond the prison walls there is something else. *What* else there is, or how we might formulate this something else and think about our relation to it, is another question. As we have seen, following Irigaray, Cornell initially names this something else, this beyond that exceeds the current culture, "the feminine"; a substantively open and futural *ideal* in which Cornell places a lot of emancipatory stock. Butler, however, is skeptical about the function of such an ideal for three reasons.

First, she raises the question of where particular ideals, for example, of femininity, *come* from? For Lacan, ideals are engendered by unconscious desires. In Butler's account, however, ideals are *socially* produced using figures of abjection to constitute, patrol and secure the borders of femininity, masculinity and even human intelligibility.[69] In order to enforce "what counts as 'intelligible' identity," the *abjected* other, expelled to the outside of the social order, is crucial. This is a point that Lacan's totalizing structuralist theory of the symbolic simply cannot account for. And the question Butler raises here is whether the constitutive outside that Lacan fails to account for amounts to "what *cannot* or *ought not* to be represented or comprehended."[70] Is what is outside the degraded other that consolidates a certain masculinist, heterosexual reality, or does this outside "constitute that limit that actively contests what we already comprehend and already are?"[71]

Clearly, Cornell affirms "the feminine" as the beyond or outside that contests reality. Indeed, this is her very definition of what an ideal is: "not a goal, but a horizon of the future...."[72] For Cornell, ideals function as challenges to the stability and integrity of the real. It is the very incommensurability between what is and what we imagine could be that *makes* the "what is" start to break up. In so far as cultural orders are "governed by fantasy," Cornell argues, "they cannot be firmly grounded and therefore are always open to transformation."[73] Thus ideals are things we are *only* ever striving for and can never real-ize or achieve. But instead of figuring the impossibility of embodying ideals as a cause for dejection, Cornell values this gap, this striving, this *failure*, as the very "horizon of the future."

This is the second point about which Butler is skeptical. What is the effect of taking failure "as the ground for a new set of social relations"?[74] What is the effect of this valorization of striving? What is the effect of figuring ethics as the gap between an always breaking up real and an always only logically possible ideal? Butler's first concern here is that Cornell ignores the line of thought developed by Nietzsche and Foucault, which "calls into question the subjection, if not enslavement, from which unrealizable ethical ideals originate."[75] Cornell seemingly fails to recognize the extent to which "what constitutes 'the logically possible' will be regulated by power."[76] Or again: ideals are socially, and thus historically, constructed through exclusion of certain others; they are not simply the logically possible outside to the current structure of meaning and representation. Butler's second concern here, no doubt related to her understanding of the role of power and exclusion in the construction of impossible ideals, is that, though Cornell casts her approach as inherently utopian, "The result could just as well be (a) the degradation of the ideal, (b) proliferation of other ideals, (c) the closing of the gap between the ideal and what is realizable, (d) permanent disappointment, disillusionment, rancor, and doubtless numerous other possibilities."[77] Butler thus raises the question of the potential for Cornell's approach to undermine hope about the future.

The third point about which Butler is skeptical concerns Cornell's attempt to figure the preeminent ideal of "the beyond" specifically in the language of "the feminine." Butler questions why Cornell continues to participate, albeit critically and creatively, in the preservational economy of the categories of masculine and feminine. In "The Future of Sexual Difference," Butler admits that she is persuaded to some degree "by the use of the feminine as a category that does not describe something that already exists but actually inaugurates a certain kind of future within language and within intelligibility."[78] But she ultimately concludes, "I just can't talk about the feminine," "...what I feel I can talk about is the category of woman, but for [Cornell], that is not necessarily the salient category. The category here is the feminine, which is, in a really significant way, beyond contemporary categorization. It is the beyond of categorization."[79] The issue for Butler is whether casting the beyond of categorization in terms of "the feminine" does not in fact further consolidate both sex and heterosexuality as the privileged categories of human being. Cornell believes that the feminine as open, uncaptured, unsymbolizable "not yet" and "nowhere" can work to trouble the terms of the present. But Butler argues that embracing the feminine, even if only as an affirmative allegory, functions "to give it a fundamental status which I won't give it."[80]

On this point Butler persuades Cornell, who comes to recognize that "Lacan [and Irigaray] inescapably privilege, and in spite of themselves, ontologize, the divide between idealized masculinity and the feminine other."[81] She does not reject the persistence, and thus relevance, of the categories of masculine and feminine per se, but she does move away from *naming* the future "the feminine." On the question of ideals themselves, however, Cornell remains steadfast. She indirectly acknowledges Butler's concerns, admitting that, "even the grandest of ideals, as soon as they are articulated and defended—even the ideal of humanity—can become exclusionary at the very moment of their defense."[82] Yet we *need* ideals, because people "are willing to fight to change the world because of the power of their appeal."[83] Placing herself squarely in the Kantian tradition, particularly as brought into political philosophy by Rawls, Cornell explains that in her work "the question of the role of the ideal and the question of representation are brought together in a reconceptualization of the role of the aesthetic as crucial to both the critique and the elaboration of new configurations of ideals in law and political philosophy."[84] The term "aesthetic" here suggests the affective, emotional aspects of life, or "new ways of imagining who we are" and could be.[85] In response to the dilemmas exposed in her discussions with Butler, however, Cornell ultimately shifts to figuring the ideal of a space beyond contemporary categorization in terms of what she now calls "the imaginary domain."[86]

CORNELL AND THE IMAGINARY DOMAIN

Cornell's notion of the "imaginary domain" is the effect of her encounter with Lacan, Derrida, Irigaray and Butler. It is also her unique way of bringing the insights of those thinkers into the local context of American legal feminism, which Cornell argues has been "plagued" by the equality/difference and difference/dominance debates that she hopes to overcome.[87] While the law is a permanent fixture in Cornell's intellectual landscape, she never clearly locates "the feminine" in the context of legal theory. When she refigures the ideal of a space beyond current categories in terms of the "imaginary domain," however, she defends it as a matter of legal right, and largely in language that recollects liberal theory as much as postmodern feminist theory. Cornell defines the imaginary domain as "that psychic and moral space in which we, as sexed creatures who care deeply about matters of the heart, are allowed to evaluate and represent who we are."[88] She *describes* "the imaginary domain" in a number of ways. It is a "heuristic device," a framework for recognizing, or giving symbolic form to, what is actually happening in contemporary society, namely new dances of sexual difference.[89] It is an ethical and utopian ideal, the space within which future imaginaries, or projections of a sense of self-identity over a lifetime, can find sanctuary from the capture of current categorizations.[90] The imaginary domain is "the space of the 'as if' in which we imagine who we might be if we made ourselves our own end and claimed ourselves as our own person."[91] Finally, she describes the imaginary domain in terms of a new theory of legal equality, in which equal access to the psychic space for the self-representation of "sexuate being" is secured for all "persons" as a matter of right.

The language used here is crucial, as it aims to integrate poststructuralist and psychoanalytic ideas about sexuality and subjectivity with liberal ideas about personhood, individual rights, moral community, and the primary good of self-respect. Cornell uses the term "sexuate being," which she appropriates from Irigaray, as an ontologically anti-essentialist and intentionally indeterminate concept-term. She intends it to supplant the neutered, abstract, universal individual of liberal theory and to avoid the gender/sex, constructivist/essentialist debate of feminist theory. Sexuate being is meant to replace, or at least unsettle, sex and gender as categories of political philosophy and law *without* imposing any substantive meaning or identifications on people. The term "sexuate being" thus also functions to signify that Cornell's approach is not a narrowly feminist one, in the sense of being of and for "women." Cornell uses the term "person" to get away from the idea of an individual subjectivity that is innate, stable and, by definition, free. She also uses the term "person" to recall Hegel's claim that the person is "constituted by recognition that she is a person with rights."[92] Personhood, for Cornell, is "an aspiration," "a project," and something we struggle for over the course of our lifetimes.[93] The freedom and responsibility to "personalize" ourselves—represent our selves to our selves as we see fit, differently at different times—is contingent on conditions that enable us to undertake that struggle. Cornell describes these as "minimum conditions of individuation," including "bodily integrity," and "access to symbolic forms sufficient to achieve linguistic skills permitting the differentiation of oneself from others."[94]

What the idea of the imaginary domain entails is a claim that the state has a legitimate interest only in securing the conditions we need as equal beings that should each be the sole source of our own meaning. The law cannot legitimately denigrate certain forms of sexuate being "as inherently antithetical to personhood," for "such a devaluation would run counter to the fundamental premise of a politically liberal society that each one of us is to be regarded as a free and equal person."[95] The law cannot legitimately bind women or men to current structures of meaning and identification, by substantively defining them in terms of existing cultural associations. The law, in Cornell's account as in many other postmodern feminist critiques, is a dubious tool. Yet unlike those who find engagement with legal rights irreconcilably problematic, Cornell stays directly engaged with law. To the question, "Why enter the preservational economy of law at all?" Cornell responds, "we have inevitably already been entered into it. Our demand is to enter it differently, on the basis of the equivalent evaluation of our sexual difference."[96]

In her defense of the imaginary domain, then, Cornell figures law as the legacy of the past, congealed in the present, but susceptible to a fundamental reworking in and for the future.

Cornell remains attuned to the here and now, but refuses to be held hostage by it. Similarly, she continues to acknowledge the hold of the masculine and feminine, but refuses to reinscribe those normative identifications in law. Thus within the imaginary domain, the *space* for the equivalent evaluation of sexual difference is protected, not particular people who embody certain recognized sexual identities. And in this space, difference that has been naturalized in binary terms, in "the two," might come to be symbolized as multiplicity in the future.

There is a genuine sense of longing that animates Cornell's notion of the future. There are not many details about what that future might look like, however, because Cornell longs for a future that is "not identifiable as the evolution of the same" but is rather something "totally new."[97] Somewhere between MacKinnon's prescriptivism and Butler's skepticism, Cornell seeks to safeguard the possibility of this wholly other future by writing into present law the right to the space in which to imagine and craft ourselves in as of yet unimaginable ways. In this sense, Cornell mobilizes the law in the service of utopia as she conceives it, namely as the idea that "what is possible cannot be known in advance of social transformation."[98] This is clearly an unconventional "post-positivist" understanding of utopia, a term typically associated with a substantive blueprint. Yet Cornell would suggest that theories that do nothing but conflate possibility with reality are utopian in name only. The beyond must be protected *as* beyond, not brought into the terms of the present. When future possibilities are articulated in present terms, they cease to be futural. What this means is that truly utopian thinking, contra Thomas More, is largely unspecific, open, and not defined.

In Cornell's notion of the imaginary domain as the utopian beyond, we see the reflection of Lacan's ideas about what is and is not culturally symbolizable, Derrida's commitment to not instating new concepts in place of old ones, Irigaray's ideas about the evocative and metaphoric, and Butler's cautious hope for a feminist future. We see Cornell working these notions over, again and again, as she appropriates these critical traditions into the practical context of American legal feminism. In stark contrast to those who claim that postmodernism produces a "retreat from utopia within feminist theory,"[99] Cornell's work ultimately exemplifies a distinctly utopian impulse that is not only *not* confounded by postmodernism, but is seemingly engendered by elements of it.

NOTES

1. Judith Butler, "Contingent Foundations: Feminism and the Question of 'Postmodernism,'" in *Feminist Contentions: A Philosophical Exchange*, Seyla Benhabib, Judith Butler, Drucilla Cornell, and Nancy Fraser (New York: Routledge, 1995), 37.
2. Drucilla Cornell, *Beyond Accommodation: Ethical Feminism, Deconstruction and the Law* (New York: Rowman and Littlefield, 1999), 207. See also Drucilla Cornell, "Civil Disobedience and Deconstruction," in *Feminist Interpretations of Jacques Derrida*, Nancy J. Holland, ed. (University Park: The Pennsylvania State University Press, 1997), 155 n.11.
3. Drucilla Cornell, *Just Cause: Freedom, Identity, and Rights* (New York: Rowman & Littlefield, 2000), 15.
4. Cornell, *Just Cause*, 15.
5. Ibid., 12.
6. Judith Butler, "Against Proper Objects," in *Differences: A Journal of Feminist Cultural Studies* 6, no. 2-3 (Summer-Fall, 1994): 1.
7. Elizabeth Grosz, *Jacques Lacan: A feminist introduction* (New York: Routledge, 1990), 124.
8. Sigmund Freud, "The Transformation of Puberty," in *The Basic Writings of Sigmund Freud*, Dr. A. A. Brill trans. (New York: The Modern Library, 1966), 612.
9. Grosz, *Jacques Lacan*, 123.
10. The degree to which Freud was concerned with the penis as organ and not symbol is a matter of debate. Lacan himself argued against this interpretation. See Jacques Lacan, *Écrits*, Alan Sheridan trans. (New York: W.W. Norton, 1977), 285. The degree to which Lacan really got away from Freud, and succeeded in refiguring the phallus as utterly unrelated to the penis, is also a matter of debate. Irigaray disputed Lacan's claims on this matter. We might say here, however, that Lacan was interested in what was going on in our fantasies, not our pants (or skirts, as the case may be), where Freud was arguably interested at least partly in the latter.
11. Grosz, *Jacques Lacan*, 122.
12. Lacan, 289.
13. Grosz, *Jacques Lacan*, 143.
14. Ibid., 124.
15. Lacan, 287.
16. Charles Shepherdson, *Vital Signs: Nature, Culture, Psychoanalysis* (New York: Routledge, 2000), 2.
17. Cornell, *Beyond Accommodation*, xxviii.
18. Drucilla Cornell, in Pheng Cheah and Elizabeth Grosz, "The Future of Sexual Difference: An Interview with Judith Butler and Drucilla Cornell," *Diacritics* 28, no. 1, Special Issue: Irigaray and the Political Future of Sexual Difference (Spring, 1998): 19–42, 24.
19. Cornell, "Civil Disobedience and Deconstruction," 150.
20. Drucilla Cornell, "What is Ethical Feminism?" in *Feminist Contentions: A Philosophical Exchange*, 75–106, at 91. Hereafter cited as "Ethical Feminism."
21. Ibid., 77.
22. Ibid., 91.
23. Ibid.
24. Cornell, "Civil Disobedience and Deconstruction," 150.
25. "Choreographies," an interview with Christie V. McDonald, *Diacritics* 12, no. 2 (Summer 1982), 66–76, at 69.

26. See, for example, sections 59–75 of Book Two of *The Gay Science*, Walter Kaufman trans. (New York: Vintage Books, 1974).

27. Jacques Derrida, *Spurs: Nietzsche's Styles, in A Derrida Reader: Between the Blinds*, Peggy Kamuf, ed. (New York: Columbia University Press, 1991), 373.

28. Ellen K. Feder, Mary C. Rawlinson, and Emily Zakin, Introduction, *Derrida and Feminism: Recasting the Question of Woman* (New York: Routledge, 1997), 1.

29. Derrida, "Choreographies," 69.

30. Ibid., 68.

31. Ibid.

32. Ibid., 72.

33. Ibid., 75.

34. Jacques Derrida, "At This Very Moment in This Work Here I am," in Kamuf, *A Derrida Reader*, 430.

35. Derrida, "Choreographies," 72.

36. Ibid., 76.

37. Margaret Whitford, *Luce Irigaray: Philosophy in the Feminine* (New York: Routledge, 1991), 129.

38. Elizabeth Grosz, "Ontology and Equivocation," in *Feminist Interpretations of Jacques Derrida*, Nancy J. Holland, ed. (University Park: The Pennsylvania State University Press, 1997), 78, referencing Braidotti's claims in *Patterns of Dissonance* (Oxford: Polity, 1991) and *Men in Feminism*, Alice Jardine and Paul Smith, eds. (New York: Routledge, 1989). See 105–106 of *Patterns of Dissonance* for Braidotti's claim that Derrida's "disconcerting conclusions emanate from a misunderstanding and downright ignorance of feminist texts, of the history of women's struggles, and from a carelessness as regards the theoretical aspects of feminism, coupled with the determination to denigrate them."

39. Cornell, *Beyond Accommodation*, 18.

40. Ibid., 107.

41. Ibid., 2.

42. Drucilla Cornell, *Transformations: Recollective Imagination and Sexual Difference* (New York: Routledge, 1993), 58.

43. Ibid., 59.

44. Catharine MacKinnon, "Points Against Postmodernism," 75 *Chi.-Kent L. Rev.* 687, (2003), 689.

45. Ibid., 688.

46. Cornell, *Beyond Accommodation*, 18.

47. In "What is Ethical Feminism?" Cornell writes, "If the privilege of the phallus as the primary signifier of difference fixes man in his subject position, it dislocates woman from any fixed position on which to ground her subjectivity. What is left over, for Lacan, is beyond expression. The feminine imaginary cannot be given form because it cannot find the symbolic 'stuff' to register the diversification of feminine sexual difference. ...As the figure of the castrated Other, women can only signify what is not there" (91).

48. Cornell, *Beyond Accommodation*, 166.

49. Ibid., 100.

50. Ibid., 11.

51. Ibid., 7.

52. See Whitford, supra. note 37.

53. Cornell, *Beyond Accommodation*, 156. In *This Sex Which is Not One* (Ithaca, NY: Cornell University Press, 1985), Irigaray writes that mimesis means for a woman to "resubmit herself...to ideas about herself that are

elaborated in/by a masculine logic, but so as to make 'visible' by an effect of playful repetition, what was supposed to remain invisible: recovering a possible operation of the feminine in language" (76).

54. Cornell, *Beyond Accommodation*, 148.
55. Ibid., 169.
56. Of course, myths and allegories are not necessarily liberating, but can be deeply conservative, functioning not to challenge but rather to consolidate and affirm a particular order.
57. Judith Butler, "Poststructuralism and Postmarxism," *Diacritics* 23, no. 4 (Winter, 1993): 3–11, 4.
58. Supra note 18.
59. In "The Future of Sexual Difference," both Cornell and Butler reference an influential exchange they had in 1995 at Berkeley, after, and presumably as something of a continuation of, *Feminist Contentions*.
60. Judith Butler, *Undoing Gender* (New York: Routledge, 2004), 186. While on its face this description seems to fit with the one offered by Irigaray above, namely that sexual difference is situated at the junction of nature and culture, Butler believes that though Irigaray may not regard sexual difference as a mere biological fact, she does regard biology as a mere fact. Butler, in contrast, sees "biology" itself, the materiality of bodily dimorphism, as a cultural construction. See Judith Butler, *Bodies That Matter* (New York: Routledge, 1992).
61. Butler, *Undoing Gender*, 185.
62. Judith Butler, "For a Careful Reading," in *Feminist Contentions*, 142.
63. Butler, "Against Proper Objects," 10.
64. Cornell, *Beyond Accommodation*, 81.
65. Ibid.
66. Cornell, "Civil Disobedience and Deconstruction," 152.
67. Cornell, "Ethical Feminism," 86.
68. Cornell, *Beyond Accommodation*, 18.
69. Butler, "For a Careful Reading," 142.
70. Ibid., 143.
71. Ibid.
72. Drucilla Cornell, *Defending Ideals: War, Democracy and Political Struggles* (New York: Routledge, 2004), 19.
73. Cornell, *Just Cause*, 24.
74. Butler, "Poststructuralism and Postmarxism," 6.
75. Ibid., 8.
76. Ibid., 10.
77. Ibid., 7.
78. Butler, "Future," 19.
79. Ibid., 24, 23.
80. Ibid., 24.
81. Cornell, *Just Cause*, 28.
82. Cornell, *Defending Ideals*, ix.
83. Ibid.
84. Cornell, *Just Cause*, 6–7.
85. Ibid., 7.
86. Cornell, "The Future of Sexual Difference," 21.
87. Cornell, *Just Cause*, 17.
88. Drucilla Cornell, *At the Heart of Freedom: Feminism, Sex, & Equality* (Princeton, NJ: Princeton University Press, 1998), x. Hereafter cited as *Heart of Freedom*.

89. Cornell, *Just Cause*, 19.
90. Cornell, *Heart of Freedom*, 36.
91. Ibid., 8.
92. Ibid., 62.
93. Drucilla Cornell, *The Imaginary Domain: Abortion, Pornography & Sexual Harassment* (New York: Routledge, 1995), 5.
94. Cornell, *Imaginary Domain*, 4, 8.
95. Cornell, *Just Cause*, 19.
96. Cornell, *Imaginary Domain*, 235.
97. Cornell, *Beyond Accommodation*, 13.
98. Cornell, *Heart of Freedom*, 185.
99. Seyla Benhabib, "Feminism and Postmodernism," in *Feminist Contentions, Seyla Benhabib, Judith Butler, Drucilla Cornell, and Nancy Fraser* (New York: Routledge, 1995), 30.

List of Contributors

Mark Bevir is a Professor of Political Science at the University of California, Berkeley.

Peter Eli Gordon is a Professor of History at Harvard University.

Jill Hargis is an Assistant Professor of Political Science at California State Polytechnic University, Pomona.

David Hawkes is an Associate Professor of English at Lehigh University, Bethlehem, Pennsylvania.

Melissa Lane is a University Senior Lecturer in History at Cambridge University, UK.

Paul Patton is a Professor of Philosophy at the University of New South Wales, Australia.

Robert Resch is a Professor of History at Texas A&M University, College Station.

Sara Rushing is an Assistant Professor of Political Science at Montana State University, Bozeman.

Simon Stow is an Associate Professor of Government at The College of William and Mary, Williamsburg, Virginia.

Richard Wolin is a Distinguished Professor at the Graduate Center of the City University of New York.

Index